NEARLY
REACHED
THE SKY

NEARLY REACHED THE SKY

Steve Blowers

FootballWorld

First published 2005 by
Football World
Tel: 01708 744 333
Website: www.footballworld.co.uk

Printed by Biddles Ltd, King's Lynn, Norfolk

Cover Photography: Steve Bacon, *EX Magazine*

Cover Design: Marios Flourentzou

Distributed by Football World
103, Douglas Road, Hornchurch, Essex, RM11 1AW
Tel: 01708 744 333
Email: editorial@footballworld.co.uk

Set in Times New Roman

ISBN: 0-9548336-8-6

To Lynn, Sam and Harriet

Contents

Foreword

By BILLY BONDS MBE

When I agreed to sign for West Ham United in May 1967, I never envisaged that I would be staying at Upton Park for 27 years. Charlton Athletic were a second division side and suddenly I was going to be at a big Division One club with the likes of 1966 World Cup winners Bobby Moore, Geoff Hurst and Martin Peters.

I'd met Mooro as a 14-year-old when he did an end-of-season presentation at my junior football club and I was in awe of him then because he was already a star. To think that I would end up playing with him and then take over the West Ham captaincy was beyond belief.

And when I went to the Boleyn Ground with Charlton manager Bob Stokoe to complete my transfer, as I sat on the other side of Ron Greenwood's big, polished mahogany desk, I never dreamed that one day it would be mine, too.

Moving to West Ham was a huge step for me but it worked out well. I played almost 800 first-team matches before going on to manage the club in nearly 250 games.

I enjoyed every minute of my time at Upton Park and in both Ron Greenwood and his successor, John Lyall, I was lucky enough to work with two great managers.

As soon as a contract ended, you were happy to sign a new one. I loved playing for the club, I never wanted to go anywhere else and there were several other players who felt the same way as I did.

It's a different ball game now.

Today, players will sign a five-year deal but as soon as somebody comes in and offers them more money, they'll be off. In those days that just never happened.

Everyone knew everyone, too. Mooro and the rest of us would be on first-name terms with everybody – from the groundsman's assistant to the gateman and the bloke who swept the terraces.

Before I could drive, I'd even get a bus to Upton Park on matchdays.

And whenever we played at Burnley, for example, our hotel was about half-a-mile from the ground. At around 1.30pm Ron Greenwood would get us together so that we could all walk through the high street to Turf Moor. That included Mooro, Hurstie and Martin Peters. Imagine that – it was probably the equivalent of David Beckham, Roy Keane and Thierry Henry doing it today.

No matter how badly the team did on the pitch, there was always loyalty around the club. The fans knew that most of the players would still be there next season and probably the year after that, too. We always seemed to have half-a-dozen good players at any one time and even when we got relegated nobody got on their bike to go to another club. Instead, they loyally stayed and battled it out to get promotion back to Division One.

John Lyall epitomised West Ham United Football Club. People talk about Arsene Wenger, Jose Mourinho and Sir Alex Ferguson but in terms of man-management and coaching, he was on a par with them. He was a great coach who improved players on the training ground and he would certainly stand up to any of the modern day ones.

The club might have stood by him when we went down in 1978 but, in return, he showed a lot of loyalty to West Ham, too. John could have moved on to QPR and, perhaps, doubled his money but he chose to stick with us and was responsible for some of the most successful times in the club's history.

In 1985/86, West Ham played some tremendous football on their way to third place but when John wanted to strengthen the squad with two or three players for the next season, he didn't get the financial backing he needed. It had been a marvellous achievement by a small group of players and it was the time to really push on but perhaps the board didn't have the money available for him.

And when one or two of the players started to get inflated ideas demanding bonuses and the like, I began to think that it could all start to go wrong for the club.

Even though the team was relegated in 1989, I never understood why the board sacked John.

Looking back, I just think that the club wanted to go down a different route. One or two directors had fanciful ideas but whatever they were, they just didn't work.

Personally, I could never knock Lou Macari but players had seen that John Lyall knew what he was talking about and they believed that he could make them better footballers. John was a huge act for anyone to follow and it was never going to work for Lou because the players didn't have the same level of respect for him.

And whereas players had generally shown loyalty in the past, the Paul Ince saga was one of the first examples of home-grown youngsters, backed by their agents, looking to move on, regardless of their contract situation. When I was a player, we all heard rumours that clubs were interested in us but we stayed put.

Following Lou's departure, I think the board saw that I was a West Ham man who could come in and stabilise the club for them. Whether they viewed me as a long-term solution is another thing altogether.

In hindsight, maybe they didn't look at me like that but I'd like to think that in the wake of Lou's departure they knew they had somebody at the club who would be respected by the players and the fans. Just a few weeks earlier, less than 15,000 had turned up for a game against fourth-placed Oldham Athletic, and now West Ham were in 14th-spot in the old second division, without a manager.

The club was on its knees but my appointment worked. I gained instant respect from the players because they had been my team-mates and they gave me everything they had. There wasn't much money about, though, and I could never, for example, bring in a top-drawer striker.

Although they still talk about West Ham being a family club, that hasn't been the case for quite a while now. Even when I was manager, to cut costs they were trying to sack the car park attendant who was on about a fiver a game. I saw lots of old faces – including some I'd known since 1967 – disappear from the club.

Harry Redknapp and myself had known each other a long, long time. We were good mates and he was even Best Man at my wedding.

In 1992, Harry said he was fed up managing Bournemouth and wanted to come to West Ham, help out and be part of the team.

I trusted him but, as I know now, it didn't end up turning out that way.

At first, we got promoted and did ever so well with the squad we had somehow assembled. I had a collection of wholehearted battling players, a handful of tricky ones, a few free transfers and some older, experienced lads. To finish 13th in the Premiership in that first season following promotion was a tremendous effort.

Harry was a big help to me but he had his own ambitions and he was always going to be a manager rather than just a number two.

The board wanted him to manage the team and I wasn't going to hang around once I knew that. I wasn't one to 'go upstairs' and just sit around in the directors' box doing nothing or helping out with a bit of coaching here and there. If you're not wanted, then it's time to go.

I realised that once I'd taken the 'Big One' – the manager's job – there was never going to be any way back if anything went wrong, because that's not my style.

I always knew that I would need to leave altogether. After giving 27 years of my life to the club it was a wrench to go and I won't say that I didn't miss it.

I learned a big lesson from the Harry Redknapp episode but I'm not bitter about it any more. After all, I've got lots of good things around me in my life including my family and two lovely little grand-daughters. It's all water under the bridge for me now and there are far more important things in life.

Looking back, I'd be lying if I said that I enjoyed managing but I'm pleased that I did it. I don't feel that I failed. We might have been relegated but we were promoted twice, we got to an FA Cup semi-final as a second division club and our 21-game unbeaten run from the start of the 1990-91 season is still a club record.

I got the club back on its feet and stabilised things. I'm very proud of that.

By keeping us in the Premiership, it also meant that funds became available to buy players after I left. Harry spent a lot of money and it's for others to judge whether that was right or wrong, although from where I'm standing it looks like the club is still getting over it. When I left, the wage bill was just under £3m and the highest-paid player was on about £3,000 per week but it went crazy after that.

So many players were coming and going that I don't think the crowd recognised half of them from one week to the next! And a lot of signings who came just for the wedge took a lot of money out of the club.

I think the crowd enjoyed Harry being at Upton Park. Sure, there were some poor buys but he bought some terrific players, too. Just look at Paolo Di Canio. Harry certainly entertained them. You could never knock that, because we saw some great games, but there was a long-term price to pay, financially.

I'm sure that Glenn Roeder did his best when he came in and took over from Harry. He finished seventh in his first season and the side that was relegated under him should have finished in the half of the table, at least, the following season, too.

Instead, it was ridiculous that a team with that quality went down. Glenn was managing one of the strongest squads the club has ever had but, by Christmas, it was obvious that something needed to be done or there was going to be no turning back. Players such as Di Canio didn't help with their antics, either, because that rubbed off onto others and undermined Glenn. It certainly didn't help his cause.

I don't think Trevor Brooking ever saw his future in management but you could not have asked for a better man to have come in and filled the gap between Glenn Roeder and Alan Pardew. Everyone has respect for Sir Trevor.

Since taking over, Alan Pardew has had a difficult job to do. Some of the fans still haven't taken to him but supporters can be fickle and management is a results business. They talk about entertainment but if your crowd-pleasers get beaten 10 games on the trot, then you're going to be in trouble no matter who you are. As a manager you live and die by your results and Alan got the club promoted within 20 months of his arrival.

Alan Pardew's done the job that he was brought in to do and now he can, hopefully, consolidate the club's position in the Premiership. He's an ambitious man and hopefully he can push on and take West Ham United forward.

You only have to look at a Sven-Goran Eriksson England squad to realise that if the club had managed to keep an almost endless list containing the likes of Rio Ferdinand, Frank Lampard, Joe Cole, Jermain Defoe, Michael Carrick and Glen Johnson together, then – with the right signings around them – the future would obviously have been very bright indeed. Those lads are still maturing with every season and are such talented players that they would have blossomed anywhere, not just at the likes of Manchester United, Chelsea and Tottenham Hotspur.

Like it or not, though, West Ham are one of the smaller clubs and you have to accept that they would always have been susceptible to clubs coming in for them.

And remember there's no loyalty in the game today, especially with the large amounts of money floating around.

The club has had to sell a lot of terrific, young players and that's hurt the supporters. West Ham fans have had to put up with a lot but they've still stuck with the team and hopefully, after all the turmoil of recent years, they can be rewarded by seeing the club retain its Premiership status in 2005-06 and build upon that.

For me, personally, the events of 1994 left a sour taste in my mouth and when I'm doing my radio work I don't particularly enjoy going back to Upton Park, but I do still support West Ham United and I now look at it as being my club again.

I enjoyed my time there because it was a fantastic place to play football and every time I ran down the tunnel I got a tremendous lift from the fans.

Having fulfilled lots of dreams during my career, I've only got one obvious regret and although the club has now also changed beyond recognition, make no mistake, if I was young enough, I'd sign for West Ham United tomorrow and do it all again.

Billy Bonds MBE
August 2005

Chapter 1
SUMMER 1989

THE LOSS OF LOYAL LYALL

It was a telephone call of simply seismic proportions.

A summons that was destined to rock West Ham United to the core.

And one that would forever change the orbit of a club that had charted a steady course throughout its 94-year existence.

On the morning of Monday, June 5, 1989, John Lyall was beckoned to a 10:30am meeting at the home of chairman Len Cearns.

With the players on their summer break, the Hammers' manager had been at the club's Chadwell Heath training ground plotting the pre-season training and friendly schedule with his coaching staff.

At the weekend, he would be embarking upon his only break of the entire year – a week's fishing holiday on the Norfolk Broads – where he could spend hour-upon-hour enraptured by the solitude of the riverbank, further scheming his just-relegated club's instant return to the top flight.

Lyall had done it once before. He could surely do it again.

But after making the 20-minute drive to the periphery of Epping Forest in his Mercedes and walking up the leafy pathway of 1 Meadow Way, Chigwell, the unsuspecting Lyall quickly realised that all was not rosy as he was ushered into the dining room by 'Mr Len' without even the customary offer of a cup of tea.

Stability abounded. Cearns, who had been a director of the club since 1947, moved into the house before World War Two, while Lyall, the eponymous, greying, chain-smoking, Ilford-born son of a police sergeant had been at Upton Park for 34 years, undertaking virtually every job bar turnstile operator.

The left-back had joined West Ham as a 15-year-old, £4 per week apprentice in June 1955. He trained on Tuesday and Thursday afternoons, played on Saturdays and used the mathematical brain nurtured at Ilford County High school to double as the club's wages clerk back at the Boleyn Ground, each day.

Footballs, not farthings, were his passion, though, and while he struggled to concentrate in an office environment, the experience was to prove invaluable, for he started to see how a club was run.

After playing in the 1958 FA Youth Cup final defeat against Manchester United, Lyall earned his full debut in a 4-2 win over Chelsea in February 1960, before going on to make just 31 first-team appearances for the club.

Sadly, a collision with Arsenal's Tommy Docherty – another player destined to become solid managerial stock – effectively ended his playing days.

After granting him an April 1964 testimonial that garnered their crocked servant a princely nest-egg of £3,797, the paternal Hammers then arranged for Lyall to make up the wages in the mornings and coach at local schools in the afternoons.

Taking over as part-time Youth Team manager, the eager coach impressed sufficiently to be handed the role full-time in 1967 and, within four years, his appetite for the game and thirst for knowledge saw him elevated to the first-team coaching staff by the wily Ron Greenwood.

While his 13 years at Upton Park had seen Lyall's career unluckily ended by injury, there was nothing unfortunate about the way sorcerer Greenwood – who had conjured up FA Cup (1964) and European Cup Winners' Cup (1965) triumphs – was grooming his apprentice for bigger and better things.

By the early 70s, West Ham United's born and bred 1966 World Cup winning trio of Bobby Moore, Geoff Hurst and Martin Peters were nearing the end of their association with the club that had spawned them.

That the three failed to replicate their international glory on the domestic stage with the Hammers once more remains one of the game's greatest mysteries.

Indeed, observational, future boss Harry Redknapp once quipped: "The other eight of us were crap!"

But there was still a rich bedrock of cockney talent and the Hammers' cornerstone of Trevor Brooking, Frank Lampard and Billy Bonds – a £49,500 bargain buy from Charlton Athletic – ensured that there would still be enough talent in the Upton Park locker room to bring some more silverware back to the East End.

In September 1974, Lyall took over as team manager, while Greenwood moved upstairs before eventually leading England into an unbeaten, yet failed, 1982 World Cup campaign.

He was destined to enjoy instant success for on May 3, 1975, West Ham beat Moore's Fulham in the FA Cup final to claim the trophy for the second time.

And 12 months later, having pitched himself in among some of the continent's finest, Lyall had seen off Eintracht Frankfurt in an unforgettable European Cup Winners' Cup semi-final victory that set up a showdown with FC Anderlecht in Brussels' ill-fated Heysel Stadium.

There was no shame in the 2-4 defeat against future Hammer Francois Van Der Elst and the Robbie Rensenbrink-inspired Belgians, for Lyall had proved that, on his day, he was tactically astute enough to mix it with the best on both English and foreign soil.

But the legacy of inconsistency left by the Hammers' sides of the 50s and 60s was destined to percolate through to their successors in the 70s, too.

After several close scrapes, West Ham inevitably succumbed to relegation following a 0-2 defeat against Liverpool in April 1978.

However, while many footballers of the post-Bosman era would be looking to scramble from the club like rats from a sinking ship, the players of the day commendably held up their hands and vowed to put right the wrongs of a season that had seen them gather just 32 points from their 42 games to leave them languishing in 20th place.

Lyall and his supportive board soon realised that patience would have to be a virtue as an instant return eluded them.

Not even the presence of Brooking, Bonds, Lampard and the emerging Alan Devonshire could lift them back to the top flight at the first attempt, but the directors' confidence in their manager enabled him to make spectacular forays into the transfer market.

The February 1979 capture of Queens Park Rangers' Phil Parkes for £565,000 – a world record for a goalkeeper – and the subsequent £430,000 purchase of Ray Stewart from Dundee United (a British record for a teenager) just six months later, proved a clear signal of his intentions.

On May 10, 1980 – 57 years after they had lost 0-2 to Bolton Wanderers in Wembley's first-ever FA Cup final – second division West Ham captured the trophy for the third time against high-flying Arsenal.

The famous white horse of 1923 was not on duty this time around as West Ham galloped to an improbable victory over the Division One side. It was, arguably, Lyall's finest 90 minutes as his East End underdogs shot down the Gunners thanks to Brooking's rare 13th-minute header that secured a 1-0 victory over Terry Neill's heartbroken Highbury troops.

Not only had Brooking deposited a collector's item into the Hammers Hall of Fame but Lyall put on a tactical master-class by fielding the selfless David Cross in a lone front-running role that simply left a Gunners side, containing the likes of Pat Jennings, Liam Brady, Frank Stapleton et al, trying to fathom how to mark the deep-lying Stuart Pearson.

As a remarkable 1980-81 campaign kicked off, money was no object as Lyall again broke the bank with the record £800,000 capture of QPR striker Paul Goddard.

"There was no need for an agent when you were dealing with John Lyall," said Goddard. "If he said he'd do something for you, he would. It was all done on a handshake and the paperwork always followed, just as he had promised it would."

Bolstered by Goddard's arrival, it was soon obvious that the Hammers' boss had an embarrassment of riches as his peerless West Ham side strolled to the Division Two championship, suffering just four defeats along the way to a post-war record haul of 66 points.

The disappointing surrender of the FA Cup to Wrexham in a third round replay was mitigated by a barnstorming run to the League Cup final, where the ever-reliable Stewart drilled in a last-gasp, extra-time penalty – one of 76 conversions from 86 attempts – to secure a 1-1 draw against Liverpool and a Villa Park replay.

Meanwhile, back in Europe, another Cup Winners' Cup sojourn endured as Hammers saw off Real Madrid's feeder club – Castilla Club de Futbol (aggregate 6-4) – and Romania's Politehnica Timisoara (4-1) on their way to a quarter-final showdown with the highly-organised Georgian outfit, Dinamo Tbilisi.

The eastern Europeans had knocked the mighty Liverpool out of the European Cup the previous season and, again, they proved the grandmasters with a technically convincing 4-1 win at Upton Park

Not to be outdone, just four days after forcing that energy-sapping 1-1 draw against the Merseysiders at Wembley, Lyall and his tired troops made the gruelling trip to Tbilisi, where Stuart Pearson's 87th-minute goal earned Hammers a 1-0 second leg win.

That victory in front of 80,000 Georgians at the Lenin Stadium may have restored some London pride but it was to prove the club's last competitive European action for nearly two decades.

And despite taking the lead through Goddard in the League Cup final replay, weary West Ham then saw Liverpool recover to claim the trophy with a 2-1 win. However, the cup runs had been a mere sideshow in a season where the main event had always been promotion back to the top flight.

When Bonds lifted the second division championship trophy on the final day of the campaign, the Hammers – six wins and a draw clear of runners-up Notts County – had simply cantered, hands and heels, into the first division with that 13-point cushion.

The board's patience and confidence in Lyall had paid off, for during their three seasons away from the big time, he had managed to retain class acts such as Brooking, Bonds, Devonshire, Lampard, Parkes and striker Cross while nurturing the budding talent of Alvin Martin, Geoff Pike, Paul Allen, Goddard and Stewart in readiness for the inevitable return.

The 1980 FA Cup final victory over Arsenal had been Lyall's singular greatest 90 minutes, while that subsequent runaway 1980-81 campaign had been one of the most emphatic in the club's history.

After spending the next four terms consolidating themselves back in the top-flight, during which period both Brooking and Lampard retired and Father Time began to catch up on the seemingly indestructible body of the ageless Bonds, Lyall was to star as the chief architect behind the club's most sensational season ever.

Having finished in 16th place in May 1985, West Ham had nail-bitingly managed to avoid relegation by just two points.

Indeed, there was little optimism around Upton Park when Lyall dusted down the cheque book during the close-season to acquire Frank McAvennie (£340,000), a former Glaswegian painter and decorator turned deep-lying St Mirren striker, and Mark Ward (£250,000), a former baker's boy cum Oldham Athletic winger.

Certainly, an opening day defeat at Birmingham City suggested another year of frustration and fight, but an injury to Goddard forced McAvennie into a more prominent striking role alongside the free-scoring Tony Cottee.

It was to prove a marriage made in heaven as 28-goal McAvennie and Cottee (25) spearheaded an unlikely Hammers' charge for the title that saw them embark on an 18-game unbeaten run as they strode up alongside Liverpool and Everton in a surreal race for the title.

The harsh winter of 1986 had taken its toll, however, for as they headed into the final furlong, the back-log of postponed matches called upon them to play 13 games inside 38 days.

Going into the penultimate game of the season at West Bromwich Albion, the unlikely lads from the East End were in second place, four points behind Liverpool

NEARLY REACHED THE SKY

with a game in hand.

But again the Reds proved Lyall's nemesis as Kenny Dalglish's goal at Stamford Bridge secured both victory over Chelsea and the Division One championship, rendering Hammers' 3-2 win at The Hawthorns academic.

Just 48 hours later, the leggy Londoners headed to Goodison Park in what could so easily have been a title showdown, but by now their spirit was broken and a 3-1 win secured runners-up spot for the Toffees.

"To sustain a challenge over 42 games against the best teams in the country is the pinnacle of achievement in the game. It is a prize only a few have lifted. Most managers can spend a lifetime in the game and not get close. At least I got close," said Lyall after that tremendous third-place finish.

Life, though, would never be the same again down West Ham way and that was destined to make things sticky for Lyall as expectation levels rose all round.

Never before had West Ham even got close to sniffing the Brasso on the Championship trophy but now the anticipation was tangible as they headed into the following campaign.

The tragic events at the Heysel Stadium in Brussels, where 39 Italian supporters were crushed to death before the 1985 European Cup Final between Liverpool and Juventus, meant that English clubs were still banned from European football.

An inaugural assault on the UEFA Cup was denied.

Through no fault of his own, the gnomes of Zurich had slammed the door firmly shut on Lyall's opportunity to pitch his technical wit against those from the continent once more.

Remarkably, during that 1985-86 campaign, West Ham had used just 18 players to reach that best-ever third-place finish.

And typically, Lyall was determined to remain loyal to that squad.

His apparent reluctance to bolster his resources meant that he was also reliant upon a second injury-free campaign if he was to reach the heady heights of the season gone by.

"You must always try to move on and there can be reasons why you don't and whatever I wanted to do is irrelevant to what we did," Lyall cryptically told the acclaimed *EX*, the unofficial West Ham retro-magazine, in autumn 2004. "Some things are private. We were trying to do things and we were doing it to the best of our ability. If it doesn't work, put your hands up and say so.

"No one had told me who to sign at the end of the 1985-86 season but when things start to go wrong they then tell you who you should have signed. People will, quite rightly, start to criticise but if we all knew the answers and football was that easy, there wouldn't be any need for coaches and managers."

Alvin Martin's form that year saw him head to the Mexico World Cup finals, where he played in the 3-0 second round win over Paraguay before being inexplicably dropped by Bobby Robson for the infamous 'Hand of God' quarter-final defeat by Argentina.

Capped 17 times, Martin had been all but hand-reared by Lyall since heading south from his native Bootle as a raw teenager. The Merseysider's career path under his mentor epitomised the nature of Lyall's management style.

16

"John Lyall never got the credit he deserved and people don't understand how good he was. John was a father figure whom you knew you could always turn to," recalled the former West Ham skipper in *Boys of 86*. "The most disappointing thing is that he's no longer at the club. He should be on the board. I don't think that there was one player who didn't get on with him. Even the difficult ones, like the teenage Paul Inces of this world, had great respect for him.

"He treated the club's money as if it was his own and was always trying to balance ambition with the budget. Even when you tried to negotiate a new contract with him it was as if it was his own money you were talking about. That was the way he did the job. It was his club and he wasn't going to bankrupt it.

"At the end of the 1985-86 season you could have said to John: 'Go out and buy the best three players you can, say, Kenny Dalglish, Graeme Souness and Alan Hansen.' But he wouldn't have done it. John would've said: 'I don't think we can afford it. What if it goes wrong? We'll suffer.' He had a wonderful attitude."

But Martin, who made 595 appearances for West Ham United between 1978 and 1996, agreed that Lyall should have taken the plunge. "When you looked around the dressing room you'd think: 'Yeah, this is alright.' But can you imagine what it would've been like if two or three top-quality players had come in? Liverpool always went out and bought two new players even if they'd just won the championship. West Ham never got to that stage. The following year we needed a central defender, a left-back, and, possibly, another striker. Instead we tried to get through with what we already had."

By the time the unpopular, injury-prone Stewart Robson was signed from Arsenal for £700,000 in January 1987, it was obvious that West Ham were never going to come close to replicating those historic events of the previous 12 months.

And having come so near to sipping champagne from the Championship trophy, some of the Boys of 86 were now thirsty for yet more success. Indeed, McAvennie headed to his beloved Celtic for £800,000 in October 1987 before the ambitious Cottee moved to Everton for a then British record £2.05million in July 1988.

He may have been awash with cash, but by now Lyall's touch in the transfer market was, unfortunately, deserting him.

The ageing Liam Brady and Julian Dicks may have brought some quality to the squad, but the likes of Tommy McQueen, Gary Strodder, David Kelly and Allen McKnight were, quite simply, not up to the job and the knowledgeable East End public quickly realised that.

"In the space of three seasons the squad had changed considerably. I know I made mistakes, I'd be the first to hold my hand up and say that. But I'd also say, I must have got something right. It's a debate and that's the beauty of it," admitted Lyall, who was powerless to stop that second relegation in 1989. Not even a last throw of the dice in the shape of the record £1.25m recapture of McAvennie in March 1989 could stop the slide.

Now just weeks after seeing West Ham crash 1-5 at an Anfield still deeply mourning the loss of 96 fans crushed to death in the previous month's horror of Hillsborough, he found himself sitting in chairman Len Cearns' dining room.

Again Liverpool had condemned West Ham to Division Two and again Lyall was intent on steering the club back to where it belonged.

With his four-year contract set to expire on June 30, the man in the Upton Park hot seat had barely settled into his chair when Cearns – a retired property contractor – demolished the building blocks that his manager had meticulously assembled across three loyal, Lyall decades at the Boleyn Ground.

The board, comprising Cearns (chairman), his brother Will, son Martin, plus property developer Jack Petchey and solicitor Charles Warner, had made their decision and, surrounded by papers spread across an impromptu desktop, the chairman cut straight to the chase.

"I'm sorry John," he flinched from the opposite side of the large table. "But the directors have had a meeting and by a majority decision have decided not to renew your contract. I don't want to go into details. The decision is irreversible."

With trademark dignity, a shell-shocked Lyall replied: "Fair enough, Mr Len."

After opting not to accept the chairman's offer to put a gloss on the departure with a hastily contrived resignation, the dismissed Lyall then further declined the incredulous gesture of a second testimonial. Instead, he was later to settle for an ex-gratia payment of around £100,000 and the club Mercedes that propelled him back to Chadwell Heath, where he broke the news of his departure to his stunned and tearful coaching staff, Mick McGiven, Ronnie Boyce, Tony Carr and Bonds.

In his autobiography, *Just Like My Dreams*, he admitted: "I had no hint beforehand that they were about to relieve me of my job. There had been some speculation that I might move 'upstairs' as general manager but my thoughts until that moment had all been about preparing for the new season.

"Inevitably, the atmosphere was difficult, strained. Suddenly we were no longer on the same side, sharing the same triumphs and defeats. It was a tense moment for the chairman. We had known each other for a long time. Even so, I couldn't say that I noticed much sympathy, reluctance or emotion on his part as he terminated my 34 years with the club. He was chairman and was accepting his responsibilities. He obviously believed that what he was doing was the right course of action for the club.

"It was not the traditional way of doing things at West Ham United but the truth of the matter was that they had sacked me. If one thing upset me more than anything else, it was the fact that there was no personal acknowledgement or thank you from Mr Len. We didn't shake hands. I left the table, walked out of the dining room and let myself out of the front door."

From boy to man to godfather, Lyall's 34 years at Upton Park were worth just 73 words in the following terse statement:

'West Ham United FC Directors have decided not to offer John Lyall a new contract as Club Manager at the end of his present contract which expires on June 30. The Directors would like to thank John Lyall for his long and loyal service to the club. Ron Boyce and Mick McGiven will formally take charge of the players and management until a new manager is appointed. The vacant position will be advertised.'

From that moment on, West Ham United would never, ever be the same again.

Chapter 2
1989-90

LOU'S LOSING GAMBLE

The crestfallen Lyall returned home to paint his upstairs windows, his ponderous brushstrokes punctuated by frequent trips back down the ladder to turn aside the five-figure bids that the tabloids were offering him to spill the beans on his reign at Upton Park.

Typically, the former Hammers' boss remained tight-lipped, honourably preferring to maintain a dignified, brilliant white gloss on his 34 years at the Boleyn Ground, in deference to a tacky, thin, £10,000-lick of red-top sensationalism.

Having swapped his tracksuit for his decorating overalls, Lyall's trusty lieutenants Ronnie Boyce and Mick McGiven were given the caretaker role as the five-man board of West Ham United set about advertising for his replacement.

With the Situations Vacant column of the *Newham Recorder* never likely to unearth the candidates required to return the club back to the top flight, they spread their net far and wide, while the press trawled up the names of Ray Harford, Gerry Francis, Steve Coppell, Don Howe and Peter Shreeves.

Prematurely, Trevor Brooking was also tipped to cut his managerial teeth some 14 years ahead of his eventual 2003 call-up, while intriguingly, the 47–times capped England midfielder's former Hammers' team-mate Harry Redknapp was also being linked with a possible return to his native East End from Bournemouth.

A right-winger who made 175 appearances in a seven-year Upton Park career that ended in 1972, 'Arry Boy was seen by many as a Cockney wide boy in every sense of the word. Having taken the Cherries to the third division championship in 1987 and 12th spot in the recently finished 1988-89 campaign, Redknapp was seen as the pick of the bunch.

But down on the Dorset coast, ballistic Bournemouth chairman Jim Nolan was making waves, accusing director Martin Cearns – son of Mr Len – of engineering a back-door approach for his manager who had famously masterminded a legendary FA Cup third-round victory over mighty Manchester United in 1984.

"I told Mr Cearns that he had done wrong and I refused him permission to speak to Harry again," the furious Nolan told the *Daily Mirror* as he closed the door on the man the board wanted to become only the fifth post-war manager of the club.

Such had been the determination of the men in suits to secure the services of Redknapp, that they had been readily prepared to sacrifice the possibility of Lyall moving upstairs into a Director of Football capacity, given the supposed long-running feud between the two which, reportedly, would have made it untenable for them to work alongside each other.

With Redknapp now ruled out of the equation and Francis extending his contract at Bristol Rovers, QPR coach Shreeves and Swindon Town manager Lou Macari emerged as front-runners.

As Shreeves prepared to fly back from a family holiday in Portugal, he was to discover that life can be a beach. For a courtesy call from Green Street to the Algarve brought him the unwelcome news that horse-racing fanatic Macari had sprinted up the standside rails to claim the job.

The new man knew that he was taking over from an Upton Park icon and one of his first tasks was to telephone his predecessor and offer to take him out for a meal at any time. And while, understandably, Lyall was never to take him up on the proposal, it was a gesture that was appreciated by the former Hammers' boss.

Macari, a tigerish, tee-total former Scottish-international midfielder had started out at Celtic, where he made 56 league appearances before going on to enjoy a distinguished career at Manchester United.

Ironically, he made a scoring debut at Old Trafford in a 2-2 draw against West Ham in January 1973, the first of his 392 senior outings for the Red Devils, before leaving in July 1984 and earning a disciplinarian reputation as Swindon Town's boss, where he also made 36 appearances as player-manager.

But despite having *played* for Britain's two biggest clubs before heading to sleepy Swindon, the 40-year-old was soon to discover the huge chasm between *managing* under the bright lights of London as opposed to the wilds of Wiltshire.

"I just don't understand the lack of responsibility and loyalty," he grimaced as he strode through the Boleyn Ground gates to face the potential of an instant mutiny from a team still reeling from both relegation and Lyall's departure. "There would be chaos in football if clubs gave in to players who signed contracts and then wanted to get away after a few months."

Pre-Bosman, the balance of power still rested with the clubs ahead of the players, whose freedom of movement was still largely restricted.

Meanwhile, despite their threats to leave, the contracted scholars of Upton Park's Academy steadied themselves for a change in the deep-rooted, pure footballing brand that was West Ham United.

Edinburgh-born Macari had lived in nearby Leytonstone for over a decade as a youngster, and he was acutely aware of Cockney tolerance levels.

But while he knew that the long-suffering East End had always favoured footballing entertainment over an all too familiar win-at-all-costs mentality, the new boss still insisted that it was time for change.

"Their style didn't do them much good last season otherwise I wouldn't be sitting here today," he declared. "Maybe the skill emphasis tended to overshadow the need for a battle. Now we need a more robust attitude and I want a fighting spirit on the pitch."

There was certainly plenty of spirit *off* the pitch.

As England Under-21 midfielder Paul Ince battled every inch of the way to seal a dream move to Manchester United amidst his contention that he was disgusted by Lyall's dismissal, the pumpkin-like Macari returned to the Swallow Hotel at Waltham Abbey just before midnight, where he bumped into the club's own 24/7 entertainment centre, Frank McAvennie.

"Have you had a good night, son?" asked the new manager at the end of an exhausting first day at the Hammers' helm.

"I don't know yet," replied the suited and booted blond bombshell who still remained goal-less in his second spell at West Ham following that record return back in the spring. "I'm only just going out!"

For long-standing senior professionals such as Phil Parkes, Alvin Martin, Tony Gale, Alan Devonshire, Liam Brady and McAvennie brought up under Lyall's law, Macari's training regime was certainly a culture shock.

"I've seen tales that players are being forced to train in the afternoons as well as mornings," stated the new man. "That's what professionals all over the country are doing. The way they are reacting, you'd think that they got West Ham promoted, not relegated."

Certainly, the sweep of a frantic morning's pre-season training followed by a post-lunch coach journey to a floodlight friendly did little to enamour skilled, ball-playing craftsmen such as 33-year-old Devonshire to a new broom trying to raise his athletes' stamina in readiness for the new campaign.

"The board had made a decision to bring in someone from outside rather than promote from within and Lou had a great record at lower levels. It could so easily have gone extremely well," suggested Steve Potts, whose 506 first-class appearances still leave him at Number Nine in the all-time Hammers appearance charts. "He had this sergeant-major reputation and his own ways but, whereas his training methods had been accepted as the norm at other clubs, here at West Ham he was dealing with experienced internationals such as Liam Brady and Dev. Even Lou would admit that it was hard to get his ideas rubbing off on players like that."

The new manager was quick to observe: "There's a belief here that ability alone can win football matches. It can't, otherwise I'd just go out and sign George Best!"

Macari, while abhorring alcohol, was more than partial to a bet. And having turned his back on Swindon it was not long before *The People* reporter Bill Bradshaw was alleging that, alongside Robins' chairman, Brian Hillier, he had arranged for the club to stake a tax-paid £5,500 on Town to win the 1986-87 Division Three championship at odds of 10/1.

While County Ground shareholders claimed it was both a misuse of club funds and against Football Association rules to bet on their own team, the duo argued that the subsequently losing wager was merely an insurance policy against the pay-out of promotion bonuses.

It was a theme that was to thread itself into the fabric of Macari's tenure at Upton Park.

As finance company Avco Trust stood down, new club sponsors BAC – a Romford based double-glazing outfit – hoped that their financial backing could open the door upon an immediate return to the top flight.

Out on the pitch, Hammers continued their preparations for the 1989-90 challenge with a pre-season tour of Scandinavia but Ince – influenced by agent Ambrose Mendy – became more and more restless as he sought to engineer a move to Old Trafford.

Ince claimed that Lyall had promised him a new four-year contract prior to his departure on holiday to Malta but by the time he had flown back to Blighty, his mentor had gone. Worse still, Macari remained insistent that the £750 per week he was earning under his existing two-year deal "was enough for a kid of his age."

Elsewhere, money had never entered the mind of Barking-born Alan Dickens, who had once been tipped as the new Trevor Brooking.

After making a scoring debut at Notts County in December 1982, he won a solitary England Under-21 cap before playing a starring role in West Ham's record-breaking 1985-86 season.

But the silky midfielder was helplessly short on self-confidence and, locked in the dressing room toilet, had even been known to be physically sick both before matches and at half-time.

"I was just honoured to be playing for West Ham United and when it came to contracts I just used to accept whatever was offered to me," admitted Dickens (who made 209 starts plus 25 substitute appearances in league, FA Cup, League Cup, Full Members Cup and European matches, scoring 30 goals) several years after his £600,000 move to Chelsea in August 1989. "It was just a case of John Lyall spelling out the offer and me signing on the dotted line. I just thought it was the way it worked. My next-door neighbour was a black cabbie and he earned more than me. It never crossed my mind to ask for more.

"My first car was a Triumph 2000 which I bought for £400. The exhaust was blowing and it was a right state. I'd just broken into the first team but instead of driving into the players' car park, I used to park in a side street around the corner from the stadium and walk to the ground. I didn't want anyone to see me because the car was a disgrace," the modest, self-effacing individual wrote in *Boys of 86*.

Dicko had been raised by Lyall in tandem with Tony Cottee but, as West Ham went on the wane towards the end of the decade, his confidence had been mercilessly dented by an expectant East End who were struggling to come to terms with the decline of their team and, in particular, the mercurial midfielder.

"Sometimes I would get too nervous. It's good to be on edge and wanting to do well but to be too nervous is not a good thing," admitted Dickens, whose cause had not been helped by the departures of Cottee and McAvennie plus Paul Goddard, who had also been allowed to head to Newcastle United for a record incoming fee of £415,000 in November 1986.

Certainly, the likes of David Kelly and Leroy Rosenior were to prove nowhere near as prolific and with injuries also taking their toll, Dicko – along with lumbering centre-half Paul Hilton – was one of several stop-gap strikers somewhat unfairly employed in an unfamiliar, front-running role by his desperate boss.

Now Lyall's departure had opened the door for the out-of-contract Dickens to link up with a long-time admirer – Chelsea boss Bobby Campbell, the father of former rookie Hammers' striker and fellow Boy of '86, Greg.

"I went to see Lou just before I signed for Chelsea because I thought it was the right thing to do. He asked me to stay but he didn't say a lot more," said the agent-less Dickens, who headed to Stamford Bridge to sign a contract that was only a little better than the one that he had enjoyed at Upton Park.

An injury-punctuated three seasons followed way out west, before the 28-year-old – who was at Cardiff's Millennium Stadium to watch the club's 2005 play-off final victory over Preston North End – disastrously lost his way, drifting out of the game. In the end, he set the meter running in his own London black cab following brief sojourns at Brentford, Colchester United, Chesham United, Collier Row, Billericay Town and Purfleet.

Having just lost midfielder Dickens, Macari was also still struggling to hold onto the want-away Ince.

And when mutinous Mark Ward was refused his habitual Friday night serving of chips on the eve of the opening game of the campaign at Stoke City, the new manager suddenly found a third midfielder quite unprepared to stay and fight for the cause under his regime.

By 4.45pm on Saturday, August 10, 1989, Macari's mountainous task was taking on Everest-like proportions. A Kevin Keen opener may have been wiped out five minutes from time, but the 1-1 draw was the least of his worries as the plastered McAvennie headed south in an ambulance for surgery on a broken right ankle that would keep him out of action for nearly eight months.

An awkward clash with the Potters' uncompromising Chris Kamara had seen the Scotsman stretchered away, reportedly threatening legal action against the former Swindon Town stopper.

"Rob Jenkins, West Ham's old physio, sprinted onto the pitch carrying his bag of tricks," recalled McAvennie in his autobiography, *Scoring – An Expert's Guide*. "He looked at my injured leg and I saw his face go sickly white. He fussed over it for a little while and then asked: 'Can you get up and walk it off, Frank?' George Parris looked at him and said: 'For f***'s sake Rob, his ankle is hanging the wrong way.' And it was!"

But the threat of litigation was never an option according to the angry McAvennie and reconciliation eventually took place several years later on the *Goals on Sunday* sofa when host Kamara and guest Macca found themselves sitting together in the Sky Sports studio.

Now Macari needed yet more reinforcements. The Dickens' fee had provided the manager with an instant war chest but as he set about garnering the players whom he felt possessed the qualities required to get back to the first division, it was clear that the items on his shopping list would cost more than the funds available in his sporran.

First-up, Queen's Park Rangers' Martin Allen was persuaded to turn down the overtures of Derby County and make the move across town in a £660,000 deal. An industrious, intense midfielder, Martin was from the Allen dynasty that included father Dennis, uncle Les plus cousins Bradley, future Hammer Clive and former Upton Park starlet, Paul.

Indeed, the biased Martin habitually voted for all of the playing members of his extended family clan in the annual Professional Footballers' Association awards!

NEARLY REACHED THE SKY

After the emerging Stuart Slater bagged a double to secure a 2-0 victory over Bradford City, the energetic Allen plundered a goal on his home debut in a 3-2 win over Plymouth Argyle that made him an instant hit with the fans who had afforded him cult status by the time he left the club in 1995.

"I booked into a hotel room and spent all day and last night by myself," admitted the man who was destined to be christened 'Mad Dog' after emerging from his five-star kennel and putting on a five-star performance. "After such a busy week I didn't want to be near the phone. I just wanted to concentrate on getting it right."

By now, the Ince saga was having a destabilising effect on the entire club. And in an act of naivety over nonchalance, the petulant midfielder managed to alienate himself from the entire East End when he allowed himself to be photographed wearing a Manchester United shirt outside the Phoenix Apollo restaurant in Stratford – a haunt for footballers, Page 3 girls and soap stars.

"Ambrose Mendy suggested that as I was going to Malta I should have my picture taken in a Man U top . . . just in case a deal was completed by the clubs while I was on holiday. I didn't really want to have the photo taken but I went along with it," Ince later explained to fellow ex-Mayfield pupil, Tony McDonald, in a revealing *Hammers News Magazine* scoop, payment for which Ince insisted went to the Princess Diana memorial fund.

But from the moment the shutter of Lawrence Lustig's camera clicked, he would be re-christened 'Judas' forever.

"I was assured that the picture would remain in the photo library of the *Daily Star* and that if I decided to stay at West Ham, it would be torn up and that would be the end of it," insisted Ince. "Some geezer at the *Daily Express* – I didn't realise they were in the same building – heard that my move to Manchester United was about to go through. He went into the shared photo library and stumbled on the one Lawrence had taken. That's how it came to appear in the *Daily Express*. It caused murders!

"I felt let down by the people who were advising me and were supposed to know it all. I can understand the fans' reactions because it wasn't a nice thing for me to do. Lou Macari said: 'You can't play here, the supporters won't have it.' I would've stayed if they were prepared to forget everything but there was no point in staying if they were going to slaughter me every time I went out on the pitch."

Team-mate, best pal and master of the understatement, Potts, later observed: "You just wouldn't do it, would you? I honestly think he was misguided over the Manchester United business. He was young and John Lyall had guided him very well. But once Lou Macari took over and he was pictured in the paper in that red shirt, it was always going to be a hard one to turn around."

The enforced inheritance of Mick McGiven, 1964 FA Cup-winning hero Ronnie Boyce, youth-team manager Billy Bonds and Tony Carr meant that Macari was still without any of his own hand-picked coaching staff and confidantes.

Indeed, the local press proved his chief allies and an hour or so after every match at Upton Park, a tribe of scribes would head for the home dressing room where Macari would wheel in the sandwich trolley and open an inquest upon the events of the afternoon's – if not the week's – proceedings and, sometimes, even find himself given the keys to lock up the stadium.

Back in willowy Wiltshire, managerial power had enabled him to hold the trump cards over a Swindon Town team comprising several journeyman 'two-bob' players just happy to have a contract that would provide them with a modest living from the game they so dearly loved.

Yet here in London the pack contained a few aces with a better understanding of their worth.

Forced to work with his predecessor's coaches, Macari found that he held far less clout amidst a gaggle of senior professionals set in their ways and a clutch of youngsters itching to flee the new regime.

"Even Steve Potts has told me that he's thinking about having talks with Brentford," confided the man – who had interrupted his discussions with the defender to watch a televised horse race – feeling the rising temperature of the hot seat. "Brentford for God's sake! Whatever next?"

Judas' position at the club was by now untenable but in a bizarre twist in the tale, the excited youngster almost talked his way out of his dream transfer when he revealed that he had a twinge in the pelvic region and subsequent x-rays revealed a mystery condition that saw the heartbroken 21-year-old fail his medical.

As United splashed out a British record £2.3m for Middlesbrough's Gary Pallister, Ince was ordered to rest for three months while his five-year, £3,000 per week deal was tossed into the Old Trafford furnace.

Back in Harley Street, Ince was given the all clear and although Hammers' own orthopaedic surgeon concurred that there was nothing wrong, United refused to return to the table. The furious Mendy, fearing his agent's commission had just gone up in flames, threatened legal action, claiming that the Manchester giants had 'degraded themselves'. Macari, himself, later admitted that he, too, had felt intimidated throughout the protracted negotiations.

"It had got a bit lively and there were threats going back and forth across the table," the Scot told *EX*. "I had been told that if I didn't let him go there could be trouble for me."

There were problems for David Kelly, too, when he was dismissed in a 1-1 draw at Hull City.

But that red card could not dampen Macari's spirits, for Hammers were top of the second division after just four games, and an added bonus came in the form of Devonshire's welcome decision to sign a new one-year contract.

"After all that's gone on around here lately, that kind of loyalty is something of a rarity," declared Macari pointedly. "It's meant a financial loss for Dev because he had several better offers."

Paul Hilton (60+19 apps 8 gls) was less fortunate. After four knee operations, the 30-year-old wisely decided that he did not wish to spend his later days as a cripple. The signing of Hilts had been an ironic by-product of West Ham's record 10-0 victory over Bury in October 1983. For just weeks after seeing four-goal Cottee lead the charge through the Shakers' defence in a Milk Cup second round, second leg tie at Upton Park, Lyall spent £90,000 on the centre-back who had also attracted Manchester United and Liverpool.

NEARLY REACHED THE SKY

"I hoped to follow Billy Bonds' example and keep playing for as long as possible but things haven't worked out," said the dejected Hilts who, fortunately, was to discover that Hammers' paternal streak was still in evidence a few months later when they offered the married father of two a coaching role and a testimonial.

Another Allen goal helped Hammers to a 1-1 draw against Macari's old club Swindon Town before a 0-3 defeat at Brighton & Hove Albion led to Julian Dicks being given the captain's armband for the opening of the Littlewoods Cup campaign at his former club, Birmingham City. Hammers won 2-1 at St Andrew's and a 1-1 draw in the second round, second leg tie at Upton Park set up another trip to the Midlands for a third round match at Aston Villa.

Aged 21 years and 42 days, Dicks had become the second-youngest ever Hammers' skipper behind Bobby Moore, who was 21 years and nine days old when he led the side out against Arsenal in April 1962.

Following 16 days of pensive reflection way up north – and sensing the chance of stealing Ince – wily Manchester United boss Alex Ferguson returned to the table with one of the game's first-ever pay-as-you-play deals that were to become so prevalent in the modern game.

The headstrong Ince (87+7 apps 12 gls) eventually won 53 England caps during a career that also took in Inter Milan, Liverpool, Middlesbrough and Wolverhampton Wanderers. Conversely, just how far the self-styled Guv'nor would have progressed in his native East End remains anybody's guess.

West Ham got more than 30 pieces of silver for their prize asset, who was destined to go on and make 206 league and 75 cup appearances in United's colours but the £2m sought took its time coming via an £800,000 down-payment and £5,000 per game over the five-year term of his contract.

Despite being forced to settle for a cash-flow sapping HP deal, the board continued to dig into their pockets to support their new manager.

Next up came Colin Foster, a gangly centre-half who had left neighbours Leyton Orient to join Nottingham Forest in a £50,000 deal in March 1987.

Sensing a handsome profit, Brian Clough was rarely a bad judge of a player and he had not wasted any time offloading his gentle-giant of a defender when Macari arrived at the City Ground with an enormous £750,000 cheque two-and-a-half years later.

"Remember, all you can do, young man, is win!" said Clough who, having trousered that huge profit for Forest, no doubt felt that the least he could do was to impart some free managerial wisdom to Macari, as he set about heading back to London with his expensive capture who would threaten the long-standing, central defensive axis of Martin and Gale.

Foster made his home debut in a 1-0 win over Watford and his away bow also saw a 1-0 victory at Portsmouth.

But his arrival could not have come at a worse time for Gale, who soon found himself sidelined by match-winner Vinnie Jones' scything tackle in Leeds United's 1-0 victory at Upton Park as Hammers – having previously been defeated 2-3 by West Bromwich Albion – slumped to a second successive home reverse.

Despite victories over Sheffield United (2-0) and Sunderland (5-0) plus a 2-2 draw at Port Vale, by October 25, 1989, West Ham had slid into mid-table. After refusing to board the coach to the Midlands for a Littlewoods Cup tie at first division Aston Villa, Ward was put on the transfer list at the sixth time of asking.

The intervention of the PFA secretary Gordon Taylor saw Ward persuaded to drive to Villa Park, where he was forced to watch the goalless stalemate from the stands and given a suspended fine.

The following evening, the board insisted that he should honour the remaining two-and-a-half years of his four-year contract before the PFA finally persuaded them to relent ahead of a 1-1 draw at Redknapp's Bournemouth, where Ward returned as a substitute.

While the £1m-rated Merseysider was to remain firmly in the shop window, Macari's continued lack of communication skills with his players sunk to a new low at Wolverhampton Wanderers.

As Ward and the rest of the squad waited impatiently in the dilapidated, derelict Molineux dressing rooms with kick-off edging closer and closer, the Hammers' manager was nowhere to be found.

A steward suggested he may possibly have gone in search of a sponsors' lounge in order to watch a televised horse-race and when Macari finally returned to the fold, his worried players asked him to reveal the line-up.

"The team's as per the programme," he announced.

"Oh, we'd better go out and buy a programme then!" retorted the disenchanted Gale before discovering that, despite being fit again, he had failed to find his way back into contention.

While Macari's friendship with club photographer Steve Bacon and the local media continued to develop, he still lacked a footballing shoulder to lean on.

"I don't think the players respected Lou but I liked him," said Billy Bonds. "He was good to me and I think that Ronnie Boyce and Mick McGiven would say the same. Where Lou went wrong is that he should have brought in his own people and got rid of his backroom staff.

"Lou was a different type of manager to anything the club had ever had before. The players had been brought up on the ideas of Ron Greenwood and John Lyall so it was always going to be difficult for Lou to win them over. He was a culture shock to a lot of them."

In early November, Macari tried to lure former Old Trafford team-mate Ray Wilkins from Glasgow Rangers. To coin the 84-times capped midfielder's catchphrase it was, potentially, a 'super' move.

Not only would the canny Scot be recruiting a chosen ally to Upton Park but the capture of the 34-year-old ex-England skipper – the professional's professional – would also mean that he was bringing a steadying influence to the club.

Unfortunately for Macari it did not turn out so super and just hours after a Dicks screamer had seen off Villa in the Littlewoods Cup third round replay, his joy was tempered by Wilkins' promised telephone call that sadly conveyed the news that he would be heading to QPR instead.

Although McAvennie had had the pins removed at the Roding Hospital in Redbridge, with auxiliary striker Leroy Rosenior still on the injured list, too,

NEARLY REACHED THE SKY

Macari set his sights on signing Justin Fashanu in a one-month loan deal from Manchester City. And the striker who was once signed by Brian Clough for £1m before almost being forced to retire with a knee injury, quickly drew puzzled looks in the dressing room when he installed his own portable heat lamp while, upstairs, his entourage wasted no time commandeering the directors' box.

A goalless draw against Newcastle United left West Ham in seventh place but as he drove home from Upton Park that Saturday evening, Macari's world was about to be rocked by the thud of the Sunday newspapers crashing onto his doormat the following morning.

This time *The People's* busy Bill Bradshaw claimed that Swindon Town Chairman Hillier had staked £6,500 at 8/13 on his own club to lose an FA Cup tie at St James's Park in January 1988. The seemingly well-informed hack produced a copy of a Ladbrokes cheque for the £4,000 winnings apparently paid to Hillier after the Magpies soared into the fifth round with a spectacular 5-0 win.

While Hillier denied he had placed the wager, the FA launched an immediate investigation and stated that they would also be contacting Macari given he was Town manager at the time.

But while all hell was breaking lose in London, across the Irish Sea Macari was enjoying some brief respite in the form of a short break to the Emerald Isle for a friendly that officially marked the switching on of Limerick's floodlights.

In the thickening fog, Slater netted the only goal before 7,000 fans as West Ham beat a Munster Select XI but, importantly, the trip gave Macari the perfect opportunity to try and bond the old and the new with their manager.

Despite Sunday's scandalous sensation, Macari remained in good form.

Indeed, the impish boss wasted no time showing that he could still be one of the lads with a prank on club clicker Bacon, the rotund, thirty-something renowned for his portly frame at grounds up and down the country.

In the adjoining hotel room, Macari could hear the snapper running his evening bath. Listening intently against the wall, the smiling Scot waited until the very moment he heard the plop and splash as the unsuspecting lens man levered his ample torso down into the bath tub.

Bacon did not even have time to grab the soap, for within moments the ear-splitting pitch of the hotel fire alarm was screeching through the bathroom. Frantically, the giant of a man clambered out of the bath and with just an under-sized bath towel to cover his modesty he hurried for the fire exit.

But no sooner had he dashed into the corridor than he was stopped in his tracks by the sight of the mischievous Macari, his coaches and a handful of players already gathered outside his bedroom door in readiness for the false alarm and the oblivious Bacon's very own version of *The Great Escape*.

That short break was to prove the last semblance of peace for the beleaguered Hammers' boss as he brought his team home to face lowly Middlesbrough.

The demanding, self-confident Fashanu was paraded before the Upton Park crowd prior to a comfortable 2-0 win ahead of an upcoming Littlewoods Cup fourth round tie with Wimbledon.

And as former Hammer Bobby Gould brought his Crazy Gang to Upton Park,

Macari witnessed at first-hand just how a floodlit Upton Park could boil over into a cauldron of vitriol.

While Arsenal slid to a 1-3 defeat at Oldham Athletic and Tottenham Hotspur found themselves scrapping out a 2-2 draw at Tranmere Rovers, back in London, the Hammers and the Dons were matching each other kick for kick.

'The ball was largely an irrelevance,' observed *The Times,* while the disgusted *Daily Mirror* declared that 'soccer is in the gutter' after Dicks was sent off for a vengeful, scything lunge on Dennis Wise. For reasons best known to himself, referee Alf Buksh dismissed only one player during the 90-minute 'war'.

In the closing minutes, 10-man West Ham limped into the quarter-finals thanks to that man Allen, who boosted his East End street credibility yet further with, according to *The Times,* 'a goal which gleamed like a diamond amid a sea of mud stretching from one end of the ground to the other.'

"That was my favourite ever game in my whole life!" howled Allen recalling an evening of anarchy. "It was the night I was crowned 'Mad Dog'. I was playing at right back in front of the Chicken Run where I had a rumble in midfield and kicked Eric Young in the child-making equipment area with all six studs.

"Then after I put us in front, I tried to waste some time by making out I was sprinting upfield before turning and creeping on tip-toe, just like the Pink Panther, back along the Chicken Run while my marker obliviously returned towards his own goal. Now unmarked, Phil Parkes rolled the ball to me and I simply passed it back to him and sprinted back up to the halfway line. It was all done just for fun. My wife Gabriella used to say: 'Why do you do things like that?' And to this day I honestly still don't know!"

Macari remained defiant. It had not been pretty but at least he had seen his side stand toe to toe with their foe and fight them every inch of the way for the right to a quarter-final place.

"Ask our supporters whether or not they would rather be in the next round," he implored.

Upon seeing the X-rated video evidence, however, the FA immediately ordered an inquiry that was to lead to a £20,000 fine for each club.

Macari may well have been under siege but, ever media-friendly, he kept his promise to allow *Hammers News Magazine* reporters to travel with the team to Blackburn Rovers in order that that an away-day diary feature could be prepared for the club's upcoming Christmas 1989 annual.

It was clear that the Hammers' boss still had strong links with Manchester United for, during a long journey north up the M6, Macari managed to arrange an impromptu coaching session at his former employer's Cliff training complex.

Spotting the rare chance of a sauna, Parkes decided on a more leisurely Friday afternoon's relaxation while the rest of his team stretched their muscles following the long coach journey.

Emerging from the treatment room, the cock-sure Ince was quick to gloat about the greener grass of Manchester and as the Hammers' team-coach prepared to continue its journey, several first-teamers delayed boarding in favour of twisting the window-wipers and aerial on the shiny new BMW which their former team-mate had obviously traded in for his Dagenham-built Ford Escort XR3i.

By the time the weary squad sat down for their eve-of-match meal, Ward's chagrin at the continuing French-fries famine was there for all too see. But, by now, Macari's innovative players had devised other ways of satisfying their less discerning appetites.

After playing a few games of pool under the watchful eye of the coaching staff, the players started heading to their rooms in readiness for the local pizza delivery scooter's arrival at the rear fire escape.

Still downstairs, the parched Parkes had a thirst to quench.

Under Lyall's law, a modest pre-match nightcap had been tolerated, even encouraged, but Macari's rule called for absolute Friday night abstinence.

But how could another non-playing, paying guest of the travelling party refuse when the amiable 'keeper asked that a covert brandy be slipped into his hitherto alcohol-free Coke?

Long-standing physio Jenkins was certainly more at home with the old school rather than the modern treatment techniques practised by the new-age sports science graduates with their state-of-the-art gizmos.

Jenkins – the son of legendary 60s trainer, Bill – was renowned for the pre-match tots he readily dispensed to any players requiring them, while post-match Sunday treatment would cost the injured first-teamers a standard tariff four cans of lager.

And anyone struggling to sleep on the eve of a big game only had to ask Rob for something to help them on their way.

Sleep was not a problem for Macari, who was one of the first down to breakfast where, again, he was quick to seek counsel from *Hammers News Magazine* scribes as to the attributes of Devonshire – a player to whom he had yet to give a start.

And after giving the eight-times capped England midfielder the thumbs up, the manager rode shotgun on the team coach down into Blackburn High Street, where he asked the driver to pull the otherwise passenger-less vehicle up onto the pavement, whereupon he dashed through the Christmas shoppers and into the bookies with his selections for the day.

Back at the team hotel, David Kelly was asked whether he would be playing.

"You'd better ask Stevie Bacon!" came the caustic response from the out-of-favour striker who was destined for another Saturday off.

By 3.00pm, Devonshire was firmly installed in the starting line-up but, as the interval neared, Rovers were already 4-0 ahead before Brady pulled one back on the stroke of half-time. Heading for the tunnel at the break, the West Ham manager had every right to cast a quizzical glare towards the *Hammers News Magazine* photographer as an eye-opening weekend had deteriorated yet further.

And just 30 seconds into the second period Lenny Johnrose put barnstorming Blackburn 5-1 ahead.

Yet somehow, Hammers began to stage an incredible comeback against a complacent home side. And by the time the final whistle blew, a Dicks' penalty plus goals from Slater and Ward had reduced Rovers to a bundle of nerves as West Ham came so close to grabbing an equalising fifth goal.

Goalless, Fashanu (2+1 apps 0 goals) returned from the 4-5 defeat at Ewood Park to discover that his wage demands were simply too great for West Ham and, while his loan spell had been far from memorable on the pitch, he still left them with lingering legacies in the shape of the string of unpaid parking fines incurred in the club car. Tragically, after being outed as a homosexual, he was to hang himself in a lock-up garage just a few miles from Upton Park, some years later, after being accused of sexually assaulting a youth in the USA.

A 5-2 victory over Plymouth Argyle counted for little in the much-maligned Zenith Data Systems Cup when a crowd of just 5,409 – the lowest since 4,500 witnessed a 0-1 defeat against Doncaster Rovers in 1955 – went through the Upton Park turnstiles to see West Ham secure a third round tie at Chelsea.

The serious business of sustaining a promotion challenge was uppermost in their minds and by the time Public Enemy No.1 Kamara rolled into town with Stoke City three days later, 17,704 were there to see a goalless draw.

Another northern defeat at Bradford City, where Jimmy Quinn netted an 89th-minute winner, left Hammers on 30 points, and that meant that Leeds United (39) and Sheffield United (38) had begun to pull away at the top of the table.

While six-goal, £600,000 Kelly had failed to make the transition from Walsall to West Ham, one of the undoubted catalysts for Lyall's downfall in his ill-fated final season had been his insistence on sticking with Allen McKnight.

As understudy to injured Republic of Ireland goalkeeper Packie Bonner, the Northern Ireland international had taken his chance with both gloves during the Celts' centenary 1987-88 campaign. The Antrim-born custodian played a dozen games as Celtic romped to a 35th Scottish championship and he also appeared in a 2-1 Scottish Cup victory over Dundee United where a McAvennie brace helped the Bhoys to the double.

But Bonner had returned to the fold and McKnight wanted another taste of the big time.

Lyall – anxious to find a successor to 38-year-old Parkes and Tom McAlister (35) – offered cash-strapped Celtic £200,000 for McKnight in a deal which seemed to suit all parties.

Within days of his arrival, McKnight had spent an evening at the Phoenix Apollo promising his new club-mates, and anyone else who would listen, that he would be loved at West Ham, thanks to his ability to dribble outside the box and pull off acrobatic saves.

Unfortunately the reality was to be so much different.

Following a relatively steady start, the relegation-bound Hammers were suffering a crisis of confidence alongside their shaky keeper.

Indeed, the tall, blond, 10-times capped international looked more at home in nightclubs such as Hollywoods, Secrets and the other local Essex venues that he regularly frequented, than he did in the goal of a football club.

"Allen McKnight was the worst keeper I have ever seen at that level," wrote the uncompromising Devonshire in *Boys of 86* after witnessing calamity upon calamity unfold between the sticks and the tabloids roll out the all too frequent 'McKnightmare' headlines.

Bereft of confidence, the keeper eventually conceded 58 goals in 36 league and cup outings at Upton Park. In February 1989, the arthritic Parkes had bravely cut-short his recovery to help Lyall in his time of need, and a 1-0 FA Cup fifth round win over Charlton Athletic on his return to the fold proved an immediate endorsement of the confidence in which he was held by the likes of Gale, Martin and the surviving boys of 86.

But the damage had already been done and, by the time injury forced McKnight's recall for the final two games of the season, his last league appearance for the club had ended in that 1-5 defeat at Anfield that confirmed relegation.

The nationwide media coverage meant that Macari had seen events from afar and from Day One he was determined not to endure a McKnightmare of his own.

"Midway through the first pre-season training session of the summer, Lou pulled me to one side and said to me: 'You will never play in one of my teams.' He set me back so far that I never recovered," timber merchant McKnight claimed in EX having set up his own business following his premature retirement.

Macari knew that those arthritic knees of Parkes were not going to hold out forever, though, and he desperately cast the net far and wide to find a replacement.

The *Evening Standard* duly announced that the little-known Czech international goalkeeper Ludek 'Misloska' was about to join the club from Banik Ostrava in a £300,000 deal

And on a wintry Sunday morning, Brentwood & District Sunday League side Havering Nalgo took advantage of an abandoned match to train in the astroturf-carpeted sports hall at Hammers' Chadwell Heath training HQ.

The claret and blue bedecked Nalgo had more connections with West Ham United than they did with the local government union. Trevor Brooking had often starred in midfield or up front, Ray Stewart trained them on Thursday evenings, while club secretary Tom Finn faced a weekly battle to hold down a first-team place in a back four containing various members of the Hammers' press corps.

As the keen amateurs changed, Macari strolled in with his son Michael – a promising teenage striker – and a towering, smiling giant of a man who clearly did not understand a single word of English.

"Meet our new goalkeeper," said the pint-sized Hammers' boss looking skywards at the nodding Ludek Miklosko.

Upon seeing the players heading towards the pitch, Macari was adamant that the poor Finn's weekly fight continued as he peeled off his tracksuit, donned a fluorescent bib and joined in with Nalgo's hastily arranged six-a-side kick-about.

Bemused, Miklosko spent his first weekend outside Czechoslavakia watching his new manager Macari – a 1978 World Cup veteran and proud holder of those 53 Scotland caps – kick lumps out of the battered and bruised club secretary at each and every opportunity.

The liberated Ludo was determined to be one of the first eastern Europeans to take flight to England while an ant-like line of Trabants drove through the now crumbling Berlin wall amidst the freedom of *Glasnost*.

With David Blunkett still making his way up the political ladder, though, Ludo had no option but to return home to Prague and wait in the minus 12 degrees centigrade cold for the Department of Employment to issue his work permit.

Meanwhile, Macari knew that he could not gamble on Parkes' knees holding up during the impending, heavy Christmas programme.

Back on September 12, Liverpool had beaten Crystal Palace 9-0 as the Reds swept goal after goal beyond beleaguered Eagles' keeper, Perry Suckling (6 apps) Now, he was at Upton Park on one-month's loan.

One local reporter mischievously speculated that Macari had meant to get Brighton & Hove Albion's unsettled Perry Digweed instead.

Suckling was pitched straight in for a 0-2 defeat at home to Oldham Athletic. Costly Foster was decisively substituted before the half-time whistle had even blown, in an opening period that had seen the central defender compound the agony of Mike Milligan's opener with a sloppy, indecisive own goal.

Parkes was equally unhappy at having been discarded without consultation.

"I vowed never to play for West Ham again while Macari was the manager," said the livid 'keeper after being stood down for half-a-dozen games. "He didn't even bother to tell me that I'd been dropped."

Meanwhile, Ward still wanted away and as Hammers headed to Stamford Bridge and a 3-4 ZDS Cup defeat – where promising young Paul Kelly (0+2 apps) made his debut as substitute – representatives from Real Sociedad pondered a move.

And as Christmas drew near, he at last looked set to be granted his wish even if it meant taking Spanish steps.

But Finn could not disguise the cocktail of exhaustion and excitement as he climbed aboard the Havering Nalgo minibus for the team's festive night out.

With the evening over and the early editions about to hit the streets of London, he finally shared what, on the face of it, was about to make up the most unlikely of morning headlines.

Some sensational wheeling and dealing had seen the relieved Macari agree to swap his unsettled Scouser for Manchester City's Ian Bishop and Trevor Morley. Ward (206+3 apps 14 goals), one hell of an unhappy Hammer, had been traded for a silky midfielder and a hungry striker.

"Obviously it was disappointing to drop out of the first division having gained promotion with City," said Morley. "But West Ham are a good team with good supporters. With a wife and three children it's a bit of an upheaval but moving down with 'Bish' does make it that little bit easier."

City boss Howard Kendall announced: "The signing of Ward is not for now. Mark's for the future, for winning trophies."

Only time would tell.

After a Boxing Day defeat at Ipswich Town (0-1), Bishop and Morley went straight into the side that also lost 0-1 at Filbert Street on December 30, 1989, whereupon the Hammers' boss announced that he was also about to sign Bradford City's Northern Ireland international striker Quinn after, ironically, selling him to Leicester City in June 1988 while the pair were still at Swindon Town.

It was all too much for one local hack, who recalled a conversation he had had with Macari a few months earlier.

"Lou was telling me that he couldn't believe he had managed to get £220,000 from Leicester for Quinny. And now here he is buying him again for £340,000!"

NEARLY REACHED THE SKY

But it was to prove money well spent for the 46-times capped striker went on to score 19 league goals in 34 starts for the club.

Going into 1990, Hammers may have progressed to the Littlewoods Cup quarter-finals but the autumnal slump in their league form meant that they were in 11th place, now 17 points off leaders Leeds United.

And off the pitch the problems continued to mount.

Still the whiff of the Swindon betting scandal would not go away, while Macari's plan to take the squad to the relative tranquillity of Waltham Abbey's Swallow Hotel on New Year's Eve equally went up in smoke.

With his side due to play Barnsley the following day, the Hammers' boss organised a gentle road jog which simply turned to farce.

Furious that certain sections of the squad were not taking the session seriously enough he later revealed that he had levied a fine on striker David Kelly, claiming that it had been the first time he had ever imposed such a financial penalty on a player during his entire managerial career.

Following the eve-of-match meal back at The Swallow, Macari ordered a glass of champagne for each player and told them to get to bed early before he retired to his room, determined to ensure that the New Year at Upton Park would provide a clean start and prove far less problematic than the previous six months of his life.

For 1989 had witnessed 12 of the most traumatic months in the history of West Ham United Football Club, too.

Sadly, for both employer and manager, Macari's hopes and dreams for the New Year were set to be scotched before Big Ben had even finished ringing in the new dawn that was 1990.

According to the *Daily Express*, Dicks, McKnight, Kelly and Gary Strodder had the riot act read to them by the Hammers' boss after news leaked back to him that there had been 'incidents' in the early hours.

And in another chapter to the tale, an 18-year-old girl from the Hammers' commercial department, spotted by Macari at the hotel, subsequently divided her now free-time between shopping in the January sales and looking for a new job.

"I looked around and just couldn't believe she was there!" the disgusted manager told the gaggle of local scribes assembled in the Upton Park locker room. Despite the potential distractions of the night before, West Ham had managed to win 4-2 thanks to a Keen double, a Dicks penalty and a stunning Allen volley.

But the pack-like mentality of the national press ensured that there was more than enough fuel to feed the roaring fire of shame and scandal burning like a beacon at the Boleyn Ground.

Add in a drink driving conviction received by one of the club's out-of-favour Essex-based internationals and a report in *The Times* that Brian Blower had taken legal advice for an incident which the *Daily Express* further claimed centred upon a gate-crashing McAvennie having an alleged dust-up with the commercial director at Palms Hotel in Hornchurch, and the club was simply in turmoil.

Coach Mick McGiven had, according to his boss, been in tears when Lyall bade his farewell the previous June. But following the events of recent weeks, the centre-back who played 55 games between 1973 and 1978 following his £20,000 move from Sunderland, had decided that it was now time to say goodbye, too.

Macari spent an age trying to get McGiven to change his mind but, by now, there was no stopping his coach from heading to first division Chelsea to take up a new post as reserve-team coach.

"It was no longer the club that I'd served so long," McGiven later told *Hammers News Magazine*. "When someone drops their standards that doesn't mean that everyone's got to drop their standards. I knew that Lou needed help but it just didn't feel right."

Back in July, the chairman had refused to accept McGiven's resignation yet now there was even talk of 76-year-old Mr Len quitting, too.

And on the eve of the tricky, albeit surmountable, FA Cup third round tie at Torquay United, the under-siege Macari – holed up in his hotel room –was facing the prospect of a possible life ban after being charged by the FA in connection with the Newcastle-Swindon bet.

In the cloying Devon mud, Youth Training Scheme rookie Paul Hirons' solitary 77th-minute goal ensured that West Ham were slain by the fourth division giant-killers to heap yet more misery on Macari in the McGiven-less dug-out.

It was around this time that the bemused Bishop, Parris, Morley and McAvennie were ordered to a health farm by Macari on the pretext that they were 'too fat'.

Bish claimed that his manager cryptically announced: 'Just because you're thin doesn't mean that you're not fat.' And according to Morley, only the vehement protestations of the spindly Keen prevented the waif-like winger from being press-ganged into going, too.

Once there, the minute portions on offer saw the players head out for McDonald's and a pub crawl while another guest, bearing an apparently remarkable resemblance to Hillier, suddenly appeared at the farm, leaving them to suspect that they had, perhaps, been set up as the fall guys in order that a clandestine meeting could be arranged.

By now, Macari's all-consuming passion appeared to be that of preparing his defence against the various allegations speeding along the M4 from Swindon to Green Street.

And indeed he would often head back to Wiltshire at bizarre hours in a bid to stem the damage to his increasingly diminishing reputation.

West Ham themselves were back in the west country seven days later, for a second division clash at Plymouth Argyle and, as the Londoners made the long trek home following the 1-1 draw that left them in 10th place, 17 points off leaders Leeds, yet more alleged Swindon shenanigans were rolling off the presses.

As Town's behind the scenes power struggle snowballed, *The People's* mole had been digging again, and this time the column inches contained claims that a string of irregular cash payments had been made to Robins' players. Ironically, one alleged that Kamara – the slayer of McAvennie on Day One of the season – had been offered a £2,000 promotion bonus, £30 per week cash and a sponsored club car when Macari was boss.

While West Ham kept a stony silence on a river of revelations flowing from Fleet Street, Trevor Smith – a respected local journalist who had reported on the

Hammers each and every week since the 1950s – was simply aghast at the incomprehensible chaos engulfing the club. Never one for gratuitous criticism, he declared in the *Newham Recorder*: 'Whatever action the present board take over the current problems, they will find it hard not to reflect wryly upon the shock decision to part company with John Lyall who, whatever his faults, would never have allowed the club to find itself in such a squalid spotlight."

More indiscipline followed when Allen was sent off in a 1-1 draw with Derby County in the Littlewoods Cup quarter-final, and following the subsequent, humiliating 1-2 home defeat by lowly Hull City, Macari announced that he had just nine senior players available for the replay at the Baseball Ground.

On the face of it, Stewart Robson had looked every inch a West Ham United player when Lyall bought him in January 1987. At the time, some questioned why Arsenal were prepared to let their highly-rated midfielder join their London rivals so easily, especially just seven months after West Ham had claimed third spot in the league compared to the north Londoners' seventh-place finish.

Robson, who ironically made his Arsenal debut in a 2-1 win at Upton Park in December 1981, had won six England Under-21 caps and was widely tipped to achieve great things in the game when he moved eastwards following an autumn 1986 hernia operation.

A fearless, combative midfielder, 'Robbo' appeared a prize acquisition but his aloofness made him equally unpopular with his team-mates.

"Quite a few players didn't get on with Robson – he'd come from Arsenal and thought that he was above the rest of us," claimed Dicks in his authorised biography, *The Terminator*.

"If going into hotels, generally being rude, shouting and swearing and verbally abusing waitresses in restaurants is the way to behave then, yes, I was different and above all that," replied the Brentwood public schoolboy who it was rumoured had also been showing interest in one of McAvennie's Page 3 friends.

In *Boys of 86*, Devonshire observed: "We needed a central midfielder but Robbo just wasn't a West Ham player. Playing for West Ham was all about one and two-touch passing but Robson couldn't play that way. We didn't need Robbo. He wanted to take all the corners and throw-ins and play against the style we were used to. The fans loved him because he ran about, but they didn't realise that when he was on his arse, not winning the ball, we were all suffering in midfield."

And Gale added: "Robbo was a good player in his own right but he wanted to be Roy of the Rovers. What we thought was going to be one of the best signings turned out to be one of John Lyall's worst. I don't mean it offensively but he was the wrong player for West Ham."

Robson later admitted: "I honestly thought I could get West Ham back on track but, unfortunately, the move never materialised into what I wanted it to. They were frustrating days for me because John Lyall and his staff were smashing people. However, he didn't know what was going on in the dressing room and they just couldn't get the players to work hard and go on from there. We went backwards and it all went off the rails."

An allegedly familiar face in the dressing room following defeat but one supposedly liable to make a quick dash down Green Street in victory, the injured Robbo became more alienated when he was sidelined by a career-threatening groin injury that led him to take an unusual, drastic course of action.

"After another operation, West Ham's consultant Brian Roper kept telling me to rest and I knew that my career was on the line as a mere 24 year old," he recalled. "I certainly wasn't prepared to let it all slip away and I went for a second opinion and paid £7,000 for treatment at a Chiswick clinic. There was a lot of controversy surrounding my decision to undergo private treatment and training but in the end I was proved right because I did come back."

And how he returned.

As the injury-depleted Hammers headed to Derby for that quarter-final re-match, Macari desperately needed Robson to play.

Sporting navy blue cycling shorts to protect his fragile groin, for 87 tireless minutes Robson made home run after home run in the Baseball Ground mud as he put on one of the most courageous shows since the bloodied 'Chief' Bonds famously wore his 'Geronimo' head bandage in the FA Cup fourth round victory at Leyton Orient in January 1980.

"I hadn't even played a reserve game but I told Lou Macari that I'd do a job. It was a very proud moment for me and there was a lot of emotion that night because I'd been off the scene for so long."

Despite an injured Allen opting to stand on the away supporters' terraces leading the West Ham war cry – and a cameo loan appearance from Manchester United's Ralph Milne (0+1 app) – the game ended goalless after extra-time.

Skipper Gale called it right when the coin was tossed to decide the venue for a second replay and this time around, West Ham made home advantage count when goals from Slater and Keen gave them the 2-1 victory that set up a two-legged semi-final against Oldham Athletic.

With McKnight's confidence at its lowest ebb, West Ham had crashed out at the semi-final stage the previous season at the hands of Luton Town. But having beaten three Division One sides – Aston Villa, Wimbledon and Derby County – along the way, their self-belief was greater this time around.

A 3-1 home win over Brighton & Hove Albion may have left Hammers in 11th place, 20 points adrift of top of the table Leeds United, but it kept the squad in good heart as they prepared for the long journey to Boundary Park.

However, there was still that FA charge hanging over Macari in respect of the Newcastle-Swindon bet.

Following a four-hour hearing, the £1,000 fine incurred for his involvement in the dodgy wager that saw subsequently banned chairman Brian Hillier collect £4,000 winnings, provoked uproar on all sides. For Macari it was too much. For the baying press pack it was a paltry and gutless punishment meted out by the men in suits.

Macari pleaded that his part in the placing of the £6,500 bet was restricted to phoning a friend who could put the club in contact with Ladbrokes.

"Everyone has been saying that I have come out of this affair well," grimaced Macari, who saw his former chairman banned from football for six months and the

NEARLY REACHED THE SKY

Robins fined £7,500. "But as far as I'm concerned, I've been fined £1,000 for making a single telephone call."

While acting against FA rules, Macari had hardly phoned a friend to make himself a millionaire. The £6,500 bet was, after all, a plausible hedge against the cost of Swindon's FA Cup weekend on Tyneside.

Defeat would see the modest £4,000 winnings cover hotel and travel expenses, a draw may see the loss of the £6,500 stake but that would pale into insignificance given the lucrative gate receipts that a County Ground replay would generate, while, again, victory would produce a money-spinning fifth round tie.

The more serious allegations of the illegal payments to players were still being investigated but, for now at least, West Ham were standing by their man.

In an official club statement, Finn declared: *"It is apparent from the punishment imposed on Mr Macari that his minimal involvement in respect of this matter is accepted by the FA. For the last six weeks Mr Macari and his family have been subjected to intense media pressure, at times amounting to harassment. Now that this matter is behind him we trust and hope he will be allowed to return to a normal life and concentrate on his duties as manager of West Ham, commencing with the Littlewoods Cup semi-final at Oldham."*

Ironically, the club secretary had joined West Ham after spending 11 years at Athletic, where he forged a strong friendship with boss Joe Royle.

Certainly, the Manchester-born Finn had divided loyalties as he headed back to his old love on February 14, 1990.

And with sleet blowing down off the Pennines and onto the plastic Boundary Park pitch, West Ham were subjected to a St Valentine's Day massacre as the shots rained in on poor Parkes.

It was 6-0 before referee Lester Shapter blew the full-time whistle that put Hammers out of their misery.

"We just couldn't handle them," admitted the shell-shocked Macari cutting a lonely figure in the visitors' dressing room. "From the word 'go' one team was gliding all over the pitch and the other was in trouble."

"It's hard to know what went wrong," said substitute Devonshire scratching his head. "That pitch helped them but I'm not using it as an excuse. Everything they hit just went into the net but we should have done better for our fans who stood in the rain all night."

Alas, that defeat was to prove the end of an era in more ways than one.

Neither Parkes nor Devonshire would play for the club again.

And with the following morning's headlines all set to highlight the fact that West Ham had just gone 'down the Lou', it was also destined to be Macari's last game, too.

For as the squad climbed aboard the team coach for the trip to his old club Swindon Town the following Sunday, the boss was conspicuous by his absence.

Plaistow-born Peter Storrie, a 41-year-old Hammers' fan and director of a furniture company, had been invited to join the board and, alongside his fellow directors, he waited patiently for the missing manager to arrive at the Swallow Hotel in Waltham Abbey.

As the clock ticked down, however, they could delay no longer and the driver was ordered to head west in anticipation of Macari making his rendezvous at the team hotel in time for lunch.

With his work permit in one hand and a Czech/English phrasebook in the other, the equally anxious Miklosko nervously tucked into his pre-match meal awaiting the absent Macari's confirmation that he would be making his first-team debut later that afternoon.

But as the waitresses cleared away the half-eaten plates of scrambled eggs and baked beans on toast from the hotel table, the chances of Macari arriving in time to take his seat on that team coach were receding by the minute.

"Of course I was worried," revealed new boy Ludo. "I really didn't know what was going to happen to me."

And as the club officials opted to head for the County Ground in the vain hope that their AWOL manager would materialise at the stadium, the ashen face of newly installed chairman Martin Cearns spoke volumes.

The People had decried Macari's role in the Swindon betting scandal, but as Bradshaw returned to the scene of the crime he was to be disappointed for Macari had, indeed, decided not to make an awkward return to Wiltshire.

Instead, in a hastily convened meeting, Boyce, Bonds and Tony Carr gave Miklosko his debut as ex-Robins' striker Quinn plundered a double in a 2-2 draw.

An emergency board meeting saw Boyce put in temporary charge of 'team affairs' and the next morning – Monday, February 19, 1990 – Macari resigned.

To have, effectively, quit on matchday was typical of the Scot's impetuosity.

But having appealed against his FA fine and realising that an extension of the whole sorry saga would only heap more unwanted publicity on himself and the club, he walked.

"I felt embarrassed for the club so, in what I can only describe as a moment of madness, I decided to resign," the candid Scot later told *EX*. "Tom Finn said I'd be daft to quit and that the board were right behind me. There was no need to go. Tom tried to talk me out of it, he said that the Swindon business was just a storm in a tea cup. But I made a bad, stupid reaction to a combination of a lot of things that had been mounting up.

"I now very much regret quitting and can still hear Tom's words ringing in my ears. I was crazy to resign. Looking back, I suppose it really was no more than a storm in that tea cup and the board were never anything but supportive of me.

"My first big mistake was leaving the club and the second stupid, crazy thing I did was to go without even bothering to try and negotiate any kind of pay-off.

"I didn't think that I was entitled to anything, but Tom left me in no doubt that the board would probably have been willing to sit down a negotiate some settlement on the remaining two years of my contract.

"You certainly can't imagine any football manager walking away with nothing in today's world, but I thought it would've been a bloody cheek on my part to have even asked for anything.

"I didn't think that I deserved it."

Certainly, there had never been a dull moment during the previous seven-and-a-half months but, all so often, the hitherto reclusive Hammers had been forced kicking and screaming under the scrutiny of the media spotlight far too many times for comfort.

For each Macari wrong, there was a Macari right and while feelings towards him were mixed, the unpredictable Scot had proved to be a likeable, chirpy man who retained his sense of humour throughout his ordeal.

The tabloid crusade had been intense. It was ironic that Macari had cultivated such an excellent relationship with the local press only to find himself scythed down by the nationals.

Had the club cat got pregnant it would, by now, have been front page news.

Macari inherited a poisoned chalice but had started to find the antidote, taking Hammers to within a few paces of Wembley and moulding the side into his own.

Certainly his sergeant-major image had been a myth and the feared long-ball game had failed to materialise, too.

It was a personal tragedy that the Swindon skeletons jumped out of the County Ground closet because, arguably, Macari was, indeed, the new broom that was needed to sweep away the cobwebs that had accumulated towards the end of the Lyall reign.

But having inherited a bunch of mutinous players, how he could have done with his predecessor sitting 'upstairs' at the Boleyn Ground and a hand-picked ally – such as Ray Wilkins – or two in the dug-out.

In the transfer market, his hand had been forced by the want-away Ward, Ince and Dickens but in their places he left West Ham with a lasting legacy in the shape of want-to-play stars.

With the exception of Foster (110 league and cup appearances) and Quinn (57), Ludek Miklosko (373), Ian Bishop (304), Martin Allen (232) plus Trevor Morley (204) each went on to play key roles in the evolution of the club through the 90s.

Lou Macari's Managerial Record:

League:	P-28	W-10	D-8	L-10	F-41	A-35
League Cup:	P-9	W-4	D-4	L-1	F-8	A-10
FA Cup:	P-1	W-0	D-0	L-1	F-0	A-1
ZDS Cup:	P-2	W-1	D-0	L-1	F-8	A-6
TOTALS:	P-40	W-15	D-12	L-13	F-57	A-52

"After all the Incey problems, we then had the trouble at Torquay when all the gambling stories came out," said Potts after seeing Macari leave the Hammers in 11th place, 20 points off table-topping Leeds United. "West Ham was his first big club and it was probably a stepping stone for him to go onto bigger things. He made some good signings – Ludo, Bish, Trevor Morley and Martin Allen.

"Things were starting to go okay and could easily have got better but no-one will ever know what would have happened, will they?"

Chapter 3
1989-90

ENTER THE LEGEND

So, just eight months after showing John Lyall the door, Len Cearns and his fellow directors were looking for the club's seventh manager.

Feelings were running high and West Ham were an easy target for anyone wanting to take a pot shot.

Certainly, Emlyn Hughes wasted no time in accusing Macari of running like a scared rabbit. Quite what Macari-gate had to do with the former Liverpool and England skipper remains anyone's guess but perhaps it was the smell of the tabloid pound notes and a deep-seated dislike of the Scot stemming back to his Manchester United and Scotland days?

But when Hughes – who tragically died from a brain tumour in 2004 – started skinning West Ham, too, the *Daily Mirror* reported that he was issued with a death threat by a disgruntled Hammers' fan.

"I ask you, what other club would have got their appointment of a manager so wrong," wrote Hughes. "Now they are in a mess of their own making. It always makes me laugh when Upton Park is called the Academy. What total rubbish. Academy of what? Certainly not success. They're just dreamers."

Lyall, who was helping England boss Bobby Robson prepare for the Italia 90 World Cup, emerged as many fans' choice to be recalled, but personal pride dictated that notion as a non-starter, while Bournemouth chairman Jim Nolan again attempted to block any move for Harry Redknapp.

Peter Shreeves, now back from the Algarve, and Ray Harford were again being mentioned in many circles but West Ham had just been on the end of the most painful lesson for not appointing from within.

Three of the previous six managers – Syd King (1902-32), Ted Fenton (1950-61) and Lyall (1974-89) – had each pulled on a claret and blue shirt, while Charlie Paynter (1932-50) had done everything except kick a ball for the Hammers in his role as an influential, long-serving trainer.

That meant only Ron Greenwood (1961-74) and Macari (1989-90) had arrived at Upton Park bearing no previous ties to the club.

And now it was time to appoint a tried and trusted individual once more.

A lack of managerial experience may have been a distinct disadvantage but, with an intimate 23-year working knowledge as to what made West Ham tick, unlimited, undoubted integrity and an empathy with the Hammers' fans, Billy

NEARLY REACHED THE SKY

Bonds emerged as the only real candidate to steer the club back onto the rails.

"Bonds is a symbol of much hope," wrote James Lawton in the *Daily Express*. "He may have slender managerial qualities but if his experience is slim he has one asset that Macari or any young driving figure coming in from outside may never have acquired in years of scuffling for a foothold in the first division. He is of the Hammers."

Indeed.

The oldest of three children, William Arthur Bonds was born on September 17, 1946 in Woolwich, south London, just a Sam Bartram drop-kick away from both the River Thames and The Valley.

Arthur Bonds – a bus driver – was a keen footballer and Charlton Athletic fan and, alongside his wife, Barbara, he had no qualms about taking son Billy to watch their favourites when he was just a three-month old baby.

Young Bill began playing the game from an early age but, upon leaving school as a 15-year-old, his parents persuaded him to get a trade in the local propeller factory earning £2.50 per week instead of joining the Charlton groundstaff.

Not surprisingly, the lure of professional football proved too great and just a couple of months later, Bonds found himself riding his bicycle to The Valley, where he would deal with the laundry, clean boots and sweep the terraces looking for the odd dropped coin to supplement his modest wage.

It was a valuable grounding that held him in good stead for the rest of his career.

For not only did the thought of returning to the factory drive him on to make it as a professional, but throughout his career he never lost sight of the common man.

Bonds made his Charlton debut in a 0-1 second division defeat at Northampton Town in February 1965 and went on to make 95 league appearances before joining West Ham for £49,500 in May 1967.

Even then, he was still a mere cyclist and had to be taken by car to Upton Park by manager Ron Greenwood, who had seen off a late approach from Sunderland to capture his signature.

Little did the 20-year-old realise then that he was about to become the driving force behind West Ham United, spending 27 seasons on the other side of the Blackwall Tunnel.

"Billy Bonds proved a magnificent buy, a perfect example of a good, hard professional," wrote Greenwood in his autobiography, *Yours Sincerely*. "To begin with he wondered how the crowd would react to him because he is a sensitive sort of chap, even a little introverted, but he had no reason to worry. He started off at right-back but later proved to be equally at home at wing-half or in central defence in a career that was to take him right through the 70s and well into the 80s. Bonds was a resolute, tireless winner and, if every buy had proved as good, then life would have been very sweet."

Leading by admirable example, Bonzo had captained Hammers to FA Cup victories over Fulham (1975) and Arsenal (1980) on his way to amassing a club record 663 league and 132 cup appearances.

After making his Hammers debut against Sheffield Wednesday (2-3) on August 19, 1967, he made the last of those 795 outings in a 1-2 defeat at Southampton on

April 30, 1988 at the incredible age of 41 years and 226 days.

Upon retiring, the four-times Hammer-of-the-Year took up the role of Youth Team Coach where he sometimes found the application and dedication of a younger generation falling below his own high standards.

Indeed, it was not unusual to see team selection decimated by a half-term holiday and a young starlet being hauled off to Butlins with his family, in deference to the chance to prove that he had all the necessary mettle to make it as a professional.

But now Billy Bonds MBE, the choice of the people, was well and truly in the Upton Park hot seat.

The relieved Ronnie Boyce, having been put in charge of team affairs, felt more comfortable stepping aside to become Bonds' number two, while Paul Hilton was in the right place at the right time to succeed him as Youth Team Coach.

For many, Bonds was a reluctant manager whose hand was forced at a time when the club needed him most.

"I wouldn't have been disappointed if I hadn't got the job," he announced, adding fuel to the theorists' fire. "And I have always said that this is not something that I have craved for. I've been given the job now and I'll do it to the best of my ability but if I end up getting the sack I won't lose any sleep over it."

But to others he was a natural figurehead to continue spreading the gospel of Ron and John in the hope that, one day, the West Ham United traditions and values would finally find a place at the top end of the table.

"You've got to attack sensibly and defend sensibly but we've also got to remember that we're here to try and entertain people. There must always be room for that," he insisted. "I don't expect anything from the players except to go out and do their best. That's all you can ask. What I don't like in a player is lack of enthusiasm, lack of desire and lack of effort.

"The lads know that if they step out of line, I'll tell them straight to their face," continued Bill after introducing his own disciplinary code of fines that would hopefully arrest the slide in standards. "They know I'll be honest and I won't give them any bull. If they're not doing their job properly, then they'll get a rucking. If they're doing well I'll pat them on the back. It's as simple as that.

"The only area where I feel any pressure is with the fans. Although they don't mean to do it, they expect so much from me and while I'm not worried about getting the sack, I would be bothered if I upset the supporters. In a year's time they could be booing me. That certainly happened to John Lyall and it's something that I wouldn't like to happen to me because I've had a great relationship with them over 23 years. It would hurt if they turned against me now."

Certainly Bonds did not need to have any worries in his opening game as he took a standing ovation before an Upton Park crowd numbering 20,054.

And although Jimmy Quinn fired Hammers ahead against Blackburn Rovers, Scott Sellars levelled to take the edge off his first day.

At Ayresome Park, Martin Allen's late goal gave Bonds his first victory as Hammers returned from Middlesbrough with a 1-0 win in readiness for their very own mission impossible.

Chasing that six-goal deficit from the Littlewoods Cup semi-final, first-leg savaging at Oldham Athletic was a thankless task.

But when Alvin Martin, Julian Dicks and David Kelly halved the Latics' advantage, Joe Royle was forced to scamper from the directors' box to the dug-out to oversee operations and help ease the jitters as Oldham duly steadied the ship and predictably reached the final, 6-3 on aggregate.

West Ham still had slender hopes of making the play-offs, though, and Bonds had galvanised his side into action. A 2-1 win over Portsmouth lifted them into 10th place, 18 points off leaders Leeds but just five behind fifth-placed Oldham.

Another 1-0 victory at Watford meant that unbeaten West Ham had gathered 10 points from the first four games of Bonds' reign.

And he had his first serious taste of man-management when he agreed that fringe-players Allen McKnight, Kelly, Gary Strodder, Tommy McQueen and Eamonn Dolan could each leave the club.

Within days, Kelly (48+15 apps 14 goals) joined Leicester City for £400,000 to draw down the curtain on a disappointing two years at Upton Park, after West Ham were said to have seen off Paris Saint-Germain, Bayern Munich and Tottenham Hotspur to secure his £600,000 move from Walsall.

As Hammers headed to table-topping Leeds United, history was being made at Upton Park, where 30 televisions were arranged in a 5 x 6 formation to provide a giant screen receiving a live beamback from Elland Road. A crowd of 8,200 turned up to watch the biggest single video wall event ever screened in Europe which was, unfortunately, blighted by technical gremlins.

Sadly, there was to be disappointment for both the travelling fans and those sat in the West Enclosure back at the Boleyn Ground as future Hammer Lee Chapman and Gordon Strachan netted in the 3-2 victory that condemned Bonds to his first managerial defeat.

A 5-0 win over second-placed Sheffield United in midweek saw West Ham lay down a powerful marker to the rest of the division. But by the weekend their promotion hopes had been dented further with a 3-4 reverse at Sunderland, while two missed penalties in a 2-2 draw with Port Vale back at Upton Park only served to see them fall yet further off the play-off pace.

Watching from afar, Macari lost his appeal against the £1,000 fine imposed in that Newcastle betting rap, while Hammers secured valuable away victories at West Bromwich Albion (3-1) and Oxford United.

It was at the Manor Ground where Bonds' managerial integrity first shone.

A 2-0 win against Oxford had, in the final reckoning, counted for little given the other play-off contenders – Newcastle United, Swindon Town, Sunderland and Blackburn Rovers – had each won and there were now only seven games left.

The point was not lost on the gaggle of journalists who contended that the rest of the season – starting with a midweek fixture against Bournemouth – was merely evaporating into an academic exercise.

In the City of Dreaming Spires, Bonds' steely, shocked stare quickly gave his corrected questioner a reality check.

"There are people who will be going to work in factories on Monday so that they can earn money to come and see us on Wednesday," he said. "It's a game of football. It's West Ham United. We won't let them down by just going through the motions."

Four days later, Redknapp returned to Upton Park to face the club whom he had come so close to managing during the close season.

"It's the only job in football that would appeal to me," he had said and now, sitting in the opposite dug-out was Bonds – West Ham United manager and former team-mate for whom he had been Best Man back in 1967.

True to his word, Bonds had made nonsense of any notion that his side were about to go through the motions as Hammers secured a commanding 4-1 victory in front of 20,202 fans.

Redknapp gave son Jamie his debut but, with his side languishing perilously close to the relegation zone, how he must have coveted the riches at his friend Bonzo's disposal.

That victory gave the East End a glimmer of hope that play-off qualification was still achievable, and a 1-1 draw at Barnsley left Hammers in seventh spot just one point behind Sunderland, over whom they had a superior goal difference.

The revolution continued with a 2-0 win over Ipswich Town but, once again, Oldham's plastic pitch was to prove Hammers' undoing. They may have done twice as well as that 0-6 Littlewoods Cup semi-final slaughter but, even so, a 0-3 loss at Boundary Park was equally damaging, while a 1-2 setback at Newcastle meant that their fate was no longer in their hands.

Kelly endured a miserable return to Upton Park as West Ham beat Leicester City 3-1, but other midweek results conspired against them. And with the play-off berths now irrevocably booked, the final game against Wolverhampton Wanderers was one of celebration for different reasons.

After Dicks was named Hammer-of-the-Year, Liam Brady (106+13 apps 10 goals) played his last game of an illustrious journey that had seen him enchant the fans of Arsenal, Juventus, Sampdoria, Inter Milan, Ascoli and West Ham.

Robson's sensational strike had already put West Ham into a match-winning 3-0 lead, and as injury time beckoned, the entire East End was willing Brady to shoot as he got within range of the Wolves' goal.

But no-one in their wildest dreams could have imagined the scenes that followed. For with his last kick of a distinguished career, that legendary left-foot curled a 20-yarder around keeper Mark Kendall and high into the South Bank net to make it 4-0 and spark a pitch invasion that persuaded referee David Allison to blow the whistle on the campaign as soon as play restarted.

While the Irishman was enjoying that fairytale finish, the beleaguered Macari was still enshrined in a nightmare. Just days earlier, he had been awoken in a Manchester hotel room and arrested for suspected criminal conspiracy to defraud the Inland Revenue. Swindon Town chairman Brian Hillier, club accountant Vince Farrer and team captain Colin Calderwood were also rounded up in the west country and, although a Football League inquiry was about to be launched, the allegations of illegal payments to players had now projected the scandal into a far more serious arena.

Long-time front-runners Leeds United and Sheffield United won automatic promotion, and in an ironic twist to the tale, Swindon went on to beat Sunderland in the Play-off final, before the Robins' wings were quickly clipped when they were found guilty of committing those financial irregularities.

Initially demoted to the third division, on appeal, Town managed to retain their second division status but it was the sixth-placed Wearsiders who headed into the top flight on the basis that they had been runners-up at Wembley.

Back at Upton Park, Bonds had gallantly galvanised West Ham into a late rally that had seen them get to within one place and two points of the play-offs.

It had been a long, traumatic campaign blighted by far too many off field distractions.

Ironically, the root cause had occurred several months earlier at *another* club where those wild events, way out west at Swindon Town, had seen Hammers veer helplessly off course.

But Bonzo was now at the helm, the old was gone and the new had now bedded down. With 11 victories and three draws from his first 18 matches there was a buzz in the air. That feel-good factor was returning and bringing with it a renewed confidence that West Ham United could, once again, find their way back to Division One.

"I hope that this time next year we are celebrating our return to the first division," said Bonds signing off for the summer. "We will do our best, but we make no promises."

PLAYERS IN

Martin Allen	Queens Park Rangers	£600,000
Ian Bishop*	Manchester City	£650,000
Colin Foster	Nottingham Forest	£750,000
Ludek Miklosko	Banik Ostrava	£266,430
Trevor Morley*	Manchester City	£260,000
Jimmy Quinn	Bradford City	£340,000

LOANS IN

Justin Fashanu	Manchester City
Ralph Milne	Manchester United
Perry Suckling	Crystal Palace

PLAYERS OUT

Liam Brady	Retired	
Alan Dickens	Chelsea	£600,000
Paul Hilton	Retired	
Paul Ince	Manchester United	£2,000,000.
David Kelly	Leicester City	£400,000
Mark Ward*	Manchester City	Swap Bishop/Morley

Chapter 4
1990-91

UP, UP, HOORAY!

On the eve of the new season, bookmakers William Hill announced that West Ham United had become the best backed side in the Football League and they stood to lose £70,000 if the 6/1 shots won the Division Two title.

Having seen Liam Brady depart in the final game of the previous campaign, more of the Upton Park old school headed for the door.

The Czech Republic's Italia 90 World Cup keeper Ludek Miklosko had now bedded himself in, and that was the cue for Phil Parkes (439 apps) to decide that it was time to quit the Hammers.

And after playing 45 minutes each for both West Ham and Ipswich Town in his testimonial which ended 1-1, he headed to the Suffolk club on a free transfer to link up with the new Portman Road boss . . . John Lyall.

Alan Devonshire (431+16 apps 32 gls) also departed on a free transfer to Watford. A £5,000 signing from non-league Southall in October 1976, the waif-like, wide boy notoriously collapsed in training soon after arriving at Upton Park. But he recovered to forge a breathtaking partnership with Trevor Brooking and become a Hammers' legend.

Dev possessed unique dribbling skills that would certainly have earned him more than the eight England caps he won before sustaining a career-threatening knee injury in 1984. Thankfully, the popular Londoner recovered to become a key player in the record breaking 1985-86 season, even though his joint was irreversibly crippled.

Certainly, Devonshire's fragile frame belied his penchant for the huge Wimpy breakfasts which the non-driver devoured at Barking station before hitching his daily lift to training at Chadwell Heath. Although the unsuspecting Lou Macari would have frowned upon such an unhealthy diet, it was on football matters where they had not seen eye-to-eye, resulting in Devonshire's fall from favour.

By the time former team-mate Billy Bonds took charge, a hamstring injury had robbed him of the chance of a recall to the first team and, sadly, for all his good times, Devonshire departed in virtual anonymity.

"Bonzo asked me whether I wanted to join the lads up in the directors' box where they traditionally say goodbye after the final match of the season," he revealed. "But I left the ground half-an-hour before the end of the Wolves game. It wasn't the way I wanted to say ta-ta to the supporters."

Another person on his way to Vicarage Road was 64-year-old director Jack

NEARLY REACHED THE SKY

Petchey. After spending a dozen years on the Hammers' board, the property tycoon said 'goodbye' and headed down the yellow brick road to purchase Elton John's 97% stake in Watford for a reported £2m.

"The club will be run on business lines," he declared.

Indeed, it was not long before the Hornets' supporters were being cross-sold time-shares as, not for the first time, the entrepreneurial Petchey tried to conjure up a cocktail of soccer and sunshine.

"Jack owned a villa in the Algarve," wrote Frank McAvennie in *Boys of 86*. "And just before the Mexico 86 World Cup he invited me to go over to Portugal and enjoy myself at his penthouse. All the boys at West Ham were saying that Jack never did anything for nothing but I just put it down to the fact that he must have liked me.

"When I got out there, everyone I bumped into greeted me like a long-lost friend. I thought it was strange. But, knowing that I'd be going to his place for a few days, Jack had arranged to display a giant poster of me, promoting the name of the apartment complex with the words printed big and bold: *'We wish Frank McAvennie good luck with Scotland's World Cup campaign.'* I'd been stitched up. He had used my name to drum up interest in his holiday villas! I wouldn't mind but he even locked the room where he kept all the booze!"

Twelve months after seeing his ankle smashed at Stoke City, McAvennie made his first full start – since that horrific Chris Kamara tackle in the opening game of the 1989-90 season – at Middlesbrough.

The Scot came through the goalless stalemate unscathed and then bagged his first goal since that £1.25m return from Celtic in a 1-1 draw at Portsmouth.

Devonshire soon found himself back at Upton Park with the Watford squad but, again, he left on a sour note after not even making the bench and then seeing Julian Dicks' penalty divide the teams as Hammers notched up their first win.

A 2-1 victory at Leicester City and a 1-1 draw with Wolves meant that West Ham were still unbeaten when Lyall brought his Ipswich side to Upton Park.

And the former Hammers' manager guided Town into an interval lead before Billy Bonds got one over on his old boss as West Ham battled back to win 3-1.

Successive 1-1 draws at Newcastle United and Sheffield Wednesday were sandwiched between a 3-0 Rumbelows League Cup win over Stoke City.

On the transfer front, Bonds generated around £250,000 by off-loading two fringe defenders who had failed to establish themselves at Upton Park.

Gary Strodder (73+8 apps 2 gls), a basic centre half signed from Lincoln City in 1986-87 for £150,000, moved to West Bromwich Albion for £190,000 following a tribunal hearing, while gentle Scot Tommy McQueen (27+9 apps) – a £150,000 signing from Aberdeen in 1987 – headed back across Hadrian's Wall to join Falkirk in a £60,000 deal.

Leroy Rosenior, his career blighted by a serious knee injury, also returned to Fulham on loan.

On the other side of the coin, home-grown, steady Steve Potts quietly continued to provide cover in the absence of an injured Ray Stewart. Curiously born in Hartford, Connecticut, he had soon returned to his parents' native east London aged just one.

While baseball, basketball and American football lost out Stateside, Potts' trans-Atlantic repatriation saw him become one of the club's most loyal servants.

An introvert, unassuming defender, the Dagenham-raised teenager, who once played alongside Arsenal's Tony Adams as a schoolboy, made his debut as a 17-year-old against Queens Park Rangers on New Year's Day 1985.

As understudy to Stewart, he emerged as a reliable right-back in his own right but, as he was to prove in later years, it was not his natural position.

What the 5ft 7ins, England youth international may have lacked in terms of height and presence, though, he more than made up for with his pace, speed of thought and ability to break down attacks with precision-timed interceptions.

And while Stewart scored those 84 goals (including 76 penalties) in 431 appearances, when Potts went into his 117th Hammers' outing against Hull City at Upton Park, the fans could count on one hand the number of times the goal-shy defender had ventured over the halfway line, yet alone threatened the keeper.

But at 3.31pm on Saturday, October 6, 1990, upon receiving the ball from Ian Bishop, Pottsy ventured forward into the Tigers' half where he let fly with a hopeful 25-yarder bobbler that squirmed through the clutches of Ian Hesford and into Upton Park folklore.

"Nobody came towards me so I just unleashed a back-pass and paid their keeper afterwards!" joked the embarrassed Potts after finally breaking his duck in a 7-1 victory that heralded the 10-game unbeaten Hammers' best-ever start to a season. "One goal over all those years is a disgrace, isn't it? But people wouldn't talk about it if I'd scored more than once."

For the 19,472 present inside Upton Park it was to prove one of those precious 'I was there' moments. And despite making 506 league and cup appearances, commanding that ninth place in the club's all-time appearance chart and twice winning the Hammer-of-the-Year award, poor Pottsy will mostly be remembered for that solitary goal of his career.

With his young stopper preferring defence over offense, Bonds – an attacking right-back himself in his younger days – pulled out the cheque-book to make Luton Town's Tim Breacker the first signing of his managerial career.

At £600,000, it was a brave plunge into the transfer market but the Hatter was a strong, attacking full back.

And at that price he was clearly not at West Ham just to sit on the bench.

"Although I didn't think so at the time, Tim's arrival was probably the best thing that ever happened to me," said Potts after seeing the high of *that* goal turn to a disappointing low within days. "In the end, there were a few injuries at centre-half so I was moved across and I felt quite comfortable there."

A Rumbelows League Cup second leg victory at Stoke City (2-1) was followed up with a 1-1 draw at Bristol City and a league win at Swindon Town (1-0). Home victories over Blackburn Rovers (1-0) and Charlton Athletic (2-1) saw West Ham – unbeaten in 14 games – climb up into second spot, just four points behind equally undefeated Oldham Athletic.

Following Petchey's departure, Barking-born Terence Brown – a life-long

NEARLY REACHED THE SKY

Hammers fan and proprietor of The Sussex Beach Holiday Village at Bracklesham Bay on the south coast – accepted an invitation to join the board.

Holder of four Academy Lounge season tickets, Brown was a perfect candidate for a board looking for supporter representation. He had served on several testimonial committees while also arranging benefit weeks for players at Sussex Beach. He had also provided Tony Gale with a sponsored car.

Having been elevated from the South Bank to the directors' box over the course of many seasons, the 48-year-old described his graduation as 'a long journey.' But events would dictate that the qualified accountant had an even greater trek ahead.

As injury-ravaged Hammers headed to Oxford United for a Rumbelows League Cup third round tie on October 31, 1990, Bonds had his work cut out, too.

And had he not failed to register himself for the competition he would have handed himself a record 796th league and cup appearance.

The hitherto undefeated Hammers were now kicking off their 17th game of the campaign and, although Trevor Morley put them ahead, the lead was wiped out by Martin Foyle before Jim Magilton's injury-time strike sent plucky West Ham reeling to their first defeat of the season.

Back in the league, Morley's sensational strike secured all the points at Notts County where Tottenham Hotspur's on-loan, 51-times capped, Republic of Ireland defender, Chris Hughton, made his debut after a knee injury to Dicks proved more serious than first thought.

And there were fireworks at Upton Park on Guy Fawkes night when Paul Hilton's kids showed that the explosive, winning mentality was flowing from top to bottom through the club, as five-goal Michael Macari led the young Hammers to a massive 21-1 win over Hampshire outfit Horndean in the FA Youth Cup.

Amidst a massive police presence, scuffles, clashes, the glint of riot shields and 15 arrests, a crowd of 20,591 paying record receipts of £106,839 delayed the kick-off by 15 minutes at The Den, where McAvennie's 73rd-minute equaliser secured a 1-1 draw against Millwall.

Subsequent victories over Brighton & Hove Albion (2-1) and Plymouth Argyle (1-0) meant that unbeaten West Ham had finally made it into top spot. Bonds' efforts had not gone unnoticed and his Barclays Bank Manager of the Month award for November nestled fittingly next to the one he had won in October, too.

It had been another good month for Bonzo who – alongside Alvin Martin – was the only other Hammer ever to have two testimonials. In December 1978, a crowd of 21,081 saw Bonds score a penalty as Hammers beat Tottenham Hotspur 4-2.

Some 12 years later, Spurs also provided the opposition when Bonds again scored from the penalty spot as 10,443 fans rolled back the years to see Parkes, Lampard and Devonshire return to a Hammers' team that ran out 4-3 winners.

On December 1, 1990, a 3-1 victory over West Bromwich Albion meant that Hammers had gone a club record 19 league games without defeat.

A subsequent win at Portsmouth (1-0) followed by a goalless draw with Middlesbrough saw them move three points clear of second-placed Oldham, whose own unbeaten run had been wrecked by back-to-back defeats at Port Vale and Bristol Rovers.

"We've made a bit of history but anything can still happen," warned Bonds, typically keeping his feet on the ground.

Just like its predecessor, the Simod Cup, the Zenith Data Systems Cup was an unwanted distraction. These descendants of the Full Members Cup were supposed to generate income for the lower league clubs playing the top sides who were given the tantalising lure of a Wembley final.

That was the theory. But the reality of this optional competition saw the glamour clubs abstain as a result of potential fixture congestion and no European carrot, while most of those that did enter merely played weakened teams. In turn, the fans voted with their feet, the clicking of the turnstiles fell silent and the entire competition degenerated into a huge white elephant until Wembley typically became around half-filled for the final.

And so it came to be on a cold Wednesday evening, less than a week before Christmas, that West Ham travelled to Luton Town to play a ZDS second round tie in front of just 5,759 people on the inhospitable Kenilworth Road plastic pitch.

The fixture was the last thing Bonds wanted ahead of an upcoming festive programme and not wishing to risk Ludek Miklosko – a keeper who had conceded just 12 goals in 21 league outings – reserve keeper Allen McKnight was recalled to the side for the first time since the 1-5 defeat at Liverpool in May 1989 that confirmed relegation and Lyall's subsequent departure.

Lou Macari may have refused to play him but now, 19 months on, Bonds had handed McKnight what was to be his last senior appearance for the club.

Again, Hammers lost 1-5 and once more the tabloids dusted down their all too familiar headlines.

"Billy Bonds' injury-ravaged West Ham side turned in a McKnightmare," hollered *The Sun*.

In an ironic post-script to his blighted Hammers career, despite his protestations that he was injured, McKnight – the only goalkeeper at the club still available for selection – was subsequently called up for the reserves' final game of the season against Crystal Palace the following May.

"They insisted that there was no-one else," he later told *EX Magazine*, looking back on a 0-11 defeat that marked his last appearance for the club who desperately – and without success – tried to suppress news of the embarrassing reverse.

"I couldn't have cared if it had been 20 by then. I just wanted to go," confessed McKnight (36 apps), who headed to Stockport County, Rotherham United and Walsall before drifting into non-league football and a move into the timber trade.

While the Hammers' team coach would again be found parked up on the pavement in a busy shopping thoroughfare 12 months on, this time around there was not a bookies in sight. Instead, it was merely Bonzo's back-room staff in the Barking Road bakers stocking up on an assortment of cakes to be washed down with endless cups of tea on a long journey north to Yorkshire.

And when they arrived, Miklosko was back between the sticks at Oakwell. But all good things must come to an end and, after 21 unbeaten league matches, Mark Smith's 20th-minute goal for Barnsley's bruisers meant that West Ham had finally been stuffed just three days before Christmas.

NEARLY REACHED THE SKY

In 1985-86, Hammers went 18 league games without defeat and, previously, they had also strung together an 18-game run, in 1980-81, before going another nine games without defeat in 1981-82. Ironically, Bonds had been ever-present in that overall 27-game streak.

And as he headed back down the frosty M1, he could at least enjoy his Christmas dinner knowing that he had now overseen an intra-season record 21-game stretch.

Normal business was soon to be resumed, for Hammers leapfrogged over Oldham with a warming 2-0 win at Upton Park on Boxing Day, a goalless draw against Port Vale and a New Year's Day, high noon, 1-0 win at Bristol Rovers.

On the transfer front, on-loan Chris Hughton completed a free-transfer from Tottenham Hotspur while striker Eamonn Dolan (14+7 apps 4goals) headed to Birmingham City in a £30,000 deal. With 12 'O' levels and one 'A' level, the intelligent, twice-capped Republic of Ireland Under-21 international had been plagued by a shoulder injury that had punctuated his career and, apart from his double-barrelled blast against Sunderland the previous season, he had done little to convince his managers that he was a long-term, attacking solution.

Indeed, in September 1989, 'The Professor' had notched a hat-trick inside 70 minutes as the reserves romped to a 5-1 victory over Southampton's second string but still the watching Macari observed: "Apart from scoring those four goals, he didn't do anything!"

Dolan later had to literally fight for his life after contracting testicular cancer, but he bravely battled back to enjoy a managerial spell at Exeter City before becoming Reading's youth team coach in 2004.

In the FA Cup, poverty-stricken Aldershot managed to get the third round home tie switched from their tiny Recreation Ground to Upton Park. Standing in 20th place in the fourth division, they were given little chance against the second division leaders, but with former QPR keeper – and 1982 finalist – Peter Hucker in inspired form, the Shots battled and scrapped to force a goalless draw.

It really was a double-money deal, for not only did the underdogs rake in an estimated £50,000 from the 22,929 gate, but they were in line for a similar pay day come the January 16 replay, again played at Upton Park.

Trevor Morley's strike against Alan Devonshire's Watford gave West Ham victory at Vicarage Road where Simon Clarke (0+3 apps) made an 89th-minute debut ahead of eventually moving to Kettering Town on a free transfer a few seasons later.

And there were no mistakes against Aldershot this time around, either, as two-goal Morley was again on target to set Hammers on their way to the comfortable 6-1 victory that booked a fourth round tie at Luton Town.

George Parris secured a 1-0 league victory over Leicester City but the result was tempered by the news that Dicks' knee ligament injury would keep him out of action until the summer.

Parris hit the net in the FA Cup, too, and this time there was no ZDS-like capitulation at Luton where Hammers forced a replay following a messy tie. And Parris's rich vein of scoring form saw him finding the target again as Ian Bishop, McAvennie and two-goal Morley eased West Ham to a 5-0 win over the Hatters in the Upton Park re-match that set up a fifth round tie against Crewe Alexandra.

January's hat-trick of league wins saw Bonds win his third Barclays Bank Manager-of-the-Month award out of four but as soon as he collected another jeroboam of champagne, he found that West Ham were succumbing to their second defeat of the season at Wolverhampton Wanderers (1-2)

Still in the Midlands, a year after walking out on the Hammers, Macari returned to management at Birmingham City insisting: "A lot of what has been heard about Swindon hasn't been the truth. That will come out eventually."

As struggling third division Crewe came to a snow-dusted Upton Park, their manager Dario Gradi warned that there could be a goals avalanche. But, in fact, it was West Ham who were in danger of slip-sliding out of the FA Cup as Miklosko boosted his burgeoning reputation with a string of fine saves before substitute Jimmy Quinn finally bagged a 77th-minute winner.

That set up a quarter-final tie against Everton after two-goal, ex-Hammer Tony Cottee had rescued a 4-4 draw in a dramatic fourth round replay against Liverpool ahead of the Toffees winning the second replay (1-0).

Throughout the season, Stuart Slater had come to prominence with a host of scintillating displays and following a 3-1 win over Millwall, Lions' boss Bruce Rioch bullishly observed: "He is not dissimilar to Eusebio in the way he runs with the ball at his feet."

Following a goalless draw at West Bromwich Albion, Hammers were two points clear of Oldham with 16 still to play and in the last eight of the FA Cup. Compared to the events of their previous calamitous campaign, all appeared to be calm.

But in the early hours of Monday, March 4, 1990, that tranquillity was destroyed by the news that 16-goal, top-scorer Morley had been stabbed in an attack at his Waltham Abbey home. According to *The Sun*, his wife Monica was quizzed by police for 12 hours after the striker was found in a pool of blood with two knife wounds on the drive of his £250,000 home.

Morley was said to be 'comfortable' in Harlow's Princess Alexandra Hospital while 28-year-old, Norwegian-born, Monica Morley was released on bail pending further enquiries.

Two days later, Parris missed a late penalty as Hammers were forced to settle for a 2-2 draw against Plymouth Argyle and while the 'satisfactory' Morley found his condition improving, the Upton Park conspiracy theorists had a field day as they each brought their scurrilous, unfounded rumours to the table.

One school of thought had Morley being attacked by his missus after returning home late from a drinking session with long-haired team-mate Ian Bishop, while another ludicrous rumour suggested that the former Manchester City pair were having a homosexual relationship.

Indeed, with this mischievous, malicious gossip subsisting for several months, even Bonds reluctantly called Bishop into his office to satisfy himself that there was no substance in the terrace claims. And as a parting shot, the manager suggested that the bamboozled Bish might want to have his flowing locks cropped in a bid to project a more masculine image.

Bishop, for his part, had indeed been out drinking with Morley at a players' function. But their wives had been there, too, and the last he saw of the couple was when they headed for home early following a row.

Meanwhile, an alternative theory – again with no substance to the speculation – centred upon Morley being attacked by one of his three children during a heated argument with his wife, from whom he subsequently separated.

Morley later gave his version of events.

"The wound was caused by an accident," he claimed. "The biggest mistake I made was not commenting on it because the newspapers accused me of all sorts of stuff. The gay thing came up with me and Ian and that was a hard time. It was a drunken accident but the papers wanted a story and they camped on my doorstep.

"They said my wife caught me in bed with another woman and I think they were trying to trick me because they said they were going to write it in the Sunday papers. But I wouldn't comment because I'd been advised not to by my solicitor.

"Then they came up with the line that one of my kids had done it, or one of my kids had caught me in bed with another woman.

"Eventually it came round to: 'Your wife caught you in bed with another man'. Then it came round to me and Bish being together!

"They never actually printed the story but I wish they had because I'd have been a rich man after suing them."

Bonds began scouting for a replacement to fill the void left by the wounded Morley and Luton's Iain Dowie seemed to fit the bill. As Hammers prepared to make an approach for the Northern Ireland forward, Nottingham Forest flyer Franz Carr (1+2 apps) joined on loan, as Stewart Robson (83+1 apps 6 gls) – later destined to be handed a free transfer – headed to Coventry City on a similar basis.

In Carr's eyes, Bonds could not have been any more different than Forest boss, Brian Clough.

"One day, we came off after a poor first half and were sitting in the dressing room just about to have our half-time cuppa," revealed the England Under-21 winger recalling a recent Cloughie 'moment' back at the City Ground. "Then the door swung open and the manager walked in shouting: 'Tea? You lot don't deserve tea! Put your drinks down and get back out there NOW!' It was too embarrassing to go onto the pitch so the whole Forest side just stood in the tunnel waiting for the other team and the ref to go out there for the second half."

Throughout the previous two seasons, the so-called Eusebio-like Slater had been rapidly emerging as the latest special youth product to emerge from the Hammers' academy. For all his precocious talent, however, the gifted, Sudbury-born youngster was a shy, unpretentious teenager who led a relatively sheltered life.

Living in Chelmsford with his grandparents during the week, he would pick up his best mate Dolan and head down the A12 to training, talking nothing but football.

"I'm really a normal kind of guy and I don't think about the money," he insisted. "I realise how fortunate I am to be playing professional football when I think of my mates who weren't lucky enough to make it."

At weekends, Slater would go home to the house his builder father had constructed – complete with a pair of darker-shaded Hammers cleverly incorporated into the brickwork – where a football was never far from his feet.

Back at Chadwell Heath, Slater left team-mates amazed at his ability to maintain 11,000 keep-ups, stopping only because his aching ankle could take no more and, while he always preferred an attacking role, most observers believed that while he could undoubtedly take on and beat defenders, his inability to conjure up a killer finish made him more of a goal-maker than a goal-taker.

Certainly, his Hammers' career tally of 18 goals in 179 outings suggested that he was not a natural predator of the ilk of, say, 146-goal, 336-match, Tony Cottee but on Monday, March 11, 1991, the scintillating Slater scored the goal of his life in a peak performance that was to propel him into the national reckoning.

Ironically, Cottee was in the Everton squad that headed to Upton Park for the FA Cup quarter-final clash in front of an expectant East End crowd of 28,162, but by the time he emerged from the bench to a crescendo of jeers on the hour, Colin Foster's falling volley had already given Hammers the advantage.

Having caused panic all evening, the destructive Slater's probing run and cool finish soon doubled the lead before Dave Watson's late strike simply proved to be too little too late, for the Blues.

"Stuart Slater was the difference between the sides," conceded Everton boss Howard Kendall. "When I first came back from Spain, the first match I saw was Blackburn against West Ham. I said that afternoon that I had seen a million-pound player. I was talking about Slater and he did me tonight."

After the Lord Mayor's Show comes a dustcart. And a demanding fixture pile-up asked West Ham to play at Oxford just 48 hours after that draining FA Cup win.

The exhausted Slater was put on the bench as Hammers succumbed to a 1-2 midweek defeat at the Manor Ground before also losing 1-3 to third-placed Sheffield Wednesday at Upton Park – Bonds' first-ever home defeat.

A rare Gale goal gave Hammers a 1-0 win over Bristol City to keep them just one point behind leaders Oldham and six points clear of Ron Atkinson's Wednesday, but McAvennie's dismissal alongside Andy Llewellyn meant that he was suspended for the FA Cup semi-final clash with Nottingham Forest.

With Morley still wounded and Rosenior cup-tied following an FA Cup second round on-loan appearance for Fulham against Cambridge United back in December, Hammers were looking desperately short of strike-power ahead of that Villa Park tie.

Bonds swooped for West Ham fan Dowie in a £480,000 move from Luton Town, although he was already cup-tied.

It was testament to West Ham's prominence and dominance that Miklosko, Bishop and Morley were each voted into the PFA Division Two All-Star team. Later that season Bishop received further recognition alongside Slater when the Hammers' duo won richly deserved England 'B' Caps in the 2-1 rolling over of Switzerland at Walsall.

And when captain Bishop put Hammers ahead from the penalty spot at table-topping Oldham, they at long last looked to have mastered the Boundary Park plastic. Victory would have seen them leap-frog Joe Royle's side and snatch a three-point lead with 11 matches to play, but with three minutes left, the Hammers' skipper tripped Gunnar Halle, allowing Andy Ritchie to level and keep it 'as you were' at the top of the table.

Dowie scored his first goal for the club as Hammers came back from two goals down to beat Barnsley 3-2 and then Bishop's goal snatched a 1-0 win at Port Vale before a rare blunder by Miklosko – a reported £1.3m target for Manchester United – gifted Brighton & Hove Albion a 1-0 win. At least Morley and Stewart – who was soon to head to Scottish second division outfit St Johnstone as player-coach – had been able to return to the fold at the Goldstone Ground.

There was an air of calm hanging over their hotel on the outskirts of Walsall as Hammers prepared to take on first division Nottingham Forest in the second FA Cup semi-final of Sunday, April 14, 1991.

Back in London, Paul Gascoigne's sensational 35-yard free-kick had got Tottenham Hotspur off to a flyer out of the traps in the morning's first-ever Wembley semi-final, where a two-goal strike by Gary Lineker sealed a 3-1 win over Arsenal.

In the claustrophobic Villa Park press room, a gaunt-looking Bobby Moore was taking forty-winks ahead of his Capital Gold radio commentary.

"Are you okay, Mooro?" asked the *Newham Recorder's* Trevor Smith – the local press veteran who had known the England captain as boy, man and legend over the past 30 years.

"Yes, I'm fine thanks, Trev," replied the weary 108-times capped international, quickly and typically playing down any fuss as he opened his weary eyes.

Out on the pitch, the omens were not looking good when the team of German Shepherds, representing Forest, won the pre-match police dog display, comfortably beating the Hammers' hounds.

And when the game itself started, it turned on a single moment of controversy as the imp-like Gary Crosby burst clear of the Hammers' defence in pursuit of a 26th-minute, diagonal through-ball. As the Forest flyer became entangled with the retreating Gale, some 20-yards, out while running away from goal, referee Keith Hackett's harsh interpretation of the newly-introduced professional foul laws saw him pluck the experienced defender's first-ever red card from his pocket.

'Clumsy, not cynical,' cried *The Independent*. 'The Forest player would probably never have scored,' observed *The Times*. 'It was certainly a foul but did not warrant a red card,' stated *The Daily Telegraph*.

Parris soon struck a Forest post in defiance, but as Gale unashamedly cried his eyes out, alone in the Villa Park dressing room, the resistance of the 10-men gradually waned. Although Slater struck an upright, too, Crosby, Roy Keane and two future Hammers – Gary Charles and Stuart Pearce – sealed a 4-0 win.

Seeing the twin towers of Wembley fading over the horizon, the West Ham fans among the 40,041 crowd did themselves proud with a continuous, deafening, rousing rendition of 'Billy Bonds' Claret & Blue Army' that simply drowned out Forest's second half cheers.

At the full-time whistle, the disappointed Bonds tried to keep Brian Clough at arms length. Not that he was a bad loser – he was just determined not to let the Forest boss kiss him!

"The fans were magnificent," admitted Bishop. "We now owe it to them to win the second division title."

Back behind his typewriter, the incensed Smith thought that he had seen it all but now this was one refereeing decision too far.

"How well did this bloke Hackett sleep on Sunday night?" he demanded.

That FA Cup exit may have been a heartbreaker but at least the Hammers still had the serious, more lucrative business of promotion to secure.

Morley still looked a shadow of his old self at Ipswich Town but he soon showed that he had not lost that scoring touch as he bagged the winner in a 1-0 win at Portman Road.

Goals by Dowie and Parris then gave Hammers the 2-0 win over Swindon Town that took them onto 82 points and guaranteed promotion.

But the cameras and champagne were banished from the dressing room as Bonds set his troops the target of the title. Absolute superiority.

Nothing less would do.

Dowie found the net in a draw against Newcastle (1-1) and a defeat at Blackburn (1-3) while another stalemate at Charlton Athletic (1-1) and a win over Bristol Rovers (1-0) meant that Hammers went into the final game of the campaign on May 11, 1991 against fourth-placed Notts County, two points clear of Oldham Athletic, albeit with a two-goal inferior goal difference of plus-27:-

West Ham United	P-45	Pts-87	Goal difference +27
Oldham Athletic	P-45	Pts-85	Goal difference +29
Sheffield Wednesday	P-45	Pts-82	Goal difference +30
Notts County	P-45	Pts-77	Goal difference +20

That meant it was win-or-bust for the Latics, who were playing hosts to third-place Sheffield Wednesday.

In a strange twist of fate the top four were all in opposition.

And the Owls could still finish second with a victory over Oldham, while Hammers merely had to match the Latics' result.

Ever-present Ludek Mikslosko was deservedly presented with the Hammer-of-the-Year award, a fitting reward for the Czech who had kept 21 clean sheets – just one short of Phil Parkes' 1980-81 record.

But his hopes of equalling his predecessor's landmark were quickly dashed when Draper's quick-fire double put County 2-0 up at Upton Park.

Fortunately, Wednesday had taken a two-goal lead at Boundary Park, too, to keep Hammers on course for the Division One title.

Despite George Parris' late effort, referee Brian Hill's hasty dash from a soon to be invaded pitch signalled that West Ham had lost 1-2, while up at Oldham the sides were now safely locking horns at 2-2 – and seemingly settling for a point apiece – deep into injury time

As a swathe of the Upton Park turf was cleared of celebrating Hammers' supporters, Assistant Secretary of the Football League, Andy Williamson, and the

NEARLY REACHED THE SKY

Barclays League dignitaries were halfway down the tunnel, carrying a claret and blue decked table, the players' medals and the championship trophy.

But up in deepest Lancashire there was still just enough time for John Sheridan's last-gasp shove on the Latics' Andy Barlow to result in a championship-snatching penalty that was converted by Oldham's Neil Redfearn to give Royle's side an improbable 3-2 win and the trophy.

'Had it been fiction, Oldham's seizure of the second division title would have been dismissed as, at best, improbable,' declared *The Times*.

"Amazing!" said the victorious Royle amidst all the drama, while back at Upton Park, Bonds broke the eerie silence to announce: "That was all a bit cruel."

Champagne on ice, it was meant to be carnival time in the East End, but now the ride had come to an abrupt halt. 'Just like my dreams they fade and die' – that immortal line from *I'm Forever Blowing Bubbles* – had never been more apt.

Overall, it was an indictment of how far West Ham had come that they were desperately disappointed to have *only* finished as runners-up.

Despite seeing the silverware snatched from his grasp right at the death, it had still proved a ground-breaking season for Bonds, who had carried on from where he had left off at the end of the previous campaign.

Indeed, that 21-game unbeaten run had formed the bedrock for a season that had seen his promoted side come within just seconds of going up as champions after their 46-match marathon.

And but for Gale's harsh dismissal in that FA Cup semi-final, there may even have been a taste of Wembley glory, too.

The reluctant hero, as ever, Bonds later admitted: "Lou left me with some decent players and I took over a decent side. He had bought well at that level and I was just able to add to it a bit and then push on."

PLAYERS IN

Tim Breacker	Luton Town	£600,000
Iain Dowie	Luton Town	£480,000
Chris Hughton	Tottenham Hotspur	Free transfer

LOAN IN

Franz Carr	Nottingham Forest

PLAYERS OUT

Alan Devonshire	Watford	Free transfer
Eamonn Dolan	Birmingham City	£30,000
Allen McKnight	Stockport County	Free transfer
Tommy McQueen	Falkirk	£45,000
Phil Parkes	Ipswich Town	Free transfer
Stewart Robson	Coventry City	Free transfer
Gary Strodder	West Bromwich Albion	£190,000

Chapter 5
1991-92

DOWN TIME

"I expected West Ham to be fitter with the English season only two weeks away," scowled Sampdoria boss Vujadin Boskov. "But they weren't and they had no technique."

Inspired by four-goal Renato Buso, the *Serie A* champions had just carried out a destructive Italian job on the bewildered East Enders, winning 6-1 in the first semifinal of the four-team Makita International Tournament at Highbury.

The following day, Buso was sent off as the Italians beat Arsenal on penalties in the final.

For their part, Hammers salvaged just a little bit of pride with a 1-1 draw against Panathinaikos before suffering a Greek tragedy in another spot-kick decider.

And in their final pre-season friendly, West Ham lost 1-2 against Botafogo at Upton Park, where Frank McAvennie went nuts against the Brazilians and – alongside Roberto – received a red card from rookie referee Graham Poll.

The season had not even started but, already, it was evident that Billy Bonds had a huge task on his hands if Hammers were to avoid instant relegation.

And question marks were already being placed alongside his summer signings.

Brighton & Hove Albion's Mike Small had headed to Upton Park in a £400,000 transfer off the back of his previous campaign's heroics when he had hit a top-scoring 21 goals for the Seagulls. Kenny Brown – the son of 1964 FA Cup winner Ken – moved from Plymouth Argyle on loan ahead of a £175,000 permanent deal, while rookie striker Dean Martin – a part-time air conditioning fitter – joined from Fisher Athletic for £20,000.

But when the first presses rolled to announce the breaking news of the £500,000 signing of Michael Thomas, the Arsenal midfielder looked like becoming the bargain of the season.

In later editions, the £50,000 fee demanded by Tottenham Hotspur for defender Mitchell Thomas looked about right.

Horror swept through the East End, however, when it subsequently transpired that West Ham had got the worst of both worlds.

Mitchell Thomas for £500,000 looked very, very expensive indeed!

Jimmy Quinn (42+15 apps 21 gls) moved to Bournemouth for £40,000, while Ray Stewart (429+2 apps 84 gls) joined St Johnstone on a free transfer ahead of moving onto the Scottish management circuit.

Cruelly, Upton Park's curtain-raiser against Luton Town was dubbed the first relegation battle of the season and the goalless draw did little to suggest otherwise.

Small opened his account in an ill-tempered 1-1 draw at Sheffield United ahead of the departure of Iain Dowie (12 apps 4 gls) to Southampton in a £500,000 deal.

"One day Billy Bonds pulled me in to tell me that the club had financial problems and that I was being sold," revealed the lifelong Hammers' fan. He said: 'I've got plenty of forwards and I need to bring in defenders. We've had an offer for you.' I said that I didn't want to go but Billy told me that the club had accepted the bid from Southampton. I'd only been at West Ham for four months, so it was over before it started. Billy was up front and honest with me. He'd been the one who signed me so it must have been a boardroom thing."

When Tony Daley gave Aston Villa the lead at Upton Park, Hammers again looked in trouble before Small, Leroy Rosenior and Brown gave Bonds his inaugural first division victory.

But just four months after spoiling the promotion party, Notts County were soon back in town inflicting a 0-2 defeat on West Ham, for whom former Spurs' keeper Tony Parks (9 apps) played in goal.

Successive derby draws at QPR (0-0) and against Chelsea (1-1) were followed by defeat at Norwich City (1-2), before a timely 3-2 victory at Crystal Palace saw Hammers chalk up their first away win.

Small's double in a 2-2 draw at Nottingham Forest was sandwiched between home defeats at the hands of Manchester City (1-2) and Coventry City (0-1).

While the former Brighton striker was finding the net, Bonds was also quick to greet another visitor from the Sussex coast – his former mentor Ron Greenwood.

"I consider it a privilege to get him into the boot room for a cup of tea and a chat about the game," said the present of the past. "If I need advice I know that Ron will be only to willing to give it."

But the decision to appoint Peter Storrie as the club's first-ever Managing Director with effect from November 1 was not welcomed with so much gusto by the Hammers' boss.

"This is probably the greatest moment of my life but I wouldn't be accepting this important role if I didn't think West Ham had the ambition and capability to challenge for all the major honours," said lifelong Hammers' fan Storrie. "I know we won't start winning league titles and cups overnight but I see no reason why we shouldn't expect to finish in the top six of the first division next season."

But Bonds was far less enthusiastic about the appointment of a fan with no commercial background within the game.

"Tom Finn was a very big help to me on the administrative side – a great man who I trusted implicitly," Bonds later confided to *EX*. "The bad news for me was when they brought in Storrie. I thought it was a good idea for the club to appoint a chief executive-type, someone to take over the negotiation of the players' contracts and the finances which left me to manage the team.

"But I never had the same relationship with Storrie that I enjoyed with Tom."

Out in the heat of battle, Small again hit the target in a 2-2 draw at Oldham and by the time Hammers had seen off Tottenham (2-1), the striker had amazingly bagged a dozen goals.

The best was still to come at Arsenal, one week later, when Small struck home an 18-yarder to see off the shell-shocked Gunners. His speculative shot even stunned the scorer himself, for with the ball nestling in the back of the Clock End net, Small had to have a double-take before embarking upon the hesitant goal celebration that signalled the enormity of what he had achieved.

'Small says he wants to play for England. He's right,' insisted the watching Mike Langley of *The People,* supporting the international claims of West Ham's 'big, black handful' after his match-winning strike. "He should be in Graham Taylor's squad, for here's the man to shake up Poland.'

The nomadic 29-year-old had certainly gone the long way round. Starting off at Luton Town, he had become surplus to requirements and was sold to Dutch side Go-Ahead Eagles for £40,000 in 1982, before moving to Twente Enschede, Belgian outfit Standard Liege, the Greek team PAOK Salonika and then returning home to Brighton for £70,000 in 1990.

The coloured goal-getter had been one of the few players to cause Hammers problems in their previous promotion season and had even scored at Upton Park.

And while the bustling forward was more than capable of mixing it with his markers, he was equally good at mixing his metaphors, too.

Forget the Coleman Balls of *Private Eye*, Tony Gale meticulously kept his own log of Mike's unique Coleman Smalls from the moment the affable striker had offered to meet fellow new-boy Thomas at *Kings Pancras* station.

Indeed, upon getting ready to train with Gale at 10:30am one morning, Small confided: "I had a really long sleep last night, I must have had 12 hours."

"What time did you go to bed then, Smally?" asked Gale.

"About midnight," came the reply.

The likeable Small – a popular member of the squad – also managed to conjure up a pre-season friendly against *Patrick* Thistle and the observation that "Trevor Francis has a lot of experience after travelling all over the world in Italy."

Typically, there was yet further confusion surrounding Small's contract as he looked to trigger a pay rise via an ambitious hope clause that he had insisted upon inserting in the paperwork following his move from the Goldstone Ground.

Now four months later those pigs were not yet flying, but they were certainly revving up on the runway as the lemming-like media flock began demanding his international call-up.

And so the player versus club debate opened as to whether the optimistic England appearance stipulated in his contract constituted mere inclusion in an England squad, an England outing or an actual England start.

In the end, the West Ham wages' clerk was untroubled, for the closest Small got to hearing the roar of the Three Lions was as a standby player alongside Bishop and David James for December's subsequent 'B' international friendly against Spain in Castellon.

Just to make matters worse, the in-form Small – troubled with a niggly cartilage injury – gradually saw his goals start to dry up, too.

Although he did not know it at the time, that winning goal at Highbury was, arguably, to be the pinnacle of the inoffensive, offside-straying, striker's

Hammers' career.

Ironically, it was Arsenal who had introduced a £16.5m bond scheme to bankroll the building of their new North Stand. Glasgow Rangers had raised £7m, too, with a similar funding plan.

Already, the Hammers' fans were disillusioned by the club's relegation struggle and with only Small, Brown and Thomas to show for the previous campaign's promotion and FA Cup semi-final charge, they had long been demanding: "Where's the money gone?"

Now, as struggling West Ham United launched a £15.1m bond scheme of their own to transform Upton Park into a 25,500-capacity, all-seater stadium by 1994, little did the board know that they were about to drive an irreversible wedge between the club and its loyal supporters.

The Hammers' fans had stood to a man sending that eternal chant of 'Billy Bonds' Claret n'Blue Army' reverberating around Villa Park in the wake of that 0-4 FA Cup mauling the previous April, and the onlooking directors could not have failed to wonder just how they could exchange such loyalty in pounds, shillings and pence.

"The support at the semi-final was magnificent," Terry Connelly – a Hammers fan of then 37 years standing – told the *Evening Standard*. "I can only think that the directors looked at us fans that day and thought: 'They'll stand for anything.' The scheme is ill-conceived. Where else are you asked for a non-returnable loan? We are being asked by the board to invest in *their* future."

A slick, scare-mongering advertising campaign was launched:

We shall not be moved.

There's been a lot of talk recently about whether West Ham United can continue to play football at Upton Park.

As a result of The Taylor Report recommendations, unless first and second division grounds become all-seater by August 1994, terraces will simply have to be shut down and capacities reduced.

The club had the choice of moving to another ground or redeveloping Upton Park.

So we recently asked you, the fans, what we should do.

The answer was overwhelmingly clear: Upton Park is our home – we must stay here. So let's state here and now – West Ham United is staying at the Boleyn Ground.

To ensure we can accommodate as many fans as practicable and give our supporters much better facilities, we need to raise around £15.5m.

And to make this happen we need the continued support of Hammers fans.

You can give us this support by buying a Hammers Bond.

It'll guarantee you the right to buy a season ticket for your own seat in the new improved Upton Park.

If we club together, we shall not be moved.

But it was already becoming clear that West Ham United fans were no fools and they were not going to be parted from their money so easily despite the propaganda machine's warning that they would not be able to buy a season ticket without forking out for a Hammers Bond first.

Without a Bond, they would have no option but to join the scramble for the 6,199 remaining tickets available to members and visiting fans.

According to chairman Martin Cearns, the club's *'Looking Forward'* survey of 2,000 supporters had, apparently, revealed that 94% wanted to stay at Upton Park, 85% wanted to participate in some way in the redevelopment of the ground and 70% indicated that they would be interested in buying a bond.

In reality, the very notion that the supporters would pay up to £975 just for the guaranteed *right* to buy for the next half-century – **at additional cost** – a season ticket that would give them the *right* to sit on the seat they had occupied for so many years was simply pushing that loyalty too far.

Never before had two rights made such a wrong.

The club claimed to have received 10,000 enquiries from supporters interested in purchasing one of the 19,301 Bonds due to be released for £500 (2,182), £750 (11,866) and £975 (5,253).

Only those 6,199 non-Bonded tickets would be available within the new 25,500 capacity stadium.

In simple terms, the weary, long-suffering Hammers supporters were audaciously being asked to finance the reconstruction of an equally tired Boleyn Ground and boost its net asset value to the benefit of the shareholders and, ultimately, the board.

And having funded the redevelopment those fans would then have the mere right to buy a ticket that would enable them entrance to the directors' shiny new multi-million pound stadium.

The board countered that a straightforward share offer was unlikely to be underwritten while a traditional bank loan was considered too expensive.

"This route offers everything we are looking for in our fund-raising. We raise the money, the club remains under internal control, we do not take on huge debt and monies for the team are not affected," insisted Storrie in justification.

As the shockwaves reverberated around the exasperated East End, the next emotive missive aimed at justifying the Hammers Bond was released:-

We need to get the builders in.

We've got no choice – not if we're going to stay at Upton Park.

And we want to do that.

But to make sure as many fans as practicable can see us play and to provide our supporters with superior facilities, we need to raise around £15.5m. And to make this happen we need the continued support of Hammers fans.

If we club together, we can build a better Upton Park.'

Even the City Desk of *The Daily Telegraph* observed: 'Unfortunately, while Arsenal's bond might be a good investment for its fans, West Ham's looks like a straight cry for help. Arsenal 'bonded' a quarter of its seats but West Ham is 'bondng' three-quarters of its stadium and once three-quarters of the seats are 'special' there are not many left to be ordinary. If West Ham needs to maximise revenue, the seat discount to bondholders is almost worthless. As an investment these bonds are hopeless.'

NEARLY REACHED THE SKY

Billy Bonds, who signed a two-year extension to his contract that, significantly, would now keep him at the club until July 1994 revealed: "The club asked me to front the bond scheme but I wouldn't do it. I would never go against them because if that's the direction in which the club felt they wanted to head, then I had an obligation both to them and to the fans. But I could never come out and say that I supported it.

"All I said I would do was have my photograph taken with people who had bought the bonds but I didn't agree with what the club was asking the fans to do. It was a diabolical thing to do and I didn't agree with it one iota."

Alongside another Upton Park legend, Trevor Brooking, though, the two former Hammers' team-mates were at the launch that promoted the scheme.

Crucially, the small print of the prospectus revealed that there was an Underwriting Agreement dated November 27, 1991 between West Ham United plc and the Bank of Scotland whereby the bank agreed, in certain circumstances, to underwrite up to a maximum of £11,634,000 of the £15,112,175 issue in return for a maximum fee of £211,510 plus VAT.

After being photographed with Bonds, inspecting a prototype of the new-look Boleyn Ground, Brooking added: "I'm very optimistic that this will work.

"Upton Park is a special place for supporters and players so I'm delighted that we're staying," confided Bonds. "I'm always looking for more new players and obviously the more money that can be made available in the future the better it will be for me, the team and our fans."

For his part, speaking over a decade later, Terence Brown was adamant that the scheme was the only real way forward.

"I fully supported the Bond Scheme and we would not have had the stadium we have today without it," he insisted. "The scheme played a fundamental part in regenerating the club. Sadly our supporters have never really understood, nor indeed would they have been aware of the importance of the underwriting agreement with the banks. For an eventual fee of £145,375 we were able to underwrite the cost of building the Bobby Moore (South Bank) and Centenary Stands (North Bank).

"I knew (and still know) of no other way to finance the development of both stands, bearing in mind the need to purchase land at a cost of £1.6m and also acquire and close Castle Street – the road running behind the South Bank.

"The country was in the middle of a severe economic recession and interest rates were touching 18%. The money could not have been raised in any other way and it is a shame that such a financially advantageous arrangement, from the club's point of view, is so misunderstood by our supporters.

"Maybe, from a presentation viewpoint, matters could have been handled differently but the banks controlled the marketing," he continued. "The banks did not wish to sustain a loss from the underwriting agreement and, therefore, geared the advertising campaign to one of pressure to take up the Bonds.

"The only way we could have changed the marketing would have been to forego all or part of the underwriting."

But with the Upton Park faithful already seething at a lack of investment in a team that, week-on-week, was looking increasingly destined to return to Division Two, the Hammers Bond launch could not have come at a worse time.

Although a confidence-boosting goalless draw against Liverpool kept Hammers out of the relegation zone, a subsequent hat-trick of defeats at Manchester United (1 2) and Everton (0-4) and at home to Sheffield Wednesday (1-2) led to a slide.

The only warming news in a freezing winter of discontent was Dicks' courageous return from a career-threatening knee injury, but another Hammers' hard man was soon in trouble.

Already there was a bit of 'history' between Martin Allen and Wednesday boss Trevor Francis. When the pair had been at Queens Park Rangers, manager Francis had been infuriated by his player's decision to dash from the squad on the eve of a match so that he could be at the birth of his son, George.

And now Mad Dog's rabid tackle on the Owls' Carlton Palmer had done nothing to rebuild any bridges between the pair.

With Hammers trailing 0-1, the second half was just 22 seconds old when substitute Allen's studs tore into the Wednesday midfielder's kneecap.

"I regret the tackle," he readily admitted a few years later. "It was over the top. I'd sat on the bench watching Carlton dominate the first half and was getting all worked up when Billy said I was going on for the restart. The kick-off took place and, well…all I can say is that luckily I didn't do him any ligament damage. Fortunately Carlton just had bad bruising.

"To go over the top is so wrong and it was a big low in my career. I wrote to Carlton and apologised and I've since seen him and shook his hand."

Certainly, Palmergate will haunt Allen till his dying day.

"Picture this. It's a quiet Sunday afternoon in a nice, peaceful Berkshire village. Your two little boys are looking in nanny's scrapbooks, asking why daddy's pictured on the back page of a newspaper dressed like a mad dog. It ain't easy explaining to little George and little Charlie why those men at the papers have put all fur around Daddy's head and given him fangs. It isn't nice," barked the consequently booked midfielder, who was fined a week's wages by an outraged Bonds on the eve of Hammers' Rumbelows Cup fourth round tie at Norwich City.

Having beaten Bradford City (1-1 & 4-0) and Sheffield United (2-0) in the previous rounds, West Ham crashed out of the competition after Robert Fleck converted an injury time penalty to secure a 2-1 victory for the Canaries.

Off the pitch feelings were escalating over the Bond Scheme and opposition was running high.

It was patently obvious that, contrary to earlier claims, 70% of the Boleyn Ground's population did NOT want to buy a Hammers Bond.

Dicks – a man accustomed to red cards throughout his career – made his long-awaited return to action following a 14-month absence by drilling home an 87th-minute penalty to secure a 1-1 draw against Sheffield United, for whom Brian Deane had opened the scoring.

This time, though, the red cards were reserved for the board's Hammers Bonds as the angry supporters turned the Upton Park terraces into a sea of scarlet.

There was little seasonal goodwill as West Ham slumped 1-3 at Aston Villa on

NEARLY REACHED THE SKY

Boxing Day and even on their travels they found the Hammers Bond protests continuing as they suffered 0-3 defeat at Notts County, where the visiting supporters staged a 20-minute sit-down, chanting 'Sack the board.'

By the time champions-elect Leeds United left Upton Park with a 3-1 victory on New Year's Day, West Ham found themselves second from bottom of the table.

'A quick return to the second division is very much a reality,' announced *The Daily Telegraph*. 'And the London team seem ripe for an FA Cup upset when Farnborough Town come to Upton Park.'

Those words proved quite prophetic. For Ted Pearce – a greying, cherubic-looking British Rail administrations manager – somehow led his GM Vauxhall Conference part-timers to a 1-1 draw and a lucrative £100,000 replay.

As out-of-work former QPR, Fulham and Norwich City striker Dean Coney celebrated his late penalty leveller, West Ham were in turmoil

"The mood is bad and the morale is low, probably lower than at any time since I have been here," grimaced Dicks after some 3,000 fans invaded the pitch upon hearing the full time whistle and several hundred then refused to leave the stadium for some two hours before half-a-dozen supporters were invited to meet the board.

Hammers' last win had come in the form of a 2-0 victory over Brighton & Hove Albion in the third round of the much-maligned Zenith Data Systems Cup on November 25, 1991. Previously in the second round, West Ham had disposed of Cambridge United (2-1) but a southern area semi-final defeat at Southampton (1-2) now ended their interest.

Another Upton Park pitch invasion – and attempt to storm the boardroom – followed in a 1-1 draw against Wimbledon, and with the club claiming that seats had been broken and stewards injured, a huge police presence was lined up to prevent a third uprising in the forthcoming FA Cup replay against Farnborough.

The family club was now a family at war.

Just what Jack Helliar, the club historian, Press Officer and former programme editor, would have made of the shambles is anyone's guess. The 75-year-old had been taken ill on the morning of the first Farnborough FA Cup tie and sadly passed away on Monday, January 13.

Helliar & Sons was founded in 1902 and it began printing the club programme in 1919. Jack started writing the matchday programme in 1946 and while he may have had the gait and resemblance of Hollywood film director Alfred Hitchcock, there was no mystery about this particular East Ender.

What Helliar – a Freeman of the City of London – did not know about West Ham United Football Club was not worth knowing anyway and, alongside his son John, he was a first-class host in the Upton Park press room on matchdays as well as a first-class ambassador for the club on awaydays.

His encyclopaedic knowledge of all things West Ham earned him respect from all quarters.

Certainly, in his final days, Helliar had no need for the first prize of a signed team photograph in a *Hammers News* 'wordsearch' competition but, as ever, he could not resist validating his own learnings as he set about finding the names of 12 West Ham players hidden within the grid of scrambled letters.

Trouble was, mischievous Jack had, somehow, actually unearthed 13 Hammers to leave the red-faced editorial team shaking their heads in admiration.

As a mark of respect, both sides wore black armbands in the FA Cup replay when Hammers again struggled to break the resistance of defiant Farnborough, who were watched by the biggest crowd – 23,869 – in their history. But just when the goalless encounter looked set for extra-time, Morley spared East End blushes when he finally struck an 89th minute winner.

While Farnborough milked the applause of the crowd, West Ham headed off the pitch and into a fourth round tie with Wrexham amidst a chorus of boos.

Small had not scored a league goal since netting that winner at Highbury some 11 weeks previously, but upon his return to struggling Luton Town he bagged a 15th goal of the campaign that enabled Hammers to leapfrog the Hatters, who found themselves marooned in 22nd spot.

Giant-killing Wrexham had felled Arsenal in the third round and now Lee Jones' late leveller had earned the Welshmen a 2-2 draw at Upton Park and a Racecourse Ground replay.

A second successive league win over Oldham (1-0) kept 20th-placed Hammers in touch with their fellow strugglers, before Colin Foster's 28th-minute header averted any embarrassment in the Wrexham re-match.

In a bid to placate their angry public, the board made some tweaks to the Hammers Bond, offering a 10-year discount of up to £100 per season to bondholders who purchased season tickets.

But that gesture did little to appease the 200 fans shoehorned into the Denmark Arms pub – less than a mile from the Boleyn Ground – in Barking Road for an official meeting of the Hammers Independent Supporters' Association (HISA).

In the FA Cup fifth round, West Ham looked to have done the hard work at Roker Park, where Small's 16th goal of the season secured a 1-1 draw against Sunderland on a replay-ridden route towards Wembley.

A 1-2 defeat at Sheffield Wednesday was not the best preparation for that FA Cup re-match and, after a shaky start by Everton's on-loan Dutchman Ray Atteveld (3 apps), Martin Allen's double against Sunderland brought Hammers back from a two-goal deficit, before Byrne's late sucker punch secured a 3-2 win for the Wearsiders.

With the cup dream over, the league nightmare continued and, three days later, with West Ham trailing 0-2 to Everton, the anger finally boiled and bubbled over at Upton Park.

Prior to kick-off, HISA had released thousands of balloons in a peaceful protest but when Martin Keown went down to receive treatment with a quarter-of-an-hour remaining, a lone Hammers' supporter grabbed a corner flag and planted it on the centre spot where he conducted his own sit-down protest.

And within seconds hundreds stampeded onto the field to congregate under the directors box and let rip with chants of 'Sack the Board' while the players returned to the dressing room for six minutes.

Dowie returned to haunt Hammers at The Dell where he netted the winner in Southampton's 1-0 victory that saw them climb off the bottom of the table and dump his old club into 22nd spot, where they stayed following defeats at Liverpool (0-1) and against Arsenal (0-2).

'The only Bond the Hammers need now is 007,' suggested *The People* after the Gunners overcame two goal-line sit-ins and another corner flag protest to shoot down troubled West Ham. 'But it is doubtful if even he could save them from relegation.'

Add George Parris's frightening collapse with a heart spasm and it was another bad day at the office.

A 2-2 draw against Queens Park Rangers left the bottom-placed Hammers eight points adrift of safety with 10 games left to play.

Incredibly, a top-versus-bottom clash at title-chasing Leeds United ended goalless as the nomadic Clive Allen – a £275,000 signing from Chelsea – watched from the Elland Road stands due to a two-match suspension.

"He was at Chelsea and sounded naffed off," said cousin Martin, who orchestrated the deadline-day transfer. "Clive said he'd love to sign for us and I mentioned it to Billy Bonds who said he'd love to have him. He was a great goalscorer and it was good to have him around, even though I'm still waiting for my agent's fee from him. I haven't had a penny!"

The banned Allen had bagged 49 goals for Tottenham Hotspur during the 1986-87 campaign but the finisher extraordinaire was, again, merely a frustrated spectator upon his return to White Hart Lane, where Gary Lineker's hat-trick secured a 3-0 victory for the north Londoners.

And although debutant Allen found the net upon his quickfire return to Stamford Bridge, Chelsea's 2-1 win now left Hammers 11 points adrift of safety with just seven games remaining.

A Matthew Rush double set West Ham on their way to a 4-0 victory over Norwich City and that thwarted a planned half-time walk-out by the Hammers Bond protesters, who could not wait for the second period to start.

But it proved a false dawn as Southampton marched to a third win of the season over Hammers thanks to Micky Adams' 88th-minute winner that did finally empty the Boleyn Ground.

Defeats at Manchester City (0-2) and at home to Crystal Palace (0-2) meant that Hammers went into a daunting clash against second-placed Manchester United nine points from safety with just three games to play.

Only Coventry City could still be caught and, intriguingly, Hammers' penultimate game of the campaign was at Highfield Road, meaning that the survival quest could still go all the way to the final whistle in the final game.

With Manchester United just a single point behind Leeds United with a game in hand, Alex Ferguson was looking to move into pole position with a midweek victory at Upton Park.

Hammers had failed to score in nine of their previous dozen games but, as is West Ham United's long-established wont, they typically hurled the form book into the gutters of Green Street, leaving apoplectic Ferguson seething at an 'obscene' performance that had seen Brown enter East End folklore with his 66th-minute winner.

"If people remember me it's always that game but I can't believe what people say about my goal," moaned the Hammers' hero. "Alex Ferguson's book and the newspapers all claim that it bobbled off my knee but that ain't right. I ran the whole length of the pitch and when Stuart Slater crossed I opened my foot up. I knew what I was doing. The ball hit me and flew in. Peter Schmeichel just sat on the floor and I was a little bit disappointed that I didn't get credit for it.

"Ferguson was slaughtering us for trying hard, asking why we hadn't done that in 15 games beforehand. Football just ain't like that, though."

But that superhuman effort counted for nothing in a win-or-bust encounter at Coventry where only victory would do. Indeed, Micky Gynn's winner for the Sky Blues left a dark, dark cloud hanging over the consequently relegated Hammers.

And as West Ham pulled down the curtain on their disastrous bond-disrupted campaign – in which Stuart Slater had incredibly failed to score in 41 league games – there was nothing to play for except pride as Forest rolled in.

Before the game, Dicks collected his first Hammer-of-the-Year award despite only having returned to the scene in mid-December. Amidst all the mediocrity dished up during the previous nine months, Upton Park's appreciative audience had clearly acknowledged the quality he had brought back to the side following that brave, successful quest to overcome his knee injury.

Hughton (40+1 apps) was on the verge of heading to Brentford on a free transfer and Rosenior (57+10 apps 23 gls) moved to Bristol City on the same basis.

McAvennie's injury-plagued second spell was also about to come to an end, too, after the club had decided not to renew his contract. In his first season at Upton Park he had scored 26 league goals in 41 games before netting a total of 39 goals in all competitions in 107 outings prior to heading to Celtic.

The five-times capped Scottish international's second spell only yielded 21 goals in 83 games as injuries, drink and drugs took their toll but, typically, the blond bombshell was destined to make an explosive exit from Upton Park.

"To my surprise, I was named as substitute," wrote McAvennie in *Scoring – An Expert's Guide*. "I reckoned that Bonds wouldn't put me on for a last farewell.

"Before the game I shared this view with Mitchell Thomas. 'No Frank, I think you're wrong. You'll get a run out today,' said Mitchell with conviction. Through a goalless first half I sat on the bench feeling as low as I could get. My last time at Upton Park and I wouldn't even get a kick at the ball.

"At half-time, I was suddenly told to get stripped and get on for the second half. 'You're replacing Mitchell,' said Bonds. 'He's taken a knock.' Like hell he had.

"I took full advantage, ran rings around Nigel Clough and scored three goals," smiled hat-trick hero McAvennie, recalling the 3-0 win that ruined Sampdoria-bound Des Walker's Forest farewell. "The fans were going wild and chanting my name. It was a perfect send off, a moment to savour for the rest of my life."

McAvennie (168+22 apps 60 gls) headed off to Aston Villa and Hong Kong's South China club before linking up with Liam Brady at Celtic, where Lou Macari ironically succeeded the Irishman. Predictably, the arrival of his former boss meant that Macca was soon on the move to Swindon Town before his career spun full circle and he ended up back at St. Mirren before hanging up his shooting boots.

NEARLY REACHED THE SKY

Retirement from the game saw him embroiled in a string of unsuccessful business ventures – including an apparent hunt for a treasure ship – and a well-publicised flirtation with jail that ultimately saw him cleared of drugs charges.

While that fairytale, farewell hat-trick may have seen Hammers end the season with a victory, it was still not enough to prevent them finishing rock-bottom in 22nd place with 38 points from 42 games.

"I'm not going to quit," insisted Bonds after a season of horror that had seen all the hard work of the 1990-91 campaign count for nothing. "I've been through the mill and I've not come through all this to jack it in now. But I have wondered if it's all worth it. The Bond Scheme had a big effect on us.

"We were halfway up the table when the club brought it in. We had just beaten Arsenal at Highbury and drawn at home to Liverpool. We were doing okay but when the Bond Scheme came in all hell broke loose. It was never easy after that."

West Ham would still kick off the 1992-93 season in Division One but now they would find the league of the elite above them.

Indeed, the lucrative riches of the newly-formed FA Premier League that was on the verge of signing a £304m contract with BSkyB, had just slipped through the grasp of a cash-strapped club that was simply in disarray and needing to comply with the all-seater stadium recommendations of the Taylor Report.

Whether they could have afforded to sack him financially is open to debate but in terms of stability the beleaguered board had no choice but to stand by their man.

Certainly, Billy was the only Bonds the furious Hammers' fans wanted.

And as the battered boss trudged off into the close-season with his wife Lyn and daughters Katie and Claire to re-charge and plot a second promotion push, help in the form of a familiar, friendly face was about to head his way.

PLAYERS IN

Clive Allen	Chelsea	£275,000
Kenny Brown	Plymouth Argyle	£175,000
Dean Martin	Fisher Athletic	£20,000
Tony Parks	Tottenham Hotspur	Free transfer
Mike Small	Brighton & Hove Albion	£400,000
Mitchell Thomas	Tottenham Hotspur	£500,000

LOANS IN

Ray Atteveld	Everton

PLAYERS OUT

Iain Dowie	Southampton	£500,000
Chris Hughton	Brentford	Free transfer
Frank McAvennie	Aston Villa	Free transfer
Tony Parks	Stoke City	Free transfer
Jimmy Quinn	Bournemouth	£40,000
Leroy Rosenior	Bristol City	Free transfer
Ray Stewart	St Johnstone	Free transfer

Chapter 6
1992-93

NEVER FEAR, HARRY'S HERE

**It was widely reported that Ray Harford was being lined up as Billy Bonds'
new assistant but the Hammers' boss wanted to secure his own Best Man.
Literally.**

"I'd had a few phone calls from Harry Redknapp telling me that he was fed up
at Bournemouth, fed up with management itself and that he would be happy to
come and work with me on my terms," Bonds, who first met Redknapp at an
England Youth trial in 1964, told *EX*. "Harry wasn't a top drawer coach but he was
good out on the training ground and good with players."

In *Harry Redknapp – My Autobiography* – the profits from which he generously
donated to the children's charity Leukaemia Busters – the former Upton Park wide
boy claimed: "When they were relegated Bill gave me a call. I immediately
thought something must be up because he never phoned anyone. He told me he
could do with a bit of help.

"I'd had enough of managing. I'd had nine years at Bournemouth and that was
plenty. When Bill rang that summer and started talking about someone assisting
him at West Ham, I thought I wouldn't mind some of that.

"I enjoyed coaching and thought I could earn a nice little living at Upton Park,
getting out with the players without the worries and stresses that go hand in hand
with being a full time boss.

"But what I first saw at Upton Park shook me to the core. It was frightening. The
club was going absolutely nowhere.

"If they were capable of turning in a display like they did against Manchester
United once they'd been relegated the previous season, then how come they
couldn't manage it more often when survival was still a very real prospect?

"I was happy to work alongside Bill. He deserved success for everything he'd put
into the club but morale was at a low ebb. Things were bad. A few players in the
squad just didn't care and the general confidence level was zero."

Ian Bishop, who had played under the new assistant at Bournemouth, was not so
convinced that Harry was as unambitious as he, perhaps, portrayed himself.

"Harry would sell his own gran to manage West Ham," warned the perceptive
Scouser.

According to investigative author Tom Bower, Redknapp had increased
Bournemouth's debts from £150,000 to £2.6m between July 1987 and June 1992.
Ultimately, these would hit £4.4m and in his award-winning book, *Broken*

Dreams, he claimed that, while the club had made some £848,000 profit on its transfer dealings, H had increased the wage bill to £1m per annum by providing his acquisitions with generous contracts.

"There was a degree of irresponsibility in Harry's actions," the Cherries' financial adviser Roy Pack told the *News of the World*. "It has developed into the mess we are now desperately trying to resolve. What happened is almost unbelievable and in a business sense it is ludicrous."

And upon arriving at Upton Park, Redknapp, the master wheeler-dealer, wasted no time thumbing his way through his contacts book in a bid to inject some fresh blood into a club low on credit with both its bankers and its supporters.

Although he had been dragged off Cherries' chairman Ken Gardiner in front of some 150 people following an argument over an alleged slur the Bournemouth executive made against his best friend Brian Tiler – the club's former managing director who was killed in an Italian car crash at the 1990 World Cup finals in which Harry was seriously injured – Redknapp had no qualms about returning to Dean Court to sign Mattie Holmes for £40,000.

Meanwhile, despite the unrealistic attempts of Southend United to make their tigerish midfielder appear as a player akin to the new Pele, Peter Butler's transfer fee was set at a sensible £170,000 by a tribunal.

"I've played for smaller clubs and that will certainly make me appreciate things more. At Southend we'd all have to clean our boots and wash our own kit and after training we'd be lucky to get a cup of tea yet alone a meal," admitted the Yorkshire tyke who was as honest as the day is long.

And in a further endorsement of his humble upbringing in the lower leagues, Butler was soon bemusing his new team-mates with a weekly meat raffle – the profits being split between the players' Christmas party fund and charity.

Whereas Liam Brady had brought casino chips aboard the team coach to use as currency in the high stakes poker games, here was Butts dishing out raffle tickets for the chance to win a bag of steaks to go with a bag of chips.

Following an eleventh-hour call from Redknapp, tricky winger Mark Robson joined on a free transfer from Tottenham Hotspur, penning a one-year contract with West Ham and turning down Dutch side De Graafschap.

Dagenham Motors, the country's largest Ford dealership, also became the club's new sponsors after signing a one-year, £250,000 deal with the club.

Ever since Stuart Slater had scorched into the spotlight with his precocious performance in that scintillating FA Cup sixth round victory over Everton in March 1990, he had been hot property.

Celtic manager Liam Brady – his one time advisor – had been his biggest courtier but Hammers' £3m price tag had simply been too much for the hard-up Glasgow club.

With Julian Dicks still on his way back from injury, apart from Ludek Miklosko and Slater, there were few glistening jewels in the tarnished Upton Park crown.

And despite his own cash constraints, Bonds knew that he had to offer the England 'B' international the biggest contract in the club's history if he was to retain Slater to spearhead the push to the promised land of the all-new Premiership.

"After all that Howard Kendall had said following that Everton cup tie, I just wasn't any old run of the mill player any more. Suddenly, I had a huge price tag pinned on me and if I had a bad game it was highlighted," admitted Slater.

"Liam's mate – Clinton Durie – became my agent when he was appointed Celtic manager. I'd been in contract talks and that was a big, big thing hanging over my season and then West Ham made me an offer that just blew my head off. I was thinking: 'All this money.' It was a new four-year deal that would've paid me more in one year than I'd earned in the whole of the previous three seasons. Even today, it would still be classed as average money in the Premiership.

"West Ham had just put a contract on the table that was the best one they'd ever been prepared to give, yet my agent just looked across the desk and said: 'No!'

"I was young and naïve and just wasn't strong enough to say that I wanted to sign because West Ham United was my club.

"We walked out and when Billy Bonds heard I'd turned it all down, the club's management naturally thought that I wanted to move.

"I'd obviously been influenced by Liam and his people outside the game," confessed Slater, who became Celtic's club record signing when Brady finally captured him for a knock-down £1.5m despite Redknapp's attempted eleventh-hour intervention. "When I left West Ham I wasn't told about any interest from any other teams. Liam's mate had only ever told me about Celtic.

"I should have been my own person because I probably would have stayed at Upton Park and been a one-team man but I don't hold anything against Liam."

In truth, beset by Achilles problems, Slater never fulfilled his undoubted potential and, as Celtic's own financial plight worsened, he was reunited with John Lyall at Ipswich Town in an £800,000 move south, before being heading to Watford in 1996.

"Without doubt, I under-achieved," confessed Slater (171+8 apps 18 gls) who embarked on a brief sojourn to Carlton Soccer Club in Melbourne before finally ending up back at Upton Park coaching Hammers' Under-11 side.

Slater-less West Ham headed to Barnsley for the opening game of the 1992-93 campaign and, although Mike Small was sent off for disputing one of the hundreds of offside flags he habitually saw during his time at the club, Clive Allen's classy strike secured a 1-0 victory.

Homeless Charlton Athletic may have been mere tenants at Upton Park but they upset their landlords as Alan Pardew's 31st minute goal condemned West Ham to a 0-1 defeat.

Kevin Keegan's Newcastle United then kept up their 100% start to the season with a 2-0 victory at St James's Park, where the much-maligned ex-Hammer David Kelly found the net and Dicks found the jaw of his former on-loan team-mate Franz Carr, to collect his second red card for the club. It also proved a painful introduction for Holmes, who broke his nose in another collision

The much-maligned Zenith Data Systems Cup had been replaced by the Anglo-Italian Cup – a competition that had been reasonably popular in the 70s – after the Football Associations of England and Italy had taken the opportunity to create a tournament aimed at rebuilding the bridges, so devastated by the tragic deaths of those 39 Juventus fans, as they fled from Liverpool's stampeding supporters, before the 1985 European Cup Final at the Heysel Stadium.

A mere 4,809 fans turned up at Upton Park for the opening tie against Bristol Rovers when Dicks' double earned a 2-2 draw as debutant 'keeper Steven Banks (1 app) endured a baptism of fire in his one and only outing before subsequently joining Gillingham in the spring.

With season ticket sales down by 8,000 on the previous season, there were only 11,921 present as the Allens – Martin and Clive – secured a 2-1 win over Watford.

A 3-1 victory at Peterborough was followed up with an even more impressive 5-1 win at Bristol City where Redknapp was accused of gesturing to an angry crowd.

Those two free-scoring awaydays should have brought the crowds back in their hordes but still just 11,493 shuffled through the Upton Park turnstiles – the lowest league crowd since 1957 – to see Hammers held to a 1-1 draw by Derby County.

"Everyone at the club is disappointed at the attendances and we all have to work together to make sure that we come up with the right methods to persuade our supporters to come back," announced spin-doctoring Peter Storrie, anxious to play down the catastrophic effect of the Hammers Bond. "The simple situation at the beginning of last season is, by all means, that we would have spent £2m, £3m or £4m in the transfer market if we'd had that to spend. But you simply cannot spend what you cannot borrow or do not have.

"We all want West Ham United to be successful and we will constantly do everything we can to improve the squad but finance is extremely tight.

"We are making changes and cuts in the organisation which is the start of our plan to build a stronger future. We will look in-depth into the pricing situation which will hopefully enable us to do something positive in the near future."

Martin Allen was equally concerned with helping to bring the fans flooding back along Green Street.

"It's up to us to show the supporters that there's something good going on here," he accepted. "They want to see a successful team and after last season we've got a few bridges to build."

Cousin Clive's fifth goal of the campaign then earned what was ultimately to prove a crucial 1-0 win at Portsmouth.

Back in the Anglo-Italian Cup, another 3-0 win at Southend United left West Ham with an identical 5-2 goal tally to that of Bristol Rovers which called for a bizarre post-match ritual.

The competition rules stipulated that the group winners would be decided by a three-way telephonic toss-up at the Football League's London offices. After a Rovers' official called 'tails' from down in the West Country, Bonds – waiting patiently on the tripartite conference line back at Roots Hall – then learned that the coin had landed 'heads' up to leave Hammers dusting down their passports.

There was little joy in the Coca-Cola Cup second round, though, where third division Crewe Alexandra followed up a goalless draw at Upton Park with a 2-0 win at Gresty Road to dump flat West Ham out of the competition.

A few days before, Hammers had drawn 0-0 at Molineux and, yet again, Dicks was dismissed, this time for tripping Steve Bull. In the surreal scrap that followed, Bonds found himself charging down the touchline from his makeshift dug-out to prevent his hot-headed, twice-booked defender from becoming further embroiled in an ugly fracas with Paul Birch.

It had been a wretched day for the Hammers' boss and a trio of travelling fans who returned to the car park to find their vehicle stolen. But upon learning of their plight as he climbed aboard the team coach, the sympathetic Bonzo, typically, organised an impromptu whip-round amongst his players to rustle up the cost of three train tickets back to London.

Still the crowds refused to return to Upton Park, though, and a sparse attendance of 10,326 witnessed a 6-0 slaughter of Sunderland before the free-scoring, second-placed Hammers returned to Bristol to plunder a 4-0 win over Rovers.

And still in Bristol, skipper Martin Allen enjoyed one of the highlights of his career when he scored a sublime goal for Glenn Hoddle's Football League side in a 3-1 victory over their Italian counterparts at Ashton Gate.

George Parris, who had been given the all clear following his worrying collapse back in March, was dismissed for a professional foul in a 0-1 defeat against Swindon Town that was followed by a 1-2 reverse at Cambridge United. The goals machine had inexplicably seized up.

A 1-1 draw on a proverbial wet, Tuesday, November night in Grimsby preceded the return of Forest Gate-born world heavyweight title contender Lennox Lewis, who arrived home to witness Hammers finally land a vengeful knockout punch on Notts County with a 2-0 victory at Upton Park.

The concept of reviving an Anglo-Italian Cup tournament certainly had some merits, given it had attracted 100,000 fans paying £500,000 in gate receipts for England's domestic preliminary rounds alone.

But, for their part, Hammers only attracted 4,809 fans to Upton Park for the draw with Bristol Rovers – while just 6,482 had turned up at Southend's Roots Hall.

Furthermore, their two trips to Italy would cost the club £40,000 and, with their autumnal promotion push now spluttering into life, it was readily apparent that the last thing Hammers needed was the midweek commitment of four games against a quartet of second rate Italian sides.

Forget AC Milan, Internazionale, Juventus, AS Roma, Sampdoria *et al.*

Forget the European Cup.

This was the Anglo-Italian Cup and Hammers – alongside Bristol City, Derby County and Tranmere Rovers – found themselves pitted in Group B, where they would play two home games against AC Reggiana and Pisa and travel to Italy to face Cremonese and Cosenza.

A series of spiteful gladiatorial encounters that typified the entire tournament were destined to follow.

Desperate to see Hammers return to the 'European' stage after a 12-year absence, many of the travelling English supporters paid £89 (including match ticket) to travel from Green Street by road some 22 hours ahead of the scheduled 2:30 pm kick-off in Cremonese.

Despite the negotiation of a *seven-minute* delay to the kick-off, with no floodlights available the game simply had to start and when those coaches finally chugged into Cremona, the second half was already underway. Indeed, those weary West Ham fans arrived just in time to see Slovenian Mattheus Florjancic's double seal a 2-0 win for the *Serie B* table-toppers.

Five players were booked and as the lights on the scoreboard displayed the digits 1639 they were not highlighting the time, but an attendance heavily swollen by several hundred East Enders who easily outnumbered the uninterested Italians.

A £12 refund was subsequently given to each coach traveller, rising to £25 for those unfortunate souls whose vehicle broke down on the return leg.

Among those flying back was director Will Cearns who, upon being spotted by the anti-Bond brigade, made doubly sure that he was securely strapped into his seat as the chorus of 'Let's chuck Cearnsey out the plane!' rang around the cabin.

Back in Division One, the atmosphere was even more tense during an ill-tempered 1-2 defeat at Millwall, where an angry Dicks returned from a five-match suspension to find himself stripped of the club captaincy.

The Hammers' bad-boy responded with a two-goal salvo in an Alvin Martin-skippered 5-3 win over Oxford United.

"That sort of game could give you a heart attack," warned Bonds, who could not have failed to be impressed by jinking Joey Beauchamp on the Oxford wing.

In another niggly Anglo-Italian clash at Upton Park, Trevor Morley became the fifth dismissal of the season when he got his retaliation in first against AC Reggiana's Gianluca Francesconi.

"Punching? Headbutting? It doesn't really matter. Morley went," said a furious Bonds after seeing Clive Allen's double give his side a 2-0 win. "Trevor thought the bloke was going to pop him and he got in there before he did!"

Morley was back to doing what he did best three days later when he joined fellow scorer Clive Allen on the dozen goals mark following the 3-1 win over Birmingham City that lifted Hammers into third spot in the first division.

That set up an intriguing clash with second-placed Tranmere Rovers. It was West Ham's first visit to Prenton Park for over 50 years and, after John Aldridge's hat-trick condemned them to a crushing 2-5 defeat, they left Merseyside hoping that they would not have to return for another half-century.

By now it was also obvious that the Hammers Bond scheme would not work in 50 years either.

Indeed, to the underwriters' embarrassment, just 780 Bonds had been sold.

Following the stand-off that had seen the supporters vote with their feet, discussions with HISA and the influential fanzines led to a ceasefire whereby the club reduced seat ticket prices and made various other concessions.

Rebel supporters whose under-estimated power had certainly been brought to bear upon the absentees, now sent out a reluctant rallying call to bury the hatchet.

Phil Daniels, author of the critically-acclaimed Bobby Moore biography *Moore than a Legend* and contributor to the fanzine *Over Land and Sea*, urged the fans to return to the fold.

"Signs of improvement are showing. Heading in the right direction at least. Wouldn't it be a shame if we can't meet them halfway?" he wrote. "My message is this: It's time to get back to Upton Park. Renew your season ticket, go back to the terraces, take your seat. Go back for all the good reasons that you went to West Ham in the first place. For the magic, the identity, the therapy and the pleasure. We can now put our club where it deserves to be, by showing our strength: Forgiveness and common sense. The damage will be irreparable. Let's make this a joint victory. Not a fight to the death."

Notwithstanding the net-busting antics of Morley and Clive Allen, Bonds was still looking for reinforcements in the striking department as he closed in on Montreal Supra's £200,000-rated Canadian international striker, Alex Bunbury, who needed a work permit.

There was no such problem for former Yardley's soap factory worker Steve Jones, who was signed from Billericay Town in a £22,500 deal.

As they flew to rain-lashed Cosenza, Jones was about to be thrown in at the deep end on a heavily waterlogged pitch that was the subject of two pitch inspections by English referee Roger Dilkes.

Indeed, with time ticking away on the runway parking meter, Billy Bonds even offered to forfeit the match rather than keep the chartered flight waiting on the Italian tarmac for another night.

"It's a great opportunity for the lad," said Redknapp after the Mossley official finally passed the pitch fit. "Steve has definitely got something to offer the club."

The previous evening the Cosenza officials had hosted a pre-match meal high in the snow-covered mountains where they enhanced Anglo-Italian relations while craftily wasting no time trying to elicit the English game-plan.

"Do you play zonal defence or man-to-man marking?" asked Cosenza.

"I don't know," replied the guarded Bonds. "You tell me your system first!"

Come matchday, only 800 Italians were prepared to sacrifice their Bank Holiday to brave the monsoons, while 50 saturated Hammers' fans saw debutant Jones wade through the ankle-deep water to set up Clive Allen for a brilliant match-winning volley.

Back home, Allen and Morley were on target again in a 2-0 win over Southend United before Hammers' 'European' involvement ended following a goalless draw against Pisa at Upton Park.

Matthew Rush became the sixth Hammer to be dismissed since the campaign started following a dust-up with Giovanni Fasce that saw the warring duo sent off.

Shamefully, 18 players – nine from each country – were red carded in Anglo-Italian skirmishes that had seen the 32-game tournament become a whole new brawl game.

With the focus back on the serious business of the league, another goalless stalemate followed at Brentford, before Hammers also grabbed a point in a 1-1 draw at The Valley where Charlton Athletic – having now vacated Upton Park and returned to their spiritual home – were still unbeaten.

A further draw followed against Luton after Hammers surrendered a two-goal lead but there were no such slip-ups in the FA Cup third round tie at The Hawthorns, where Clive Allen and Robson secured a 2-0 victory over West

NEARLY REACHED THE SKY

Bromwich Albion.

Another 2-0 win followed at the Baseball Ground but, for the third time since the start of the season, Dicks was sent off after collecting two bookings inside the opening half-hour.

"Mr Bonds must clean up West Ham's act," demanded *The Daily Telegraph* as Dicks became the seventh Hammer to be dismissed. "Otherwise, the self-styled Academy of Football will become the Hammer House of Horror."

"Julian Dicks' talent was never in doubt," conceded Redknapp. "But if I say he was a pest I am guilty of an outrageous understatement. He was, and I stress *was*, the most disruptive footballer I've ever come across. An absolute nightmare. He got sent off for two absolutely horrendous tackles yet for the next hour the West Ham fans chanted his name. He was completely out of order. He let the team down and left them to work their socks off for an unlikely victory. Yet his team-mates didn't get a mention. It was all 'Julian Dicks this' and 'Julian Dicks that.' That's how it was at the club at that time."

As Dicks counted the cost of the £8,000 fine imposed by the club, West Ham again rustled up another telling 2-0 win over Portsmouth at Upton Park where an improving 18,000-plus crowd came through the turnstiles for the second successive game.

In the FA Cup fourth round at Barnsley, Hammers were run out of town by the Yorkshiremen as they crashed 1-4.

With only promotion to concentrate on now, wins over Bristol City (2-0) and Leicester City (2-1) left Hammers in second place, 11 points adrift of runaway leaders Newcastle United.

Jones marked his full league debut with a goal in the 1-1 draw against Barnsley at Upton Park and he was also on target in a 2-1 victory over Peterborough United.

West Ham extended their unbeaten league run to 11 games with a 2-1 win over Watford but despite having closed the gap on Kevin Keegan's Magpies to just four points, the victory was soon overshadowed by the news that 51-year-old Bobby Moore was battling against bowel cancer.

"I have a battle to win," he said on February 15, 1993.

Tragically, this was to be one fight the 108-times capped England legend was destined to lose.

The gaunt 1966 World Cup-winning skipper looked a shadow of his imperious self as he sat in the press box at the scene of the country's greatest-ever sporting triumph, co-commentating for Capital Gold Radio on England's 6-0 win over San Marino in a USA 94 qualifier, at Wembley, two days later.

The following Sunday, Moore was due to be at Upton Park to witness Hammers' goalless draw with leaders Newcastle United but, typically, he abandoned what would have been a further pilgrimage back to another career defining venue for fear of being mobbed by well-wishers.

And at 6.36am on February 24, 1993, he sadly lost his battle.

Robert Frederick Chelsea Moore OBE was born in Barking on April 12, 1941.

After signing amateur forms for West Ham United in August 1956, he made his debut against Manchester United in September 1958 and went on to make 642 appearances for the club.

In the mid-60s he trotted up Wembley's 39 steps in three successive seasons to collect the FA Cup (1964) and the European Cup Winners' Cup (1965) before famously wiping his hands to collect the ultimate prize of the Jules Rimet Trophy from HM The Queen on July 30, 1966.

Moore was a golden boy of the swinging sixties who famously liked nothing more than a beer or three with his mates. England's only World Cup-winning captain was certainly of the highest profile but, crucially, he knew how to conduct himself both on-and-off the field, unlike so many of the low alcohol-tolerant players of the modern game.

In 1974, he moved to Fulham, where he ironically faced Hammers in the 1975 FA Cup final before heading to the USA's North American Soccer League. Upon his return to England, Moore embarked on brief managerial stints with Oxford City and Southend United before becoming a media pundit with the *Sunday Sport* and, more popularly, with Capital Gold in his later years.

Yet, incredibly, prior to his premature passing, the man who had so much to give was wastefully given so little to do by West Ham United.

"The manner of his leaving was in keeping with the man's way of living," wrote friend and *Daily Mail* journalist Jeff Powell. "No commotion, no complaint, no thought for himself and, most typically, no loose ends. The meticulous attention to detail, the scrupulous care with appearance, the exact precision of time-keeping, the constant observation of manners which maketh a gentleman out of a hero, all were with him to the premature end. The loss is ours. England has lost a distinguished ambassador, the world of football has lost a giant."

Prime Minister John Major added: "Bobby Moore enhanced sport by his example and his behaviour as well as his skill."

And long-standing friend and respected TV chat show host, Michael Parkinson observed: "He looked and played like a hero and he behaved like one, too."

Sir Alf Ramsey, manager of the 1966 World Cup winning side added: "Bobby was my right-hand man, my lieutenant on the field, a cool, calculated footballer I could trust with my life."

As the nation mourned the loss of one of its iconic sons, a few scarves, a Hammers' shirt and several bouquets of flowers were attached to the main gates in Green Street. The makeshift shrine grew by the hour, as mourning men, women and children made the pilgrimage to Upton Park to pay their last respects.

Some had been privileged to see him play, others had lost a part of their childhood, while the kids 'just knew' that Moore was the greatest-ever Hammer.

The tears flowed as quickly as the 75-yard sea of mementoes and bouquets had meandered its way along the main forecourt.

And there was barely a dry eye in the house at Roker Park as Hammers faced Sunderland in their first match since Moore's death.

On an afternoon laden with emotion, snippets of Kenneth Wolstenholme's immortal 'They Think It's All Over' commentary were played ahead of an impeccably-observed minute's silence that saw the muted Roker Roar reduced to a chilling, self-inflicted hush.

NEARLY REACHED THE SKY

Hammers escaped with a second successive goalless draw against north-eastern opponents but football was always secondary on a sombre day for the game.

The Sun announced it was to back a memorial game at Wembley and more than a decade later that promise had still be delivered.

But at the suggestion of *Hammers News*, one fitting tribute was observed when the Number Six shirt was retired for the following week's home game with Wolverhampton Wanderers.

While Ian Bishop prepared to revert to the Number 12 jersey, Moore's fellow 1966 heroes Geoff Hurst and Martin Peters, accompanied by Ron Greenwood, carried a giant floral tribute in the shape of Bobby's Number Six shirt into the centre circle as West Ham's biggest crowd of the season – 24,679 – paid tribute with another vacuum-like 60 seconds silence prior to a subdued 3-1 victory.

"We would normally have expected a gate of around 16,000 for this game. So many extra people came to pay their respects – it just shows you the stature of the man and how much he is loved," said Bonds. "Bobby Moore is a legend."

Three days later, Dicks – the heartbeat of Hammers promotion push – struck twice inside the opening 11 minutes as West Ham notched up a 2-1 win over Grimsby Town at Upton Park.

Despite a 0-1 defeat at Notts County, second-placed Hammers were still six points clear of Swindon Town, Portsmouth and Millwall, who were all on 60 points as they desperately tried to keep tabs on the top two.

With just 15 minutes to spare before the transfer deadline passed, Southampton's David Speedie – who had been lent to West Bromwich Albion – joined Hammers on loan in time to play in a 2-0 victory over Tranmere Rovers at Upton Park.

Andy Melville headed Oxford United to a 1-0 win at the Manor Ground, where Dicks collected his sixth booking for a wild tackle on Beauchamp and, added to those three sending-offs, his latest ban meant that he would miss a total of 13 games through suspension.

Elsewhere, 'Mad Dog' Martin Allen headed to the Football Association after becoming the first player to reach 41 disciplinary points.

"I picked up those bookings up in record time – I'd get there even quicker these days – but I must admit I enjoyed that visit to Lancaster Gate, sitting there with all the hobnobs," recalled Allen. "I'd prepared my piece well and spoke for half-an-hour in my defence. Billy Bonds just sat there mesmerised.

"I then proceeded to get heavily fined and banned for loads of matches!"

Indeed, the 13 bookings he had collected in his over-enthusiastic quest for Premiership football cost Allen a £1,000 fine plus a four-match ban.

Speedie had an equally aggressive reputation and when Hammers – minus the suspended Dicks and Allen – scrapped out an absorbing 2-2 draw against Millwall at Upton Park, his two appalling quick-fire misses did little to enamour him to an angry Upton Park crowd who were feeling the pressure of Portsmouth's late burst.

"Those two minutes were an absolute nightmare," admitted the fiery forward whose tenacity when playing for Chelsea against the Hammers in the same win-or-bust games of the mid-80s had clearly neither been forgiven nor forgotten.

On the day when the Aintree Grand National was abandoned after a false start,

Hammers had not even got into their stride when Andy Saville gave Birmingham City an 11th-minute lead at St Andrew's. But somehow West Ham conjured up a storming finish as late, late goals by Kenny Brown and Ian Bishop gave the visitors an unlikely victory.

Ironically, George Parris (266 | 32 apps 18 gls) had been sold to the Blues just a month beforehand in a move that was encouraged by Redknapp.

City boss Terry Cooper had only called to sound him out over a deadline-day move for his former Bournemouth star Paul Moulden but it ended up costing Birmingham £100,000 when 'H' took the opportunity to offload the popular Ilford-born utility man.

"With respect, you can pick up players like George Parris in any division if you look hard enough," claimed the assistant manager, no doubt satisfied that new midfield marauder Peter Butler had proved himself an adequate replacement.

And in a surreal post-script to the game, Parris – who was still training occasionally at Chadwell Heath – returned to London aboard the Hammers' team coach, sharing his man-of-the-match champagne in lieu of paying a fare.

"I'll do anything to get a decent crowd at my testimonial!" he joked.

The short-trip to lowly Southend United looked set to give Hammers the chance to put some daylight between themselves and the chasing pack but they succumbed to their worst league defeat in terms of divisional standings since 1979 when Fulham, in 21st place in the second flight, won 3-2 at Upton Park.

With the Shrimpers in 23rd-spot, Stan Collymore invited Brett Angell to net the only goal of a game on a night when West Ham slipped down to third place behind unstoppable Newcastle and in-form Portsmouth.

Having seen the crowd bay for his blood following those misses against Millwall, Speedie scored twice in a 3-0 win over Leicester City, before drawing a blank in 0-2 defeat at Luton Town, where Dicks was lucky to escape with a fourth red card after somehow only receiving a seventh booking of the campaign for a deliberate goal-line handball.

In a dramatic climbdown, the rhetoric of Storrie's clouded, half-hearted attempt to claim that the Hammers Bond was still alive and kicking was undermined by the fact that the board had taken an embarrassing U-turn, while the equally red-faced underwriters took a hit and the club scaled back its ambitious redevelopment plans.

"The Bond Scheme has not been scrapped and it's still in existence," he insisted before revealing that the ill-conceived plan to get the fans to finance the rebuilding of Upton Park had, indeed, been all but scuppered. "But now supporters have a genuine choice. You do not have to buy a Bond, you will not lose your seat to a Bondholder but when you see the season ticket prices for next season, you will see what a genuine saving it is to actually have a Bond. It is entirely and utterly your choice but you do NOT need a Bond to get into Upton Park."

Alan Dickens returned to the East End with Brentford and although Hammers (79 points) comfortably turned in a 4-0 victory, Pompey (82) remained three points clear in second spot with just three games to play.

The heavily barracked Speedie had another hit-and-miss outing against Bristol Rovers at Upton Park, where he missed a sitter, won a penalty and finally stuck his head where few would put their studs to net a last-gasp winner that saw him require lengthy treatment.

He may have only been on loan, with no chance of signing permanently for cash-strapped West Ham, but Speedo was still giving his all to the promotion cause.

"It's disgusting," said Bonds after the 2-1 victory. "He took terrible abuse and I have apologised to David on behalf of the club."

Portsmouth's shock 1-4 defeat at Sunderland suddenly opened the door for West Ham as they headed to Swindon Town for their penultimate game of the season, 24 hours later.

And they grabbed that lifeline with both hands as substitute Clive Allen stepped from the bench, after a four-month absence with a calf injury, to inspire Hammers to a 3-1 win that saw them leapfrog Portsmouth into second place.

"That was the most important result since I've been at West Ham because the pressure was on and we knew that we had to win," enthused Allen, who struck the crucial second goal.

While both sides were level on 85 points, West Ham had scored 79 goals and conceded 41 while Pompey had netted 78 and let in 45.

But Hammers' superior goal difference would count for nothing in the final reckoning, though, as the Barclays League rules stipulated that promotion would be decided by most goals scored and, if level, the least goals conceded.

Hammers had the edge as they took on relegation-threatened Cambridge United, while mid-table Grimsby had little to play for as they headed to Fratton Park.

Earlier, Steve Potts had collected his first Hammer-of-the-Year award, and as their 56th competitive game of the campaign entered its final minutes, West Ham were 1-0 up against the Us thanks to Speedie, while Portsmouth led Grimsby, 2-1.

A late Pompey goal – an 81st of the season – would have elevated them from a play-off spot into second place but back in the East End, Clive Allen sealed a Hammers' victory with a last-gasp tap-in in front of the South Bank terraces that were about to be re-developed into the all-seater Bobby Moore Stand.

As time ran out on Portsmouth, Allen's crucial, promotion-confirming goal – number 81 of the campaign – was the cue for an excited pitch invasion from the biggest crowd of the season (27,399) and lift-off to the Premiership.

Love him or loathe him, the utterly committed Speedie (11 apps 4 goals) had brought both a telling tenacity and a compelling contribution during his brief loan spell at Upton Park.

"David Speedie has been fantastic for this club. He's run his ticker off for us and has been brilliant. I've shaken his hand and told him that if he ever wants to drop in for a cup of tea he's more than welcome," said Bonds, no doubt wishing that he could offer him a contract rather than just a cuppa.

During the course of the season Hammers had transfer-listed Tony Gale, Ian Bishop, Tim Breacker, Mitchell Thomas and Mike Small, while several clubs had been sniffing around £3m-rated Dicks despite his dismal disciplinary record.

Now Hammers would need all the quality they could muster in their bid to retain Premier League status that they had just battled so fiercely to attain.

There had been a frosty reconciliation between the club and its supporters during a promotion campaign that had been clouded by the tragic, untimely death of Bobby Moore. But Bonzo and H had complemented one another, bringing their own skills to the promotion party.

"Harry worked well with the players, they liked him," said Bonds a few years later. "We worked well together in that first season, sharing everything we did. I gave him as much responsibility as me. We talked about players and he was a good foil. I could talk to him like I'd done with Ron Boyce. It was my responsibility for picking the team and bringing in new players and if it went wrong I'd have been the one to get the bullet. But Harry had an important input, too."

There was little time to savour success, though, for within hours of that win over Cambridge United, *The Sunday Telegraph* had already delivered a quick reality check. "While it is always good to have West Ham back in the top drawer of English football, it will be little short of a miracle if they stay in the Premier League next season," wrote Colin Malam. "Rarely can a club have looked and sounded more like relegation candidates on the day they were promoted."

It had been a season of triumph and tragedy and, as they cracked open a beer and relaxed on the dressing room treatment tables in the dungeons of the Boleyn Ground, Bonds and Harry knew that much serious hard work now lay ahead.

"There is a good spirit and attitude at the club now. I've got players who will give blood. People like Peter Butler epitomise that and with lads like him about we've always got a chance," insisted Bonds before suggesting that the Premier League could be split into three – the championship/European competition chasers, the mid-table safety merchants and, finally, the relegation strugglers.

The cautious, realistic Hammers' boss knew just how far he could set his sights as the club prepared to kick a ball in the Premier League for the first time.

"I just hope to be top of that bottom group," he announced. "But even that's going to be bloody hard!"

PLAYERS IN

Alex Bunbury	Montreal Supra	£200,000
Peter Butler	Southend United	£170,000
Mattie Holmes	Bournemouth	£40,000
Steve Jones	Billericay Town	£22,500
Mark Robson	Tottenham Hotspur	Free transfer

LOANS IN

David Speedie	Southampton

PLAYERS OUT

Steven Banks	Gillingham	Free transfer
Simon Clarke	Kettering Town	Free transfer
Paul Kelly		Released
Simon Livett	Leyton Orient	Free transfer
George Parris	Birmingham City	£100,000
Stuart Slater	Celtic	£1,500,000

Chapter 7
1993-94

OUT OF THE FRYING PAN...

The pack simply had to be shuffled. Having guaranteed their passage into the top flight by scoring that solitary, single goal more than Portsmouth, Hammers had hardly been promotion kings. And now extra aces were needed if they were to avoid becoming the Premiership's jokers.

A fan at heart, Managing Director Storrie turned fantasy football management into reality as he orchestrated the £750,000 acquisition of the long-admired Dale Gordon from Glasgow Rangers.

While playing for Norwich City, the tricky winger had proved a consistent menace against West Ham. Indeed, his acutely angled goal following a touchline dance past the hapless, stranded Allen McKnight at Carrow Road on Boxing Day 1988 was the catalyst for the much-maligned 'keeper's confidence crisis that was, ultimately, a significant factor in the club's 1989 relegation.

Capped four times by England at Under-21 level, Gordon had moved to Rangers in November 1991 for £1.2m and Hammers sensed that they had secured a bargain as they brought the former Canary back across Hadrian's Wall.

Having hand-reared the pair at Bournemouth, Redknapp could not resist returning to Dean Court to sign 21-year-olds Keith Rowland and Paul Mitchell in a combined £150,000 deal.

Gerry Peyton had also been at Bournemouth for five years under Redknapp, and when the 33-times capped Republic of Ireland goalkeeper became available, his former boss swiftly snapped him up on a free transfer from Brentford.

And there would have been more. Nottingham Forest's Gary Bull and Watford's Paul Furlong came under close scrutiny as Hammers looked for another striker, while Leeds United's Lee Chapman pitted the club against Portsmouth in a spiralling auction.

"At 33, Chapman would have been one of our top earners," said Storrie after letting the journeyman striker head to first division Pompey as salary won the day over status. "We were being traded against each other and we had to call a halt."

Simon Webster was also signed from Charlton Athletic for £525,000 but, disastrously, after playing in just one pre-season friendly at St Albans, the defender broke his leg in two places in an accidental training ground clash with Julian Dicks, just 22 days after heading through the Blackwall Tunnel.

"It was a complete accident," insisted Webbo after fracturing his leg for the second time inside five years.

And Dicks was in the thick of things again at Brisbane Road as Hammers took on Leyton Orient in Kevin Hales' Testimonial, when Bonds was told to make an enforced substitution by referee John Moules, who patiently kept his red card in his pocket following the defender's fiery clash with the O's Warren Hackett.

"I went for the ball and he smacked me in the mouth," claimed Dicks following the 1-0 victory. "I turned round and had a go back. It's natural. It's the way I am."

Young midfielder, Simon Livett (2+1 apps) headed to the O's in more civilised circumstances, joining Orient on a free transfer.

Alongside Mark Robson, home-grown Kevin Keen had been one of the chief architects behind West Ham's recent rise. The bow-legged, waif-like winger had blown hot and cold in past seasons but his fine flank play had brought him into the spotlight and won over the hitherto indifferent West Ham supporters.

But having also been part of the side that had failed to set the top-flight alight two seasons earlier, Bonds and Redknapp knew that a £600,000 bid from Wolverhampton Wanderers was simply too good to resist for a player whose Premiership pedigree was still being debated by an undecided jury.

It proved a sensible move for Keen and following a year at Molineux he headed to Stoke City for a six-season stint, before joining Macclesfield Town, where he became player-manager, gaining his UEFA 'A' coaching badge and rejoining the Upton Park coaching staff in 2002.

Where the casino chip supplying Liam Brady had once been chief croupier, Keen (237+42 apps 30 goals) had been the prince of board games, forever turning the team coach into a sub-branch of Hamleys for those long, arduous away trips.

There had been nothing trivial about John Fashanu's pursuit of Lawrie Sanchez during Wimbledon's pre-season training routine, though, and the powerful striker had caused furore with a *kung-fu* style kick on his team-mate.

All was forgiven, though, when the Dons' duo bagged a goal apiece to give the visitors a 2-0 victory at Upton Park on the opening day of the season.

Hammers had endured a baptism of fire in the cauldron of the Premier League and Bonds admitted: "This game told us everything that we already knew about the Premiership – it'll be very physical."

But just as he was about to conclude his post-match conference, the furious West Ham manager could contain himself no longer.

As his eyes welled in sheer anger, there was a trembling in his tone and a juddering in his jaw as the pens of the hushed press pack froze in mid-sentence.

Clearly, this was nothing to do with the disappointment of defeat in Hammers' first-ever Premiership outing.

"We have only just buried Bobby Moore, who stood for everything decent in the game, but today Wimbledon have been an absolute disgrace. Sam Hammam did his club no credit at all," he gasped before revealing that the marker pen-wielding Wimbledon chairman had sneaked into the visitors' dressing room before the match and scrawled obscenities all over the walls.

In a warped bid to motivate his team, the controversial Dons' owner had wanted to make it look like it had been West Ham who had penned the guttural graffiti.

And as Storrie conducted a behind the scenes tour as part of the matchday hospitality packages, he was horrified to discover the disgusting diatribe seconds before women and children were about to follow him through the door.

"I have told the police about it," added Bonds, still unable to regain his composure, knowing that Chief Superintendent Ivan Brown would be sending a report to the Football Association via Scotland Yard, although, ultimately, the club stopped short of pressing charges.

And West Ham's inability to make their on-pitch actions speak louder than Hammam's moronic words choked him yet further.

Incredibly, despite vandalising his hosts' property, Hammam was adamant that he was the one who had been wronged.

According to the *News of the World* he defiantly declared: "Bonds and Redknapp wanted me to get rid of the graffiti but I told them what we did in our own dressing room was our own business. They had no right to interrupt our preparation."

Indeed, goalscorer Fashanu – no doubt relieved that Hammam had deflected the *kung-fu* kick headlines away from him – held court in the player's car park defending his chairman.

"Hey guys, it's just a bit of fun," insisted Fash. "We go into dressing rooms and it's written that Fash is this, Dennis Wise is that. It's Sam's way of winding us up."

Gary Speed's goal at Leeds United then condemned Hammers to a second successive Premiership defeat before the new boys started to turn the corner.

Indeed, Gordon scored Hammers' first-ever Premiership goal on 45 minutes at Coventry City before Dicks took the definition of first-half injury time quite literally when he felled Sean Flynn in a touchline tangle.

Everyone at Highfield Road bar Dicks – who had bizarrely been awarded the resulting free-kick – expected him to be dismissed but, incredibly, he escaped with just a booking.

And that sparked an amazing interval interlude.

"Dicksy should have been sent off – how he was never sent off I will never know. He was completely out of order," recalled Redknapp. "At half-time Bill had a right go at him. 'What are you doing?' he asked. 'We're 1-0 up!' 'Ah, p*** off' replied Dicks and the next minute he wanted to fight Bill in the dressing room. Then he threw a sulk, took his boots off and refused to go out for the second half. But it all got sorted out and he went out and played."

In *Terminator – The Julian Dicks Story*, the player described his take on events.

"I went in at half-time and Billy and Harry started having a pop at me," he concurred. "We had quite a flare-up really and Harry said: 'Take him off.' So I took off my shirt, threw it on the floor and said: 'Take me off then!' Billy calmed it down though and told me to get ready for the second half. If Harry had been manager, he'd have taken me off and chucked me out."

No shrinking violet himself, the watching Liverpool manager Graeme Souness – oblivious to the half-time tantrum – remarked to Redknapp afterwards: 'Dicksy did alright. Puts it about a bit, doesn't he?'

Clive Allen's double secured a 2-0 win over Sheffield Wednesday as Hammers chalked up their first-ever Premiership victory.

But just a few days later, the euphoria of the expectant East End evaporated at

Upton Park, where a Les Ferdinand-inspired QPR coasted to a 4-0 win before an almost inevitable 0-3 defeat followed at early pace-setters Manchester United.

On Saturday, September 4, 1993, watched by his proud father, young 15-year-old Frank Lampard junior made his Hammers' debut in a South East Counties League clash against Cambridge United. West Ham won 4-2 and In a remarkable weekend, young Frank then cracked an unbeaten 57 runs as Ardleigh Green Under-16s won the Mobil Matchplay Trophy at Essex County Cricket Club.

At first-team level, that defeat at Old Trafford had set the alarm bells ringing sufficiently to ensure that the players were banned from attending Tony Gale's Testimonial dinner.

"It's important that we prepare professionally," insisted Bonds ahead of a goalless draw against fellow Premiership new boys Swindon Town.

Again, Souness witnessed the proceedings.

"Maybe he was watching £2.5m-rated Julian Dicks," suggested *The People*. "But for a man with a heart condition, Souness is stretching it a bit to even contemplate Dicks and Neil Ruddock in the same defence."

But that combustible Coventry confrontation had been the last straw for an Upton Park management team who also recognised the need to cash in on their most saleable asset if they were to bring in bodies and avert instant relegation.

The sale of cult hero Dicks was never going to be a popular move in the eyes of the supporters. But the player was becoming bigger than the club. Anxious to keep their dressing room credibility intact, Bonds and Redknapp knew that they could not be seen to be undermined.

Dicks had to be sold.

On Friday, September 17, 1993, the club entered into a frenzied day of transfer activity that saw Dicks swapped for the Liverpool duo of left-back David Burrows and midfielder Mike Marsh, while the previously reluctant Chapman finally moved from Portsmouth in a £250,000 deal.

While he lacked the aggression of Dicks (203 apps 40 gls), the likeable, controlled, accomplished Burrows was already on the fringes of the England squad and more than able to fill the chasm left by his predecessor.

The mischievous Marsh, an archetypical Scouser, was Liverpool through and through. Indeed, as a kid the grubby faced scallywag would commando crawl under the turnstiles and nuzzle his way to the front of Anfield's legendary Kop.

An earlier enquiry had seen Bonds quoted £1.5m for Marsh alone, and when Souness offered a straight exchange of Burrows for Dicks, the wily Hammers' boss – perhaps egged on by Harry – suddenly saw the chance of a straight two-for-one swap which the Merseysiders duly accepted.

Lincoln-born Chapman, who had bagged a top-scoring 16 goals for Leeds United in their championship-winning 1991-92 season, preferred to portray himself as a cut above the rest.

Indeed, following a spell with French side Niort, an aloof Chappie returned from across the Channel with a somewhat unique passion for wine which was to leave him open to constant jibes from Bournemouth restaurateur, Redknapp, as he planned his frequent post-match dinner parties with his actress wife Lesley Ash.

"I haven't met anyone in football with quite the same passion for wine as I have," claimed the striker. "Football is to a large extent a very working-class game and I suppose that is why there are relatively few who are interested in wine. I get accepted for what I am. People don't take the Mickey."

But cutting through the pomposity of it all, on one occasion Harry Redknapp teased: "Oi Chappie! I could give you a bottle of *Piat D'Or* to take home and you wouldn't know the difference!"

Former Bordeaux striker Clive Allen looked on, sheepishly admitting that upon moving to France he certainly did not know his Claret from his Chablis or his Merlot from his Muscadet.

Indeed, deep in the heart of red wine country, the equally red faced goal-getter had once even asked his new chairman for a glass of white Bordeaux.

"I made a big mistake joining Portsmouth," admitted Chapman. "And I knew for the sake of my career that I had to get back into the Premiership quickly."

As the new-look Hammers lined up to take on Blackburn Rovers on Saturday, September 18, 1993 AD (After Dicks), it was the striker who uncorked a classic, 33rd-minute tap-in to set the determined Londoners on their way to a 2-0 win at Ewood Park.

And as the squad climbed back on board the coach for the long journey back down the M6, the change of atmosphere was tangible. Even Ivan the driver and Joe, his much-abused steward, had smiles upon their faces knowing that they could almost certainly look forward to an early night back at the depot, given the vehicle was now unlikely to be trashed with litter by Dicks and his cronies, who were like lost souls without their leader.

The whip hand looked to be back with the management. The case for divide and rule had never looked sounder.

Had they turned on the radio they would also have heard the anger on the airwaves as the red population of Liverpool jammed the post-match phone-ins complaining about Souness's Friday afternoon brainstorm.

Ironically, Dicks' debut was marred by former Hammers' team-mates Mark Ward and Tony Cottee, who had given Everton a 2-0 win over Liverpool, in a Merseyside derby that saw even more aggression in the shape of Steve McManaman's skirmish with his own keeper, Bruce Grobbelaar.

"I have just locked my season ticket in the drawer and I'm not getting it out again until Souness gets rid of Dicks and Ruddock. They are just not Liverpool players," boomed one angry caller, mirroring a popular theme of an evening that suggested the beautiful game had gone down the Mersey.

Burrows was quickly on target in a confidence-boosting 5-1 win over Chesterfield in the Coca-Cola Cup second round that also saw Chapman and Morley grab two apiece.

That Kenny Brown – a surprise late call-up to the squad – even made it onto the pitch for a Premiership clash at Newcastle United was a miracle in itself when it was discovered that his gear had not even been packed.

Eddie Gillam, the club's resourceful kit-man, spent Saturday lunchtime trawling

Tyneside in the quest for a replica West Ham United shirt. After much pleading, he persuaded the bemused assistant in Eldon Square's Dixons Sports to undress the tailor's dummy promoting that afternoon's clash, sell him the jersey for £40 and then iron on the number '15' plus letters 'BROWN'.

How Jeroen Boere must have wished that his shirt had been left behind, too.

After netting a brace for the reserves against Arsenal, the self-confident Dutch striker was signed from Go-Ahead Eagles for £165,000 and quickly found himself at the centre of controversy in the 0-2 defeat at St James's Park.

The Holland 'B' international arrived as a 64th-minute substitute but he found it all double-Dutch when he was red carded two minutes from time after clashing with both Kevin Scott and then Barry Venison within a split-second of each other.

"Everyone will remember this and I could get a reputation," protested Boere. "I caught Scott when I turned in the air but I thought he hit my wrist and then I collided with the other guy. I could accept a yellow card for the second challenge but it's the first time that I've ever been given a straight red card and I just hope that people don't judge me on one incident."

The influx of proven forwards saw Hammers cool on former air-conditioning technician Dean Martin (1+2 apps) who was moved out to Kettering Town.

Hammers' clash with Chelsea on October 2, 1993 was preceded by a poignant pre-match ceremony that saw a time capsule placed into the foundations of the proposed new Bobby Moore Stand.

Bobby's widow – his second wife Stephanie – was joined by Geoff Hurst, Martin Peters and other dignitaries as chairman Terence Brown 'topped out' the sealing of the casket containing a dozen Moore-related items.

Ironically, Brown had once fallen victim to a large piece of rust falling off the old South Bank roof where it, irritatingly, lodged firmly in his eye. As he later joked, that could well have been his motivation for rebuilding the new structure that would take the club into the 21st century.

Trevor Morley's stunning 25-yarder gave Hammers victory over the Blues, who were subsequently reduced to 10 men after Wise was dismissed for an awful lunge on Burrows.

The injured Clive Allen may not have been fit enough to line up alongside his team-mates against his former club, but he was still able to keep them entertained with his tales of Wise's Stamford Bridge antics that involved all manner of pranks.

With Vinnie Jones constantly bemoaning the fact that he was the only player ever to keep the post-training biscuit barrel topped up, Wise would often mischievously offer the McVitties chocolate digestives to the young apprentices cleaning the changing rooms, knowing full well that the apoplectic Hollywood hard man was on the brink of returning to find his stocks being seriously depleted by the oblivious Blues teenagers!

Having already been sent off at Newcastle, Boere made a happier reappearance from the bench to score in a 2-0 win in the Coca-Cola Cup second round, second leg tie at Chesterfield.

Successive goalless draws followed against Aston Villa and at Norwich City, where the injured Gordon was confined to the bench for a return to the club he had left nearly two years earlier. The second-placed Canaries had just beaten Bayern Munich in a UEFA Cup tie at the Olympic Stadium and, as the Hammers' coach rolled into the redeveloped Carrow Road, Gordon surveyed the stadium before claiming: "They built that new stand with the money Rangers paid for me."

"I think you'll find that they actually only managed to tarmac the car park!" came the cutting riposte from Tony Gale who was to later reveal that Gordon had, apparently, missed a day's training on account of the fact that his wife was being terrified by a stray mouse in the marital home.

Having netted just six goals in 12 league outings, Hammers were the lowest scorers in the country and a 1-2 defeat at Nottingham Forest in the Coca-Cola Cup third round compounded an agonising start to the season.

On October 28, 1993, following a long illness, Leonard Cearns died aged 79. He was first appointed a director of the club in 1947 and was chairman from 1979-90.

The Cearns family had built both the West Stand (1925) and East Stand (1969) and it was, perhaps, poignant that just four days after Mr Len's death, Upton Park turned on the new floodlights of a Bobby Moore stand that had risen from the rubble of the South Bank terracing.

Equally fittingly, Hammers discovered their shooting boots to produce a dazzling 3-1 win over Manchester City, before finding it business as usual in a 0-2 defeat at Liverpool, where the injured Dicks was forced to sit out the action, while Burrows and Marsh received a warm welcome upon their first return to Anfield.

Following his free transfer from Tottenham, Robson had been a revelation during the previous season's promotion campaign, but just like Keen there was a question mark hanging over his ability to carry his skills onto the Premiership stage.

The amiable Robbo, a lifelong Hammers fan, was another example of Redknapp's 'horses for courses' policy whereby players had been brought in to get the club out of the second flight before being discarded for those capable of keeping Hammers in the Premier League.

It was a continuous change programme designed to maintain improvement to a team that simply could not afford to succumb to continuous yo-yo-like relegation and promotion. And this time the management reckoned that Gordon and Mattie Holmes could bring more to the Premiership party than Robson and Keen.

Robson (42+8 apps 9 gls) was a reluctant departee when Charlton Athletic made a £125,000 bid to sign him.

"I had only one season at West Ham but it was fantastic," declared the distraught Stratford-born winger, who unashamedly left the club in tears after making just one start and two substitute appearances in the Premiership. "I never got the opportunity to prove that I could do it in the top flight. I don't think that Bill and Harry thought that I could cut it and, looking back, perhaps they were right. It just would've been nice to find out if they were correct!"

World Cup qualifiers resulted in a break which saw West Ham head to the south coast for some golf, a day's racing at Fontwell Park and a friendly against Poole Town which ended in a 2-2 draw.

What goes on tour stays on tour. Just how reserve goalkeeper Gerry Peyton sustained what appeared to be a facial injury upon his return to his old

Bournemouth stamping ground remained cloaked in mystery, but when Hammers returned to face Oldham Athletic, rookie Martin Peat was called up for his one and only appearance on the bench.

Back in the Premiership, though, there were signs of that continuous improvement.

A 2-0 win over the Latics was followed by a goalless draw against Arsenal, who had David Seaman dismissed, before a 2-0 victory at Southampton took West Ham into 10th spot – their highest league placing for seven years.

Thanks to an eighth clean sheet in 11 matches, things were looking up for Bonds and his assistant Redknapp, who were offered new three-year contracts in the same week that predecessor Lou Macari took over the reins at Celtic.

Conversely, John Lyall, another man twice removed from the Upton Park managerial merry-go-round, ruled himself out of the running after being strongly linked to follow in the footsteps of his own forefather, Ron Greenwood, and take over as England's caretaker manager, following Graham Taylor's departure in the wake of his failure to steer England to the USA 94 World Cup finals.

A Chapman double on the eve of his 34th birthday secured a 2-1 win at Wimbledon. With Burrows and Marsh bedding in, too, the decision to offload Dicks was being vindicated.

Finding Allen, Morley, Chapman and Boere well ahead of him in the pecking order, Canadian international Alex Bunbury (3+3 apps 0 gls) headed to Portuguese side Maritimo for a cut-price £50,000 after failing to play anywhere near the required 75% of first-team games needed to retain his work permit since his £200,000 arrival from Montreal Supra.

In his place came striker Malcolm McPherson, a £30,000 capture from Yeovil Town, who had impressed while guesting in that friendly at Poole. Having had a fruitless day at Fontwell on the same trip, the Hammers management were hoping that maybe, just maybe, they would reap big dividends from their small outlay on the novice outsider.

Second placed Leeds United brought Hammers' good run to an end with a 1-0 win at Upton Park. But three days later, Ferenc Puskas was at the Boleyn Ground to see West Ham beat Coventry City 3-2, when goalscoring Peter Butler had the game of his life in front of the Hungarian legend.

"They are very good and play intelligent football," observed the Galloping Magyar who clearly gave the East Enders ideas well above their station ahead of a 0-5 defeat at Sheffield Wednesday.

A 1-1 draw at Ipswich Town seemed to have arrested the slide the day after Boxing Day, but just 24 hours later, Hammers surrendered an early lead to lose 1-3 at home to Tottenham Hotspur, a defeat that saw them go into 1994 in 13th spot.

Tim Breacker's first-ever goal for the club secured a 1-0 win at Everton on New Year's Day and, after being held to a goalless draw against Sheffield United, West Ham saw off Watford (2-1) to secure an FA Cup fourth round tie at Notts County.

Before heading to Villa Park and a 1-3 defeat, Bonds and Redknapp signed the new, three-year contracts that would seemingly keep the partnership together at the club until 1997.

NEARLY REACHED THE SKY

And despite signing a one-year contract, reserve keeper Peyton (0 apps) decided to quit in mid-season to take up a coaching role in Japan.

"I'm not pleased to say the least. We gave Gerry a good contract and expected him to honour it, but he says that if we don't release him, he'll retire," said an angry Bonds, who quickly tried to sign Yugoslav Dragan Lekovic from Red Star Belgrade only to be foiled by the red tape entangling a refused work permit.

After Steve Jones gave Hammers an early lead, they had to rely on Morley's late leveller to secure a 3-3 draw against Norwich City, when the lower tier of the new Bobby Moore South Stand was opened for the first time. And Jones was on target again in that FA Cup tie at Notts County, forcing an equaliser in a 1-1 draw.

In the Upton Park replay, Chapman finally broke the deadlock to shoot down the Magpies with his 118th minute winner that set up a potential banana skin tie at non-league Kidderminster Harriers,

Young defender Paul Marquis stepped from the dug-out to make an 88th-minute debut in the goalless draw at Manchester City, where Bury's on-loan keeper Gary Kelly (0 apps), filled the void left by Peyton on the bench.

At a sold out Aggborough, 8,000 fans saw Kidderminster frustrate West Ham for 69 minutes before Chapman broke the minnows' resistance with a looping header. The Vauxhall Conference side, whose average crowd was just 2,250, had staged the tie magnificently but their efforts counted for nothing come May for, despite winning their league, Harriers were denied elevation to the Football League on the grounds that their stadium was inadequate. They would have to wait until 2000 to finally earn that status before returning to the Conference in 2005.

Paul Ince knew that he was going to be playing in a cauldron of hate upon his first return to Upton Park since that acrimonious move to Old Trafford in September 1989.

And 'Judas' was not to be disappointed as the abuse rained down on him.

Like a Koi carp growing to the size of his pond, Ince would not have developed into the player he was had he remained in the stifling confines of his native East End. Indeed, by the time he returned with mighty Manchester United, he had already won a dozen of his 53 full England caps but he looked like suffering the ignominy of defeat after Mark Hughes' early effort was wiped out by quick-fire strikes from Chapman and Morley.

However, after enduring 87 minutes of bananas and venomous vitriol being hurled at him, the self-styled Guv'nor smashed home a late equaliser for the champions-elect, who extended their unbeaten run to 33 games.

Shielded by two burly bouncers smuggling him out of the stadium, all the typically, self-satisfied smugness had returned when he paused to declare: "Today, I faced the music and danced!"

After taking a point against the top side, Hammers managed to repeat the feat against the Premiership's bottom team when they were held to a 1-1 draw at bottom-place Swindon Town.

A welcome distraction from the league campaign came via the Bobby Moore Memorial Match, which was staged to mark the official opening of the £4.9m, 7,630-seat capacity Bobby Moore Stand at the south end of the Boleyn Ground.

Out of the frying pan...

Before the game, Stephanie Moore unveiled a bronze bust of the Hammers' legend in the foyer of the new stand, while a Who's Who of West Ham United stars took to the field to cut ribbons suspended to the 28 metre-high roof of the structure. Geoff Hurst, Martin Peters, John Bond, Eddie Bovington, Ron Boyce, Ken Brown, Brian Dear, Peter Brabrook, Alan Sealey, Jack Burkett and Joe Kirkup were there alongside Johnny Byrne and John Sissons who flew in from South Africa, while Jim Standen had made the trans-Atlantic trek from the United States.

As for the football itself, raising £200,000 for the Bobby Moore Fund for Imperial Cancer Research, 20,311 fans turned up to see Billy Bonds' side take on a Premiership XI managed by George Graham. Each of the Premier League's 21 other clubs was represented by one of its players who played 45 minutes each, while Liam Brady made up the numbers with a second half appearance.

"I see you've made a comeback?" said the Irishman upon seeing veteran Alvin Martin warming up.

"I've made three since you left!" replied the Merseysider.

Fundamentally, both Dicks and the previously heckled Tony Cottee returned to represent George Graham's side and both received a hero's reception.

While Dicks was only ever going to be welcomed back into the East End fold, compellingly for Cottee, it signalled that he might just have been forgiven for his record-breaking, £2.05m exit to Everton in 1988.

Following an impeccably-observed minute's silence held in driving rain, not even TC's 15th-minute goal for the Premiership XI could dampen the crowd's enthusiasm, before goals from Boere and Clive Allen secured a 2-1 win for West Ham on a night when football was the real winner.

"It was a wonderful tribute and a marvellous evening that couldn't have gone better," noted Stephanie on one of the few occasions that West Ham United Football Club could justifiably claim to have got everything just right.

"There was one word which seemed to be on everyone's lips last night – class. A class act, different class," wrote Ken Dyer of London's *Evening Standard*. "It echoed around the deserted Bobby Moore stand long after the fans had gone."

"Bobby Moore? He was just class," concurred Bonds.

In the FA Cup sixth round, Luton Town held Hammers to an unwelcome goalless draw at Upton Park where the prize for the winners was a semi-final encounter against Chelsea.

A 2-4 home defeat at the hands of Newcastle United had hardly been the ideal preparation for the replay, but as West Ham headed to Kenilworth Road they were in confident mood.

Clive Allen was clearly looking forward to playing his part in helping to secure a last-four meeting with his old club but, upon arriving at the ground, he suddenly found himself dropped, whereupon he was invited to become a Sky TV pundit.

And as he sat in the makeshift studio watching a topsy-turvy cup tie unfold, the still track-suited striker could only watch on helplessly as Scott Oakes – the son of a Showaddywaddy band member – took his own *Three Steps to Heaven* with a hat-trick.

With the scores deadlocked at 2-2, Steve Potts made an uncharacteristic mistake which allowed Oakes to net the winner for the Hatters, who simply went mad as Hammers found the road to Wembley crumbling beneath their feet,

"Without a doubt that was the lowest moment of my career," admitted the normally reliable central defender. "I mis-controlled the ball and as Oakes raced clear I was just praying that Ludek Miklosko would save it, but he didn't. It was a major, major disappointment. I felt that I'd let everyone down."

A transfer deadline day move for Oxford United's Joey Beauchamp collapsed but, while Hammers' 'In' tray remained empty, papers piled high in the 'Out' box.

He did not realise it at the time but heading to that Luton replay, Clive Allen (46+4 apps 21 gls) had already played his last game for Hammers as he moved to Millwall – his seventh London club – in a £75,000 deal.

Following a loan spell at Notts County, Colin Foster (104+6 apps 7 gls) headed to Watford for £80,000 – a huge discount on Lou Macari's £750,000 purchase price – while Boere moved on loan to Portsmouth.

After his two minutes of fame, Marquis (0+1 apps) joined Doncaster Rovers while Mitchell Thomas (48+1 apps 3 gls) returned to his first club, Luton Town, also on a free transfer.

Over-priced and under-played, the gangly defender had failed to impress following his £500,000 move from Tottenham. Indeed, alongside Mike Small, at the start of the 1993-94 campaign, he ran into an Upton Park cul-de-sac when he was not even allocated a squad number from the 32 shirts issued.

Certainly, for some, after nearly half-a-century of matches, Thomas will merely be best remembered for his off-pitch ability to single-handedly ransack beers from the team coach fridge, upon arriving home from an away trip, than what he ever actually achieved on the field of play.

Meanwhile, following loan spells at Wolves and Charlton Athletic, the lame Small (52+9 apps 18 gls) was released.

A 0-2 defeat at Chelsea was Hammers' third successive loss but, after taking a two-goal lead at Sheffield United, that trend looked set to be reversed, only for the Blades to recover and cut down Hammers with three goals.

That quartet of blanks meant that going into April 1994, West Ham had not won a league match since New Year's Day and were now just seven points off the drop zone with nine games to play.

By Easter Saturday it was clear that, while Chapman may have been top of the Upton Park goalcharts, his lumbering style and propensity to miss more than he scored had hardly endeared himself to a fanbase determined not to see their side get dragged into an unwelcome and unwanted late relegation dogfight.

And when Bonds replaced his veteran striker with Matthew Rush, he received an instant dividend as the youngster returned from a loan spell at Swansea City to spectacularly fire Hammers towards a 2-1 win over Ipswich Town.

Having waited so long for that league victory, just like buses, two came along together as Hammers beat Spurs 4-1 at White Hart Lane, where Jones entered Upton Park folklore after stepping from the bench midway through the first half and firing his side towards Premiership safety.

Incredibly, aside from his scandalous FA Cup semi-final dismissal in 1991, Gale picked up his first yellow card for five years for disputing Teddy Sheringham's penalty. Before that his last booking had come in April 1989 . . . at White Hart Lane for dissent minutes after Terry Fenwick had converted a spot kick.

After netting in that Bobby Moore Memorial Match, Cottee relished another return to his goal-rich scoring fields of Upton Park. While West Ham were now nine points clear of relegation with seven games remaining, Everton had just a two-point safety cushion. But TC went some way towards easing the Merseysiders' fears when he bagged a 72nd-minute winner.

West Ham then conjured up a 2-1 win at struggling Oldham who were not so well-placed and, indeed, consequently found themselves in even more trouble.

"That should end all talk of relegation," smiled Bonds after leaving the Division One-bound Latics in the bottom three.

Following hot on the heels of Cottee, Dicks also made a second homecoming as Liverpool rolled into town. It looked like being an unhappy return when Martin Allen put Hammers ahead after just 58 seconds but Robbie Fowler levelled before Ian Rush stole onto Gale's poor backpass to nick a late winner.

Blackburn Rovers were still chasing Manchester United in the Premiership title race and future Hammer Ian Pearce netted a late winner at Upton Park to give the Ewood Park outfit a 2-1 victory that kept them just two points behind United.

Mitchell had finally been handed his debut when he made a late substitute appearance – his one and only outing for the club – against Blackburn. And this time around, youth team starlet Danny Williamson received a late call from the bench, whereupon his first touch set up Martin Allen for a spectacular goal to clinch a 2-0 win over Arsenal at Highbury. That ended a 19-game unbeaten run for the Gunners, who were preparing for their midweek European Cup Winners' Cup final against Parma, which they were destined to win 1-0.

A goalless draw at Queens Park Rangers led West Ham into the final game of the season against Southampton, who were still far from safe. And as the Hammers' fans standing on the North Bank terracing for the final time celebrated Williamson's first goal for the club, the Saints looked in deep trouble.

But inspired by Matt Le Tissier, Southampton fought back to lead 3-2 before a false-start saw the inevitable North Bankers' pitch invasion halt play for 11 minutes, during which time the Saints marched off to learn that they were now already safe at the expense of Swindon, Oldham and Sheffield United.

And when the teams returned to play out the last four minutes of the final match of the day, Ken Monkou's academic own goal merely made it a 3-3 draw to leave both sides taking a point apiece from their closing match of the campaign.

One year on from that promotion campaign, Hammers returned to the directors' box to milk the applause from an appreciative crowd, thankful that they had finished the campaign in 13th place.

Everyone at Upton Park was well satisfied that, using Bonds' analogy, the one-time relegation favourites had finished up towards the lower reaches of the Premiership's 'second group' rather than at the bottom of the 'third group' that he had alluded to a year earlier.

NEARLY REACHED THE SKY

Now going into the summer, Bonds knew there was little time to relax if he was going to consolidate the club's Premiership status, during what promised to be an equally tough 1994-95 campaign.

PLAYERS IN

Jeroen Boere	Go-Ahead Eagles	£165,000
David Burrows*	Liverpool	
	with Marsh for Dicks (£2.5m est)	
Lee Chapman	Portsmouth	£250,000
Dale Gordon	Norwich City	£750,000
Mike Marsh*	Liverpool	
	with Burrows for Dicks (£2.5m est)	
Malcolm McPherson	Yeovil	£30,000
Paul Mitchell	Bournemouth	£40,000
Gerry Peyton	Brentford	Free Transfer
Keith Rowland	Bournemouth	£110,000
Simon Webster	Charlton Athletic	£525,000

LOANS IN

Gary Kelly	Bury

PLAYERS OUT

Clive Allen	Millwall	Free Transfer
Alex Bunbury	Maritimo	£50,000
Julian Dicks*	Liverpool	
	Swap for Burrows & Marsh	
Colin Foster	Watford	£80,000
Tony Gale	Blackburn Rovers	Free Transfer
Kevin Keen	Wolverhampton W.	£600,000
Paul Marquis	Doncaster Rovers	Free Transfer
Dean Martin	Kettering Town	Nominal fee
Gerry Peyton	Retired	
Mark Robson	Charlton Athletic	£125,000.
Mike Small	Released	
Mitchell Thomas	Luton Town	Free Transfer

Chapter 8
1994-95

TROUBLE AT THE TOP

Oblivious to the storm clouds looming on the horizon, Billy Bonds wasted no time reinforcing his side ahead of another tough Premiership campaign.

Towering 6ft. 6ins. Yankee goalkeeper Ian Feuer – brother-in-law of Hollywood hell-raiser Mickey Rourke – joined from Los Angeles Salsa in a £70,000 deal, closely followed by John Moncur, an £850,000 capture from just-relegated Swindon Town. The son of Tottenham Hotspur's Youth Development Manager – John senior – Moncur had cut his teeth at White Hart Lane, where had had forged a strong friendship with fellow practical joker, Paul Gascoigne.

Indeed, Moncur had pulled off his favourite prank with the Geordie jester.

"We were staying in our hotel near Hyde Park on the eve of the 1991 FA Cup final when Paul Allen came back telling us how there was an old camper van parked down the road in Park Lane, with a bloke who had stopped to get some shut eye," recalled Moncs. "Apparently the lads had looked through the curtains, seen the fella asleep and rattled on the side of his van. He'd got the right needle. Gazza and me went down there, quietly climbed onto the top of the motor and then started banging on the sides. He kept getting out of his van going nutty. In the end, he'd totally lost it. The bloke was walking around waiting for this person to come back and rattle his van, yet all while we were hiding up on his roof! Every time he got back inside we started hitting the sides again. We had him on a bit of string."

And the tigerish, technically-able midfielder was quickly to establish himself as Upton Park's court jester, too.

But having joined on the same day, fellow signing Joey Beauchamp was, equally, to prove himself an altogether different kind of joker.

After missing out on transfer deadline day, back in the spring, Bonds had finally got his man when he signed the lively Oxford United winger for £850,000.

"I've lived in Oxford all my life and only had a short time to make up my mind in March and it was a big wrench to leave," revealed Beauchamp. "Earlier this week, I was all set to sign for Swindon. I regret not joining West Ham in the first place and thought that Billy Bonds had forgotten about me. Now I can't wait to play in the Premier League."

But it was soon obvious that it was a match made in hell as Beauchamp barely gave himself the chance to settle, before incredibly going public and declaring that he wanted out before the new season had even begun.

"Joey Beauchamp was trouble from Day One," declared Harry Redknapp. "He came up to me and said: 'I should have gone to Swindon.' I thought he had got lost on the M4 motorway on his way to training but it was soon obvious that he was talking about a transfer. 'This is too far from home,' he added. I couldn't believe it. Here was a guy on £2,000 per week before bonuses complaining about travelling. It got worse by the day. We couldn't get him to raise a gallop in training. He said he wanted to carry on living in Oxford and then rang in to say that he was too tired and stressed from sitting in a traffic jam. He drove Billy crazy."

Indeed, having discovered that half of his transfer budget had been expended on a player who did not wish to play for the club, Bonds was understandably furious.

"Both Harry and I felt let down by him," he said. "When we first spoke to Joey he wasn't that sure about the move and, looking back, we should have ended any thoughts about signing him there and then.

"The boy was a total wimp and it was disastrous for the club because we'd paid £850,000 for him. What could I say to the kid? I couldn't threaten him. I just told him to keep his nut down because the fans weren't going to be too happy."

Only a few days later, the club experienced yet more difficulties on Beauchamp's manor when Redknapp arranged for a heckling Hammers' fan to borrow Lee Chapman's boots and take to the field in a friendly against Oxford City.

Ironically, H had kicked off his managerial career at the Ryman League club as assistant to Bobby Moore.

"Always remember that Harry Redknapp started out as Mooro's bag carrier at Oxford," one member of Moore's colt side frequently reminded his friends.

And 27-year-old, father of two, Steve Davies, was another who wasted no time haranguing Harry, either.

"You've got all the mouth. You seem to know the tactics, go and show us what you can do," Redknapp exclaimed before sending the man with all the opinions onto the field for a second half run-out in place of the injured Chappie.

"The lad did well but I won't be signing him – it was only a 45-minute contract," insisted Redknapp after the 4-0 victory, before arranging to give the £200 per week courier Chappie's shirt.

Homesick? Lovesick? The insular, 23-year-old Beauchamp's situation was hardly helped by the trek north for Hammers' pre-season tour of Scotland.

Upon returning to the hotel at gone midnight, the West Ham management team were aghast to discover their new signing still on the telephone to his teenage girlfriend – an Oxford student – in the lobby.

Beauchamp was phoning home more often than Steven Spielberg's ET.

He was doing nothing to enamour himself to his new team-mates either and once the fans got wind of the mutinous winger's desire to leave, he was never going to be able to stay.

Sadly, Bonds was soon to find his position untenable, too.

The Beauchamp battle was not the only problem to hit the club's sojourn beyond Hadrian's Wall and it really was Scots on the rocks as the Bonds/Redknapp alliance ran irreversibly off course.

"I had received a call from Geoffrey Hayward, a former chairman at Dean Court who told me that he wanted to buy Bournemouth on one condition – that I went back there," wrote Harry in *Harry Redknapp – My Autobiography*. "He said: 'If you come back, I'll give you the club. Whatever you want Harry, it's yours. You can be managing director, manager, whatever. Just ask.' It was a hugely tempting offer. I thought: 'Harry you're pushing 50, why not settle for an easier life?'

"When I told Bill about the offer his attitude was: 'I don't blame you, Harry, but I don't know what I'm going to do without you.' Then he said: 'If you go, I'll go.'

"What do you want to do that for?" I asked. 'Aah, I don't want to do it anymore,' he replied. So I told him that if he was taking that attitude, then I was staying put. I didn't want to be responsible for Billy walking out on his beloved West Ham.

"At times Bill got fed up with things in the game. He got fed up with people who didn't show the same standards as he did."

Bonds, for his part, had kept a dignified silence over the exact circumstances surrounding his consequent departure, but speaking in *EX* in 2003, he candidly revealed more than ever before.

"Harry came in with talk that Bournemouth wanted him but whether that was just to try and bump up his wages, I don't know," said the astute Bonzo. "He was always talking about being wanted elsewhere. Before Bournemouth it had been Oxford. I used to say to him: 'Well if they want you – go. I'll miss you but if you want to leave then do it.' I think the board got wind of the fact that Bournemouth were after Harry and they clearly wanted to keep him."

According to Redknapp, Terence Brown approached him to ascertain what was going on.

"Why are you leaving us?" the chairman asked. "You want to be manager, don't you? What happens then if we make you manager and we make Bill the director of football?"

By Redknapp's reckoning, he reaffirmed his reluctance to jump into the Hammers' hot seat, telling Brown: "My only options are to carry on as Bill's assistant or leave and return to Bournemouth who are going to pay me what I'm earning here – and it's where I live."

At six o'clock that evening, an emergency summit meeting was held in the team's Scottish hotel and, in a throwback to the mid-70s Ron Greenwood/John Lyall shuffle, it was suggested that Billy could move upstairs as director of football, while Harry would take charge of team affairs.

Again Redknapp – whose influence on the managerial partnership had undeniably ballooned – gave his version of the evening's events. "Bill said to the board: 'It's quite obvious that you want Harry to take over from me. You think he's better than me. You want him to be manager.' Things were getting very uncomfortable for me but then the chairman outlined the functions of the director of football and said it was a job for life."

Bonds recalled: "When I got to the room at six o'clock on the dot, the whole lot of them – the board members, Peter Storrie and Harry – were already sitting around. I'm not a mug and I got the strong vibe that they had already discussed everything and that Harry wanted to have more say in team matters.

"I didn't feel needed or wanted anymore. I don't think that the directors wanted me to leave the club, but I would imagine that they wanted Harry to take on a more senior management role. I told them that I knew where I stood and that I'd resign but they wanted me to go on the board. I would have been the first manager to go into a director of football-type role but I'm not one for staying around if I feel that I'm not really wanted. I suppose I was hurt by it. That's life. It happens."

As the club rounded off a tour that saw them lose 0-1 at Dunfermline and draw 0-0 with St Johnstone, Bonds remained in the managerial chair while the *Bournemouth Echo* persisted with its scoop, this time publishing a front-page lead speculating that Redknapp would be returning to Dean Court both as manager and a director.

"Bill had asked for some time to think things over and confided to me that he was in two minds as to what to do," claimed Redknapp. "No aggravation? A job for life? I thought to myself: 'I could do that!' I could well understand his dilemma."

Upon their return back across the border, the entire Hammers' squad was taken to the south coast for a fitness assessment in which the 47-year-old Bonds finished in 12th spot.

Shortly afterwards, Beauchamp was confined to the bench in a 1-1 draw at Portsmouth after arriving for the friendly announcing that he was 'tired and stressed up' as a result of his entrapment in a traffic jam.

"He has to pull his finger out," said the frustrated Bonds who, according to *The People*, had even fined his new signing £2,500 for a public attack on his new club. "Every time we ask him how he is doing he says 'not very well' and I have even had him crying to me."

As Hammers lost 0-2 at Southend United, the West Ham supporters had managed to make the trip down the Thames estuary on a hot, August evening in the busy rush-hour traffic and stifling oppressiveness of the commuter-packed trains, without getting too stressed.

And once there, they ensured that the heavily barracked Beauchamp endured more torrents of abuse as he warmed up prior to being called into action in the dying moments.

Bonds was not even at Roots Hall, having already decided earlier in the day that, after 27 years at the club, he now wanted out, too.

By the following morning he was officially gone.

"Bill rung me up and said he was going. I jumped into the car and raced to the ground to try and persuade him not to go," claimed Redknapp. "We arrived in time but neither Ronnie Boyce nor myself could get Bill to change his mind."

"The chairman then said: 'Bill's going. Will you be the manager?'"

According to Redknapp, who was offered a five-year contract, Bonds said: 'Take it, you'd be a fool not to. Don't worry about me, financially I've had it off and I've been well looked after.'

At an earlier press conference, Storrie had made no mention of the club wanting to replace Bonds with Redknapp.

But as the departing Hammers' legend revealed the board's apparent desire to shuffle the pack, Storrie changed tack, unconvincingly trying to clarify the circumstances surrounding Bonds' exit: "It wasn't a case of taking the managership away from Bill. We wanted him to stay as a director, but he wanted a break. There are no hard feelings. It was difficult for both Bill and Harry but their friendship is as strong as ever. If Harry had gone to Bournemouth there was a good chance that Bill would have resigned anyway, so we were in a no-win situation. We're sad that Bill is going and it's a big blow, but it's time to move on and we have appointed a great manager."

'It will be perceived as a sad and badly handled departure for Bonds,' observed *The Daily Telegraph*. 'Most West Ham fans will feel he deserved better. While the club may deny that Bonds was sacked, they wanted to relieve him of his manager's job with a post "upstairs". Those who know Bonds realise he would not be happy in a boardroom sipping gin and tonic and talking to directors. Bonds' environment is the boot room and that is where he hopes to be after a break."

Under the headline 'The knifing of Bonzo' *The Sun* cried: "No-one thought that West Ham would treat Billy Bonds like this. They hurt John Lyall when they sacked him and now they've cocked it up again."

Redknapp, who claimed that he, too, was on the verge of quitting in the wake of the accusations that were flying around, conceded: "Looking back, I allowed myself to be pushed in too quickly and that was a mistake. I stayed the entire week in Bournemouth thinking things over and also picked up a paper and read a story that I'd knifed Bill in the back. But that's not my game. It's not my nature.

"How could I go on and look people in the eye when people were saying that I'd stabbed Bill in the back? I've never felt so bad about something in my life.

"I'm not ambitious enough to jeopardise a friendship for the sake of a job and certainly not Bill of all people. 'Look Bill,' I said broaching one of the things that was really worrying me. 'If I take this job, it'll look like I've done a bad 'un on you, like I've stitched you up.' Bill replied: 'Don't worry. You and I both know you haven't. Take it.' In the early days after his departure I rang him for a chat on a few occasions but looking back it must have been very hard for him. He'd fallen out with the chairman and fallen out big time with Peter Storrie. We just drifted apart, but I still love him to bits.

"I don't know if Bill bears me any ill-will. It bothers me more than anything to think that he might. Of all the people in football, he'd be right up there at the top. I'd rather not have had the job than anyone think that.

"You don't reach the half-century mark in life without harbouring some regrets. And one of my biggest is the break-up of my friendship with my best mate."

Certainly, the Redknapps have not received a Christmas card from the Bonds for a decade.

"Don't get me wrong, no-one should be guaranteed a job for life," concluded Bonds, who reportedly received a pay-off of around £500,000 before becoming youth team coach at Queens Park Rangers and then Millwall manager prior to moving into radio punditry. "It's the biggest job you can have at a football club and you know that one day you'll get the bullet.

"I'm glad that I had a go at management. You hear people say: 'Oh Bill wasn't cut out to be a manager' but I think that I was reasonably successful.

"I'm just sorry that I left West Ham in the circumstances I did. All I will say is that I was a very bad judge of character where one person was concerned. It doesn't bother me now. It's all in the past. I always sleep at night.

"Being totally honest, though, I never enjoyed management. It was a way of staying in the game. But for me it could never replace playing."

Speaking nearly a decade later, Brown confessed: "I believe that we should have handled the Billy Bonds situation far better than we did. I can't expand upon it, but Bill had every right to expect more from the club."

Billy Bonds' Managerial Record:

League:	P-193	W-82	D-52	L-59	F-262	A-212
FA Cup:	P-21	W-10	D-7	L-4	F-33	A-23
League Cup:	P-13	W-7	D-2	L-4	F-25	A-11
Anglo-Italian:	P-6	W-3	D-2	L-1	F-8	A-4
ZDS Cup:	P-4	W-2	D-0	L-2	F-6	A-8
TOTALS:	P-237	W-104	D-63	L-70	F-334	A-258

Following a long meeting with Storrie, almost inevitably, Redknapp opted to stay and, keeping it in the family, immediately appointed his brother-in-law Frank Lampard, a Hammers' veteran of 663 games, as his Number Two.

According to Bonds, Redknapp also phoned to explore the possibility of the former management partnership being pictured together to show that they were still mates. Needless to say, Truprint were not disturbed as that particular notion was kicked far, far into touch.

As he settled in on the other side of the manager's desk, determined to look forward and not back, Redknapp was only too aware of the fact that he had also inherited the poisoned chalice that was the Beauchamp saga.

"I made it my first task to get rid of him," said 'H', who immediately found himself at loggerheads with who, up until then, had to be Hammers' worst signing of modern times.

It really was damage limitation, and after negotiating a deal with Swindon whereby West Ham would receive £300,000 and former Leyton Orient centre-half Adrian Whitbread in exchange for Beauchamp (0 apps), the gob-smacked Hammers' boss incredibly found himself embroiled in further argument.

"Beauchamp's asked for a £35,000 signing-on fee and then demanded £350,000 to leave," announced an exasperated Harry after Swindon Town and the PFA entered the fray and finally convinced their member that he should leave quietly.

"It was like a black cloud had been lifted," sighed Redknapp after seeing the bundle of trouble head to the quiet backwaters of willowy Wiltshire just 58 days after arriving at Upton Park.

It had certainly been a summer of turmoil down Upton Park way.

And it had been a traumatic few months for unemployed Tony Gale, too. But as he stepped out to take part in the FA Charity Shield against Manchester United, the Blackburn Rovers new boy was still pinching himself.

One minute he faced a toss-up between the dole queue and a spell with FC Zurich. And next the likeable central defender was walking down the Wembley tunnel after making an 11th-hour dash to link up with his former mentor at Fulham,

Ray Harford, who was now assistant manager at Ewood Park.

Certainly, 34-year-old Gale's departure from Upton Park was not befitting of someone who had loyally served the club for a decade following his £200,000 transfer from Craven Cottage during the summer of 1984. Having been awarded a richly deserved testimonial, Galey was also expecting to be handed an extended contract given he had helped Hammers retain their Premiership status.

Gale's wicked sense of humour had earned him the nickname of 'Reggie' after the one of the notorious East End Kray twins.

"I'm glad it wasn't Ronnie because he was the queer one," joked Gale (359+9 apps 7 gls), who certainly had not laughed when Bonds handed him a free transfer when he arrived for his benefit game against a Republic of Ireland XI heading for the 1994 World Cup finals.

Less than 24 hours earlier, Hammers had drawn 3-3 with Southampton in that final game of the 1993-94 campaign, and several of Jack Charlton's USA 94 squad had a run out as West Ham recorded a 4-2 victory.

Gale's long-time central defensive partner – 36-year-old Alvin Martin – proved another winner, too, when he was handed a new 12-month contract by the club.

With the West Ham management deciding that they could not retain both veterans, two did not go into one, but two did go into the Rovers' net at Wembley as Manchester United recorded a 2-0 Charity Shield victory.

While he did not realise it at the time, Hammers' harsh decision to release him was, ultimately, destined to send Reggie on a simply wicked and wonderful journey beyond his wildest dreams.

For his part, Redknapp had already endured a nightmare before a ball had even been kicked and things were to get no better as the season started.

Indeed, after three games, a goalless draw against Leeds United 0-0 and defeats at Manchester City (0-3) and Norwich City (0-1) meant that Hammers had not even scored their first goal of the season

They did find the net in their second home game of the new term, though, when Don Hutchison, a £1.5m capture from Liverpool, netted a penalty against Newcastle United on his debut, although his 87th-minute spot-kick was too little, too late to prevent a 1-3 defeat.

Having exhausted the patience of Reds' boss Roy Evans, the long-coveted Hutchison had been transfer-listed following yet more high jinks on his close-season holiday in Cyprus with flat-mate Jamie Redknapp.

Unfortunately for the Gateshead-born attacking midfielder, a semi-naked picture of him using a strategically placed Budweiser beer bottle label to cover up his manhood had appeared in the *News of the World* and, not for the first time, his off-field antics had overshadowed his on-field abilities.

While some pundits suggested that he had real trouble if a mere beer label could hide his modesty, Hutch – who was also sent off playing for Liverpool reserves in front of the watching Harry – conceded: "I created a lot of my own problems by doing silly things and I hold my hands up."

After scoring seven goals in 45 appearances for the Merseysiders following his £300,000 transfer from Hartlepool, Hutchison was shown the Anfield door.

"Nobody knows that boy better than me," insisted Harry after breaking the bank and hearing the Bobby Moore stand welcome the club record signing with a chant of 'Get your k**b out for the boys!' "After all, he's always trying to lead Jamie astray!"

Indeed, some conspiracy theorists even suggested that Harry had only signed the former £100 per week fork-lift truck driver – who had taken a pay cut to join Hartlepool as a £27 per week Youth Training Scheme trainee – to break up a disruptive alliance with his son Jamie, who needed to focus on his blossoming career.

But the overriding motive behind the move was surely Redknapp's long-held desire to acquire a goal-scoring midfielder whom he had seen play many, many times for Liverpool.

Harry was not finished on Merseyside, either.

For less than a week later, Cottee's absolution for that record-breaking 1988 move to Everton was complete when he returned to Upton Park in an exchange deal for David Burrows (35 apps 2 gls) that also saw West Ham receive a £300,000 cash adjustment.

The affable Burrows had proved a more than competent replacement for Julian Dicks but, again, he had to be sacrificed for fire-power and Cottee – who was also being courted by John Lyall at Ipswich Town – was the perfect replacement.

"I didn't want to leave Liverpool, I admit that," declared Burrows. "But the move to Upton Park worked out very well for me and I was very happy at West Ham."

The same could not be said for out-of-favour Cottee, who had gone from the high of scoring a hat-trick in a 4-0 win over Newcastle United on his Toffees' debut in August 1988, to the low of playing against his £10 per week window cleaner for Everton's 'A' team at Morecambe.

As former Red Burrows set about acquainting himself with the blue half of Liverpool, Redknapp still had unfinished business in the city.

And this time around, he was lining up an even more audacious raid on Anfield.

Like Hutchison, Dicks had fallen out of favour with Evans but his reported £7,000 per week wages all but ruled out any Hammers' move for him.

A crowd of 3,000 turned up on a damp Devon evening to see West Ham take on Exeter City in a testimonial for Eamonn Dolan, whose career had been cruelly cut short by testicular cancer.

And there was a surprise in store as guest Dicks – a former Upton Park team-mate of Dolan – scored in a 4-1 win for the Hammers.

That merely heightened speculation that the tough-tackling defender was on his way back to Upton Park, his salary still proving a huge obstacle.

Left behind by Evans for Liverpool's pre-season tour of Germany, the 'unfit and overweight' defender was given a huge steer as to where his future lay.

"I remember Jamie came in to training and told me off the record that his dad wanted to sign me," recalled Dicks, who had been forced to train with the youth team. "I said: 'Here's my number get your father on the phone.' But Harry knew he had to do things properly and go through official channels."

Memorably, Cottee had scored against Tottenham Hotspur on his first West Ham

United outing, on New Year's Day 1983 under Lyall, but there was less joy on his second Hammers' coming.

For his reckless, revengeful, 55th-minute tackle on Liverpool's Rob Jones – another future Hammer – saw him red carded at Anfield.

However, seven days later, TC got back to doing what he does best on his second home debut, netting an 86th-minute winner in the 1-0 victory over Aston Villa.

Hammers' Coca-Cola Cup second round first leg defeat at Walsall saw a bizarre own goal by Charlie Ntamark eclipsed by Steve Potts' similar effort which gave the Saddlers a 2-1 win.

And Martin's training ground bust up with Matthew Rush saw the veteran defender apologise to the youngster.

"I lost my head and that disappoints me because I thought those days were behind me," admitted the remorseful Merseysider. "At my time of life I should've learned to control myself."

Redknapp played down the fuss.

"I've seen worse fights at weddings," he insisted, clearly more concerned by the sight of future Hammers' striker Ian Wright helping Arsenal towards a 2-0 win at Upton Park, where the booked Hutchison's two-footed lunge on Alan Smith raised eyebrows.

Peter Butler may have impressed Ferenc Puskas in the previous autumn's win over the Sky Blues of Coventry City, but there were now desperately dark clouds hanging over his Hammers' career.

"Anyone who's prepared to settle for the reserves shouldn't be at the club," he declared with the typical Yorkshire grit and honesty that had mirrored his on-field mantra, after finding himself in the West Ham wilderness. "I'll just have to get my nut down and work even harder, but I'm not going to run off with my bat and ball just yet."

But Redknapp had decided that Butts was by now dispensable and he needed to generate cash to bring Dicks to Upton Park. Indeed, he had already lined up the £400,000 sale of the surplus midfielder to first division Notts County.

Meanwhile, Martin Allen netted Hammers' first away goal of the season at Stamford Bridge before Moncur secured a 2-1 win over Chelsea.

And as the *Hammers News Magazine* team headed for home, they almost succumbed to a cardiac arrest as a shaven headed yob emerged from a Kings Road telephone box screaming: 'Come on West Ham!'

The relief was tangible as the barking aggressor proved to be 'Mad Dog' himself, who crumbled into laughter at seeing the fear on the writers' faces.

Moncur was also proving himself to be a practical joker at Upton Park, too.

"They were painting up the changing rooms at Chadwell Heath and I turned up a bit late for training," he recalled. "All the other lads were already out on the pitch, so for a laugh I got the decorator to emulsion my hair. I jogged out and spent the whole morning training with a white head."

Moncur was on target again in the 2-0 second leg victory over Walsall in the Coca-Cola Cup and, after also scoring against the Saddlers, Hutchison then netted the winner in a 1-0 victory over Crystal Palace.

NEARLY REACHED THE SKY

"Hutch'll always score goals for you because he's got great ability," enthused H, who had also finally persuaded Butler (78 apps 3 gls) – whose seriously ill mother had just died – to make a £330,000 switch to Meadow Lane. "I see what he can do every day in training."

Eric Cantona ended that hat-trick of victories after scoring the only goal of the game at Manchester United, before Dicks' long-awaited return to Upton Park was sealed.

"Everyone thought I was off my rocker. Everybody opposed it. They all thought: 'What are we doing taking him back here? I'm talking about directors and coaching staff, people who had been at Upton Park during his time before. They didn't think that it was a very good idea!" said Redknapp after carving out an Ince-style pay-as-you-play deal that saw Hammers lay out an upfront £100,000 with further payments of £50,000 for every 25 games that Dicks' dodgy knee stood up to the rigours of the Premiership. "Julian wasn't in the best of shape when he left West Ham and he wasn't in the best of shape when he came back!"

So just 399 days after heading to Anfield, the shaven-headed Dicks had returned.

And 48 hours later, the uncompromising left-back with the cannonball shot and billiard ball head received a hero's welcome as Hammers beat Southampton 2-0 to climb to 12th-place in the table.

"It was even money Julian got booked today, wasn't it?" conceded Redknapp after referee Joe Worrall took just an hour to pluck a yellow card from his pocket to caution the returning idol for flattening ex-Hammer Paul Allen with a tackle that would have floored a rhino.

Hutchison's fourth goal in eight outings gave Hammers a 1-0 win over Chelsea in the Coca-Cola Cup third round, while Butler inspired new club County to a shock 3-0 victory over Tottenham Hotspur.

Having won five out of their last six games, as West Ham headed to White Hart Lane for another derby clash, the last rites were already being administered to Ossie Ardiles.

But, for once, the Spurs' boss found his star-studded, Famous Five strikeforce in electrifying form, and although Rush found the net for West Ham, Jurgen Klinsmann, Teddy Sheringham and Nicky Barmby gave the Argentinian a brief stay of execution with a 3-1 win that also saw Romanian 1994 World Cup star Ilie Dumitrescu in fine fettle.

Typically, just three days later, the benevolent Hammers – giving Beauchamp-transfer makeweight Whitbread his first Premiership start – also helped to delay win-less Mike Walker's departure from Goodison Park as Gary Ablett secured bottom-placed Everton's first victory of the season at the 13th attempt.

Redknapp's frustration at those two unexpected defeats was compounded by Hutchison's 33rd-minute dismissal for two reckless tackles on Leicester City's Lee Philpott.

"It's personal with me and Hutchison," he fumed, his anger only being marginally tempered by Dicks' penalty that had secured a 1-0 win over the Foxes. "If he's gonna let me down, he'll let anyone down. He's got talent to burn but he's letting himself down behaving like that. I'm so disappointed, I couldn't tell you.

"You've got a chance with disciplined people and no chance with undisciplined ones – that's the problem."

Sent home by the ranting Redknapp at half-time, Hutchison was already back in his room at the Swallow Hotel by the time the final whistle blew.

"I don't know what came over me," he said after receiving a four match ban. "I've never been a tackler in my life but since I came to West Ham I've been tackling left, right and centre. Perhaps I've been trying too hard to please."

Following his training ground clash with Dicks back in the summer of 1993, Simon Webster had still not kicked a ball for West Ham. And while the Hammers' hard man had now gone full circle and returned from Anfield, Webbo had suffered both ankle complications and a further setback, after slipping down some steps.

With his first-team chances limited, striker Steve Jones (11+11 apps 5 gls) headed to Redknapp's old club Bournemouth.

"I don't think that he's good enough for what we need at this level and I swam the ocean to get £150,000 for him," contested Harry, before jetting to France to snap up Northern Ireland international Michael Hughes on loan from Racing Club Strasbourg.

Veteran, Bethnal Green-born goalkeeper Les Sealey – the nephew of two-goal 1965 European Cup Winners' Cup hero Alan – joined on a free transfer from Blackpool and H also found time to sign Danish international Marc Rieper on loan from Brøndby.

A 0-1 defeat at Trevor Francis' Sheffield Wednesday was further complicated by Martin Allen's cracked rib and punctured lung.

"I was taken to the NHS ward of the living dead in the oldest hospital in Sheffield," recalled Mad Dog, whose career-threatening lunge on Carlton Palmer a few seasons earlier looked set to make him the loneliest man in Yorkshire. "I remember it vividly. It was the night of the first National Lottery draw – by the way I could be sitting on £8m because to this day I don't know where the ticket in my tracksuit went – and it was 10.25pm when the head sister said Trevor Francis had arranged to phone.

"I wasn't sure whether I was still under anaesthetic! We hadn't spoken since the day I left QPR but he said he hoped I was okay and asked if I needed anything. Trevor was very professional – he even sent his physio to see me – and we've since spoken. Life goes on."

Tony Cottee had managed just a solitary goal in 10 games since his return from Everton and his drought continued in a 0-1 home defeat against Coventry City.

TC may have found the net in the Coca-Cola Cup against Bolton Wanderers but his 82nd-minute consolation came far too late to prevent West Ham from skulking off the Upton Park pitch to predictable chants of 'What a load of rubbish'.

Inspired by two-goal John McGinlay, the first division outfit – who were destined to make it all the way to a Wembley final defeat at the hands of Liverpool – had trotted to a 3-1 victory to end Hammers' interest in the competition.

After months in the wilderness which had also seen fruitless, goalless loan spells at Portsmouth and West Bromwich Albion, Jeroen Boere returned to score in a 1-2 defeat at Queens Park Rangers, where Hammers slumped to a fourth-successive reverse after shipping first-half goals to future Hammers Les Ferdinand and Trevor Sinclair.

And an unwelcome five-timer looked on the cards as West Ham fell two goals behind at Elland Road, too. But then it all went double Dutch for the Leeds United defence as Boere – the forgotten man of Upton Park – scored twice to rescue a draw.

Mid-December 1994 was approaching yet, incredibly, the Dutchman was now leading scorer with a grand total of three goals.

Elsewhere, Ipswich Town's Lyall resigned with the Suffolk strugglers wallowing helplessly at the bottom of the Premiership and, in an ironic twist, ex-Hammers' striker Paul Goddard took over as caretaker-boss at Portman Road as he began to take his first tentative steps on a managerial ladder that would, one day, reach towards Upton Park.

And Frank McAvennie rocked the game when he confessed to the *News of the World* that he had taken drugs during his playing days at Upton Park – a claim he was later to repeat in his autobiography, *Scoring: An Expert's Guide*.

"The first few times I tried coke I was playing football for Celtic but they were one-offs and on nights at least a couple of days away from a match. Now at West Ham I was on a cocktail of painkilling and anti-inflammatory pills and didn't see why that should stop me from having a few drinks," he wrote, recalling his time on the sidelines as a result of the broken leg sustained in that clash with Chris Kamara at Stoke City back in 1989. "And it was around this time that I started hitting the cocaine.

"It was seen as a recreational drug of choice and if you weren't carrying it, you weren't up to par.

"When I got the all clear to go back to football in summer 1990, though, the sessions on the p*** were cut back and the coke put aside as an occasional treat. I even cut back on the fags."

While Macca was dropping his own headline-making sex 'n drugs bombshells, his clean-cut former striker-partner Cottee was just pleased that he still had enough pages in his legendary scrapbooks to record altogether different scoring feats of his own.

Indeed, as McAvennie battled to save his ailing career, the parched TC finally ended his own personal Premiership goal drought with a welcome hat-trick in West Ham's biggest win of the season – a 3-0 victory over Manchester City.

McAvennie may have left the club, but there was still a handful of Hammers willing to fill his drinking boots. And the 1994 Christmas Party was a case in point.

"There was a little group of players who couldn't behave themselves," wrote H in *Harry Redknapp – My Autobiography*. "They were forever having booze-ups and causing aggravation. Dale Gordon was head of the club's entertainment committee and for Christmas he wanted to hire an open-top bus to trawl through London's West End. 'Are you out of your mind?' I said to him. 'We're struggling in the league and you want to go around looking like you've won the bleedin' FA Cup!' Instead they hired a minibus to take them to the Phoenix Apollo in Stratford. One or two of them had too much to drink and set light to the seats on the bus at the end of the night. Boere could be a handful and someone said he may have been involved."

While it was certainly never proven whether the Dutchman had played any part in those juvenile shenanigans, the *Daily Mirror* later claimed that seats had been urinated on and slashed, while a replacement vehicle also sustained damage, leading to a bill of £1,162 from Dan's Minibus Hire Limited – a sum subsequently rustled up via a Gordon-led players' whip-round and their furious manager.

Back on the pitch, Cottee's treble against City had taken him back to the top of the Upton Park scoring charts and he found the net again on Boxing Day in a 1-1 draw against the returning Goddard's Ipswich, who were about to persuade 35-year-old Chapman to move his wine cellar for the 12th time in his career.

A 0-1 defeat at Wimbledon and criticism of a long-ball approach was soon tempered by a superb passing display in a 3-1 win over Nottingham Forest as the on-song Cottee again hit the net to help Hammers go into 1995 in 16th place.

With four of the Premiership's 22 teams destined to be relegated in a downsizing of the Premiership, Hammers were still looking over their shoulders.

That was something Tony Gale had constantly found himself doing during his days down West Ham way.

But now this time around, the Blackburn Rovers defender was glancing behind from the comparative luxury of the top of the table as he greeted his former team-mates to Ewood Park on January 2.

Ian Bishop greeted referee Kelvin Morton's award of a penalty to the tumbling hat-trick hitting Alan Shearer with a pinch of his nose and the pulling of an invisible toilet chain, a little New Year charade that cost him a yellow card.

And an odious start to 1995 was compounded by a 2-4 defeat at the hands of the table-toppers when another Cottee strike – his 99th league goal for the club – coupled with a deadly Dicks effort were not enough to prevent the Champions-elect from taking all three points.

When West Ham headed to Wycombe Wanderers, desperate to avoid an FA Cup giant-killing, BBC TV's *Match of the Day* cameras were at Adams Park all set to record a third round upset.

But Alan Hansen left hugely disappointed as goals by Kenny Brown and, yet again, Cottee, without reply, ensured that Hammers avoided a slaying.

As West Ham contemplated an FA Cup fourth round tie at Queens Park Rangers, Marsh (58+3 apps 2 gls), citing Beachampitis, engineered a £500,000 move to Coventry City so that he could be a little nearer to his native Merseyside.

Bizarrely, Marsh did not stay at the half-way house that was the Midlands for long. And in total navigational malfunction, he was soon heading to Turkey to link up with former Liverpool boss Souness, who was now in charge of Galatasaray. With the lure of the Lire no doubt easing the homesickness, he remained there for just two months before linking up with fellow Liverpudlians Ronnie Whelan and Martin at Southend United before a knee injury forced his retirement from the professional game.

Unperturbed, Marsh then headed into the Conference where he guided Kidderminster Harriers to promotion but, given the insurance pay-out he had received for that injury precluded him from ever playing again in the Football League, he eventually joined up with Ian Bishop at Unibond part-timers Burscough before embarking upon an unlikely career as a care worker and paramedic.

There was another move behind the scenes, too, as club secretary Tom Finn took up a similar post at Wolverhampton Wanderers. Having joined from Oldham in the latter days of Lyall's reign, the experienced Finn had proved the perfect confidante for Lou Macari and the less-experienced Bonds.

But the likeable northerner had suddenly found himself the odd man out, as Storrie's relationship with Redknapp now made him the suit with the power. Already at the club, Richard Skirrow – a former qualified chartered accountant with Touche Ross – moved along the corridor into Finn's office.

Back in the league, Boere's opener was wiped out in a 1-2 defeat against Tottenham Hotspur before a 0-2 loss at the hands of Sheffield Wednesday saw Hammers finish with nine-men after referee Paul Danson's farcical 10th-minute dismissal of Martin was followed by Tim Breacker's later red card.

Martin's offence was later commuted to a yellow card, but the damage was already done and a win-less January ended with a fourth successive defeat as future Hammer Andrew Impey clinched an FA Cup fourth round victory for Queens Park Rangers.

"I said: 'Come on chaps, wake up please!'" announced helpless Harry looking back on his hopeless half-time attempt to rally West Ham to cup glory. "We left ourselves with a lot to do."

With a Beaujolais noveau bill looming, no doubt, the out-of-favour Chapman (43+8 apps 11 gls) had stood firm in his quest for an Upton Park pay-off before heading to Portman Road and the twilight of his career, a new life as a restaurateur and squalid reports of a stormy relationship with his actress wife Lesley Ash.

Indeed, notwithstanding her role in the hit comedy series, the tabloids' unproven claims suggested that it was Chappie who was the *Man Behaving Badly*.

So 488 days since Bonds and Redknapp engineered the four-way move between Dicks, Burrows, Marsh and Chapman, none of the four remained at their destination club.

Moncur admitted to being a man behaving madly ahead of Hammers' next clash at Leicester City.

"On the night before the game I sneaked out of the team hotel to go to a nearby petrol station," confessed the team joker. "I bought every packet of dog biscuits the geezer had and went back to Martin Allen's room, pulled back the blankets, smothered his entire bed with them and then covered it all back over. Mad Dog wasn't happy when he climbed into bed!"

Indeed, it was never safe when Moncur was in the vicinity of a service station.

"On another evening we went for a walk down to the local garage," recalled Moncs. "Hutch, Dicksy and Martin Allen each bet me that I wouldn't go through the car wash. It was about minus two degrees at the time but I didn't care, I stripped down to my pants, they put the token in the machine and I battled it out through the spinning brushes right to the end. The only trouble was that Mad Dog paid me in dog biscuits!"

There had been no such smiles for team-mate Cottee, who had found himself all washed up on the goals front for over a month.

But it was finally ton-up TC at Filbert Street, as the Hammers' hit man set his team on the way to a 2 1 win over the bottom-placed Foxes.

The goal ace had once hit 99 goals in a season for schoolboy side Romford Royals and he had also fallen one short of his century at Everton.

"I knew it would come eventually," said the relieved Cottee after moving into fifth place in Hammers' all-time scoring charts with his strike at Leicester. "There are still a lot of goals left in me."

Indeed, he immediately moved onto 102 with a double against his old club, Everton, as somehow Hammers twice surrendered the lead in a 2-2 draw at Upton Park to leave themselves in the bottom three.

And how Redknapp was going to be reliant on his master marksman as Storrie attempted to lock the Upton Park safe.

"We drew up our budget at the beginning of the season," he announced, suggesting that the club had to sell before it could buy. "And we have already exceeded that figure by spending up to £3m net on transfers. That's more than at any time in West Ham's history. We believe the money given is as much as any club in the Premiership other than Newcastle United and Blackburn Rovers, who have benefactors in Sir John Hall and Jack Walker, while Manchester United have vast off-the-field resources.

"Of course, I sympathise with supporters worried about relegation but we do not have £1m to change things. You cannot spend what you do not have. We simply cannot afford to buy our way out of trouble."

New boss Ron Atkinson looked on as Marsh – who was about to be joined by £1.1m Burrows – netted for Coventry City in their 2-0 win at Highfield Road.

"Everyone will say: 'Ron's come in and they've done this and they've done that.' But Coventry were crap!" fumed Harry after 'Bo Jangles' got his City managerial career off to a Sky Blue start. "If it was only two to be relegated we'd be sitting quite pretty now, but with four going down, anything can happen. It's so close."

A 1-2 defeat at home to Chelsea left Hammers in dire straits before Don Hutchison gave Hammers a shock, confidence-boosting 1-0 win at Arsenal.

But all that good work was undone with a 0-2 defeat at Newcastle, before Cottee single-handedly salvaged a 2-2 draw against ten-man Norwich City with a late, late double in a farcical afternoon of officiating. Innocent Andy Johnson was ushered forward by his team-mates in place of the already booked Prior, in the vain hope that he would only be cautioned for the second serious foul committed by his team-mate. But it all backfired when substitute referee Martin Sims produced a straight red card to send Johnson for an early shower instead.

At Southampton, the subsequently cleared Bruce Grobbelaar's preparations were disrupted by match-fixing allegations that only saw him released from police custody just three hours before kick-off. But apart from picking Hutchison's 39th-minute header out of his net, replacement Dave Beasant had little to do in a 1-1 draw at The Dell where Redknapp suggested to his Saints counterpart Alan Ball:

NEARLY REACHED THE SKY

'Let's go to Cheltenham races, it's gotta be better than this!'

But as Hammers found their backs against the wall in a frenzied finale, Hutch's lack of defensive application drove his manager wild. Indeed, in a quite literal throwback to their bust-up following the attacking midfielder's autumn dismissal against Leicester, the ranting Redknapp launched the post-match sandwich platter at his record signing.

"Hutch stood there wearing all this ham, cheese and tomato and all I could think was: 'Harry, what have you done that for? You're starving!'" he recalled.

And as the transfer window slammed shut, the beleaguered 'H' managed to sign 31-year-old, eight-times capped, German striker Dieter Eckstein on loan from Schalke 04 at the eleventh hour.

But in a surreal turn of events, deadline beater Dieter was sidelined by a *blister* and never kicked a first-class ball for the club!

"Yeah, it's like passing strangers and Dieter's enjoying his holiday," groaned 'H' after seeing the sum total of the German's efforts come in the form of a run-out in George Parris's testimonial against Ipswich Town. "He's going to have a look around the Tower of London in the morning!"

Certainly, Parris, a loyal servant of the club, deserved more than the 1,379 who turned up to see him score in a 2-3 defeat in his own benefit match. Having fallen out of favour with Birmingham City manager Barry Fry, 'Smokey' was on the verge of joining Liam Brady's Brighton & Hove Albion, where he would see out his playing days, before becoming a milkman and holding down a job as a schools football and cricket coach while bravely battling against his desperate gambling addiction.

Following his sensational confessional, McAvennie knew his football career was over, but he made one last return to Upton Park to sign off with a goal against Town.

"That's my last game," insisted the hyperventilating 35-year-old following his 90 minute run-out. "I was dying to come off for a sit down. I'm knackered. I wouldn't mind but when they paid me to play here, they couldn't wait to get me off!"

Back in the Premiership, Hammers may have gone to Villa Park still in the bottom four, but a 2-0 win over Aston Villa sent them three points clear of safety, while a 1-1 draw at Nottingham Forest and a 3-0 win over Wimbledon eased them into 17th place.

West Ham were hardly out of the woods, though, and while they demolished Dorchester Town by four goals in a south coast friendly, according to the *Daily Mirror*, some of the squad also smashed up Room 164 of the squad's Dormy Hotel on the outskirts of Bournemouth.

Following the previous December's minibus incident, an unruly element had clearly not learned their lesson and the raging Redknapp – who, again, was obviously not involved – received an invoice for £531.63 for smashed glasses, spilled alcohol, food scattered over walls and carpets as well as a ripped snooker table cloth in the club room.

Ironically, Cornish hotelier Martin Bodenham was in charge for Hammers' next match where the fight for survival, quite literally, continued at Portman Road.

Boere's 94th-minute leveller salvaged a 1-1 draw against bottom-placed Ipswich Town, but moments earlier, all hell had broken loose when Dicks – booked for the 50th time in a claret and blue shirt – chopped Claus Thomsen before Hutchison then became embroiled in an ugly skirmish as he tried to pick up the grounded Dane.

Mr Bodenham had been generous in merely flashing one yellow card.

"The referee must have some unruly visitors to his guest house if he thinks Dicks' behaviour was normal," suggested *The Daily Telegraph*, clearly oblivious to the unreported events of a few weeks earlier.

"I asked Kenny Brown what happened out there," revealed Redknapp. "He said: 'Hutch has gone to pick the fella up and he's accidentally caught him on the head with his boot!'"

Blackburn headed to Upton Park having reaped 86 points from their 39 games and that left them eight points clear of second-placed Manchester United, who had a game in hand.

But goals from Hutchison and Rieper threw the Premiership title race wide open while, in the nether regions of the table, Hammers headed into 16th-spot three points clear of safety with four matches to play. And the icing on the cake came in the form of substitute Webster's long-awaited Hammers' debut, nearly two years after his £525,000 move from Charlton.

A goalless draw against Queens Park Rangers witnessed dismissals for Allen and future Hammer Rufus Brevett, before Hammers' eight-game unbeaten run ended with a 0-1 defeat at struggling Crystal Palace.

With a daunting, ironic visit of Jamie Redknapp's Liverpool set to be followed by an equally difficult Upton Park clash with title-chasing Manchester United, Hammers were still looking vulnerable with just two matches remaining.

But Hutchison's double against his former club gave West Ham a 3-0 win over the Merseysiders to fully secure their Premiership status.

Hammers were safe after 41 matches, but the outcome of the Premiership title was still going to boil down to the outcome of the 42nd and final match of the season.

With United at Upton Park and Rovers playing at Anfield, the top of the table read:

Blackburn Rovers Played-41 Points-89 Goal Difference +42
Manchester United Played-41 Points-87 Goal Difference +49

Premiership football was guaranteed at Upton Park for another season and, with the certainty of cashflow to see off Turkish predators Fenerbache, West Ham were able to sign Rieper for £1.1m before the teams took to the field for the final game of the campaign.

And when Hughes quickly put Hammers 1-0 up at Upton Park and Shearer fired Rovers ahead at Liverpool, the title certainly looked to be heading to Ewood Park.

But throughout a roller-coaster afternoon, the fate of the trophy was never certain.

Indeed, when Brian McClair levelled for United and John Barnes equalised for Liverpool suddenly the race was thrown wide-open, once more.

NEARLY REACHED THE SKY

Try as they might – with frustrated second-half substitute Andrew Cole firing blanks against the brilliant Ludek Miklosko – United just could not muster the decider that would transform one point into three, while way up north, Gale kneeled in the Anfield dug-out praying that his old muckers would hang on to preserve his Premiership winners' medal

As the clock ticked down, United still could not score for neither love nor money, and that proved all the more galling for the barracked Paul Ince when Redknapp struck an injury time free-kick to give Liverpool a 2-1 win over Rovers, just seconds after the final whistle had blown at Upton Park.

Staring stony faced at the final league table, Alex Ferguson did not need reminding that he had just seen Hammers emerge from an Alamo-like assault to claim the point that had wrecked his title dreams yet again.

"We had to defend for quite a long time and they had most of the play," confirmed Miklosko, the master of under-statement, who was all but given the freedom of Blackburn after Rovers secured their first title in 81 years. "Having already beaten Blackburn and Liverpool we again wanted to show that we could compete with the best teams in the country. And, of course, we all felt good for our old team-mate Galey who was one of the best defenders I have ever played with."

Back in 1992, Fergie had fumed at relegated West Ham's 'obscene' victory over his side.

Make no mistake, he was equally annoyed that Hammers – despite having nothing to play for except Cockney pride – had again wrecked his team's title aspirations.

This time, however, he was just a little bit more forgiving in defeat.

"We couldn't have done any more," he asserted after seeing the title tantalisingly elude him by a solitary point. "The goalie did fantastic. He had a marvellous game."

Before the coach left the Upton Park car park for the long, silent journey home to Old Trafford, the United boss stood in the aisle, summoned all of his deflated players and urged them: "Do not forget how badly we are all hurting. We never, ever want this to happen to us again."

At youth level, Hammers' youngsters miraculously overturned a 1-4 first leg, Upton Park deficit in the South East Counties Cup final against Chelsea. Inspired by the unknown Rio Ferdinand, the youths had won 5-2 at Stamford Bridge to level the tie 6-6 on aggregate before teenager Frank Lampard drilled home the penalty shoot-out decider in front of the excited Harry Redknapp senior.

With a rich vein of youth talent finally beginning to ease its way down the academy's production line, the future now augured well for his son, who also knew that West Ham United would return from their Centenary Tour to Australia still in the Premiership.

There had been times during a season of trauma when the Hammers' boss had been so tense that he could not even turn his neck to reverse his car.

"I don't want to go through all this hassle again," declared Harry before heading off into the summer in the vain hope that a crate of vintage Bollinger would be heading south from an eternally grateful Rovers' manager Kenny Dalglish. "It mustn't be like last year. I'm not going to go through next season continually standing there saying: 'Yeah, played well but got beat'."

PLAYERS IN

Joey Beauchamp	Oxford United	£850,000
Tony Cottee*	Everton	
	Swap for Burrows + £300,000 (in)	
Ian Feuer	Los Angeles Salsa	£70,000
Don Hutchison	Liverpool	£1,500,000 (Record)
John Moncur	Swindon Town	£850,000
Marc Rieper	Brøndby	£1,100,000.
Les Sealey	Blackpool	Free.
Mark Watson	Sutton United	£50,000
Adrian Whitbread$	Swindon Town	
	Swap for Beauchamp + £300,000 (out)	

LOANS IN

Dieter Eckstein	Schalke O4
Michael Hughes	RC Strasbourg

PLAYERS OUT

Joey Beauchamp$	Swindon Town	
	Swap for Whitbread + £300,000 (out)	
David Burrows*	Everton	
	Swap for Cottee + £300,000 (in)	
Peter Butler	Notts County	£330,000
Lee Chapman	Ipswich Town	£50,000
Steve Jones	Bournemouth	£150,000
Mike Marsh	Coventry City	£500,000
Trevor Morley	Reading	Free Transfer

Chapter 9
1995-96

A VERY FOREIGN AFFAIR

The crestfallen Manchester United players climbed into their beds to endure the recurring nightmare of Ludek Miklosko still repelling everything that they could throw at him.

And while the Red Devils were left to rue their missed Premiership title, the West Ham United squad prepared to make the 10,000 mile journey to Australia to mark the club's centenary.

Founded in 1856 on the banks of the River Lea at nearby Canning Town, The Thames Iron Works and Shipbuilding Company Limited went on to build almost 150 battleships and nearly twice as many lifeboats together with iron ships and the Royal Yacht HMS Fairey.

The company's paternal owner Arnold S. Hills had also formed a number of clubs and societies for his employees including – as every self-respecting East Ender knew – the forerunner of West Ham United, Thames Ironworks Football Club, in 1895.

Now, 100 years on from its inception, the club decided to take a Centenary Tour Down Under.

As John Moncur prepared for the flight with a liquid breakfast in the bar of the Swallow Hotel at Waltham Abbey, it was not the first time that a long haul and the Hammers had threatened to produce an alcoholic cocktail of potent proportions.

Indeed, Phil Parkes recounts an epic tale of Hammers' end-of-season tour to Tokyo, 10 years earlier, when he was assured by John Lyall that he would not be playing in the opening game of the Japan Cup tournament.

And that was the green light for Parkesy and physio Rob Jenkins to embark upon a flight-long bender all the way to the Far East.

Upon arriving at the stadium to face their unfancied opponents, however, deputy Tom McAllister had not travelled too well himself and the hungover No.1 was called into action.

As Hammers stormed towards a predictable interval lead, right on the stroke of half-time, Parkes dived post-wards as a hopeful, harmless 30-yarder flew straight into the middle of his goal.

Walking off at half-time, the embarrassed keeper begged Tony Gale to say that the ball had taken a wicked deflection off his boot but the central defender was determined not to be an accessory to the crime.

"What happened with their goal then, Phil?" enquired the wily Lyall, clearly unhappy that his keeper, to the detriment of the team, had now paid the price for keeping the trolley dollies working overtime quenching an in-flight thirst.

As Gale looked at the floor, the silence was deafening and, realising he was on his own, Parkes sheepishly replied: "Sorry John, I saw three balls coming at me and I just didn't know which one to go for!"

Not that Moncur would have realised but, back on the Essex/Hertfordshire border, the Aussie-bound squad set off for Heathrow Airport four men light.

With Harry Redknapp taking a brief end-of-season holiday with his long-suffering wife Sandra in Jersey, it was his assistant Frank Lampard's turn to endure all the stress for once.

But as he arrived at the terminal, the acting headmaster was, at least, relieved to see Don Hutchison, Kenny Brown, Julian Dicks and Matthew Rush emerge from a stretch limousine.

And having endured former Burton's shop-window dresser Mark Watson – a £50,000 signing from Sutton United – holding up check-in proceedings thanks to his unsigned passport, Lampard then found himself bailing out young Malcolm McPherson who, having lost the key to the safe of his Singapore stop-over hotel, needed to fund a £100 surcharge.

Looking for some brief respite, if not spiritual guidance of a more conventional kind, the assistant manager then removed his shoes to visit an ancient temple only to exit to a barefoot walk home after finding that his loafers had been stolen!

A crowd of 10,000 delayed the start at the Western Australian Cricket Arena in Perth, as Hammers kicked off their tour with a 2-2 draw before losing 3-5 on penalties to the home state.

Western Australia's Stan Lazaridis was certainly having a cracker at the WACA until the exhausted Tim Breacker ended his involvement with a crunching tackle that was also to deprive the flying left-winger of the chance to guest for West Ham on the next leg of their four-match tour.

McPherson levelled to make it 1-1 before Watson hit Hammers' second equaliser. Although the only likeness was his complexion, Watson, who had gone from fitting dummies to trying to sell them, had already been cruelly nicknamed 'Pele' by his fellow travellers.

Danny Shipp rescued a 1-1 draw against Victoria in the shadow of the Melbourne Cricket Ground but the English performance was greeted with derision by the 3,500 present at Olympic Park. A cocktail of jet-lag, Fosters and a midnight screening of Everton's FA Cup final victory over Manchester United made for a lethargic, injury depleted Hammers' side who were even forced to put Lampard senior on the bench.

Clearly, the Australian public had expected to see a full-strength West Ham team, but the reality was that the likes of Miklsoko, Ian Bishop, Alvin Martin, Mattie Holmes, Jeroen Boere, Marc Rieper, Keith Rowland and Michael Hughes were still back in England, while the lame, known names such as Tony Cottee, Dicks, Moncur and Rush were there for PR purposes only.

"We've had a long trip and quite a few injuries but it was a below-par performance," conceded Lampard who was just relieved to see the unknown Shipp salvage some pride and the accident-prone Simon Webster receive an X-ray all-clear, following a clash with his own keeper Ian Feuer.

"I'm disappointed that West Ham didn't give a good account of themselves," fumed Victoria boss Ian Dobson, fanning the flames of Aussie anger.

The arrival of Harry Redknapp, minus Sandra, was the catalyst for a workmanlike 1-0 victory over the Australian Olympic-bound Under-23 side – the Olyroos – in Sydney's Marconi Stadium. That placated the angry locals a little, but the top-dollar paying crowd – who again had delayed kick-off – was still coming to terms with the absence of established Premiership stars in a Hammers' side that relied on McPherson to net the decider.

As wily, Birmingham-bred tour promoter Gary Williams again played down the attendance to his fellow Poms, his mathematically challenged calculation of 4,100 was blown out of the water by the PA announcer's definitive confirmation that there were, in fact, 5,764 paying punters inside the arena.

The midweek departures of Steve Potts, Breacker and Martin Allen – whose father Dennis was seriously ill – did not help matters, and Harry literally had to pluck a player off the beach following his chance meeting on the sand with former Bournemouth YTS apprentice Gary Peters.

Hutchison managed to pick up his third booking of the four-game 'friendly' tour in the return against the Olyroos, as Hammers simply capitulated in front of 6,998 frustrated fans in Brisbane.

"It was a disgrace!" bellowed Redknapp from the dungeons of the Suncorp Stadium after seeing his weary side sign off with a humiliating 0-4 defeat in which the awestruck Peters enjoyed a brief run-out.

The year of 1995 really was the summer for the anniversary.

While the modern day Hammers were Down Under, 20 years on, the 1975 FA Cup final was re-staged at Craven Cottage between two West Ham and Fulham sides looking a little greyer and heavier. This time around, the Cottagers avenged the Alan Taylor-inspired 0-2 defeat at Wembley with a 2-1 victory, after Billy Jennings had beaten Peter Mellor to put Hammers ahead.

And the senior squad was on the move again in July when the 1965 European Cup Winners' Cup final was marked by a competitive friendly against TSV Munich 1860 that saw two-goal Martin's 37th birthday celebrations gate-crashed by Bernhard Winkler's last-gasp strike in a 4-3 win for the Germans.

Since returning from May's Australasian tour, Redknapp had plunged into the transfer market to buy Marco Boogers from Sparta Rotterdam for £1m and, on Lampard's recommendation, the fit-again Lazaridis had been flown in from Australia for a trial.

Record signing Hutchison was conspicuous by his absence in Germany, seemingly left at home following a training ground row with 'H'. Lampard, however, diplomatically suggested that there was "not enough room on the plane!" for the enigmatic £1.5m Geordie, overlooking the fact that Peter Storrie's friend, Neil Waite and Stadium Manager, John Ball, had still been aboard the flight.

The new season was just a fortnight away, but it was readily apparent that goals – just as they had been last season – were going to be equally as hard to come by during the months ahead. Only the centre-halves – Martin and Rieper – had got their names onto the score sheet, while the overly aggressive Boogers had missed some gilt-edged sitters against the match-fit Germans.

Lazaridis, had shown some good touches down the flanks and probably looked worth a punt at the proposed £300,000 or so fee but there was certainly trouble ahead.

Dutch superstars Ruud Gullit and Dennis Bergkamp may have moved to London but the likes of Messrs Koeman, Jonk and Winter were still plying their trade in Italy and Spain. In a vain attempt to add a touch of credibility to their surprise, unknown acquisition, it was boldly announced that Boogers had been voted into third spot in the previous season's player-of-the-year poll in Holland.

But in the cool of the club's Bavarian retreat, Redknapp thoughtfully mulled over the last few morsels of his meal and openly admitted that the Dutch striker was, perhaps, not the answer.

"At £600,000, it's a gamble," he confided, slashing Boogers' reported fee by £400,000. "But give me £6m and I'll get you Les Ferdinand. Now that's not what I'd call taking a chance!"

That 3-4 reverse in the Grunwalder Strasse Stadion had been equally hard for Harry to swallow and, with the season looming, he immediately placed a curfew on the team, thus barring any notion Martin had of celebrating his 37th birthday in the beer cellars of Munich.

"Didn't stop us emptying the mini-bar, though, did it?" announced a defiant Moncur, showing passers-by the bare fridge of his hotel room the following morning.

One man destined not to kick-off the new campaign with the club was Trevor Morley (188+26 apps 70 gls). Having overcome that horrendous 1991 stabbing, the striker had recovered sufficiently to be voted Hammer-of-the-Year in 1993-94, but injuries and competition had started to take their toll, too, and he was handed a mutual free transfer.

The former fruit and vegetable stallholder subsequently joined Reading, where he overcame a serious head injury sustained in an on-field collision, before taking up a coaching role in Norway, where he met his second wife.

By the time fancied Leeds United rolled into town to kick-off the 1995-96 campaign, Redknapp had wheeled and dealed that little bit more by selling Matt Holmes (76+13 apps 6 gls) to champions Blackburn for an amazing £600,000 plus another Aussie, Robbie Slater.

"I loved Mattie as a player and a lad but that deal was important," admitted Redknapp after sending the reluctant Holmes to Ewood Park.

"I was never the type to chase glory or money, I just wanted to play regular football at a club where I was happy and I already had all of that at West Ham," replied the likeable midfielder in an echo of Stuart Slater's early 90s plight. "I was flattered that the Premiership champions wanted me but I was never positive about the move. I was driving up to Blackburn thinking: 'I don't really want to be doing this' even though they'd offered me a package that meant I'd doubled my wages."

Holmes made a promising start to his Rovers' career but as Sir Jack Walker kept bankrolling new buys, he found himself sliding down the pecking order in an ever increasing squad. In the end he returned south to join Charlton Athletic in a £250,000 deal before the wild boots of Wolverhampton Wanderers' Aussie hatchet man, Kevin Muscat, ended his career with a thuggish tackle that shattered his tibia.

On a fine day for English football, Muscat decided to return to Melbourne in 2005, but for many battered and bruised Brits that was, alas, a decade too late.

Holmes eventually received an out of court settlement of around £250,000 plus costs as his outraged advisors pursued the manic Muscat through the courts and it was testament to one of the game's good guys that he then made an unsolicited donation towards Charlton's Youth Academy.

And Rush (35+20 apps 5 gls) joined Norwich City for £330,000 rising to £500,000 with a certain level of appearances. A sell-on clause provided that extra degree of comfort, but only time would tell if the powerful winger could fulfill his undoubted potential. As it happened, Rush found himself moved on to Oldham Athletic, where a knee ligament injury sadly ended a career of under-achievement that had always promised so much yet delivered so little.

Having already expended that £1.1m on Rieper just before the curtain had fallen on the previous term, Redknapp was conscious of the fact that he simply could not afford another Joey Beauchamp fiasco this time around. And Boogers, the club's biggest signing of the summer, was certainly not happy to find himself on the bench as the new 1995-96 season kicked off against Leeds United.

But Harry's decision looked to have been vindicated when Danny Williamson put them ahead at 3.05pm. Given it had taken West Ham 357 minutes to get off the mark in the previous season, things were certainly looking up, before livewire Tony Yeboah struck a second half double to leave West Ham wallowing in defeat and Redknapp bemoaning an acute lack of cash.

"Everyone else has bought Dutchmen," he declared casting an envious eye towards Stamford Bridge and Highbury where Gullit and Bergkamp had just arrived in town. "We've only managed to get a couple of Aussies so that means that when Slater's fit and Lazaridis has sorted out his passport, we'll just have two Australian wingers hopping up the touchline."

Four days later, Hammers made the daunting trip to a wounded Manchester United still smarting from the events of May 14 – the day they had again failed to win the Premiership title at Upton Park.

Following a critical outburst over team selection, the bemused Boogers – aptly pronounced 'Bookers' – found himself on the bench once more. And by the time he was pressed into action, the overawed Hammers were trailing 1-2 to an unimpressive United side that was destined to reclaim the Premiership trophy come the first week of May.

However, Mad Marco lasted just 18 minutes! A crazy clog on Gary Neville saw the Dutchman deservedly – albeit sensationally – red carded, and that only added to the speculation that he could be heading back from whence he came.

"It was a bad tackle," confessed 'H' who, two years earlier, had seen 'Bookers' fellow countryman Boere dismissed at Newcastle United on his Hammers' debut, too. "It's not in Marco's nature at all. Maybe he was trying to impress. But his name is Boogers – not Beauchamp. He has a future here at West Ham."

But the press call ended in chaos thanks to Harry's parting riposte: "Stan Lazaridis, our record £300,000 signing, still isn't available. He's shagging sheep in Australia at the moment!"

Hammers stayed on amidst the peaceful surroundings of Cheshire's Mottram Hall hotel, preparing to head south to face Nottingham Forest. It was far from relaxing for Redknapp, however, as he looked to get win-less West Ham off the mark.

Having released Morley, he knew that Boere lacked the vital Premiership pedigree to sustain a season-long strike-rate, while the future of Boogers was already teetering on the edge of the Upton Park precipice.

Redknapp was often heard to justify the more unorthodox actions of his reign with the declaration: 'Desperate times call for desperate measures.'

D-day had arrived once more. And the morning after the night before he made the shock decision to lure Iain Dowie back from Crystal Palace for £500,000.

For the West Ham fans, these were, indeed, desperate times. The awkward marksman had managed just a dozen games last time around, before moving on to Southampton in September 1991 and then heading to Selhurst Park at the beginning of 1995.

The majority feeling in the East End had been that Billy Bonds had done well to get his half-million pounds investment back on a player who just could not win over the fans during that brief stay. Indeed, not even his four goals in that promotion push had prevented him from being cruelly jeered during the club's 1991 celebration banquet at London's plush Hilton hotel.

Rocked by the death of his father, Dennis, the want-away Martin Allen headed West Ham ahead at the City Ground before future Hammer Stuart Pearce's penalty rescued a 1-1 draw for Forest. The disgraced Boogers had never looked like getting off the bench, while in a farcical finish, H panicked, sending on defender Martin for striker Cottee, a move that only succeeded in heightening the pressure on his embattled defence.

Afterwards, the normally street-wise Redknapp curiously played all his cards by admitting that Dowie topped his shopping list.

"I'm looking to play with wingers," he confessed with an honesty bordering on naivety. "And if I'm going to do that I need someone who can head the ball."

And yet another press conference turned into farce as Harry responded to an enquiry regarding the craggy striker's propensity to get on the end of crosses. "Yeah, judging by the look of Dowie's face, I'd reckon he's headed a lot of balls!"

Acknowledging that he had now crossed the line between comedy and outright cruelty, and not wishing to upset his top target, he compensated with an impromptu rendition of a song he claimed he had been singing to himself the previous evening: "There's only one Iain Dowie!"

As the Sunday newspapers crashed onto the doormat of Palace chairman Ron Noades, the 'We want Dowie' headlines simply invited the Palace chairman to crank up the negotiations.

The frustrated Storrie confided: "Noades keeps sending us faxes varying everything we've just discussed, and then he goes and switches his phone off!"

By now, Boere had entered the Dowie equation and Palace wanted to take him to Selhurst Park on loan.

While negotiations continued, Hutchison looked like securing the first victory of the season with a 25-yard screamer against Tottenham Hotspur at Upton Park, but Ronny Rosenthal nicked an equaliser that meant win-less West Ham had surrendered the lead for the third time in their opening four matches.

Boogers' stock was diminishing by the minute. It now transpired that he had only been voted into third-place in the *Sparta Rotterdam* Player-of-the-Season poll – not the Dutch *Eredivisie* – and the Boogie Wonderland headlines were, quite literally, now metamorphosing into Boogie Blunderland banners.

"Of course he's the kind of player I expected," roared Redknapp. "I knew exactly what I was getting. People are saying that I bought him off a video. I don't know who dreamt that one up!"

After again finding himself overlooked, the perplexed striker replied: "Harry tells me that I've got to settle in, but I've found a house, I know where the training ground is, I can find my way to Upton Park and my English is better than it was six weeks ago! I'm 28 and have played over 200 games in Holland. Just what is this settling in?"

Equally anxious to put the record straight, he added: "I never said: 'I want to go home.' I just told the manager to give me a chance."

But a further question mark was chalked down against his future when, after much wrangling, fellow Dutchman Boere (18+11 apps 7 gls) plus £125,000, headed to south London as Dowie finally rejoined the club.

Boere's arrogant streak had not always found favour with Redknapp, who was more inclined to bring him in to shake things up now and again, rather than look to the striker as a long-term solution.

"If it was up to Jeroen, he'd be picking himself to play for Holland," said Harry, who was equally uncomfortable with the refuelling habits of the man from the land of Oranjeboom and Grolsch.

Boere later admitted that with Bishop, Morley, Mike Marsh and David Burrows all living in the vicinity of the Swallow Hotel, his bar bill used to be £2,000 per month.

After his spell at Palace, he eventually joined Southend United before heading to Japan where he was horrendously stabbed in the eye at a nightclub, apparently, in an unprovoked attack. Forced to retire, he returned to Essex to run Epping's Half Moon pub for a while before going home to Holland.

For his part, Dowie drew a blank in his first outing against Chelsea who, inspired by their own Dutch master Gullit, painted Upton Park blue in a 3-1 win.

Unfortunately for Dicks, the Sky TV cameras were there to analyse his first-half clash with the sliding Spencer. The pint-sized Scot ended up with eight stitches on the top of his head and that led to an FA inquiry into the alleged stamping incident.

"I swear to God I didn't see it," protested Redknapp formulating a phrase that would subsequently be used with alarming regularity at Highbury by Arsene Wenger in the years to come.

"An accident!" insisted the uncompromising left-back with the beads of sweat still cascading down his shaven skull. An explanation, seemingly, accepted by the Chelsea match-winner.

Still the press wanted retribution, though, and Dicks' subsequent dismissal against Arsenal gave them the platform to pursue justice for the, by now, embarrassed Spencer.

Following three successive Highbury victories, West Ham had become the scourge of Bruce Rioch's Gunners. But a four-timer was never on the cards. Having already collected one yellow card, just before half-time, he could easily have collected a second for a wild lunge at Wright in the area which proved a double let-off when the Arsenal striker ballooned his spot-kick high and wide.

Early in the second half, however, the Terminator was terminated when he swiped another leg at future Hammer Wright and then left without waiting for the inevitable red card. Wright later made no mistake with his second penalty and, having made two substitutions, 10-man Hammers then saw Moncur retire with a scratched cornea.

Reduced to nine men, that was the cue for substitute keeper Les Sealey – wearing the number 12 shirt of outfielder Keith Rowland – to make his debut up front alongside the anonymous Dowie.

"We all agree, Sealey's better than Bergkamp," chanted the long-suffering Hammers' faithful as the game ended in farce and the suits at the Premiership merely added further insult to injury by slapping a petty £250 fine on the club for fielding Sealey in a shirt that carried neither his name nor squad number.

Having just told the withdrawn Hutch to find another club during a dug-out tirade, Redknapp then set about Dicks during the press call.

"I'm very disappointed. You can't keep making rash tackles. He got booked, he knew he was on thin ice. I told him at half time that we couldn't afford to go down to 10 men," roared H. "But we've got one or two undisciplined people at the club who let you down when the chips are down.

"When I brought Dicksy back I didn't have one bit of support from anybody at the football club. Not one bit from anyone on the staff or anybody above me. I took a gamble and up until this week Julian's disciplinary record has been excellent. But during the last two games he's let himself down and he's let us down.

"I don't want to see incidents like the Spencer one either," blasted the unstoppable H. "I've got my own opinions about it, but Julian swore to me on his kiddies' lives that he didn't mean to do it. I've got to believe him haven't I?"

With all the Dicks' furore, the mystery surrounding the absconding Boogers – apparently holed up on a Dutch caravan site – had somehow paled into insignificance.

"I've got a massive problem with him," admitted Redknapp. "He's come over here but he wants to be in Holland. What I've asked him to do he doesn't feel he should be doing, like running around and trying his best!"

To add to Redknapp's headache, Dicks was charged with misconduct for his part in the Spencer incident. And in a futile bid to win sympathy, agent Rachel Anderson revealed that the left back's twin daughters had been attacked in a carbon-copy playground incident by a 10-year-old Chelsea fan. But the FA were unmoved and, despite Spencer sending a letter to the Disciplinary Commission stating that he believed it to be an accident, following a three-hour hearing, the guilty defender was given a three-match ban.

"There's a war going on in Bosnia and yet Dicksy's daughters are on the front page of *The Sun*. What's the world coming to?" asked a perplexed Harry.

Languishing win-less in 19th place, his week was getting longer and longer by the second.

A quickly taken Moncur free-kick sealed a Coca-Cola Cup second round, first leg win at Bristol Rovers, while Storrie flew to Holland for showdown talks with Boogers whereupon he duly announced that the door was still open for Marco to pick up the pieces.

Two thunderous Dicks' penalties blasted Hammers to their first Premiership victory of the season – a 2-1 win over Everton.

However, Redknapp was clearly not eating off the same menu as his MD.

"Boogers has caused me a million problems," he winced. "The biggest problems I've ever had in football. I bought a player and within two weeks he doesn't want to be in England. He doesn't like the way we play, and he doesn't like being tackled in training. For £1m all you get is someone else's problems. It doesn't buy you a player. If they can tie up their boots they're worth a million. It's barmy! I got one who doesn't even want to tie his boots up! The best way out is for him to go back to Holland.

"He's due back on Tuesday and we're all looking forward to seeing him. I wouldn't bet on him still being here on Wednesday though!" he added sarcastically.

As it happened, Boogers, armed with a medical certificate declaring himself mentally unfit to play, and by now on unpaid leave, delayed his return for a few days more. His wife's difficult pregnancy had certainly not helped, but what had possessed Mad Marco to embark on a reported Dutch caravan holiday with the season underway was surely one only Amsterdam detective Van Der Valk could work out.

Trevor Smith, of the *Newham Recorder*, aptly described this latest debacle as one to top the previous season's Beauchamp fiasco. In a scathing attack on the club, he wrote: "Bunbury, Beauchamp, Boere, Boogers – while it can be validly argued that the combined money spent on that alliterative quartet of failed gambles would not have bought one proven quality striker, that is no consolation to Hammers followers. Whether or not it's true, they feel their hard-earned dough is dribbling down the drain . . . at the same time as they are regularly reminded the club is cash-strapped. And it is this that stops the present farce from being at all funny really."

Despite the win over Everton, there were clearly deep-seated problems down in E13. Still the gifted Hutchison was left out in the cold and with the defence still in disarray, 37-year-old Martin had suddenly emerged as the jewel in Hammers' tin-foil crown.

But the reluctant veteran was less than certain about his desire to play an active role in the inevitable battle against the drop, confiding: "I don't mind coming in for a few games now and then just to shore matters up a bit, but I'm too old to be playing week in and week out. It's getting hard at my age."

Even more alarming was Martin's revelation that, as Hammers headed to Southampton for their goalless live Sky TV encounter, Redknapp had apparently asked the former England World Cup star who he would rather partner, given Harry 'didn't really rate either Potts or Rieper!'

Dicks, Bishop and Cottee then found the target as Hammers saw off Bristol Rovers in a 3-0 Coca-Cola Cup second round, second leg victory.

Redknapp had insisted for months that he would not get involved in an auction for Michael Hughes and, after waiting and waiting before finally being blown out by Paris Saint-Germain, the Irishman returned like a breath of fresh air from Strasbourg for another season-long loan spell, while Frank Burrows joined the coaching staff as Youth Team Coach Paul Hilton and training ground 'co-coordinator' Ronnie Gale departed in quick succession.

In a throwback to the tabloid witch-hunts of the Macari era, the *Daily Mirror* soon reported the previous season's shenanigans aboard the Christmas party minibuses and inside the Dormy Hotel's room 164.

According to Redknapp, an insider had rifled his desk and sent the damming invoices to the gleeful tabloid.

"I said at the time that I was going to nail the mole," wrote H in *Harry Redknapp – My Autobiography*. "I suspected at the time who he was and my suspicions were later confirmed. In a revamp of my backroom staff I'd let a fella go who I think resented it. He felt he should have been offered a job on the coaching staff. He took the letters and sent copies to the *Daily Mirror*. The person was rumbled. It was sad that anyone should be so vindictive but I suppose that's life."

Cottee, meanwhile, had been on the trail of his first Premiership goal of the season and he duly bagged it to secure a 1-0 win at Wimbledon, while Dowie finally opened his account against champions Blackburn Rovers, for whom Alan Shearer salvaged a late, 1-1 draw.

Dowie's return to The Dell ended in disappointment when Cottee's strike was not enough to prevent a 1-2 defeat at the hands of Southampton in the Coca-Cola Cup third round.

As young Frank Lampard headed to Swansea City for an 11-match loan spell, Boogers – back in Blighty – sat on the Hillsborough bench alongside American John Harkes (7+6 apps). Although the Yank had just been sold by Derby County to the US Soccer Federation for £600,000, the enterprising Redknapp brought the ex-Owls' star to Upton Park on loan until the end of the season, pending the start of Major League Soccer Stateside.

Dowie's hopeful prod was enough to secure the 1-0 win over Sheffield Wednesday that sent Hammers up to 12th place.

Despite their five-match unbeaten run, they had always looked fragile and the arrival of Aston Villa simply blew them to smithereens. That West Ham escaped with a mere 1-4 reverse was a mini-miracle in itself.

With Martin's testimonial just seven days away, it was the worst possible result for the ageing defender who had been chasing shadows all afternoon.

Indeed, in the build up to the game against a Chelsea XI, there were no surprises when he announced his retirement at the end of the season.

And Simon Webster (0+5 apps) finally threw in the towel, too, two years after breaking his leg in that accidental pre-season training clash with Julian Dicks. Webbo subsequently qualified as a physiotherapist whereupon he returned to Upton Park before taking up a similar post at Gillingham.

One man to depart a bit earlier was loyal Ronnie Boyce, after 37 years at the Club. West Ham's hard-nosed decision to offer him the post of *part-time* Chief Scout saw him follow in the footsteps of the recently jettisoned Hilton and Gale, out of Chadwell Heath.

'Ticker' had served the club diligently as player, coach and scout and, with the likes of the invalid Dale Gordon still raking in enormous wages, it was ironic that the man who netted the winner in Hammers' 1964 FA Cup final victory over Preston North End was seemingly offered a paltry £5,000 settlement. Eventually, the Club apparently settled at around £10,000 plus his car.

"Storrie told me that the club was looking to make changes and would be letting me go. That was fair enough but the way I was treated hurt me," said Boyce, who had even recommended that the club should sign Blackpool rookie Trevor Sinclair, years before Redknapp bought the subsequent 2002 World Cup quarter-finalist for £1.5m in 1997. "All I wanted was to be shown a bit of appreciation and to be thanked for the service I had given the club. West Ham had changed, though, and it wasn't the same club that I knew and loved."

Martin, on the other hand, saw 8,710 turn up on a murky November afternoon for his benefit game. Three men with points to prove – Boogers, Williamson and Hutchison – each scored as Hammers fought back from two-down to draw 3-3. How West Ham could have done with the guesting Jamie Redknapp, Steve McManaman and Chris Waddle as permanent fixtures in the midfield.

It didn't take long, however, for Martin's ongoing disillusionment with the Upton Park regime to surface. The alleged presentation by the club of a £16,000 bill for services rendered at his game stuck in the loyal veteran's throat. Having never received a signing-on fee in 21 years, 'Stretch', conscious of the salaries commanded by the lesser-talented *nouveau* Hammers, asked for the costs to be waived in recognition of *his* services down the seasons. But the request apparently fell on the deaf ears of the board and that merely increased his desire to leave the club he had served so faithfully.

A training ground bust-up between Slater and Hutchison during an experimental six-a-side game, was then captured by the TV cameras. The Aussie was fined the PFA minimum of around £250 while, predictably, the Geordie found that his penalty was substantially more.

Not for the first time, Hutch knew he would never play for the club again, but by now the day of reckoning was drawing near.

With beleaguered Bolton Wanderers' boss Roy McFarland coming under increasing pressure, a 3-0 win at Brunton Park was topped off by Williamson's 80-yard solo dash that made the Trotters' disgruntled supporters even angrier.

"Fortunately, I had Frank Burrows on the bench alongside me!" said a relieved Redknapp, who branded the local natives 'evil' before returning to London and naming an unchanged team for a goalless draw against Liverpool.

And it was the same again against Queens Park Rangers three days later, too, as Cottee's late, late dribble settled the most tepid of London derbies to make it seven points in a week.

But those efforts were cruelly destroyed at Ewood Park, where a Shearer hat-trick ensured that the Fat Lady was singing her heart out by half-time as Blackburn Rovers romped to a 4-2 victory.

Elsewhere, Luton Town sealed the £700,000 signing of Feuer (0 apps) after making Hammers an offer that they could not refuse for an American keeper who had not played a single second's competitive football for the club.

Down on the south coast, the grieving Allen contemplated turning his loan spell at Portsmouth into a permanent £500,000 move for entirely personal reasons.

"All the time Dad was ill it just wasn't like playing proper football for me anymore," he confessed after his father Dennis succumbed to cancer.

With father watching son play each and every game, the pair had been inseparable and after every match at Upton Park they would drive to Brick Lane deep in the heart of the London's East End where they would sit eating bagels chewing over the events of the afternoon.

"Suddenly, there were no worries about the games, my life as a footballer changed from the day I heard he was ill. It was never the same for me. I lost all my inner drive and desire to make the most of myself which I'd had since I was a little kid," continued the still distraught Allen, who was rocked by the spiritual void left by his father's absence at the Boleyn Ground when Hammers had drawn with Spurs back in August.

"It was time to move on. My career was average but at least I finished with three very good games against Spurs – which was the only match Dad never saw me play at Upton Park – Manchester United and Forest."

Allen (202+30 apps 34 gls), who collected 44 yellow cards and one dismissal – ironically dished out the previous season against QPR on Dennis' final visit to Upton Park – during his six-year spell with the Hammers, signed off by mischievously sneaking back to the changing rooms and cutting up each of his team-mates' socks.

Following a stormy time at Portsmouth, he was then dismissed as Alan Pardew's assistant at Reading whereupon he developed his own unique style of leadership at Barnet and then Brentford as he became one of the rising stars of English-born managers.

With three players now chopped from the wage bill, it was rumoured that Redknapp was offered the chance to take Gheorghe Hagi on loan from Barcelona but, for reasons only known to himself, he apparently felt it was a gamble too far, and discussions had never got beyond the Romanian World Cup star's representatives.

Miklosko's disorientated, accidental clout on Everton striker Daniel Amokachi saw him sent off in a televised Monday night clash at Goodison Park. And with the

NEARLY REACHED THE SKY

East Enders – minus a substitute keeper on the bench – already a goal down, the extra large Dicks pulled on the extra, extra large goalie's jersey for the final 47 minutes.

The stand-in's first job was to pluck future Hammer David Unsworth's subsequent penalty from the net, but Dicks then stood firm amidst ironic chants of 'England's Number One', merely letting in a John Ebbrell slider as West Ham escaped with just a 0-3 defeat.

"Obviously with 10 men and me in goal, it was a case of stopping them scoring so many," said the unlikely keeper clutching an equally unlikely bottle of champers, courtesy of Sky TV. "It was good to be voted man-of-the-match but it's not the best champagne in the world, to be honest!"

After seeing the Miklosko's 160th consecutive appearance come to an abrupt halt, Redknapp fumed:

"How can that be serious foul play? It was a penalty, but I didn't think Ludo should have gone."

His counterpart Joe Royle was just as convinced about the Czech's guilt as *The Sun*, who cruelly nicknamed him *Judo Miklosko*.

"The ball's white, Dan's head is black!" insisted the Toffees' supremo.

Late goals from Cottee and Dowie wiped out Bishop's earlier own goal to give Hammers a 2-1 win over struggling Southampton at Upton Park, where Redknapp was full of praise for his match-winning former Saint.

"No disrespect, I really would have liked Les Ferdinand and Alan Shearer, but I only had £150,000 to spend. I bought a tremendous professional with my money. Iain Dowie has been a smashing buy for this football club."

Even Dell boss Dave Merrington jumped on the bandwagon: "Dowie's a player who uses what he's got in his locker to the best of his ability. He gives it everything. He'll make mistake after mistake, but you won't be able to criticise him for his honesty and his battling."

As Hammers headed to Middlesbrough, Boogers went under the knife for cartilage surgery after injuring himself playing for the reserves. Juninho, Boro's brilliant Brazilian drove Hammers nuts down by the Riverside. The diminutive South American simply roasted Redknapp's men as Middlsbrough went 3-0 up before the break.

"Suddenly, we conceded three goals and the game was over within the space of seven minutes. We defended badly," fumed Harry after seeing his side – minus Martin – fall to an eventual 2-4 defeat. "It's the blind leading the blind out there! Abysmal. We just can't keep relying on a 37-year-old."

But the Hammers' boss was already putting steps in place to replace his ageing centre-half.

Only the men in bowler hats could stop Karlsrühe's Slaven Bilic from moving to Upton Park in a club record £1.65m transfer, for the highly-rated, 19-times capped Croatian stopper still needed the work permit that would enable him to fulfill his dream of playing in the Premiership.

Fluent in English, Italian and German, Bilic, who was just one exam paper away from becoming a qualified lawyer back in the former war-torn Yugoslavia, was certainly nobody's fool and, having put in some useful displays at Chadwell Heath, everyone was anxious for him to pull on a claret and blue shirt.

Redknapp was also lining up the capture of two young defenders – Chris Coyne, a 17-year-old acquired from Australian outfit Perth Soccer Club for £20,000, and Graham Philson, purchased from Coleraine in a £30,000 deal.

After seeing Hammers' festive matches against Coventry City and Newcastle United frozen off, Sealey headed north for the New Year's Day game at Manchester City all set to make his goalkeeping debut, deputising for the suspended Miklosko.

But training just 24 hours before kick-off, the veteran stand-in ripped his calf muscle.

With Feuer sold to Luton, Redknapp's desperate attempts to by-pass the Premier League's 48-hour registration rule fell on deaf ears, and that meant an emergency call-up for youth-team keeper Neil Finn. Ivana Miklosko hastily sewed a '3' onto one of hubby Ludo's Number One shirts and started stitching on the name 'THINN' before being corrected and sending out Hammers' No 31 with the right identity thus saving the cash-strapped Hammers another £250 fine.

"There was no problem getting a keeper. Everyone wanted to help," insisted Harry after the 17-year, three-days-old YTS trainee became the Premiership's youngest-ever player in a 1-2 defeat. "But the fella at the Premier League was out playing golf and when we finally caught up with him he must have missed a few putts, because he said we couldn't have anybody. I didn't want David Seaman or Tim Flowers and I can't believe they couldn't have shown some common sense."

Finn (1 app) was soon to discover that those 90 minutes of fame would be followed by two years back in the youth team, ahead of a free transfer to Dorchester Town in spring 1998.

Meanwhile, Redknapp moved to sign goalkeeping legend Peter Shilton, who had been on loan at Coventry City. Shilts had 1380 appearances to his name including 997 league outings.

"It's quite an incentive for me to get to my thousand league appearances," suggested the record 125-times capped England international, who joined the club for an initial one-month loan spell alongside Birmingham City's veteran central defender, Chris Whyte (0 apps).

Suspension complete, Miklosko was back between the sticks for the FA Cup third round clash with Southend United who, ironically, fielded Mike Marsh, the one-time homesick midfielder who had now returned from Turkey only to still find himself 300 miles from Merseyside.

But an Upton Park giant-killing was never on the cards as Hammers won 2-0 to set up another comfortable looking home tie against Grimsby Town.

At Elland Road, Leeds United's rotund Swedish misfit Tomas Brolin hit a double to sink Hammers 2-0. And in an ironic twist, the Yorkshiremen's on-loan striker Lee Chapman was grounded, too, after his return to the scene of his greatest glories saw him red carded against another one of his former clubs, just 25 minutes into his second debut, for an over-enthusiastic aerial challenge on Rieper.

Still in Yorkshire, the out of favour, one-time record signing Hutchison

(33+6apps 13 gls) dropped out of the top flight to join Sheffield United for an initial £850,000.

"Unlike Mattie Holmes, I wasn't sad to see the back of Hutchison," announced Redknapp after finally giving up the battle to correct the wayward Geordie, who would go on to play for Everton, Sunderland and Scotland before...returning to Upton Park some six years later!

"I knew his background and thought he had talent but I felt badly let down. You don't really know people until you get them in the building. I saw him play for Liverpool reserves against Coventry in the last game before I signed him. He didn't try a leg and got sent off. Everything he did that day, he did once he came to this club, too. Every day, I'd say: 'C'mon Hutch,' or 'Well done Hutch' or 'Buck yer ideas up Hutch.' I tried everything but maybe he'll now change and grow up."

Manchester United finally got some joy at Upton Park as Eric Cantona's strike secured the 1-0 victory that put them nine points behind runaway leaders Newcastle, but their evening was slightly tempered by Nicky Butt's dismissal in a physical contest that saw another four Reds booked and Dicks heavily censured for an unpunished two-footed lunge on Andrew Cole.

On February 4, 1996, Alan Sealey, the two-goal hero of 1965 European Cup Winners' Cup victory over TSV Munich 1860, suffered a fatal heart attack, aged 53, and a minute's silence was held before the FA Cup fourth round tie against Grimsby Town, who surprisingly survived an onslaught to force a 1-1 draw.

Back in the Premiership, Hammers were leading Coventry City 2-1 when Frank Lampard junior made his Hammers debut as an 81st minute substitute, and although Noel Whelan equalised within seconds of his arrival, Dowie notched a 3-2 victory with a late strike.

Passport control was struggling to keep up with events down Green Street way.

Following a storming USA 94 that saw Romania reach the World Cup quarter-finals, £2.6m Ilie Dumitrescu had been recruited as part of Ossie Ardiles' infamous 'Famous Five'.

But the Argentine's exciting strategy of all out attack just did not get the results. While his cavalier quintet had been banging them in, his back four had been leaking goals all ends up, and following his dismissal, Ossie's successor Gerry Francis had set about reconstructing a Spurs' side with a spine.

Dumitrescu had just returned from a loan spell in Seville but, never one to miss out on a potential bargain, Redknapp's work permit-dependent bid of £1.5m was gratefully accepted by White Hart Lane chairman Alan Sugar.

However, Dumi's lack of appearances – he had not played in 75% of Spurs' games – proved problematical and not even his own union, the PFA, were prepared to support his case.

"What's the boy supposed to do? He's settled. He's got a house. He's a smashing lad and wants to play for West Ham," argued Harry after seeing his application declined. "I'm not buying him just to sit on the bench because he's played at the highest level."

"It would've been easier to buy him from his first club Steaua Bucharest," suggested club secretary Richard Skirrow after Hammers sought to apply for a new permit rather than an extension.

Such was the anticipation at Upton Park that one Sunday tabloid claimed Dumi was on a £40,000 bonus if he finished as the Premiership's top-scorer at any time during the term of his four-and-a-half-year contract.

Whether the mandarins at the Department of Education and Employment were mindful of Hammers' treatment of Canadian international Alex Bunbury, who subsequently started just two games following receipt of his work permit in 1992, is anybody's guess, but there were to be no such problems for Daniel Da Cruz Carvalho, a Portugal playboy who was well and truly set to stir the loins of the East End womenfolk.

The flamboyant 19-year-old had made his international debut against England at Wembley back in December and his Portuguese passport meant that there were no work permit obstacles to be overcome.

Indeed, he immediately went into the squad to face Nottingham Forest. And by the time he stepped from the bench to try a late, crowd pleasing, speculative 40-yard chip, Slater had already netted the goal that was to give Hammers a 1-0 win.

"Dani walked into the dressing room and all the lads said they're not bringing their wives to the games anymore. He looks like a film star. The other teams won't know whether to mark him or f*** him!" jested Redknapp.

And making his first start alongside Bilic, Dani's stock rose yet further when he netted what proved to be a fifth-minute winner at White Hart Lane that put an inflated £5m price-tag on his head.

Just 48 hours later, Hammers found themselves arriving in Cleethorpes for one of those wet Wednesday, February nights that test the loyalty of a club's supporters to the limits.

But Grimsby Town looked a club in crisis. Harry may have once given Hutchison a ham, tomato and cucumber makeover at The Dell but that was nothing compared to the alleged damage inflicted by Brian Laws on Ivano Bonetti.

For in an incandescent rage, the Mariners' player-coach had reportedly hurled a tray of chicken legs at his on-loan Italian defender, inflicting a broken cheekbone that required surgery.

And in a surreal pre-match PR exercise, Laws and the badly-bruised Bonetti staged an on-pitch reconciliation to show that they had made up following the previous weekend's serious fowl play.

However, with the feelgood factor returning to the North Sea coast, Town's 3-0 victory was not the only shock of the night as forgotten £750,000 signing Gordon emerged from the Blundell Park dug-out to make a surprise substitute appearance for the marinated Hammers – his first outing for two years.

Ironically, that secured a fifth round tie against Chelsea for the Division One side and the Blues were Hammers' next opponents, too. A 2-1 win at Stamford Bridge was followed by a sensational 2-0 victory over runaway, table-topping Newcastle United that took West Ham to within just three points of sixth place. Goals by Williamson and Cottee ensured that the Magpies' lead over Manchester United was clipped to just six points.

Future Hammer John Hartson ended West Ham's five-match winning sequence with a first-minute goal that gave Arsenal all three points at Upton Park, before a 2-2 draw at Coventry City left Redknapp targeting a top 10 finish.

Still Dumitrescu was having no joy in securing his precious work permit.

"I've had the lad in my office crying his eyes out, " claimed Harry. "All he wants to do is play football."

The equally elusive Boogers (0+4 apps) returned home to join Groningen on loan, his 95 minutes – based on a disclosed, seemingly reduced, transfer fee of £800,000 – having equated to £8,400 per minute!

"I could tell after three or four weeks that I had dropped a 'rick' with him," said Redknapp who, incredibly, later conceded that he had, indeed, bought the Dutchman on video evidence alone. "His attitude stank. Someone sent me a tape of Boogers in action and urged me to watch it. I was very impressed and for the first time in my life I signed a player purely on what I'd seen on video. The new season was upon us and we didn't have time to check him out any further."

But in one final post-script, it later transpired that the striker's reported caravan holiday had just been one greatly exaggerated urban myth.

"When Harry and Boogers fell out, Khris Raistrick from Clubcall phoned me on his mobile to ask if I had arranged his journey home," revealed former Hammers' travel agent and public address announcer, Bill Prosser. "I told him: 'Marco's decided not to fly, he may have gone by car again.' But the line was crackling and Khris thought I'd said: 'He may have gone to his *caravan.*' He put that on Clubcall and *The Sun* picked it up and ran a story about 'Barmy' Boogers going into hiding in his caravan!"

Still on the foreign front, following an agonizing seven-week wait, Dumitrescu was finally given his work permit thanks to the intervention of local MP – Chelsea fan Tony Banks.

"This is a good news story," said Education & Employment Minister, Cheryl Gillan.

"I want to work hard and, hopefully, I can do special things and score lots of goals for West Ham," smiled Dumi with one eye on the net and the other on shovelling his goals bonus into his deposit account.

The Eastern European duly made his long-awaited debut as a substitute in a 2-0 win over Middlesbrough but when Hammers were awarded a penalty, Dicks quickly swiped the ball to leave the Romanian in absolutely no doubt as to who took the spot kicks in the East End.

Sealey finally made his long-awaited goalkeeping debut at Newcastle United. But the match will best be remembered for Steve Potts' red card in a 0-3 defeat for collecting two quick-fire bookings inside the space of 28 seconds.

"That was the only time I was ever sent off," recalled Potts following a double assault on the theatrical David Ginola in a live Sky TV match that saw the Tuesday tabloids rolling out their 'Crack Potts' headlines "With the second one I actually got the ball and I thought that the referee should have been a bit more lenient, but I don't think 40,000 Geordies screaming at him exactly helped my case."

As Potts contemplated his suspension, Harry was keeping the Dean Court-Upton Park supply channel busy. Playmaker Scott Mean headed to Upton Park on loan with a view to a £200,000 permanent transfer and midfielder Matt Holland (0 apps) was reluctantly allowed to head in the opposite direction, joining the south coast club on a free transfer. That proved the springboard for Holland to go on and earn 44 Republic of Ireland caps during spells with Ipswich Town and Charlton Athletic, while Paul Mitchell (0+1 app) also returned to Bournemouth on a free transfer after playing just half-a-dozen minutes against Blackburn Rovers in 1994.

That was six minutes more than Darren Currie (0 apps) – nephew of gifted England playmaker Tony Currie – who, with his Hammers' career forced down a dead end by the influx of foreigners, joined Shrewsbury Town in a £30,000 deal.

Despite the presence of Shilts, yet another Australian – goalkeeper Steve Mautone – moved to Upton Park in a £60,000 transfer from Canberra Cosmos.

Hammers' beauty and the beast strike-force was on target in a 4-2 win over Manchester City as Dani netted his first goal for the club, while two-goal Dowie's 54th minute strike was to be his last for what would seem like an eternity. Future Hammers' skipper Steve Lomas was also sent off for fouling present captain Dicks, who also scored on a day when he discovered that, despite all the media hype, he was not going to be selected by England coach Terry Venables for the forthcoming Euro 96 warm-up against Bulgaria.

A 1-1 draw against Wimbledon meant that West Ham had taken 23 points out of a possible 33. The arrival of Bilic to partner Rieper had been a crucial factor and the Croatian's confidence had oozed through the team. Indeed, he had stood toe-to-toe with Dons' hard man Vinnie Jones in a heated stand-off, before boldly betting Dean Holdsworth a fiver that he would score from a corner.

In the end, Dowie's son proved the benefactor, for when loser Bilic paid the five-pound note to the Selhurst Park striker, he duly gave it to the youngster as a birthday present.

A lack-lustre performance at Anfield resulted in a 0-2 defeat to Liverpool, before Cottee's strike gave Hammers a 1-0 win over bottom-placed Bolton to send themselves into 10th spot.

Substitute Dani emerged from the Villa Park dug-out to set up a late Cottee equaliser against Aston Villa on a night remembered more for West Ham's unveiling of their yellowing 'ecru' away strip and a broken leg sustained by future Hammer, Gary Charles.

By now, Dani had fallen from favour with Redknapp after he released him for an Under-21 international and it subsequently transpired that he had been dropped by his Portuguese coach for going out to a nightclub.

And his socialising caused the Hammers' boss no end of trouble too.

"When he first came over to West Ham we put him up in the Swallow Hotel," wrote H in his autobiography. "A couple of days later he came up to me and said: 'Coach. Hotel no good. I have found another – The Dorchester! I want to see the sights.' In the end we got him a mini-suite at the Tower Hotel but he still wasn't happy so we rented him a flat in Docklands.

"Dani's playboy image was best highlighted when I took the players to Tenerife for a mid-season break. 'I want you down for training at 9:30am,' I said. The next day all the lads were in the lobby except for Dani. We went training without our

NEARLY REACHED THE SKY

little Portuguese film star. Come 1.30pm there was still no sign of him.

"I'd worked the lads hard and they were all relaxing by the pool when suddenly this tanned figure, walked towards us, hair immaculate, sun-glasses on, every inch the movie star. It was Dani. All the lads knew he'd picked up a bird, maybe even two or three? 'I'm fining you £1,000,' I said. 'Thank you. Thank you,' he replied. I just turned to Frank Lampard and said: 'He must have had a good night if it was worth a grand!'"

The teenager also failed to show at Chadwell Heath on the eve of Hammers' penultimate game of the season at Loftus Road, causing Harry to declare: "He's a natural without a doubt and I love him as a lad but he's got to learn that he must turn up for training and on time.

"I tried to call him all day but I just kept getting his answerphone. At 4.15pm he said he hadn't been feeling very well but it turned out he'd gone home to Portugal to sign a boot deal. How do I tell Ian Bishop and Danny Williamson, who do turn up every day, and on time, that they're not playing yet Dani is?"

Only victory could keep Queen Park Rangers' slim survival hopes alive and despite their 3-0 win over Hammers, results elsewhere conspired to condemn Ray Wilkins' side to the drop.

Watson (0+1 apps) made a 77th-minute substitute appearance that was destined to comprise the sum total of his Hammers' career, prior to a £100,000 move to Bournemouth a few weeks later.

At the final whistle, an over-ambitious Bilic tried to reassure the Rangers' player-manager.

"Slaven spoke to me in Italian first and English second. I thought: 'Good grief, this is most unusual.' He said: 'C'mon, you can stay up.' That was very pleasant . . . but wrong," revealed Wilkins, the former AC Milan midfielder who, having arrived in the home dressing room, then fittingly heard the club doctor break the bad news and prescribe relegation for Rangers.

After Dicks was named Hammer-of-the-Year, Rio Ferdinand was given his debut in the final game of the season against struggling Sheffield Wednesday, who found their Premiership status preserved by events elsewhere.

It really was a case of in with the new and out with the old. For substitutes Lampard and Ferdinand came on midway through the second half, while long-serving Martin stepped from the bench amidst a crescendo of cheers for a two-minute cameo appearance that marked the last of his 595 appearances in a 1-1 draw. And as he trudged off the Upton Park pitch for the final time to another standing ovation, the influx of foreigners had made the West Ham side unrecognisable from the team that had kicked the season off against Leeds United back in August.

By the time Dani's Sporting Lisbon came to town to contest a poorly attended end-of-season Centenary friendly in front of just 4,361 fans, it was clear that the Portuguese playmaker would not feature in Harry's plans for 1996-97 and, after playing for West Ham in a 1-4 defeat against his employers, H duly announced: "I'd have him back and persevere with him but he's earning too much money for a 19-year-old. Dani would have to be my star player for us to carry on paying him what we have been."

Dani (3+6 apps 2 gls) duly joined Ajax Amsterdam from Sporting Lisbon for a more realistic £2m and a few years later, having joined Benfica, startled officials reportedly found him sharing his suite at a five-star hotel in Estoril with six girls!

Notwithstanding the spectre of his Boogers blunder, it had been a good season for Harry who, following the stress of the previous Beauchamp-blighted campaign, had consolidated Hammers' Premiership status. Redknapp's reward came in the shape of a new five-year contract extension.

The future was bright, too, for a Hammers' squad containing Frank Lampard and Rio Ferdinand won the South East Counties League and finished runners-up to Liverpool in the FA Youth Cup final.

"I want to stay here at West Ham and I think those five years will just about finish me," Harry said after leading the club into tenth place – its highest league finish for 10 years.

Alvin Martin (588+7 apps + 34 gls) and Les Sealey (1+1 apps) moved to Leyton Orient on free transfers and just as cash-strapped Bournemouth looked to be on the brink of receivership, Redknapp made a welcome eleventh-hour swoop on his old club to re-sign Steve Jones – the player he had swum the ocean to get £150,000 for – in a £200,000 deal.

"Jonah's done smashing down there, he's got pace, can score goals and for two-hundred grand he's a very useful player to have in our squad," he said.

Capped 40-times by his nation, Miklosko declined the opportunity to be third-choice keeper at Euro 96 but he still headed to the 80-1 rated, Czech Republic's training camp to help coach his fellow countrymen to the Wembley final, where they eventually lost to the Germans' Golden Goal.

Hammer-of-the-Year Dicks had been in with a shout of making it into England's Euro 96 squad but the uncompromising defender had always been on a collision course with the FA establishment.

And the outspoken left-back all but ended his slim hopes of an England cap when he declared that he would rather spend the summer building a home for his dogs.

"The truth is I don't want to go and play for England," he declared. "If Terry Venables called me tomorrow I'd say: 'No thanks.' It would only be an after-thought. I wouldn't use the summer to build kennels though, I'd get someone to do them for me!"

Injury ruled Dumitrescu out of Romania's Euro 96 challenge, too, but as Bilic (Croatia) and Rieper (Denmark) prepared to join up with their national squads for the tournament, it was clear that the Hammers' boss had already developed a keen taste for foreign fare.

Back in April, Redknapp had flown to Spain to watch Espanyol's Florin Radicioiu in action against Real Sociedad only for the game to be washed out, but now the Romanian international striker was UK-bound.

And with the European Championships taking place in England, the summer was to prove one huge, inviting, window-shopping opportunity for Harry.

PLAYERS IN

Slaven Bilic	Karlsrühe SC	£1,650,000 (Record).
Marco Boogers	Sparta Rotterdam	£800,000
Chris Coyne	Perth	£20,000
Iain Dowie	Crystal Palace	£500,000
Ilie Dumitrescu	Tottenham Hotspur	£1,500,000
Steve Jones	Bournemouth	£200,000
Stan Lazaridis	West Adelaide	£300,000
Steve Mautone	Canberra Cosmos	£70,000
Graham Philson	Coleraine	£30,000
Robbie Slater*	Blackburn Rovers	
	exchange for Holmes + £600,000 (in)	

LOANS IN

Dani	Sporting Lisbon
John Harkes	US Soccer Federation
Michael Hughes	Racing Club Strasbourg
Scott Mean	Bournemouth
Peter Shilton	Coventry City
Chris Whyte	Birmingham City

PLAYERS OUT

Martin Allen	Portsmouth	£500,000
Jeroen Boere	Crystal Palace	£374,500
Marco Boogers	Groningen	Free transfer
Darren Currie	Shrewsbury Town	£30,000
Ian Feuer	Luton Town	£700,000
Matt Holland	Bournemouth	Free transfer
Matthew Holmes*	Blackburn Rovers	
	exchange for Slater + £600,000 (in)	
Don Hutchison	Sheffield United	£800,000
Alvin Martin	Leyton Orient	Free transfer
Paul Mitchell	Bournemouth	Free transfer
Matthew Rush	Norwich City	£330,000
Les Sealey	Leyton Orient	Free transfer
Mark Watson	Bournemouth	£100,000
Simon Webster	Retired	

Chapter 10
1996-97

A BRIGHT FUTRE?

Dogs barked and inquisitive joggers stopped in their tracks as the white stretch limousine negotiated its way along the snaking entrance to Hainault Forest, a Ludek Miklosko punt from Hammers' Chadwell Heath training HQ. Having returned from their summer breaks, the squad was just about to embark on the first of several, gruelling cross-country runs that would sweat out the Stella, Smirnoff and sangria excesses of the summer days just gone by.

But even they were distracted from their warm-up as the gasoline-guzzling, gleaming long limo pulled up at the kerbside and despatched a tardy, cigar-chomping Paulo Futre, ready in full kit, from behind its darkened windows.

Harry Redknapp had, predictably, spent the summer recruiting and the East End was full of expectation as he returned laden with cosmopolitan purchases.

Futre was his highest-profile capture. The 41-times capped Portuguese international had grown into a European superstar during a round of cross-border moves but debilitating knee injuries had restricted his ability to weave his way through statuesque defences, and mighty AC Milan duly decided to release him upon the expiry of his contract on June 30.

"Paulo has told me that ever since he was a little boy walking the streets of Lisbon, he's always wanted to play for West Ham," jested Redknapp. "On the way he's had to stop off at Sporting Lisbon, FC Porto, Atletico Madrid, Benfica, Marseille, Reggiana and AC Milan but he eventually got here!

"If he's only lost a yard of pace, though, he's still got four in hand on anyone else! We've just got to get the ball to him and he'll make something happen.

"When he gets a football he's so electric, so he needs his rests during games. But just remember, a genius doesn't have to run all over the field."

And as Derby County's Jim Smith flew confidently into Milan to seal his signature, Futre showed the Italians that he could still sell a dummy as he jetted out to Heathrow to meet Redknapp and discuss a contract containing a cancellation option should his fitness desert him.

Elsewhere, it was an open secret that Harry had been on the trail of Florin Raducioiu for several months in the hope that he could sign him before Euro 96. But the Romanian striker – with 20 goals in 32 international appearances – preferred to keep his powder dry in case he had an explosive tournament that would drive his worth yet higher.

As it happened, the 26-year-old former Dinamo Bucharest, Bari, Verona, Brescia and AC Milan goal-getter managed just one strike – against Spain – as the under-performing Romanians failed to repeat their World Cup heroics of USA 94 and a relieved Redknapp paid Espanyol a club record £2.4m for their star striker.

But the summer spending had not stopped there.

Slaven Bilic's Croatia may have come out on top over Marc Rieper's Denmark with a 3-0 win on their way to the Euro 96 quarter-finals, but despite having two international stoppers Harry still wanted further central defensive cover. And he duly acquired Richard Hall from Southampton for a fee of £1.9m.

Defender Mark Bowen, 32, also joined on a free transfer from Norwich City, while the hitherto on-loan Michael Hughes took advantage of the Bosman ruling to sign permanently upon expiry of his Racing Club De Strasbourg contract.

Some £7m had been committed in fees and wages and there was little to balance the books as Malcolm McPherson (0 apps) joined Brentford, while the squad was also forced to find a new Entertainment Secretary when the injury prone, scorer of their first-ever Premiership goal, Dale Gordon (9+2 apps 1gl), joined Bournemouth as player-coach, much to the relief of the East End minibus trade.

Scott Mean moved the other way from Dean Court in a £200,000 deal and Scott Canham (0 apps) headed to Brentford for £25,000. Graham Philson (0 apps) returned to Ireland on a free transfer to Linfield, while an inconsistent and precious Robbie Slater (22+7 apps 2 gls) joined Southampton for £250,000 following an infuriating, injury-punctuated spell at Upton Park that had, at times, left Harry tearing his hair out.

"Slater's got a broken tie-up!" the Hammers' boss had once announced as he went through the squad's casualty list.

Notwithstanding Blackburn's £600,000 cash adjustment, Slater had proved a poor replacement for Mattie Holmes and, unlike his fellow Aussie winger Stan Lazaridis, he had done little to endear himself to a demanding Chicken Run – the Hammers' aficionados seated at pitch level within touching distance of the players on the east side of the stadium.

Steve Jones marked his return to the club with the winner in a friendly at Margate, while Hall injured a tendon in a collision with a postman, in a goalless draw at part-timers Carshalton Athletic.

Having graced Milan's San Siro stadium, Futre found himself scoring in a friendly at Dagenham & Redbridge's Victoria Road ground, alongside Hughes.

Meanwhile, Raducioiu endured a hard baptism in English football when he made his debut at Torquay United. Elbowed by Jon Gittens – a player reportedly all set to be sued by Reading's Trevor Morley for allegedly fracturing his skull in an aerial challenge – this proved no pre-season 'friendly' as the fragile durability of the latest recruit to Redknapp's foreign legion was tested from Day One.

Gittens was immediately substituted at the behest of an over-generous referee who kept his red card in his pocket, before being subsequently fined two weeks' wages. "It was not an elbow, it was a punch," admitted Torquay chairman Mike Bateson after seeing Raducioiu depart with blood streaming from his wound.

With the pre-season preparations following a carefully planned exercise programme designed to optimise the squad's fitness levels in time for the opening game of the season at Highbury, physio John Green headed to Hammers' local City Limits leisure club to finalise arrangements for a group gymnasium booking.

Left in charge of a fitness session back at the Chadwell Heath, a senior member of the coaching staff had decided to round off the session by putting the players through their final paces with a series of the 70s and 80s style shuttle sprints that he had endured as a Hammers' defender.

But it was all too much all too soon. Hamstrings, thighs and the odd calf snapped like under-strength fishing lines twanging under the stress of a cantankerous carp and the gob-smacked Green returned to base facing carnage.

"I've had a million problems in the build-up to the start of the season. I was four or five players away from my best 11," announced the injury-ravaged Redknapp, whose selection problems as the curtain was about to be raised on the new campaign were compounded by a pre-match argument over…a shirt number.

A dislocated finger almost saw Miklosko make way for 46-year-old Peter Shilton and, as the injury-decimated Hammers prepared to kick off the campaign at Arsenal, it was about to become the *Highbury Stadium Mystery: Part Two* as Futre's subsequent eleventh-hour omission from the bench was inconsistently explained away.

As the team line-ups were distributed around the press room at 2.00pm, the West Ham fans at the Clock End were left asking: 'What the Radi hell's going on?'

Raducioiu nursed a torn calf, Hall and Dumitrescu also remained injured, while Futre was on the bench alongside Bowen.

For all the summer transfer activity, it was left to £200,000 Steve Jones to partner Dowie up front in an opening game that was destined to end in a 0-2 defeat.

But before the teams had even stepped onto the pitch, kit manager Eddie Gillam had to report Futre's dissatisfaction with his shirt to Redknapp. And he was not complaining about its fit.

Shaking his head, the Hammers' Number 16 was not a pleased Paulo.

"Futre wear 10!" pleaded the Portuguese prima donna pointing towards John Moncur, who had carried that squad number over from the previous campaign.

Harry frantically tried to diffuse the situation by explaining that the squad numbers had been registered at the Premier League and could not be switched.

"Futre just said: 'I f*** off. No play.' and the next minute he was in a cab and heading home," recalled Redknapp, who hurriedly persuaded referee Paul Durkin that scapegoat Frank Lampard had filled out the team-sheet incorrectly, in order that he could then pluck Rio Ferdinand from one of the Highbury lounges and frantically plonk him on the bench.

Post-match, the tabloids had a field day as Harry tried to douse the flames.

"People ought to do their homework because they write things that just aren't true," he protested with compelling plausibility. "Nothing at all happened at Highbury. On the Friday I'd spoken to Paulo about not playing because he hadn't trained. He said: 'Maybe I can be substitute.' I replied: 'No.' Paulo then added: 'Good, I'll rest for a few more days.' I drove to Arsenal because I was going home to Bournemouth afterwards and when I arrived, Frank had already filled in the team sheet and put Futre's name down and given him a shirt. Paulo was saying:

NEARLY REACHED THE SKY

'No sub! No sub!' Obviously he meant 'I'm not supposed to be one of the substitutes.' On the Sunday, all the papers are saying he refused to be sub because he wasn't number ten. What a load of cobblers."

But the truth will always out.

And as the Monday tabloids started to break the story, Redknapp then found a delegation hammering on his door.

Having told Futre, his agent and his lawyer that too many numbered shirts had already been sold to enable the change, according to Harry, the player then offered to pay £100,000 for his precious *Numero Dezasseis* shirt.

In the end, the beleaguered Hammers' boss brokered a deal whereby golf-mad Moncur could have a free two-week stay at Futre's luxury villa on the Algarve in exchange for his Number 10 squad number. Thankfully, for a relieved H, the pedantic suits at the Premier League agreed to the early season switch.

"Obviously wearing Number 16 was a problem for Paulo," said Moncs after negotiating a deal of which his outspoken agent Eric Hall would have been monster, monster proud. "To be honest it really doesn't bother me. Sure, I've played well in that number 10 but, then again, I've played really badly in it, too!"

Sporting his favoured Number 10 shirt, Futre stepped from bench to inspire a recovery as Hammers battled back to force a 1-1 draw against Coventry.

Harry may have placated his 'Portu-geezer' but already he was beginning to see that this once-purring Rolls Royce had been around the block too many times.

"Paulo tires so I'm going to have to use him in short bursts," he admitted, both lowering his sights and managing the expectations of the supporters.

Southampton were leading 1-0 when Romanian substitutes Raducioiu and Dumitrescu joined the fleet-footed Futre to engineer a thrilling recovery that saw Hughes level and Dicks blast the winner from the spot.

"There are a lot of fine footballers here now and we've got to look towards playing in Europe next season," insisted Dumitrescu after getting his first 30 minutes of the season under his belt in the 2-1 win.

The three musketeers had simply fired the imagination of Upton Park in a frenetic final half hour that had seen the sorry Saints put to the sword. And having been danced dizzy all afternoon, the bedazzled Francis Benali was also dismissed for attempting to launch the tormenting Futre into the Hammers' supporters.

"These are exciting times! The fans will love watching us," enthused a breathless H after seeing his attacking jigsaw puzzle fit menacingly together. "We'll have our ups and downs, we won't always win but we'll certainly entertain."

But that predicted rollercoaster ride started far more quickly than the Hammers' boss could ever have envisaged.

"We couldn't defend to save our lives," he roared after seeing Middlesbrough's own foreign legion of 'silver fox' Fabrizio Ravenelli, Emerson and Juninho tear Hammers apart in a 4-1 romp down by the Riverside.

The hitherto reformed Dicks received his first booking in an incredible 26 games after Boro's greying Italian fell as though fatally shot by the mafia and as the Teesside media congratulated him for his side's participation in an absorbing attacking encounter, Redknapp snarled: "Well, I'm glad YOU enjoyed it."

Hammers stayed in the north-east for their televised Sunday clash with Sunderland but it really was a choker at Roker as the sides shared a lacklustre goalless draw in which Sky TV struggled to show any action replays.

"You can't accuse me of being defensive," declared H after, effectively, seeing just seven of his outfield players battle for a point. "I started with three foreign forwards who wouldn't have a clue how to defend."

Deep down, however, Harry knew that his foreign policy had inherent flaws.

"There was a howling wind and Sunderland were swarming in on our goal and Futre, Dumitrescu and Raducioiu were standing there on the halfway line just looking on," he recalled. "I knew then that it wasn't going to work long term."

Indeed, the culture clash led to unwelcome cliques emerging in the dressing room while some of the battling British players struggled to come to terms with the apathetic work ethic of the expensive, highly-paid, imports.

And as rumours of huge pay differentials between the home-grown lads and the overseas mercenaries escalated, the chasm simply widened.

While West Ham had themselves exploited a loophole in Bilic's Karlsrühe contract that allowed him to leave the *Bundesliga* outfit if ever a bid of £1.65m came in for him, the canny Croatian had insisted in the insertion of a similar clause – this time set at £2.5m – in his Hammers' deal.

A cocktail of progressively impressive Premiership performances, coupled with his country's march to the last eight at Euro 96, had projected him to the top of many shopping lists, Manchester United and Tottenham Hotspur included.

Somehow, Spurs' Gerry Francis had discovered that £2.5m would be enough to prise Super Slav northwards across London

But as Bilic seemingly looked to invoke that clause, according to Redknapp, his lively legal mind had, for once, let him down.

"Slaven said: 'You must sell me, it says so in my contract.' I replied: 'No, I've read your contract and it says if we get an offer of £2.5m or more and *we* want to sell you and you want to go, then the deal goes through. But *we* don't want to sell you.' It took a few seconds for this news to sink in, then he reacted angrily. 'No, no, no. You have tricked me,' he argued. Bilic is a lawyer and must have thought his contract was watertight. But I went to the University of the Street in Stepney and I done him up like a kipper," gloated H in his autobiography.

Snookered on the baulk cushion, the only angle available to the disappointed Croatian was one of damage limitation.

"There was a clause that said we would either discuss a new contract after Euro 96 or I could go for £2.5m," revealed the stammering Slaven opening the way to salvage some pride. "That clause was one of the reasons why I signed for West Ham in the first place. I knew if I did well then it was my big chance. I thought: 'Slaven, you're 27-years-old and you have to play your best football to make the best deal for yourself.'

"I've never ever wanted to leave West Ham. I've read all the stories that I'm greedy, disloyal and just looking for money. None of that's true. My family is trying to lead a good and honest life and back home we even give to a charity for poor people and hospitals. That shows we are not selfish.

"But I can't stop other clubs wanting me, can I? Neither I nor my agent went to Manchester United or Tottenham and said: 'Please buy Slaven.' Anyway, I would only leave West Ham to join a big club and Spurs are just not big enough."

Former England coach Terry Venables had accused the mild-mannered defender of doubling his wages less than 20 games into his Premiership career.

"That's private!" said the law student clearly uncomfortable with the line of questioning that had seen reports of a new four-year deal worth £10,000 per week.

"We agreed to give him a new contract," confirmed Harry. "That made him the best-paid player at the club by miles. He had a new clause inserted that if a club offered anything over £4.5m for him, we would have to sell, whether we liked it or not. I was happy with that amount of money for a 28-year-old defender."

Just as Bilic had rocketed up the wages league, for several weeks, Tony Cottee had been courted by Malaysian outfit Selangor. In an on-off-on deal that suited everybody, the club had the opportunity to recoup £775,000 for their 31-year-old striker, while the prolific goal-scorer could set up one last big pay day.

"The move is a good one and helps to give my family security," confirmed TC after finding his first-team opportunities limited by the foreign invasion.

Following a 0-2 defeat against Wimbledon in which Futre retired after half-an-hour, Hammers scraped a 1-1 draw in a Coca-Cola Cup second round, first leg tie at Barnet on September 18, 1996 where Aussie keeper Steve Mautone made his debut and, more tellingly, Cottee – who memorably scored on his debut against Spurs on New Year's Day 1983 – netted what was to be his 146th, and final, goal for the club.

A 2-0 win at Forest – where Rieper was sent off – was followed by a 1-0 victory over Barnet in a flat Coca-Cola Cup second leg, in which man-of-the-match Bilic celebrated his new deal with the winner.

That tie against Barnet – a club he went on to manage – was to prove the final outing for Cottee (323+13 apps 146 gls), who carried on training at the club pending his departure to the Far East in the New Year.

The rigours of the Premier League were also beginning to take their toll on Futre and, after just four starts and a substitute outing, he was finding the going tough.

And as Hammers' physio John Green tried to help the fading star, it was clear that the road to recovery was not going to be a two-way street. Pampered on the foreign circuit, the precious Portuguese playmaker struggled to come to terms with the English ratio of one physiotherapist *per team* rather than *per player*, while all efforts to cajole him into a lap of the pitch ended with the hyper-ventilating Futre having withdrawal pangs for fags rather than football.

"Paulo seemed to associate quality with the amount of man hours spent on him," recalled Green. "You don't need a physio to count out 150 sit-ups but, sadly, he expected that. Surely players have got to do some things for themselves? He was supposed to have played for some of the best clubs in the world, but he was one of the least fit players we had at the club. I wouldn't have even let him *train* with the first team, let alone *play* for them!"

With time on his hands, however, Futre did help to persuade the twice-capped Hugo Porfirio to move to Upton Park on loan until the following July, with

Hammers having the first option to sign him for £800,000 by February 1, 1997.

"I spoke to Dani, who said that West Ham is a good friendly club," announced a diplomatic Hugo. "But I didn't talk to him about going out and about!"

On a hastily arranged journey into the inner depths of east London to find out just what was going on, Luis-Miguel Santos of Portugal's leading soccer daily *A Bola* declared: "Sporting Lisbon are mad to let Porfirio leave!"

Convinced that he had the new Futre, Harry predicted: "Hugo's a special talent and will be a good player for West Ham United for years to come. We certainly won't be letting him go. He's our player and no one can nick him!"

Bilic was also on target against Liverpool but the Merseysiders still left Upton Park with a handy 2-1 win and following that victory, the astute Redknapp sent Rio Ferdinand to the south coast where he enjoyed a two-month, 10-match loan spell.

It was all part of an apprenticeship that would see the young central defender return from Bournemouth all the more street-wise ahead of becoming one of the most sought-after commodities in Europe.

Substitute Porfirio had made his debut against Liverpool and there was to be a Mersey theme to his first full start, too, as he stepped out in a 1-2 defeat at Everton.

"That Portuguese lad looked useful!" observed Toffees' boss Joe Royle.

Another handy-looking Portugeezer was Dani, who bagged two goals for Ajax Amsterdam in their 4-1 Champions League victory over Glasgow Rangers.

"Let's face it they were only headers against Rangers," said Harry dismissing his former playboy's double-Dutch effort.

A 1-0 win over Leicester City at Upton Park was the precursor to the Hammers felling Nottingham Forest in the Coca-Cola Cup third round. Just what the dancing Dani had made of the dogged Dowie the previous season was anyone's guess.

And, on paper, there was to be another culture clash as the absence of Futre, Raducioiu and Dumitrescu again saw the determined Dowie partnering a Portuguese prodigy.

Dowie's last goals had come in the 4-2 win over Manchester City back in March when Dani had also struck and, again, an Anglo-Portuguese partnership prevailed as the craggy striker bagged a double, while Porfirio also found the net in a 4-1 victory.

Hugo's honeymoon continued in a 2-1 win over manager-less, bottom-placed Blackburn Rovers – where he had once been on trial – to further endear himself to an Upton Park faithful already urging the club to take up that option to sign him ahead of the expiry of their upcoming February option.

But conscious that there may be trouble ahead, the on-loan striker was determined not to commit himself too soon and a season-long game of cat and mouse was set to endure.

As the bronzed, muscular frame of Futre cut through the water at the Swallow Hotel gathering admiring stares from a gaggle of female swimmers, Porfirio sat pool-side trying to fathom out his manager's eagerness to sign him from Lisbon, so quickly.

"You can have this for £800,000 now," he proffered, pointing at his can of Coca-Cola. "Or you can still continue drinking it, wait a little while and then have it for nothing. Why would you want to pay so much for something you can have for free a little later?"

For Redknapp, an early plunge into the market would secure Porfirio's signature and, while accepting they would possibly see a fair proportion of the sale proceeds evaporate into agents' fees and expenses, Sporting Lisbon would also get some money for the international star they had hand-reared from the age of 12.

On the other hand, as a Bosman case, hot-foot Hugo could dictate his own signing-on fee and ongoing salary with any suitor agreeing to sign him on August 1. Provided he could sustain his early form throughout the season, he would be much more marketable as a free agent.

But he also ran the risk of there being no takers for his services at the salary levels he could secure in England at West Ham before February 1. Quite simply the decision was his. And his alone.

A 0-1 defeat at the hands of Spurs was followed by a 1-1 draw at table-topping Newcastle United, where Keith Rowland headed home what was to prove his only goal for the club.

After another 1-1 stalemate with Derby County, Hammers entertained second division Stockport County in the Coca-Cola Cup third round, where Raducioiu – making only his fifth start – finally found the net for the first time in his injury-punctuated opening to the campaign.

"It's harder in England because the game is very fast but I've tried very hard to accustom myself to the English ways," pleaded the Romanian following a disappointing, shock, 1-1 draw. "People have been waiting for some time now and I feel a little bit of pressure.

"My son is due in mid-December. I scored the goal in the first game and now I have to go to the hospital at the time of the second match with my wife Astrid!" joked Raducioiu, prophetically indicating that, torn between a possible trip to the labour ward and the long coach journey to Greater Manchester, he was not certain to make the replay.

By now, Futre's chances of a comeback were receding, while – despite seeing the chances of a work permit renewal diminishing by the hour – the club denied that it had instructed agents to tout Dumitrescu's availability around the world.

One player definitely on his way, though, was Epping-born Adrian Whitbread (6+8 apps). The unwitting pawn in the deal that offloaded Beauchamp to Swindon Town, he had not ended up at Upton Park out of mutual choice and had always seen his first-team chances severely limited.

Following a loan spell at Portsmouth, Whitbread opted to make the move permanent in a £225,000 transfer and after linking up with Martin Allen at both Fratton Park and then Reading, he subsequently became Mad Dog's assistant at Brentford when he took over as manager at Griffin Park in 2004.

After a goalless draw against Sheffield Wednesday, Hammers then slumped 0-2 at Aston Villa. Having fallen to 15th place in the league, the first rumblings of 'Redknapp Out' emerged from the Bobby Moore stand.

The academy had gone off campus. No longer were there any lads from Canning Town, Plaistow and Romford. Instead, it was all Croatia, Portugal and Romania and things looked pretty ominous as Manchester United took a two-goal lead at Upton Park through Ole Gunnar Solskjaer and David Beckham.

But, once again, that certain something about West Ham's inherent desire to scupper United reared its head, as Raducioiu showed undoubted class to pull one back, and then Dicks levelled it at 2-2 with an invasion-inducing penalty in a thrilling, late recovery that, again, left Alex Ferguson fuming.

Almost inevitably, Futre (4+5 apps) decided to call it a day and his pay-as-you-play contract was duly shredded.

"It was a fantastic idea to come to England, but I just couldn't give it my best," he said after bidding *adeus* to the East End and heading home to the Algarve to prepare for the arrival of the Moncur golfing entourage. "It was my choice, I was in too much pain with my knee and I don't want to be playing if I can't do it anymore. Believe me, it was for the best."

It was a sad day for Harry, for 'free' transfer Futre had still shown in, admittedly, short spurts just what might have been.

"I knew it was a gamble," conceded 'H' acknowledging you only ever get what you pay for. "It was a chance that we took but it just didn't work out, did it?"

By now it was pretty obvious that Dumitrescu was about to be shunted into the sidings, too. But as the Romanian sat on the team coach on the eve of that inhospitable Coca-Cola Cup replay at Stockport County, the absence of his fellow countryman was, ultimately, going to lead to the dishonourable discharge of another foreign legionnaire, too.

"We hung around for an hour while we tried to track Raducioiu down," recalled Redknapp recounting another tale that would end up in East End folklore. "Dumitrescu reckoned he didn't have a clue where he was but I reckon he knew he wasn't going to turn up. On the day of the match we again tried to track him down, too. Then a friend spotted him shopping in Harvey Nichols in London. I knew then that I had to get rid of him."

On a miserable monsoon-like Manchester night, West Ham should have fired themselves into the Coca-Cola quarter-finals. Instead they shot themselves in the foot. It looked to be going to plan when Dicks gave them the lead midway through the first half, but within two minutes, County levelled in the most bizarre fashion.

For Dowie, his neck-muscles taut and tense, outjumped everyone to power a header past a bewildered Miklosko, and shortly afterwards Brett Angell sent the sports editors racing for their 'Shockport' headlines as the second division side progressed into the last eight.

"I tried to head the ball over our crossbar," explained Dowie, dismissing the theories that he had either forgotten which way Hammers were kicking or that he had been blinded by the Edgeley Park floodlights. "Instead the ball went into my own net. It was a genuine mistake by me, a misdirected header."

"Seeing the reaction of the fans was a tough moment for me but when you do something bad they're entitled to have a go at you," continued the Northern Ireland striker, whose luck took an even further turn for the worse when he suffered a spiral fracture of the leg on the half-hour mark.

That saw the call for urgent reinforcements and as Christmas approached, Mike

NEARLY REACHED THE SKY

Newell (6+1 apps) joined, in what was destined to be a goalless loan spell from Birmingham City, ahead of a 1-3 defeat at Chelsea that left Hammers languishing in 16th spot.

Back in 1987, American property magnate Irving Brown had, according to the *Daily Express* tried to mount a £1m takeover bid for the club, only to be foiled by Lady Penelope Ogilvy – the grand-daughter of founder Arnold Hills.

Lady Penelope, lived in a Scottish mansion some 400 miles from Upton Park and she certainly came to the rescue of the Cearns family when she refused to sell her shares, just as her ancestors had done back in both 1927 and 1949, when they declined to sell in hostile bid situations, too.

Now, more than a decade on from Brown's approach, it was former Arthur Prince bookmaking chain proprietor and millionaire racehorse owner, Michael Tabor, who was to launch a takeover bid at the club's annual general meeting.

Solicitor Henry Montlake – Tabor's representative – saw his proposal to be elected to the board defeated as Terence Brown was re-elected chairman.

Montlake had circulated a letter to shareholders outlining Tabor's apparent interest in injecting £30m into the club for players and ground improvements.

According to the *Newham Recorder* Montlake's letter stated: *"I intend to try and persuade you that Mr Brown and his fellow directors have not behaved and are not behaving in the best interests of the company and West Ham United. Mr Tabor can provide for West Ham the sort of finance it needs to buy the players that must be acquired in order to be successful. He is not seeking to make any short or long-term profit but wants to make sure that a long-term benefit will be provided for the club and its supporters. Without Mr Tabor's investment, it is difficult to see how the board can achieve rendering the club viable for the future."*

For their part, the directors issued their own letter countering Montlake's claims, and with Brown and his colleagues holding a huge majority stake, Monaco tax-exile and lifelong Hammers fan Tabor had little real chance of succeeding with his hostile takeover bid.

On the goalkeeping front, the frustrated Shilton (0 apps) was still marooned on 997 appearances when commercially-astute Barry Hearn decided to unlock the value in that 1,000th league appearance.

Swapping the returning veteran, Les Sealey, for the creaking custodian, the Leyton Orient supremo duly organised a Sky TV spectacular to celebrate the milestone and, fittingly, Shilts was just grand as he kept a clean sheet in a goalless draw against Brighton & Hove Albion at Brisbane Road.

The ailing Redknapp missed the only game of his entire Boleyn Ground tenure as West Ham beat Sunderland 2-0 at Upton Park, where 85th minute substitute Raducioiu took another step towards endearing himself to the home crowd by outsprinting future Hammer Andy Melville and climaxing his 50-yard run with an unstoppable shot.

"Players get the hump when they're not in the side but Florin's as happy as a sand boy now after scoring that great goal," enthused stand-in boss Frank Lampard.

"The way Raducioiu scored West Ham's second goal was class of the highest order," announced *The Sunday Telegraph*. "The display of affection from the

Upton Park fans to greet the Romanian showed they have not lost faith in him. And they were rewarded as Raducioiu ruthlessly exposed the Sunderland defence."

But lying in his sick bed watching television, Harry had a different view of that Radi rocket.

"He tried to jump out of the way of the defender because he thought he was going to get walloped," argued the Hammers' boss, unconvincingly.

Whereas Dumitrescu had never really won over the crowd, Radi's goal-scoring reputation had convinced the locals that he could cut it and, certainly, his goals against Manchester United and Sunderland supported the view.

Unlike the moody and arrogant Dumi, Radi was more popular with his team-mates and, intriguingly, the pair from Bucharest were not overly close to each other either.

"Just because we are both from Romania it doesn't mean that we have to be friends and go out with each other," declared Raducioiu, who had endured a more testing apprenticeship at Dinamo Bucharest, compared to Dumi who had started out, as an eight-year-old, across the city at the state-influenced Steaua, where he duly became one of disgraced former president Ceaucescu's footballing pets. Dumitrescu had been treated like royalty back home. He expected the same treatment in England, too, but at times his boorish behaviour was deemed unacceptable by team-mates and restaurant staff alike.

Redknapp was back in the dug-out for the shock 0-1 defeat at home to second from bottom Nottingham Forest on New Year's Day. On an afternoon when Radi was anonymous alongside the labouring Newell, that reverse meant that the relegation bell was starting to toll for the Hammers, too, as they went into 1997.

"We were powder puff up front," moaned Harry, who immediately set about dumping goalless Dumitrescu (7+6 apps) to Mexican outfit Futbol Club De America for £1m. Following all the furore over his work permit, he was departing less than a year after he had arrived. A hamstring injury, loss of form and general taxing of Redknapp' patience reduced him to just 13 luckless, goalless outings out of a possible 34 appearances. And Hammers knew that any ambitious application for a work permit renewal would have been laughed out of court by the DoEE.

Dumitrescu claimed to be a fervent orthodox Christian who went to church before difficult matches.

"The reason why I didn't perform very well at Tottenham and West Ham United is probably because there aren't too many orthodox churches in England," added the Romanian, who subsequently returned to Steaua Bucharest before retiring just one month after his 30th birthday.

That Forest defeat was also to prove Radi's final game for the club for, ignoring East End sentiment, Harry sold him back to Espanyol.

Equally, the Spaniards paid 2.4m for Raducioiu (7+5 apps 3 gls) but whereas Hammers had sent pounds to Spain they only got US dollars back. And that meant a loss of some £900,000.

"It was a toss-up between Raducioiu and Marco Boogers for my worst ever signing," declared Harry, who clearly rated Florin a two-bob striker.

"I had problems with the manager," replied Raducioiu who, like Dumitrescu, had only made seven starts. "He wanted me to do what Dowie did but I'm not Dowie."

Born and bred in sun-drenched Portugal, Porfirio had seen neither snow nor an orange ball. But on a day when they would not even have held a donkey derby at the Racecourse Ground, Hugo looked like he had been playing in the icy conditions all his life when he scored spectacularly in a 1-1 draw.

"Are we really supposed to play on frozen snow?" enquired Harry after only seeing the touchlines and penalty areas cleared.

Desperately trying to bring some more funds into the Upton Park coffers, Harry sold rookie striker Danny Shipp (0 apps) to Coleraine for £25,000 while Kenny Brown (66+13 apps 6 gls) headed to Birmingham City in a £75,000 deal and Steve Jones (18+15 apps 5 gls) moved to Charlton Athletic for £400,000, again having failed to convince Harry that he was the finished article.

Despite their lowly position, West Ham battled their way to a gritty goalless draw at table-topping Liverpool before succumbing to a 0-2 defeat at Leeds United where future Hammer, Lee Bowyer, got on the scoresheet. That reverse left Hammers in the bottom three.

As the February 1 deadline neared, Porfirio refused to be drawn on his future.

"First we have to make West Ham safe," he insisted. "There's still time to talk."

The board was doing some talking, too, as it mulled over Tabor's offer of that £30m buy-in. But in an open letter to the fanzine, *On a Mission From God,* the angry East End tycoon wrote: 'This board by its own figures show that the club is in a worse financial position than it's ever been. If it goes down again it's going to be even more difficult to come back next year.'

MD Peter Storrie replied: "It's not true that Mr Tabor has been ignored but we are also considering other options. The offer is not as straightforward as it seems, though. Of the £30m, £22m would be in the form of loans which would, therefore, put West Ham largely in his debt.

"His intention is to buy a third of the shares with the other £8m. This would be available, along with £7m of loans to spend on players, with the balance to go on stadium redevelopment. Mr Tabor values the club at about £25m which is, in our opinion, nowhere near a true valuation.

"He has, perhaps, given the impression that he is a white knight riding in to save the club but the supporters should know that there are a lot of strings attached."

One thing of which the fans were unaware, however, was the fact that, according to Redknapp, he had already brokered a meeting with the high-rolling Tabor at the Cheltenham festival.

"I mentioned Michael's interest to Peter Storrie and he and the chairman seemed quite keen," he wrote in *Harry Redknapp – My Autobiography*. "Tabor invited the three of us to his box along with a string of top racing figures.

"We went back for dinner at a Warwickshire hotel. Discussions continued and everything seemed to be going fine, but somewhere along the line it all went wrong. Tabor made an offer that the chairman did not find acceptable and all of a sudden relations between the two groups were not the most cordial."

Following their pre-Christmas Coca-Cola Cup defeat at the hands of Stockport County – and a postponement through fog – there was to be even more cup upset as Kevin Russell's 89th-minute goal secured a 1-0 win for Wrexham in the FA Cup third round replay at Upton Park.

That slaying led to calls for Harry's head, too, as an angry mob gathered at the Green Street gates demanding his resignation, only for Bilic to walk down to the main entrance and pacify the restless natives.

"That's my worst result as a manager," confessed the black-suited, black-tied Harry following a post-match pitch invasion that left him at the end of his tether.

"The fans paid their money and I understand their frustration. Now I've got to do what's best for West Ham. If the people don't want me here then I understand. The club is more important than me but I couldn't afford to just walk away," he continued, clearly indicating that he would only leave if he was waved off with a golden handshake. "If the chairman thinks it's for the best then I understand."

According to Redknapp, however, he did offer to resign.

"I said to the chairman: 'It hasn't worked out and you probably feel that I'm responsible for the Tabor situation which is hardly helping things. I know you've got the best interests of the club at heart so maybe it's best if I call it a day'. We'd had a couple of meetings before that, too," he wrote. "And things had got personal. 'I wonder if you're trying to get us relegated so your friend Tabor can buy the club on the cheap,' he said. I left the chairman in no doubt about how I felt about this comment. He wouldn't hear of me resigning, either, and said he thought I was the best man for the job and was confident that I could turn things around."

These were trying times for West Ham United, but Redknapp was still in charge for the 1-2 home defeat against Arsenal which saw a half-time red card protest calling for the dismissal of the board and a sit-in at the final whistle. The Gunners had to wait for over an hour before their team-coach could leave a besieged Boleyn Ground where calls for the heads of Brown and Redknapp went on well into the East End night.

'It's good to talk' read the supporters placards but with his patience tested to the limit, the silence was deafening as Tabor issued a seven-day deadline that simply lapsed into oblivion with both parties claiming that the other had proved elusive.

"The bickering between the two camps had got worse," continued Redknapp. "In all honesty it couldn't have helped the team."

In the end, West Ham United raised £1.6m from a placing of 3,200 shares that was viewed by the City as a prelude to a full stock market listing.

According to *The Daily Telegraph*, 38 per cent stakeholder Brown said "The price paid for these shares and the valuation they give to the club is significantly higher than that proposed by Mr Tabor."

Returning substitute Ferdinand – on the verge of being offered a new, five-year contract – scored his first goal for the club at Blackburn Rovers, but it was to prove a mere consolation in a 1-2 defeat

"Rio's gonna be a star," insisted Harry, finding one small glimmer of hope from an afternoon that had seen Hammers' win-less run extend to seven games. "He's going right to the very top. He'll play for England one day. He's outstanding."

There were just 14 matches remaining.

And with a limited transfer kitty, plus what he had recouped on the Romanian resales, an under pressure Harry knew he had to buy the goals that were so desperately needed to stave off the looming spectre of relegation.

This time around, however, there could be no mistakes. No expensive failures.

But going into the crucial final lap of the season, those clubs still left with everything to play for were simply not prepared to release their prize assets.

With precious Premiership experience, Celtic's temperamental Pierre Van Hooijdonk, Wimbledon's Dean Holdsworth and Stoke City's Mike Sheron topped Harry's shopping list but after drawing a blank on all three fronts, he dusted down the *Rothmans Football Yearbook* and went in search of some obsolete stock that could hit the Upton Park pitch running.

At an initial £3.2m, Arsenal's out-of-favour John Hartson became his prime target alongside the redundant £2.3m-rated Paul Kitson at Newcastle United.

"I'd been impressed with Hartson every time I saw him. He was young, big and strong and he could give us a presence we were lacking. I knew he'd do a good job for the club," announced Harry after shelling out £5.5m in one last, desperate gamble. "People warned me off Kitson. They said he's a moody, miserable git but I liked him. I thought he'd work well with Hartson. Once we signed those two, I thought we'd stay up, even though we looked to be in an impossible position.

"The chairman had really pushed the boat out. Desperate situations called for desperate remedies. He knew as well as I did that if we didn't spend, we'd die. I had no money and my hands were tied. I had to take some gambles but, then again, I've been doing that all my life."

Both Hartson and former Ram Kitson made their Hammers' debuts in a 0-1 defeat at Derby County, where unsteady Croatian Aljosa Asanovic won the controversial penalty that he duly despatched to settle it from the spot.

And the tight-rope walking Hartson unluckily picked up his 13th booking of the season, and an unwelcome two-match ban, for continuing an ongoing feud with future Croatian Hammer Igor Stimac, that dated back to his Highbury days.

"Stimac must have been proud with the way he got me that yellow card," roared the Welshman as he hit 36 disciplinary points for the season against the 18th placed Hammers' league tally of 22. "But I was never going to go 12 games without getting booked again, so it's good to get it out of the way early. At least I can play in the whole of the run-in now."

A 4-3 win over Tottenham was widely regarded as one of the most pivotal victories in modern times as the dove-tailing duo marked their home debuts with conversions.

Future Hammer Teddy Sheringham had given Spurs the lead before Dicks and Kitson put Hammers ahead. Darren Anderton then levelled but, like a bull in the proverbial china shop, Hartson charged through Sol Campbell to smash the Spurs defence to smithereens. That show of sheer strength suddenly restored the genuine belief that Hartson's power harnessed to Kitson's pace could save Hammers from the dreaded drop. And although David Howells pulled it back to 3-3, Dicks' unstoppable penalty secured a vital West Ham victory.

All that good work was undone, though, when a pitiful defensive mix-up led to a 0-1 defeat at Leeds United, where Hughes was dismissed before Hammers again turned it on in another Upton Park derby.

This time it was Chelsea's turn to be turned over in a topsy-turvy game that saw two-goal Kitson bag a 3-2 win in injury time after Mark Hughes had silenced Upton Park with an 87th-minute equaliser.

With the wording of the Croatian's new, improved contract now compelling any bidder to pay £4.5m for his services, Everton's Joe Royle had also come knocking on Hammers' door with the readies for Bilic.

According to Redknapp, Royle said: 'I don't want to screw you Harry, we get on great, but business is business and we do want Slaven.'

The manager urged Bilic not to leave Hammers in the lurch, and with a signing-on fee still owing to him, the defender returned from a trip to Merseyside in March having agreed to a move that would still allow him to stay at Upton Park until May.

"We've already made him the highest-paid player in West Ham's history yet he wants to go to a big club," said H. "Slaven thinks that Everton is a bigger club."

A covert deal was struck, but it was soon football's most open secret that now not so Super Slav would move to Goodison Park at the end of the season.

"It was never a question of me leaving now," insisted Bilic, unsuccessfully trying to create an illusion that nothing was yet set in tablets of stone. "Never. I just wanted to talk to Everton. I told them: 'I can't come now. No way.' If I'd gone and West Ham then went down I would never forget it."

At Aston Villa, Frank Lampard's season ended when he cracked a bone in his leg during a goalless draw and as the tearful teenager headed to hospital, his uncle Harry became quite agitated at the sight of Porfirio being questioned by *Hammers News Magazine* in the players' car park about his future.

"Look, Hugo's got the ability to do things and he's a threat but when he hasn't got the ball there's a problem," he said, his opportunity to pay Sporting Lisbon that headline £800,000 now gone and his enthusiasm to sign him on a Bosman free transfer seemingly ebbing away. "That gives me difficulty with the balance of the team. He's a free agent in the summer and he can sign for who he wants. We can't force him to do anything."

And MD Peter Storrie added: "Hugo's had our offer on the table for ages. It's not a case of us getting into an auction with other clubs. It's a case of him making his mind up that he wants to stay at West Ham."

Knowing that he could now walk away from Lisbon's Jose Alvalade Stadium for nothing, Porfirio admitted: "I have some very good invitations from some very good clubs. I'm glad that Hartson and Kitson have signed, though, because they are giving the club other values. But at the moment I'm just the 999 of West Ham! I'm only playing for 15 or 20 minutes when it's an emergency and the team needs me or we are losing. I don't want to be that 999 all my life. And I certainly don't want to think that I'm not playing just because I haven't signed yet!"

Two players definitely on the move were goalkeeper Steve Mautone (3 apps) signed by Reading for £250,000 and the Orient-bound Mark Bowen (18+2 apps 1 gl). But the Welsh international defender was not heading to Brisbane Road. Instead, he was off to Japan to link up with former Spurs' team-mates Ossie Ardiles and Steve Perryman at J-league club Shimizu S-Pulse.

NEARLY REACHED THE SKY

Aussie Stan Lazaridis' 90th-minute equaliser – his first-ever goal in English football – could not have been more timely as Hammers secured a 1-1 draw at Wimbledon to edge a point clear of the drop zone.

And at Coventry City, two-goal Hartson simply had too much strength for the Sky Blues as West Ham overcame Rieper's early own goal to notch a 3-1 win.

But that was also to prove Dicks last game for 549 days as he spent 18 months fighting to recover from another debilitating knee injury.

As transfer deadline day arrived, Redknapp swooped for Manchester City's Steve Lomas in an eleventh-hour, on-off-on £1.6m deal that saw the midfielder signing via the faxes churning from the machine at the Northern Ireland training camp in County Down.

While Ferdinand's England Under-21 debut against Switzerland was cut short by an ankle injury, Hartson was controversially kept on the bench by Wales' manager – ex-Hammer – Bobby Gould in the 1-2 defeat against Belgium.

It was hard to decide which team had enjoyed a 17-day break and which side had just played out extra-time in a leg-sapping Coca-Cola Cup final as Hammers and Middlesbrough – having lost out on the trophy to Leicester City – settled for a goalless draw at Upton Park where Richard Hall made his long-awaited debut.

And future Hammer, Eyal Berkovic, sealed a 2-0 victory for Southampton as all the good work of recent weeks started to come undone. There were 15,245 present at The Dell compared to the 35,300 at Old Trafford who saw England Under-15s take on their French counterparts.

"England has plenty of talent to develop," wrote *The Daily Telegraph's* Sarah Edworthy. "Joe Cole for one. He lost the ball, won it back impressively, calmly threaded it through to the forwards and created chances with elegance and calm."

Unfortunately, Upton Park was short on tranquillity and long on calamity in a game of two schizophrenic halves against Everton after Kitson's double put West Ham 2-0 up inside 32 minutes. And just after the break, the reluctant striker was offered a spot-kick by nominated taker Hartson.

But it was keeper Neville Southall who claimed the match-ball after the nervy Kitson saw his penalty saved, before Everton salvaged an unlikely 2-2 draw.

"Of course I'm annoyed," roared Redknapp after seeing three points turn to the one point that left Hammers swimming for their Premiership lives in the bottom three. "I can't believe what's happened. If we score it's game over. Instead we give the ball to a boy not interested in taking penalties. Suddenly, it's like a testimonial and everyone's shouting for Kitson to get a hat-trick and keep the ball. Terrific! We're in a relegation battle. It doesn't happen in the Premiership. It's amateurish."

At Leicester City, Moncur accidentally clattered referee Roger Dilkes, forcing him to retire at half-time and, after his replacement Grant Hegley gave Hartson his 15th booking of the season, Moncs secured a 1-0 win with a late strike that lifted Hammers into 16th spot, one point clear of trouble.

And when Sheffield Wednesday came to Upton Park, Kitson did bag that elusive hat-trick, while Hartson weighed in with a double as Hammers hit five goals in a top flight clash for the first time in over a decade.

"Bilic did well," observed Wednesday boss David Pleat, who was also in on the biggest open secret in football. "But I thought the crowd were very fair to him because he's going to Everton, isn't he? They clapped him off. How strange!"

Following the 5-1 win that took his side up into 15th place, Redknapp declared: "Now everything's in our hands. Since Hartson and Kitson arrived, we've suddenly started to believe that we can get goals again."

Those successive victories certainly eased the pressure. Now with two games remaining, Hammers – on 41 points and boasting a superior goal difference – were looking more comfortable than Leicester City (P-36/Pts-41), Sunderland (P-37/Pts-40), Coventry City (P-37/Pts-38), Middlesbrough (P-36/Pts-37) and already-relegated Nottingham Forest (P-37/Pts-34).

A physical goalless draw against Newcastle United at Upton Park secured the Premiership title for Manchester United. And as the Magpies returned to the north-east with their wings clipped, Redknapp announced that he felt Hammers had beaten the drop.

"I've always said that 42 points will do it," chirped the Hammers' boss taking one last look at the runners and riders approaching the final furlong. "Yeah, I feel safe. Yet a dozen games ago it just didn't seem possible. I'd better get a bonus!"

Indeed, Harry was to be proved right just 48 hours later when duly relegated Middlesbrough only drew at Blackburn Rovers.

As West Ham headed to Old Trafford for the final game of a long, hard season full of twists and turns, so much could have rested on their clash with United.

But both teams had already achieved their respective goals, and as relegation-proof West Ham took on the already crowned champions, they rarely looked like gate-crashing the Premiership title knees-up party.

"I've got nothing to say. Today belongs to Manchester United," said Harry at the final whistle after substitute keeper Sealey – a former Red – made an emotional return to the Theatre of Dreams with an 89th-minute appearance, while Moncur also claimed the jersey that Eric Cantona had worn in his final game for United, before handing the shirt over to *The Sun* in a bid to raise cash for Great Ormond Street children's hospital.

But it was referee Lodge's first whistle that caused the most controversy.

Straight from the kick-off, Kitson received the ball and inexplicably sliced it out for a throw-in with just the second touch of the entire game.

For the watching live Sky TV audience it was an ambitious at best, atrocious at worst, opening set play.

To the mocking 55,249 crowd pleased to see United win possession so soon, it merely looked like a woeful attempt to find Dowie on the right-hand touchline.

But back in the London offices of the spread betting firms, there were few smiles. That instant throw-in had cost them so dearly.

Through the 80s and 90s, spread betting had become a sophisticated alternative to the traditional 'first across the line' type wagers laid by the high street bookies where punters could back their selections at a fixed price, or starting price.

A high risk, moveable feast or famine, the firms would lay books on a variety of potential occurrences in a sporting event, leaving backers to judge whether they wanted to wager 'over' or 'under' the designated 'spread'.

NEARLY REACHED THE SKY

For example, the spread on the number of corners won in a match could be set at 8-to-10. Backers expecting a defensive game would go 'under' and bet, say, £10 per flag kick under that lower limit of eight. Those expecting an attacking match might bet, say, £10 per corner 'over' the upper end limit of 10 flag kicks.

The layers, meanwhile, enjoyed the edge of the eight, nine and ten corners 'spread'.

If there were 15 corners, then the punters who had gone 'under' would lose £70 – i.e. £10 for every corner over the lower (eight) end of the spread. Those punters who had gone 'over' would win £50 – i.e. £10 for every corner over the upper (10) end of the spread.

Conversely, if there were only four corners, then the punters who had gone 'under' would win £40 – i.e. £10 for every corner under the lower (eight) end of the spread. Those punters who had gone 'over' would lose £60 – i.e. £10 for every corner under the upper (10) end of the spread.

Similar books were laid on goal times, bookings, sendings off and even the tally of shirt numbers of the scorers.

The potential for big gains and equally big losses was absolutely huge.

But it was the time of the first throw-in that had seen the bookies – like the Old Trafford punters – scrambling for cover. After all, on a spread set at 50-65 seconds for the first throw-in, a canny punter going 'under' would have secured odds of at least 42/1 (i.e. 50 seconds minus 7 seconds = 43 x stake) by virtue of the seven seconds that elapsed between the kick-off and that first throw-in.

One virtual certainty at Old Trafford was that the visitors would always get the opportunity to kick off.

Quite simply, if the United skipper won the toss he would nearly always forfeit the right to kick-off in favour of electing to choose ends, thereby ensuring that the Reds could play the second-half attacking their favoured Stretford End.

If the home captain lost the flick-up, his visiting counterpart could simply choose to kick-off anyway. Nowadays, there is no choice – the winner has to choose ends.

Such inside information truly was a potential 'Heads we win, tails you lose' situation for the knowledgeable spread bet punters and was open to abuse from any one looking for a flutter with the odds weighted heavily in their favour.

In *Harry Redknapp – My Autobiography*, the Hammers' manager went some way to confirming that when he wrote: "If I'd only known the stink our unsuccessful opening gambit was to cause, I'd have gladly let United kick-off."

However, it is nothing but conjecture to suggest that he, any player or official from either club was involved in any gambling activity or wrongdoing.

"Looking at the replays of his attempted pass, I'd have to admit it wasn't Kitson's most elegant ball," continued 'H'. "That match, or at least the poxy kick-off, would have been long forgotten had it not been for a story in the *Racing Post* the following week. Spread betting firm Sporting Index apparently reported a large number of sellers forcing the line down to 50-to-65 seconds.

"The inference was clear: Someone had cleared up at the bookies' expense. And the finger of suspicion was pointing at West Ham United. The press went mad. Kitson's misplaced pass looked worse and worse the more you saw it.

"I suppose you'd have to admit the circumstantial evidence was pretty strong but, believe, me that's all it was – circumstantial.

"But if you looked at all the characters involved in this supposed coup you'd realise it was all a cock-and-bull story. There were no punters at West Ham except John Hartson who wasn't even playing and Kitson knows as much about betting as I do nuclear science. I didn't even have a spread betting account. And who won this small fortune? Sporting Index claimed they saw a large number of sellers but they later said little damage had been done.

"Our kick off that day was one we and, indeed, most clubs in the Premiership followed regularly. It just didn't come off. The betting riddle made a good story, sure, but there was nothing in it. And even if there was, do you think I'd ever admit it? They'd lock me up!"

According to the *Daily Mirror* betting offices reported unusual interest in the first throw-in where the spread opened at 70-85 seconds.

Stating that a United player took the throw-in after just seven seconds, the tabloid confirmed that it had been possible to win 63 times the punter's stake. It also reported that Wally Pyrah, of Sporting Index, admitted that there had, indeed, been 'concerns' about the match plus 'one or two other games' while confirming: "We did look into that West Ham match because there were a lot of rumours."

Kitson also came in for stinging flak on BBCs satirical sporting quiz *They Think It's All Over* as each three-man team – alluding to allegations of the unproven spread bet – comically searched out a motive for the striker's wayward pass.

But fearing the full weight of Kits' legal team, the conclusion eventually drawn was that the former England Under-21 striker was just not a good player, leaving the Hammer – again in full view of a peak-time audience – to take the full brunt for something in which he was merely implicated by association.

Certainly, it was never suggested that Kitson had even bet a penny, yet alone made any profit, on the outcome of his ridiculously over-hit pass into Old Trafford's bemused, touchline crowd.

"It was just one of those things," replied Kitson. "They're just trying to get laughs out of things but I was the one out there in front of 55,000 people. It's so easy for them to sit on their backsides in a studio and come up with an opinion."

As those bookies contemplated an alleged scam, within just 72 hours of the curtain falling on the season, Bilic predictably announced that he was on his bike.

"Yes, I had a few bonuses in my contract at West Ham but, please believe me, it would still have been better for me to have joined Everton in March," said the part-qualified lawyer, pleading his case after heading to a Goodison Park outfit who, ironically, had finished below West Ham in the league. "It's not all about money.

"I know we can go on and win things at Everton. They're ambitious and I need to play for a big club.

"As far as my career is concerned it is better to go to Liverpool," added Bilic (54 apps 3 gls) using an unfortunate choice of words. Indeed, it would have been more beneficial to have gone to the red half of Merseyside, for Bilic came unstuck at the Toffees where his stay evolved into one, long, unhappy scrap against relegation.

Elsewhere, the chances of Porfirio (18+9 apps 4 gls) staying in east London receded yet further when he announced: "I'm on vacation. I just want to forget about all this transfer talk and have a break from football."

And even his mother added: "My Porfirio? He's always very slow at making up his mind on anything!"

Needless to say, it was no-go for Hugo who ended up signing for Spanish side, Racing Santander.

"We offered him a deal to stay but he got offered massive money from Spain," admitted Redknapp as he drew down the curtain on a highly eventful term.

In reality, though, he no longer needed him now that he had the double-barrelled threat of his all-British strikeforce.

"It's possible that Michael Tabor's interest indirectly saved us from relegation," suggested H in his autobiography. "I think the fans clamouring for Tabor's money, and my offer to resign, perhaps forced the chairman's hand. He knew we'd go down unless drastic action was taken and all of a sudden he found the money to buy Hartson, Kitson and Lomas, three signings which kept us up.

"Midway through the season I felt I had no chance of success," added H after seeing that brave, bold swoop for Hartson (five goals from 11 starts) and Kitson (eight in 14 games) prove the catalyst for the harvesting of 20 points from the final 13 matches. "I was putting out a team that I knew couldn't win. There was no way I could survive with Steve Jones and Mike Newell playing up front for me.

"It was an impossible situation. I don't care who had managed them, that team couldn't have won games, It just didn't have the players.

"Until Hartson and Kitson arrived there was no way we could have stayed up.

"Now I'm going to be working to try and give us a real chance next season because I don't want to be involved in another relegation battle. I'm not steering clear of foreigners, though," he continued defiantly turning a blind eye to the assorted problems encountered with Futre, Bilic, Raducioiu, Dumitrescu and Porfirio. "I think that foreigners have been fantastic for the English game. The standard of our football has really gone up. Average British players are not getting in their teams but so what? They might have to go and play in the first division, but we're seeing better players in the Premiership – and better football."

PLAYERS IN

Mark Bowen	Norwich City	Free transfer
Paulo Futre	AC Milan	Free transfer
Richard Hall	Southampton	£1,900,000
John Hartson	Arsenal	£3,200,000 (record)
Michael Hughes	Racing Club Strasbourg	Free transfer
Paul Kitson	Newcastle United	£2,300,000
Steve Lomas	Manchester City	£1,600,000
Scott Mean	Bournemouth	£200,000
Florin Raducioiu	Espanyol	£2,400,000 (record)
Les Sealey	Leyton Orient	Free transfer

LOANS IN

Mike Newell	Birmingham City
Hugo Porfirio	Sporting Lisbon

PLAYERS OUT

Slaven Bilic	Everton	£4,500,000 (record)
Mark Bowen	Shimizu S-Pulse	Free
Kenny Brown	Birmingham City	£75,000
Scott Canham	Brentford	£25,000
Tony Cottee	Selangor	£775,000
Ilie Dumitrescu	F C de America	£1,000,000
Paolo Futre	Retired	
Dale Gordon	Bournemouth	Free transfer
Steve Jones	Charlton Athletic	£400,000
Steve Mautone	Reading	£250,000
Malcolm McPherson	Brentford	Free transfer
Graham Philson	Linfield	Free transfer
Florin Raducioiu	Espanyol	£1,500,000
Peter Shilton	Leyton Orient	Free transfer
Danny Shipp	Coleraine	£25,000
Robbie Slater	Southampton	£250,000
Adrian Whitbread	Portsmouth	£225,000

Chapter 11
1997-98

THE YOUNG ONES

One player who had certainly improved the quality of the Premiership was Eyal Berkovic, as Hammers had found to their cost back in mid-April when he engineered Southampton's 2-0 win at The Dell.

Down the years, Harry Redknapp had developed a good relationship with former Liverpool boss Graeme Souness, especially when the Anfield Road-Green Street trade route became a heavily trodden path a few seasons earlier.

And when Southampton boss 'Souey' quit the south coast club at the end of the 1996-97 campaign, H somehow discovered that the Saints' hold on Berkovic was not quite what it seemed.

Indeed, while most of football was under the false impression that the impish Israeli international had already signed a permanent deal, he was, in fact, still only on-loan from hometown club Maccabi Haifa.

Certainly, Redknapp did not need any further prompting to persuade Berkovic to march out on the Saints, whereupon the Hammers' boss promptly outsmarted Tottenham to sign his man from the Israeli outfit for a bargain £1.5m.

French defender David Terrier was also signed on a free transfer from FC Metz on an initial three-month deal, while Canadian international goalkeeper Craig Forrest joined from Ipswich Town in a £500,000 transfer.

Hammers still had that overseas feel. But it was not all imports, and closer to home Andrew Impey was snapped up from Queens Park Rangers in a £1.25m deal that was delayed by the wide man's foot condition curiously called 'Hammertoes'.

The lure of European football with former team-mate Kenny Dalglish's Newcastle United won the day over Harry's Hammers for John Barnes, who moved to Tyneside on a free transfer from Liverpool amidst a cocktail of cockney dismay and disappointment.

And with luckless Richard Hall requiring a third operation on his troublesome foot, Redknapp had also tried to sign Derby County's injury-wracked centre-half, Paul McGrath, on a free transfer but the deal collapsed at the last minute.

Vociferously refuting rumours that his career was over, Julian Dicks was still going to be absent with a knee injury until further notice and, as the season neared, another stopper, Marc Rieper, had become a pre-season target for Celtic.

Following a three-game tour of Scotland in which John Hartson and Paul Kitson carried on from where they left off with a double apiece, Hammers ironically headed to Brøndby – the club that had sold Rieper – to play in a friendly.

"As far as I'm concerned, I'm a West Ham player and I'll remain so until at least the end of the season," insisted the Dane, trying impossibly to slam the door on all the speculation, while tantalisingly also leaving it slightly ajar. "I haven't heard anything at all about a move to Scotland but if it was felt that the transfer was right for the club or me, then we'd have to look at the situation."

At Stansted airport the difference between West Ham United and Arsenal could not have been more stark. The Gunners, be-decked to a man in their club tracksuits, sat undisturbed in the sanctuary of a glass-enclosed private lounge awaiting their flight to Amsterdam for a pre-season tournament.

How Iain Dowie could have done with such segregation as he and his casually dressed team-mates sat in the departure area amidst a tipsy tribe of Hammers' fans who had taken advantage of a *Daily Mirror* promotion that allowed them to fly to Copenhagen for £12.50 plus two cut-out vouchers.

"Ere Dowie! Why are you so ugly?" asked one Neanderthal follower, to the amusement of all his cronies, as the Northern Ireland striker merely turned to look longingly towards Ian Wright and Co. behind their glass screens.

And once aboard the flight, the mere curtain that had been swept across the front end of the cabin did little to dampen the raucous chants of 'Harry Redknapp's claret & blue army!' that simply got louder with every trundle of the drinks trolley through the fuselage.

Harry was furious that his Premiership stars had been plonked 'Business Class' onto a low-budget flight to Scandinavia with just a flimsy velvet screen to separate them from one giant jolly boys' outing.

As the rowdy passengers from London Stansted dispersed into the Danish dusk, the meeters and greeters from Brøndby could have been forgiven for thinking that West Ham's official club party had missed the flight.

Eventually, a puzzled representative from the hosts approached a lost-looking 20-strong group of waifs and strays and exclaimed: "You are *the* West Ham United? I thought that you would all be wearing the same jackets or track suits?"

Before kick-off, a pre-occupied Rieper – usually one of the most relaxed, co-operative players at Upton Park – sat in the lounge of Copenhagen's SAS Radisson Hotel with some fellow Danes, curiously insisting that no photos of him and his party should be taken.

Redknapp gave Tore Pedersen a run-out and the Norwegian trialist wiped out Peter Moller's opener before Per Neilsen secured a 2-1 win for the Danes.

And in an act of petulance, Michael Hughes lashed out at Soren Krogh to receive a straight red card from referee Jorn West Larsen. Injury-hit, 10-man, West Ham finished both defeated and facing the prospect of losing the Irishman through suspension for the start of the campaign proper.

It was not a happy Harry who climbed aboard the team-coach to declare that the niggled Northern Ireland international had been stupid to get himself sent off and, potentially, banned for the first three games of the domestic campaign.

In a bid to keep news of that moment of madness suppressed from the Football Association, however, Peter Storrie contrived to convince the English press that instead of sending off Hughes, Mr Larsen had, on reflection, decided that he had merely invited him to be substituted and with no more availability on the bench, Hammers had, in any event, to finish the friendly with 10 men.

That tale tested the bounds of credibility to the extreme and, with highlights of the game later screened on Danish TV, too, it became patently obvious that the player had, indeed, been shown both the red card and the way to the showers.

Fittingly there were no such problems in Steve Potts' long-delayed, albeit richly-deserved testimonial against Queens Park Rangers. A crowd of 12,568 turned up to see Hammers run out 2-0 winners in their final warm-up for the big kick-off.

Fortunately for Hughes, his Danish bacon was saved. A generous Mr Larsen did not report the Brøndby incident to the FA and that enabled the Irishman to escape the suspension that would have precluded him from lining up in the opening fixture of the fresh term against newly-promoted Barnsley.

Top-flight football had come to Oakwell for the first time in 110 years and to chants of 'It's just like watching Brazil!' Neil Redfearn got the Yorkshiremen off to a dream start before John Hartson equalised and Frank Lampard silenced the colliery bands with his first-ever senior goal that sealed a party-pooping 2-1 win.

As he stood in the sun-drenched Oakwell car park, Redknapp admitted that the club was in the throes of trading fit-again Danny Williamson for Everton's once-capped England defender, David Unsworth, in a switch that would also see Hammers receive a welcome £1m cash adjustment, too.

Williamson's promising early start to his Hammers' career had been blighted by injury and, indeed, he had made just 15 starts in the 1996-97 campaign.

Some medics had, apparently, suggested that the 23-year-old's right ankle might not withstand the test of time under the continued rigours of the Premiership.

However, a move to Goodison Park would possibly provide Williamson (52+6 apps 5 gls) with financial security come what may, while the adaptable Unsworth would give cover in a whole host of defensive positions.

For the first time in over a decade, Hammers made it two victories out of their first two matches with a 2-1 win over Tottenham Hotspur, as Hartson opened the scoring and Berkovic rubbed further salt into the White Hart Lane wounds by marking his home debut with a goal, too.

By the time the half-time whistle blew at Goodison Park, the returning Unsworth had every reason to smile at the fact that Hammers were, technically, top of the Premiership thanks to Dave Watson's own goal. But Williamson and the booked Slaven Bilic were to have the last laugh when Gary Speed and Graham Stuart stole a 2-1 victory for the Blues.

A 1-1 draw at Coventry City followed as Kitson combined with Hartson to wipe out Darren Huckerby's opener and net his first goal of the campaign.

"No, it wouldn't have been nicking it if we'd won, we'd have been getting what we deserved!" stormed H after it was suggested by *Hammers News Magazine* that Ferdinand might have snatched a late winner had he not scooped over.

And as the questioner walked away from Highfield Road, Harry's Mercedes drew alongside.

"Nicked it? F****** nicked it? Are you f****** sure?" he screamed, before closing the electric window and roaring off, shaking his head, towards London.

"Redknapp reckoned his side deserved to win and on their second half performance they probably did," observed *The Times* also taking a slightly more balanced view than the Hammers' boss. "But that is to ignore a first half totally dominated by the home side."

The creative Berkovic was in electrifying form as he further endeared himself to the Upton Park crowd by inspiring Hammers into third place with a 3-1 victory over Wimbledon, who had shown post-match interest in the want-away Hughes.

And it was a measure of the club's progress that Lampard was included in the England Under-21 squad for the Young Lions' game against Moldova, while Rio Ferdinand won a widely acclaimed call into the senior squad for the World Cup Group Two qualifier against the Moldovans at Wembley.

"Some people say that I get an easy ride but, personally, all the family business has worked the other way for me," said 'magistrate' Lampard, who had been forced by his uncle H to sit on the Hammers' bench no less than 26 times during the previous campaign. "Harry just can't be seen to stick me in when I'm not ready. And that's why I've always got to give that bit extra above everyone else to prove that I'm good enough to be there. I've played for England's youth team and trained with the full international squad. I've got enough belief in my ability."

On the weekend of the fatal Paris car crash that claimed the life of Diana, Princess of Wales, Lampard's best pal, Ferdinand, could not have picked a worst weekend to have been caught driving with one-and-a-half times the legal limit of alcohol in his blood. Stopped by police the Sunday afternoon after the Saturday night before, he was just hours from joining up with the full squad.

Following a five-minute hearing at Wimbledon Magistrates Court, he was fined £500 and banned from driving for one year. Having overdone the celebrating upon getting that call-up, he was now commiserating big time.

Glenn Hoddle took the only realistic, political route open to him when he axed the forlorn Ferdinand from the squad but, in an act of compassion, he still allowed him to remain at Bisham Abbey training with his international colleagues.

Rio's timing could not have been worse. But there was still a dark shadow of hypocrisy hanging over the England coach, who had previously selected the alleged wife-beating Paul Gascoigne and jailed drink-driver Tony Adams.

"It was a one-off and it's turned out to be the biggest mistake I've ever made," rued Rio as he candidly poured out his heart to Danny Francis of *Hammers News Magazine.* "I'm devastated and I've got to put it behind me. I wasn't under the impression that I was over the limit because there's no way I would have driven. I felt perfectly okay but had obviously underestimated the whole thing.

"Harry was stern but he was very good about it. He told me I'd been silly. Glenn Hoddle told me that I'd made a big mistake but that everyone makes mistakes and it was up to me to put it right. He told me that I'd be an idiot if I made the same mistake again. When he told me that I was out of the squad it was literally [sic] the biggest punch in the mouth anyone has ever given me. Those were the worst three days of my life. I can't find the words to say just how sorry I am."

Time was, however, on Rio's side.

In his *Newham Recorder* column, John Hartson incredibly wrote: "I'm not telling any tales out of school if I say Rio's bad luck was to be caught. If we are honest we must admit we have all done it. There but for the grace of God . . . !"

Redknapp was a little less sympathetic as he immediately slapped an immediate alcohol ban in the Upton Park players' lounge.

"We have got to start educating our young players," said the Hammers' boss. "Why should they want to start getting loads of drink down them? It only leads to them doing silly things and then getting into trouble. They don't do it in Italy."

There was also one thing that did not happen in Spain.

And that was the slighting of the FC Barcelona jersey with the name of a team sponsor. As one of the giants of European football, the Peseta-packed Catalans simply felt that the notion of a shirt sponsor was too vulgar.

The same could not be said for cash-strapped West Ham United, though, especially as they had recently circularised clubs with a willingness to consider 'reasonable' offers for Dowie and Ian Bishop. Yet, the Hammers and Barca shared the distinction of being the only clubs in the elite leagues of Europe with blank, logo-less shirts.

Previous sponsors Dagenham Motors wanted to renew their four-year contract but could not meet the club's asking price and drove away. Six months on from his opening discussions, Storrie was still desperately trying to land a deal with a South African airline in order that they could finally start selling some first-team shirts.

Table-topping Manchester United might have had 'Sharp' on their jerseys, but it was Hartson who drew first blood at Old Trafford as the Reds conceded their first goal of the campaign. But after Kitson then missed a sitter, Roy Keane levelled and Paul Scholes headed the winner.

"Kits will never get a better chance," reckoned Redknapp, disappointed to be returning south only in sixth-place.

That was an indication as to just how far West Ham had come.

A shock 0-1 defeat in the Coca-Cola Cup second round, first leg tie at Huddersfield Town was similarly followed by a 0-1 reverse against Newcastle United at Upton Park as Hammers started to gravitate back down towards earth.

"I'd rather play crap and win," fumed Harry after Barnes added insult to the injury of his summer snub by netting a stunning winner for the Magpies.

Hammers may have missed out on the former England international but they did secure the £2.3m signature of Blackburn defender Ian Pearce as Rieper (93 +8 apps 5 gls) inevitably headed to Celtic for £1.4m where his career would, sadly, be cut short by the amputation of a toe.

Rieper, in any event, would have been able to leave on a Bosman free transfer at the end of the season, so it was good business for Redknapp to recoup a seven-figure sum, while receiving £1.5m from Wimbledon for Hughes (90+7 apps 6 gls).

Trailing 0-4 to Arsenal by half-time, West Ham were just thankful to leave Highbury without incurring any further second half damage, but a black September of four defeats passed with Hartson and Berkovic finally engineering a 2-1 win over Liverpool at Upton Park.

"Eyal showed he's a talented footballer," enthused Harry, proudly seeing his Anglo-Israeli blend working far better than the last season's Portuguese-Romanian alliance. "The boy's got an ability to play passes that other players can't even see." Hartson's hat-trick secured a face-saving 3-0 win over Huddersfield in the Coca-Cola Cup re-match but there was a miserable return to Southampton for Berkovic. Hammers lost 0-3 as Nottingham Forest's on-loan Ian Moore (0+1 app) managed his only half-hour for the club. And the disgraced Ferdinand hardly needed Hoddle to witness the visitors' Dell destruction from the stands.

Upon his return from expert consultation in the USA, Dicks went under surgeon John King's scalpel at Mile End's London Independent Hospital in a bid to stabilise the cruciate ligament in his left knee.

"No, I don't consider that this is my last chance," he insisted, looking ahead to eight months' rehabilitation under the guidance of physio John Green, who had helped the uncompromising left-back to beat the odds last time around. Green, the physio's physio, had motivated his patient with equal measure of diligence and dedication and, fortunately for Dicks, he was still at the club. "When I had my operation seven years ago, people were saying that I was finished then.

"Football's been the biggest part of my life for 14 or 15 years – it's a big thing just to chuck away. I could have sat on my backside, collected the insurance money and had a good life. But at the end of the day I'd rather play football. Playing for West Ham again is just too much not to go for. I'm desperate to play again."

Dicks would not kick a ball all season but 13 games into the campaign, the club finally made its new home kit available in the shops *without* a sponsor's logo but *with* the promise of a free printing as and when the red-faced MD had concluded a new commercial deal.

With 3-0 becoming a common thread running through the scoresheet, Hammers saw off Aston Villa in their Coca-Cola Cup third round tie at Upton Park, where Bolton Wanderers subsequently also lost by the same margin as two-goal Hartson took his tally to a deadly dozen goals.

Berkovic, who also netted against The Trotters, moved quickly to deny tabloid reports that he already wanted to quit Upton Park.

The influential Israeli international had been instrumental in engineering Hammers' encouraging – albeit mixed – start to the season.

"Look, you must tell everybody that I'm very happy here," he urged in the company of his agent Pinchas 'Pini' Zahavi. "I want to stay for many years and be successful. The crowd likes me and I like them. There's no way I'm leaving here."

As time wore on, Berkovic was to prove that he was never shy to manipulate the press, making himself media-friendly when it suited, while hiding behind non-existent managerial 'gags' when, perhaps, it was in his interests to stay silent.

"Frank Lampard has said that I must not speak to anybody, not even the club's magazine," he later protested after reneging on an agreement to do a *Hammers News Magazine* interview amidst more intense speculation over his future.

"Can't talk?" frowned the puzzled assistant manager. "No, sorry, I don't know what Eyal's talking about. Make him talk to you!"

A 1-2 defeat at Leicester City left Hammers in 11th place with 16 points after five wins, six losses and a draw. Despite escaping a yellow card himself, Hartson branded referee Mike Reed 'a homer' after West Ham received five bookings and that earned him a misconduct charge from the Football Association, whom the East Enders were keeping busy.

"I don't regret my comments as such. I thoroughly believe that what I said was right but, obviously, I regret saying what I said because I'm on an FA charge," said the cryptic Hartson, who escaped a ban but was fined £1,000.

According to the *Daily Express*, as Sir John Smith – former deputy head of the Metropolitan Police – concluded his report into gambling in football, Tottenham's David Howells was about to force the authorities to re-open their inquiry.

The Spurs' midfielder reportedly claimed that a team playing at White Hart Lane had deliberately kicked the ball out of play to win spread bets on the time of the first throw-in. And while he did not name West Ham United, it was believed that he was, indeed, referring to the Hammers. After the unproven speculation at Manchester United, that made it the second time that West Ham's name had been implicated in a spread betting scandal.

Sir John, who took anonymous evidence from players, announced: "I did look at spread betting but it involves relatively few punters who are all vetted. I just don't see it as a serious concern."

The Sun reported that Redknapp's verdict was a terse: "It's cobblers!"

And the FA eventually took no further action after deciding that any evidence was merely anecdotal.

Ironically, the world of gambling was destined to have yet more effect on the hapless Hammers.

Neil Shipperley – a Crystal Palace striker who would break Hammers' hearts in years to come – sent the Eagles soaring into a 2-0 lead at Upton Park before West Ham mounted a radiant fightback.

Hartson reduced the arrears and, on 65 minutes, Lampard netted the equaliser. But young Lamps was still celebrating when the Boleyn Ground was transformed into an eerie darkness as a result of a mysterious floodlight failure.

Following a 30-minute wait in the Upton Park dark, referee David Elleray abandoned the live Sky TV match.

"At half-time, I'd have liked to have got my hands on those fuses," joked Harry clearly oblivious to the sinister reason behind the black-out.

"The contractors have told us that the termination of the contactors supplying power to the floodlight gantries indicated coil failure in three units," announced Storrie, following an inquest into the blow-out. "They also said it was very unusual to have three units fail simultaneously!"

A few months later, the Selhurst Park floodlights went out just 13 seconds into the second half of a televised game between Wimbledon and Arsenal, which led Scotland Yard to investigate the suspicious circumstances behind another unprecedented, unexplained black-out.

It would later transpire that a Far Eastern betting syndicate was to blame.

Indeed, the gang had subsequently bribed a security man with £20,000 to allow them to enter Charlton Athletic's ground and install remote control devices that could switch off floodlights.

But the scam was halted when a second guard reported an attempt to buy him off, resulting in the arrest at The Valley of Chee Kew Ong and electronics expert Eng Hwa Lim, while they were trying to disrupt a Charlton versus Liverpool game.

And in August 1999, Middlesex Guildhall Crown Court heard how the two Malaysians had also boasted about fixing the generators at Upton Park and halting that game between Wimbledon and Arsenal which was deadlocked at 0-0.

Scotland Yard detectives found bets totalling £30m had been placed on each match through criminal betting syndicates in Hong Kong, Malaysia and other Far Eastern countries where – unlike the UK – wagers stand regardless of any second half abandonment. The syndicate had simply plotted to stop the matches in the second half, once the score was in their favour.

Ong and Lim were jailed for four years ahead of deportation after pleading guilty to conspiracy to cause a public nuisance. Roger Firth, the Charlton Athletic security guard who was paid the £20,000, received an 18-month sentence after becoming the chief prosecution witness, while Wai Yuen Liu, whose role in the plot remained a 'slight mystery' was given a 30-month stretch.

Back at Upton Park, Richard Hall – accompanied by the dedicated physio Green – was hot on the heels of Dicks as he flew to Seattle. The defender wanted to arrange specialist surgery with world-renowned foot specialist Dr Ted Hanson in a bid to save a Hammers' career spanning just seven starts, while Ivory Coast-born striker Samassi Abou eventually jetted in from Cannes to finally join Hammers in an off-on £250,000 deal.

Sporting Lisbon's 13-times capped, Portuguese international striker Paolo Alves then followed in the footsteps of Dani, Paulo Futre and Hugo Porfirio when he signed a three-month loan deal.

Alves had scored for his country against England in a 1-1 draw at Wembley back in December 1995 and for Sporting Lisbon in their 4-1 Centenary friendly victory at Upton Park a few months later.

"I've been to London twice and scored twice!" he said, before warning that he was not as technically equipped as his compatriots who had been at the club.

The Upton Park players' bar may have been dry but Lampard and, incredibly, Ferdinand, were two of five Under-21 players who were caught over-celebrating the Young Lions' 1-0 win against Italy in Rome.

All five were banned from watching England's seniors qualify for the 1998 World Cup with a goalless draw against the Italians at the Olympic Stadium.

The drink culture continued to permeate all the way through Upton Park and into the wine cellars of the Boleyn Ground, too, and this time it was Hartson whose collar was felt for allegedly being drunk and disorderly at the Swallow Hotel.

"John wasn't really involved," said Harry after seeing the matter dropped on all fronts. "He was just trying to calm everything down."

And despite enjoying the relative comfort of mid-table respectability, Harry had to play headmaster yet again when Berkovic and Moncur flared up at one another during Hammers' 1-2 defeat at Zola-inspired Chelsea.

"You can't have players pushing and shoving each other like that – it's not on," fumed a relieved Redknapp after the warring duo were calmed down by referee Graham Barber before Moncs cheekily planted a kiss on his team-mate.

NEARLY REACHED THE SKY

It would not have even made it onto the undercard of Derek Hales versus Mike Flanagan or Lee Bowyer versus Kieron Dyer but, back home in Israel, Berkovic reportedly said: "I am not sorry. Moncur is one of the most jealous people I have ever met and he has goaded players and fans against me."

Moncur replied: "I don't have a clue what he's talking about. It was just a silly one-off incident."

Hartson's penalty at Stamford Bridge – his 13th league and cup goal of the season – had put him into top spot in the Premiership scoring charts, his powerful potential having undoubtedly been unlocked by Harry .

"Leaving Arsenal was the best thing I could have done," he enthused. "It's great to be in front of everybody else, but I want to stay there as top scorer. I've got to put all the off-the-field business behind me and concentrate on playing football."

Ferdinand finally won his first full international cap when he came on to replace the injured Gareth Southgate in England's 2-0 friendly victory over Cameroon at Wembley, before his pal Lampard struck a hat-trick in a 4-1 win over Walsall in the Coca-Cola Cup fourth round to set up a quarter-final meeting with Arsenal.

"The supporters didn't react too well to me last season – you'd have to be a fool not to have been aware of that – but it was something that I had to overcome," observed Lampard, whose treble certainly went some way towards winning over a sceptical crowd. "It's an old saying but my dad reminds me of it all the time: 'Let your football do the talking.' It's a dream of mine to play for England alongside Rio one day. I don't think anything's beyond me."

It was also gratifying for Uncle Harry to see the belief in his nephew starting to silence the ridiculous claims of nepotism, too.

"Let's be honest, when I brought Frank on as sub once or twice last season he didn't get a very kind reception, did he?" said H. "Some silly people were thinking it was all a family act and felt that he was only getting his chance because his old man was here and he's my nephew. They reckoned he shouldn't have been playing at all. None of them knew what they were looking at but I did!

"I always knew that the kid was gonna be a player, there was never any doubt."

Indeed, the teenage midfielder also put Hammers ahead at Elland Road – and celebrated with a carbon-copy of his father's 1980 FA Cup semi-final corner pole dance – before they capitulated under a late Leeds' flurry.

That 1-3 defeat was their sixth successive away reverse.

Hartson's double-barrelled blast in a 2-1 win over Aston Villa fired West Ham into 12th spot and, going into November, the striker was already on 16 goals.

The lights shone brightly as Hammers beat Palace 4-1 in the replay of that abandoned game. And as the jaded, jet-lagged Stan Lazaridis collapsed in the dressing room after returning from Australia following the 2-2 draw against Iran – a play-off game that saw Terry Venables' team fail to qualify for 1998 World Cup – there was to be more trouble ahead for the walkabout winger.

For with El Tel's Socceroos due to play in the Confederations Cup tournament, Harry had tried to persuade Stan-the-Man not to go back on international duty.

"Stan's knackered and has no energy," insisted H. "I don't want him to go to Saudi Arabia. We pay his wages. This is where he earns his bread and butter."

"I feel so divided," said the victim of the tug-of-war. "I'm stuck in the middle."

There were farcical scenes in a 0-2 defeat at Derby County, where Ludek Miklosko conceded a soft own goal before scuffing a goal kick to Dean Sturridge, who gobbled up the gift.

"Ludo made a couple of rickets," roared Harry. "Just what do you say to somebody who's done that? What are you supposed to do when your 'keeper chips the ball straight to one of their players? Don't worry Ludo, try and kick it a bit higher next time? I'd get the sack if I kept making mistakes like that!"

And on a surreal Derbyshire afternoon, the innocent, confused Alves stepped from the bench to a hail of abuse from the visually challenged Rams' fans, who spent the entire finale booing him in the mistaken belief that he was former County striker, Kitson.

Then when the coach rolled back into London, Lazaridis left his manager in no doubt as to who had won the club-versus-country battle when he took his boots out of the kit skip and headed for the airport.

Having seen Lampard and Ferdinand – who had just signed a new seven-year contract – start to flourish, Redknapp pulled off a major coup when he beat off several clubs – including Manchester United – to sign 16-year-old Joe Cole, the hottest property on the UK youth scene. And according to the *News of the World*, his £10 per week pocket money would be boosted to a sensational £5,000 per week wage once he broke into the first team – a figure rubbished by the club.

Ferdinand had been earning £40 per week as a YTS player just a couple of seasons earlier, yet now he, too, was up there amongst the highest earners.

"A lot has been said about the money I'm earning now and I've seen the 'Richest Teenager in Football' headlines but it doesn't bother me," said the boy from Peckham after being linked with a move to Manchester United. "I don't care what people say. I'm earning a lot more than I was but that's the way football is."

Kitson made a welcome return from injury to bag the winner in a 1-0 victory over Sheffield Wednesday at Upton Park, before the travel sickness reared its head again in a 0-3 defeat at Blackburn Rovers, where Steve Lomas was dismissed.

As Miklosko underwent knee surgery, Paris St Germain's former French international keeper Bernard Lama moved to Upton Park on loan.

Capped 35-times, he had been banned for two months after testing positive for cannabis which resulted in him falling out of favour with both club and country.

With the France 98 World Cup approaching, the pony-tailed keeper was desperate for some cross-Channel first-team action.

But he was only on the bench alongside Alves and Abou as Kitson again hit the target in a 1-0 Boxing Day win over 10-man Coventry City.

The three foreigners were also named as substitutes for the 2-1 win at 10-man Wimbledon that ended a run of eight-successive awayday defeats.

In the FA Cup, Hammers endured a sticky afternoon against Unibond outfit Emley at Upton Park. When Lampard struck after just three minutes an avalanche looked on the cards but shift supervisor Paul David levelled for the Yorkshire part-timers on the hour.

In the end it was left to Hartson to clinically dispense with the romance of the FA

Cup via a late winner.

"I'd be lying if I didn't think a nightmare was gonna happen," admitted a relieved Harry after seeing Hammers scrape a 2-1 victory. "People were saying to me this morning: 'Six? Seven?' I was thinking: 'Are you sure?'"

Redknapp, who frequently reminded the assembled press how the mighty Manchester United had been humbled by his battling Bournemouth side in the FA Cup in 1983, added: "These games are never easy – this sort of thing happens year in, year out."

Having secured an FA Cup fourth round tie at Manchester City, Hammers set about trying to get into the Coca-Cola Cup semi-finals. But ex-Gunner Hartson saw David Seaman save his early penalty, before Ian Wright and Marc Overmars put Arsenal in the driving seat and Abou's first goal for the club was to prove no more than a consolation in a 1-2 defeat.

"John didn't miss the penalty on purpose," said Redknapp, who was much happier a few days later to see the Welshman hit the target in a 6-0 win over rock-bottom Barnsley as Abou netted twice.

"We've got good young players at the club now," insisted the Hammers' boss. "A year ago we wouldn't have scored six goals against anybody. West Ham are a different class now.

"I'd rather be in charge of this team of kids with enthusiasm than a soured old team that thinks it knows all the answers."

The frustrated French journalists following Lama could not believe that he was merely warming the bench as Forrest deputised for Ludo between the sticks.

It was tantamount to England's *nombre un* Seaman ending up marooned in some faraway French dug-out.

"I'm very, very disappointed," announced the flamboyant, equally frustrated Lama. "I really must question why Mr Redknapp wanted me here in the first place. Sure, he made no promises but I want a World Cup place and must play. He says I *will* play but, unfortunately, he doesn't tell me *when* I will play. If West Ham do not want me, then I am sure that there are other clubs in Europe that do.

"And I am not a boy!" he roared, still getting over the experience of a reserve outing at Oxford United's Manor Ground. "I have played for the French national team and in two European Cup Winners' Cup finals. For many years I have played in the French first division. To have to go to Oxford for the reserves was incredible! I haven't had to do anything like that for 12 years."

But with Forrest in fine form, H knew he had to be fair to the Canadian, too.

"As much as I want to help Bernard, I've got to do what's right for the football club," he insisted. "I can't just kick Craig out."

One Frenchman did depart, though, as David Terrier (0+1 app) – a mere 89th minute substitute on the opening day at Barnsley – headed to Newcastle United, while Alves (0+4 apps) returned to Portugal a month ahead of schedule having failed to increase his London goals tally beyond the two he arrived with, in a quartet of trips from the bench.

Abou's honeymoon period came to an abrupt halt at White Hart Lane. He had run the Tottenham defence ragged and endured 43 minutes of sly Spurs provocation, before being dismissed by Harrow housemaster David Elleray for kicking Ramon Vega, who had whacked the Hammer and then pulled off a theatrical Swiss roll when the apoplectic Abou retaliated.

With Hammers already trailing to Jurgen Klinsmann's early, match-winning opener, the furious Frenchman then manhandled the official and refused to walk, as Redknapp – almost at the invitation of Mr Elleray – raced onto the pitch to prevent him getting into deeper trouble. And that also led to an equally unsightly showdown between the Hammers' boss and Spurs' defender Colin Calderwood.

"Abou shouldn't have retaliated," conceded H after seeing his striker subsequently receive a £1,000 fine and an additional one-match ban. "I thought Vega had fractured his leg but it was only a broken tie-up.

In the FA Cup, Lomas was on target upon his return to Maine Road as Hammers ran out 2-1 winners to set up a fifth round tie against another side from the north-west – Blackburn Rovers.

A few years earlier, the now redundant former chief scout Ronnie Boyce had been a frequent visitor to the region checking out Blackpool's £600,000-rated winger Trevor Sinclair.

But while Hammers had been consistently linked with the dreadlocked flyer, nothing had ever come to fruition. Sinclair had undoubted talent. Indeed, he had been called into full England squads and had also claimed the goal of the season with a spectacular overhead kick from outside the area for Queens Park Rangers against Barnsley.

However, the Loftus Road wide boy – who was about to see charges dropped following an alleged altercation with a taxi driver in his native Manchester – had certainly lost his way following Rangers' relegation in 1996.

Having once bullishly been rated at £10m by his manager Ray Wilkins, Sinclair needed a fresh challenge and Redknapp – despite apparently being warned that his target 'had a fat arse' – did not need to be asked twice to get out the magic dust and sprinkle it on an outrageous swap deal that was a total kick up the R's for the supporters down Shepherds Bush way.

Somehow, the Hammers' boss managed to persuade Ray Harford to swap 24-year-old Sinclair for Northern Ireland internationals Dowie (83+12 apps 15 gls) and Keith Rowland (71+20 apps 1 gl) plus £1.6m.

"I just can't afford to be a squad player so it's time for me to move on," said Rowland. "I was always involved at West Ham but I never managed to make the step up to play regularly in the first team."

Although Dowie had bagged that Porfirio-assisted Coca-Cola double against Nottingham Forest back in autumn 1996, it had all gone flat for the 33-year-old striker who had not scored in the league since March 1996 – an incredible run of 44 Premiership outings.

"Look, he doesn't miss them on purpose!" protested Harry on more than one occasion after his confidence-stricken striker had come in for a Boleyn barracking for only managing those two goals in 49 league and cup run-outs.

Harford had promised Dowie the opportunity to start coaching at Loftus Road – a move that was to have a significant impact on the Hammers, a little over six years later.

"I always gave my all for West Ham, while I also saw people come and go who didn't want to play for the club," he said in a clear blast at some of his foreign strike-partners. "I didn't score as many goals as I would have liked to have done, but I'd like to think that I earned the respect of the fans through my efforts for the club I love."

And Redknapp added: "Florin Raducioiu? I find it strange how the fans liked him. He got a smack in the gob at Torquay and he deserved it! You could give me Iain Dowie any time!"

In stark contrast to the departing Dowie's drought, sharp-shooting Sinclair marked his debut with a double-barrelled blast in a 2-2 draw against Everton.

"I'd been out of the Premiership for a while and I began to think: 'Am I still good enough to play there?' Now I've just proved to myself that I am," enthused the five-times capped England Under-21 international. "We've got some good young players here and it's a club that's going places. I want to be a part of that."

Everton's Slaven Bilic received the predictable chants of 'Judas' and, with the Blues languishing well below Hammers in the table, it was pretty obvious that the Goodison grass was not as green as he had envisaged. Reports of constant bust-ups with boss Howard Kendall coupled with three red cards and seven bookings had made for plenty of Mersey misery.

As spring approached, Unsworth conversely announced that both he and his homesick wife were longing for Liverpool.

"We're northerners through and through but it's a situation that we're going to grind out," he insisted. "I'm down here to do a job and, football-wise, the move's been fantastic for me."

Storrie certainly did not miss home as he continued to make frequent trips to Australia to gauge the progress of the strategic alliances Hammers had forged with potential feeder clubs, Blacktown in Sydney and Perth's Kingsway Olympic, in an attempt to nurture talent rather than pay top dollar in the transfer market.

"We only need to find one or two players and the investment will pay for itself," he insisted. "And West Ham are also upping the standard of all the boys which must surely assist Australian football."

But try as it might, the club just could not unearth another wizard from Oz like Lazaridis, who netted a spectacular long-range winner in a 1-0 victory at Newcastle United.

To the disgust of the French media, Lama had still not featured for the first team and, despite threatening to find another club, he remained at Upton Park, staying equally tight-lipped on his future.

"Boy, I know that it is your job," he dismissively told the "boy" from *Hammers News Magazine* seeking an indication of the French keeper's waning tolerance level. "But you just ask too many questions."

Another goalie on his way into Upton Park was promising England youth keeper Stephen Bywater, who joined on loan from Rochdale with a view to a £300,000 transfer rising with appearances.

When claims that the fee for the 16-year-old – who had yet to play a league match – could be as much as £2.3m, though, they were quickly refuted.

"Only if he captains England!" came the cries from within the Boleyn Ground.

First-team coach Frank Burrows left to take over the reins at Cardiff City and that saw the return of ex-West Ham striker Roger Cross, who joined up with his former Hammers' team mates Redknapp and Lampard after quitting Spurs.

Having seen off the northern challenges of mighty Emley and Manchester City, Hammers faced Blackburn Rovers in an FA Cup clash at Upton Park. An ill-tempered tie saw Berkovic claim that he had been the subject of anti-Semitic abuse after the consequently dismissed Kevin Gallacher clobbered him in the 2-2 draw that forced an Ewood Park replay.

"I'm here to play football and I did not come to England to get involved in other things," said Berkovic who had been linked with both Tottenham and former mentor Graeme Souness' Benfica. "It's the first time that anything like that has happened to me. I was surprised to be insulted like that."

Again, West Ham found themselves travelling across the Pennines as they drew 1-1 at Bolton Wanderers, where Nathan Blake's late strike wiped out Sinclair's opener after the visitors hit the self-destruct button by missing a hatful of chances and then having Hartson sent off.

And the FA Cup fifth round replay at Blackburn Rovers ended all-square at 1-1, too, after extra-time. In the build-up to the game it had been suggested, but never actually proved, that it was possibly Rovers' skipper Tim Sherwood who had upset Berkovic so much in the original tie.

The subsequently substituted Israeli was brutally booed for the 55 minutes that he was on the pitch, but after Stuart Ripley cancelled out Hartson's 102nd-minute opener, Berkovic had the last laugh. Hammers won 5-4 on penalties, following Colin Hendry's miss in the spot-kick decider, to set up a second cup quarter-final tie of the season with Arsenal.

But before getting down to the business of the FA Cup, the sides fought out a goalless dress-rehearsal in the Premiership, as Lama was finally handed the gloves after Forrest strained his neck.

Hammers had famously won an FA Cup sixth round tie at Highbury – thanks to two-goal Alan Taylor – on their way to lifting the trophy in 1975. And, Trevor Brooking's header had also shot down the Gunners' hopes in the 1980 final, too.

And when stand-in striker Pearce put Hammers ahead in this quarter-final to silence the red half of north London, the omens were looking good for the visitors.

But Dennis Bergkamp forced an equaliser before a string of fantastic Lama saves ensured that West Ham held out for an Upton Park replay.

"I have felt for a long time that Bernard Lama is one of the top three goalkeepers in the world," declared Gunners' boss, Arsene Wenger, giving his fellow countryman a grand endorsement. "Even when I was in France he was always a problem for my teams. You just cannot take a player like him as cover. All along, West Ham have had gold in their hands."

With Lama and Abou at the club, the French theme continued as centre-half Mohamed Berthe (0 apps) joined on loan from second division Gazelec Ajaccio, but it was soon clear that he was not up to standard and he never made it beyond the Hammers' bench.

As Lampard impressed at Under-21 level, Ferdinand became the first Hammer since Alvin Martin – in the 1986 World Cup tie against Paraguay – to start an England international when he lined up for a 1-1 draw against Switzerland.

The revitalised Sinclair, who was also doing his international chances no harm whatsoever, was on target in a 1-1 draw against Manchester United and he found the net again in a 2-1 victory over Chelsea which moved Hammers to within just one point of a top six spot.

That win over the Blues was also Ian Bishop's last appearance for the club.

For just as a defence containing the likes of Ferdinand, Pearce and Unsworth picked itself then so, too, did the midfield comprising Lampard, Lomas, Moncur, Sinclair and Berkovic. And that meant there was little room for Bishop (287+17 apps 17 gls), who was allowed to return to struggling first division Manchester City on a free transfer.

"I had to go," said Bish, who soon ended up getting relegated into the second division. "Harry was very fair to me. He said I could go on a free or sign for another year and have a testimonial. I'd only started three games all season and just didn't feel part of things anymore. I would've stayed and fought for my place but you've got to be given the chance to climb into the ring in the first place."

Despite the disappointment of relegation, Bish subsequently inspired City to a Premiership return before joining up with fellow Scouser Mike Marsh at Burscough. Having stood on the punter's side of the bar in virtually every pub in every town, Bish crossed till-side and ran the Fisherman's Rest in Southport before eventually heading to the States in 2005.

The build up to the FA Cup quarter-final replay had been overshadowed by Patrick Vieira's final whistle dust-up with Moncur and Lampard at Highbury.

And Bergkamp did little to restore goodwill at Upton Park when he was dismissed for elbowing Lomas 10 minutes before the break. Although that gave Hammers the edge over Arsenal, Nicolas Anelka gave his team the lead before Hartson equalised against his old club to send the tie into extra-time and then penalties.

But the Welshman went from hero to villain when, alongside Abou and Berkovic, he missed from the spot in the shoot-out.

"You can lose to the Dog & Duck on penalties," said the gutted Hartson. "Anything can happen."

West Ham shook off the disappointment of that cup exit with a scintillating 3-0 win over Leeds, in which goal-scoring Pearce proved a revelation at right-back.

"West Ham played some high-speed, high-calibre football to edge closer to a UEFA Cup place," observed the *Daily Mail*. "On this form they would be a credit to the country if they were to make Europe."

And although the Yorkshiremen crash-landed at Upton Park, that defeat was put into perspective when they had to make a real-life emergency touchdown as Emerald Airways flight JEM 1532 caught fire on take-off at Stansted airport.

Thankfully, the 40-strong Leeds party emerged onto the runway from the nosediving BAe 748 plane unscathed.

West Ham's good work on the field was undone by a 0-2 defeat at Aston Villa before they suffered another huge blow with the dismissal of Hartson for continuing his long running feud with Derby County's Igor Stimac.

"The game's not about punching people, it's about playing football," insisted a furious H after seeing the Welshman collect a second red card of the season that would mean a costly four-match suspension going into the final furlong. "If you wanna fight, go down to the York Hall at Bethnal Green and get Frank Warren to put you on the bill.

"The silliest thing was the crowd clapping him off. He let us all down and left us with 10 men. Hartson gets paid to play football, not to get sent off."

The goalless draw also saw Stefano Eranio later dismissed and another eight players booked.

"Hartson wasn't very bright doing that two yards from the linesman," said Rams' boss Jim Smith. "He doesn't like Stimac. That's the third time he's punched him!"

Hartson, the hell-raiser, did not disagree.

"I don't normally dislike anyone in the game but I'm just not too keen on Stimac," he confessed. "I played straight into his hands again. Harry fined me and I've got no complaints about that. But he also called me an idiot, which I didn't agree with. Then again, he's the manager so he can say what he wants about me, can't he? As for Stimac, he's probably still laughing at me, but I suppose some people would say at least he's laughing with a sore head!"

Berkovic was on target in a 1-1 draw at Sheffield Wednesday before Hartson signed off his season with a double in a 2-1 win over Blackburn Rovers.

While Kitson's campaign had been punctuated by injury, Hartson had weighed in with a massive 24 league and cup goals which would see him finish second in the scoring charts, behind only Manchester United's Andrew Cole.

"It was a fantastic season for me," he said. "And if I'd not missed seven matches through suspension, I could've scored five or six more."

Redknapp remained relaxed.

"Where are we in relation to Europe?" he replied after being pitched the question at the post-match press conference. "Not far from Dover! Whatever happens, the people here have seen a team play like they haven't seen a team play for a long time at West Ham United."

But a shock 2-4 home defeat at the hands of Southampton, followed by a 0-5 lashing at Liverpool, meant that the passports were less likely to be dusted down for a first foray back into Europe since 1981.

Injuries were beginning to bite and Redknapp declared: "I'm down to the bare bones with some substitutes who are simply not even good enough to be sitting on the bench. In fact, they're not good enough for this division or any other division in the Football League!"

Two late goals by Manny Omoyinmi rescued a 3-3 draw at Crystal Palace, before Hammers signed off the season with a 4-3 win over Leicester City, for whom substitute Tony Cottee – having returned from a Malaysian nightmare – netted twice to set up a frantic finale.

Eighth-place with 56 points represented Hammers' best top-flight finish since their record breaking efforts of 1986 but Villa, in seventh spot, had still pipped them for a coveted European berth.

"If anyone had said at the beginning of the season that we'd finish eighth, not too many people would've believed it, would they?" suggested Redknapp.

And H had every right to milk the applause for assembling the nucleus of a young squad that had every chance of going onto bigger, better and brighter things. The artful use of the cheque-book saw him mix youthful Englishmen with able foreigners.

"I went back to doing what I know best in the transfer market," he said, knowing that 29-year-old, six-times capped French international, Marc Keller, had already agreed to sign on a free transfer from Bilic's former German club, SC Karlsruhe. "This time I didn't buy at the cheap end of the foreign market, taking chances."

As Paul Gascoigne sensationally failed to make the final 22, forgiven Hammer of the Year, Rio Ferdinand, was the shock inclusion in Glenn Hoddle's France 98 squad. The youngster would not, however, feature in the Three Lions' challenge, which faltered in a controversial sudden-death, second round defeat at the hands of Argentina as petulant David Beckham was dismissed.

Keller unluckily missed the 22-man cut for eventual winners France, but Lama (14 apps) – who quit Upton Park to return home – was picked by Aime Jacquet while ex-Hammers Rieper (Denmark), Slaven Bilic (Croatia) and Ilie Dumitrescu (Romania) also prepared to make the trip to the World Cup finals.

Geoff Hurst, the 1966 World Cup hat-trick hero, was told that he would soon be crossing swords with HM The Queen after being awarded a knighthood – only the sixth in the history of the game behind Sirs Stanley Matthews, Alf Ramsey, Bobby Charlton, Tom Finney and Matt Busby.

"It's absolutely amazing," he cried. "I was really knocked sideways by the news because this is the ultimate accolade for anybody in any walk of life or industry."

As fellow World Cup winner Martin Peters declared that he would not be calling his lifelong friend 'Sir Geoffrey' their former team-mate Redknapp prepared to go cross-Channel talent-spotting.

And while Chile's Javier Margas topped his France 98 viewing list, the Hammers' boss knew that he did not need to be panicked into a Euro 96-style supermarket sweep this time around.

Instead, he already had the backbone of a talented young team and could look back on a domestic season with immense pride. The 24-goal, £3.5m Hartson (aged 23) had encouragingly carried on from where he had left off the campaign before, and while strike-partner Kitson (27) may have been injured, in his absence Abou (24) weighed in with a useful half-dozen goals.

In midfield, England Under-21 skipper Lampard (19) had come of age and taken a giant stride towards winning over the Upton Park sceptics, while Lomas (24) had added bite and Berkovic (26) and Sinclair (25) both looked sub-£2m bargains. Aussie Lazaridis (27) – when not on international duty – had skipped on in leaps and bounds, too.

In defence, England international Ferdinand (19), Unsworth (24), Pearce (24) and Impey (26) had brought pace and strength to the rearguard that also had the experienced Tim Breacker (32) and Potts (31) in reserve, alongside a determined Dicks (29) battling to save his career.

In goal, the thirty-somethings Forrest (30) and then Lama (35) had proved able deputies for the ageing Miklosko (36) ahead of a long-speculated swoop for Newcastle United's Shaka Hislop.

Harry's new look young Hammers had certainly brought more joy than pain.

PLAYERS IN

Samassi Abou	Cannes	£250,000
Eyal Berkovic	Maccabi Haifa	£1,500,000
Stephen Bywater	Rochdale	£300,000 (rising).
Craig Forrest	Ipswich Town	£500,000
Andrew Impey	Queens Park Rangers	£1,250,000
Marc Keller	Karlsrühe SC	Free
Ian Pearce	Blackburn Rovers	£2,300,000.
Trevor Sinclair*	Queens Park Rangers	
	Swap: Dowie+Rowland+£1.6m (out)	
David Terrier	FC Metz	Free
David Unsworth$	Everton	
	Swap for Williamson + £1m (in)	

LOANS IN

Paolo Alves	Sporting Lisbon
Mohammed Berthe	Gazelec Ajaccio
Bernard Lama	Paris Saint-Germain
Ian Moore	Nottingham Forest

PLAYERS OUT

Ian Bishop	Manchester City	Free transfer
Iain Dowie*	Queens Park Rangers	
	Swap for Sinclair+Rowland+£1.6m (out)	
Neil Finn	Dorchester Town	Free transfer
Michael Hughes	Wimbledon	£1,500,000
Marc Rieper	Celtic	£1,400,000
Keith Rowland*	Queens Park Rangers	
	Swap for Sinclair+Dowie+£1.6m (out)	
David Terrier	Newcastle United	Free transfer
Danny Williamson$	Everton	
	Swap for Unsworth + £1m (in)	

Chapter 12
1998-99

THEY FLEW SO HIGH

"Blimey, have you seen the size of John Hartson?" screamed Harry, looking for anyone who would listen to him, as he stormed towards the Chadwell Heath medical room on the squad's first day back at training.

"I like a beer, although I wouldn't say that I drink more than the average 24-year-old," pleaded Hartson who had also found himself in hot water with the police after being caught kicking a hanging flower basket around during a summer prank upon a return to his native Swansea. "But I do like to enjoy myself and I can put weight on. I went home for six weeks and came back a little bit heavy – about 10 pounds overweight – and that's quite a bit to shift.

"I'd scored a few goals last season and I suppose I spoilt myself a bit."

Redknapp wanted a bigger squad but this was not quite what he had in mind.

"Players have no right to come back to the club overweight," fumed H. "They get well paid and should look after themselves."

While Hartson had been occupied at the bar, the Hammers' boss had been busy in the transfer market securing, as expected, Neil 'Shaka' Hislop from Newcastle United on a free transfer that completed an amazing, circuitous route back to his East End birthplace for the amiable shot-stopper.

Having been born in Hackney, the 29-year-old goalkeeper was taken home to their native Trinidad by his parents in the early 70s. After shining in the Caribbean, he won a soccer scholarship to Washington DC's Howard University, where he also took a mechanical engineering degree. And while playing in Baltimore he was discovered by a Reading scout who brought him back to England.

Newcastle then paid the Royals a record £1.575m for the keeper who soon collected a Premiership runners-up medal before falling behind Shay Given in the St James's Park pecking order and finding himself sidelined altogether for prevaricating over the Magpies' offer to open discussions over a new contract

"West Ham have just had a tremendous season," said the wily Hislop after helping to secure his future via a Bosman free transfer. "And hopefully that will just be a stepping stone for us to build upon during the years ahead.

"The team has got some very good young players with a lot of expectation on them so this is not going to be a stroll in the park for me. The club and the fans want success and I want to be a part of it."

Certainly, that eighth place finish had given Redknapp negotiating power as he looked for new recruits and that was in evidence when Arsenal legend Ian Wright

– scorer of 185 goals in 288 Gunners' appearances – agreed to join in a £750,000 transfer from Highbury on a reported wage of £25,000 per week.

Battersea-born Neil Ruddock was signed on a three-year contract from Liverpool, where he had forged a good friendship with Jamie Redknapp.

His Anfield career was all but at an end from the first day that Gerard Houllier arrived on Merseyside.

"Hello Michael and Stevie Mac," said the Frenchman introducing himself to Messrs Owen and McManaman.

"And what's your name?" he asked Razor.

"Have you been in coma for the last 15 years?" replied the enraged Ruddock.

Razor had a reputation for playing hard, both on and off the field, and the new look, slim-line, once-capped England international certainly could not have had a more testing welcome to Chadwell Heath.

For the defender's arrival at the training ground coincided with the delivery of Hammers' new fitness assessment equipment, which called for its participants to undertake a series of paced interval runs across a set distance within an allocated time determined by an audible 'beep'. The longer the test went on, the more frequent the pulses sounded as they transformed gentle jogs into serious sprints.

The luckless Ruddock had only come to have a look around the facilities, but the opportunity was soon taken to hand him some kit so that he could be press-ganged into an inhospitable incremental speed and endurance examination…which he somehow passed with flying colours.

"These days footballers earn a lot of money so it's only right that we look after ourselves, isn't it?" said the seemingly reformed former Millwall, Tottenham and Southampton stopper, acutely aware of the fact that he had to get his act together if he was going to earn a new contract with a new club. "But I certainly haven't given up alcohol. I don't drink beer these days, instead it's white wine and soda."

And he was quick to pay homage to H's summer shopping escapades.

"Harry's just got hold of five players for about three million quid. That's gotta be great business for the club."

Redknapp's most expensive acquisition was centre-half Javier Margas, who joined in a £2m deal from Deportivo Universidad Catolica De Chile after helping his country into the second round at France 98, where they succumbed to Brazil.

Capped 55 times, Margas had excelled in Chile's 2-0 win over England at Wembley six months earlier.

"We haven't rushed into this one," insisted Peter Storrie, conscious of the cultural problems that could be encountered by a lonely South American in deepest, darkest Essex. "It's something we've been talking about over the past few months. We all needed to be comfortable.

"But if somebody can't move 250 miles, you can't say for sure that there won't be problems," he added, mindful of David Unsworth's predicament.

Indeed, in a farcical pre-season transfer, with Everton seemingly showing no interest, the geographically challenged Hammers' defender had sealed a £3m transfer to Aston Villa before quickly revealing that he had made a 'dreadful mistake' in not realising that the Midlands was still some way from Merseyside.

Beauchampitis was certainly contagious.

As Unsworth (41 apps 2 gls) sought a return to the now keen Everton, furious Villa boss John Gregory kicked his new signing out of training early, mockingly stating: "I think his wife said his dinner was ready at one o'clock."

A few days later, Unsworth made that £3m move to Goodison Park, leaving the bemused Gregory sticking the boot in again: "He's obviously confused Birmingham with Bolton. But then he is a footballer!"

And after embarrassingly letting Dagenham Motors depart before closing out the South African airline sponsorship which eventually fell by the wayside due to aviation licensing problems, Hammers avoided another blank season as Griggs Group – manufacturers of Dr Martens footwear – weighed in with a heavyweight three-year shirt-sponsorship deal.

Following 1-1 friendly draws with both Hibernian and Motherwell, West Ham kicked off the season with a 1-0 win at Sheffield Wednesday, where Wright instantly endeared himself to the Hammers' fans by bagging the winner.

"The West Ham supporters have spent the best part of a decade loathing Wright," wrote the *News of the World*. "But Upton Park has found a new hero."

And following France 98, the East End had identified a villain, too.

After being dismissed in an ill-tempered second round tie, David Beckham was still being castigated for England's World Cup exit that had followed his petulant flick at the antagonistic Argentinian Diego Simeone.

There was a siege mentality around the Boleyn Ground as Becks was ushered into the bubbling cauldron amidst tight security but, just like the goalless match itself, the afternoon passed off with little incident.

Margas made an assured debut in a second goalless draw at Coventry City and things looked to be going fantastically well when Hammers raced into a 3-0 lead against wobbling Wimbledon thanks to two-goal Wright and his former Highbury team-mate Hartson.

But as the Anglo-Chilean axis of Ruddock and Margas suffered a huge communication breakdown, the Dons amazingly battled back to win 4-3.

"At 3-0 up and having not conceded a goal all season, you wouldn't have believed what was about to happen, would you?" fumed a dumbstruck Harry after seeing his hari-kari Hammers lose their stranglehold on the game. "They pummelled us and penned us in. The crowd loved what they were seeing in the first half-hour but then it all turned into a major disappointment for everybody. When you're 3-0 up at home, you shouldn't get beaten."

Margas injured his knee, too, and a cartilage operation meant that he would be out of action until December, but it was a measure of their durability that Redknapp's men bounced back to beat table-topping Liverpool just three days later as, for the second season running, Hartson and Eyal Berkovic sealed a 2-1 victory.

But Hammers were quickly booted into touch by the Cobblers after a double by Northampton Town's Chris Freestone saw the second division outfit pull off a Coca-Cola Cup second round, first-leg shock at Sixfields Stadium.

"West Ham were outplayed by a team which normally charges around like a herd of buffalo," observed *The Sun*.

"I can't make any excuses," admitted Harry on the wrong end of yet another giant-killing. "After beating Liverpool, this is a major disappointment."

Patched-up West Ham scrapped out another goalless draw at Nottingham Forest before Julian Dicks made a welcome return to action, after an 18-month absence, for the return leg against Northampton.

"I just went out there to enjoy myself. For all I knew it could have been my last game," said the brave defender, who was given the captain's armband by the volunteering Wright. "The reception I got from the West Ham fans was unbelievable. The adrenalin then kicked in and I was off and running. It was great to prove everybody wrong. I've got 18 months left on my contract and I'd like to play every week. I don't know whether I can or not but that's what I want to do."

After seeing him play his first game since March 1997, Harry enthused: "They said he'd never play again. Dicksy's just a freak!"

Given a slender one-in-10 chance of making a return, the dogged defender had simply refused to lie down.

"I just wanted one last pop at it to prove a few people wrong," he said. "The club had even tried to pay me off before I went out to America for my operation."

But that was the only encouraging aspect on an evening when Lampard's 90th-minute strike was too little, too late to prevent Hammers crashing out of the Coca-Cola Cup 1-2 on aggregate.

In the Premiership, however, West Ham kept up their strong start to the season with a 1-0 victory over Southampton at Upton Park, where match-winner Wright celebrated his goal with a cheeky parody of Paolo Di Canio's recent shove on referee Paul Alcock.

Sheffield Wednesday's irascible Italian had pushed over the official during a bust-up in the Owls' 1-0 win over Wright's former club, Arsenal, at Hillsborough two days earlier.

And in what appeared to be a well-rehearsed sketch, Wright held up an imaginary card to Ruddock who then shoved the goalscorer to the ground in a re-run of the incident that would condemn Di Canio to an 11-game suspension.

But, ironically, on the same weekend that soccer was being shamed in Sheffield, an incident of similar gravity had taken place at Chadwell Heath in the preparations for that live Sky TV clash with the Saints.

Certainly, Hartson was the sinner as he kicked the grounded Eyal Berkovic in the head after the Israeli retaliated with an attempted slap into the Welshman's thigh following the striker's forceful training ground lunge from behind.

And just to make matters worse, the whole incident had been caught by the satellite broadcaster's cameras, who had been filming in the build up to the Monday night football special.

However, back at Murdoch Towers, the order had, apparently, come down from on high that the incident was just too horrific to beam onto the dishes of the nation.

With no incriminating photographic evidence having been published, in his weekly *Newham Recorder* column the wily Welshman was economical with his words when he wrote: "It's time for the truth to come out about the incident between me and Eyal Berkovic. I didn't think it was such a big deal but the press has got hold of it and turned it into a major controversy.

"To be honest, I think it's disgusting how much publicity the story has got so now I will put the record straight. In training, I hit Eyal with a bad tackle. It was a silly challenge but not malicious and I went straight up to him and apologised. He said everything was fine and I thought that was the end of it.

"Then I saw in the papers that Eyal has said I booted him in the shoulder and that he wants to leave the club. Let me stress that I haven't actually heard him say this. It could all be paper talk again. But if he has come out with these comments, then I admit I would lose a little bit of respect for him.

"This sort of things happens in training every day but nobody goes around making it public because we are professionals. But I will not judge him until I know the truth because I've always considered Eyal a nice guy.

"But just like always in this sport, everything has been blown out of proportion.

"Another example of this is my being dragged into court for apparently causing criminal damage to a plant pot. I was given a conditional discharge and asked to pay £40 costs. The bloke before me was caught in possession of cannabis and got a £30 fine and ordered to pay another £30 costs.

"If I'm making the papers because of a broken flower pot, imagine what it would have been like if it was me caught with drugs. I suppose the moral of this story is not to tamper with pot of any kind!

"I now want to get back to just concentrating on my football."

But for Hartson, this one was simply not going to go away.

Up until then, it had been a happy camp inside Upton Park and, going into October, Hammers had still lost only one Premiership encounter – that bizarre 3-4 defeat to Wimbledon.

But the paint on the walls of the Ewood Park dressing room was soon blistering.

"We were all over the place today," said Harry following a 0-3 reverse at Blackburn Rovers that saw West Ham concede their first goals on the road.

With an international break for the Euro 2000 qualifiers, Hartson was pulled out of the Welsh squad with an ankle problem and duly packed off to see Tiburce Darrou – a personal fitness guru – on the French Riviera, where he was treated to a harsh training regime and a diet of Mediterranean fish.

Berkovic, who was back home in Israel preparing for matches against Spain and San Marino, insisted: "I am forbidden to talk about the incident but I am okay."

But local Tel-Aviv newspaper *Ma'ariu* reported that the player had allegedly said: "If my head had been a football it would have flown into the top corner of the net."

And when the *Daily Mirror* eventually published the damming stills of the video footage that mysteriously came into its possession some 10 days later, the whole horror of the assault became clear.

"We were going to fine Hartson two weeks wages but Berkovic asked the manager not to do that. He said the matter was closed," said Storrie, reacting to media criticism that the club had not taken any action.

As the Football Association moved to charge Hartson with misconduct that would, ultimately, lead to a £20,000 fine and three-match ban, the club also docked him two weeks wages and sent the post-tax sum to the Leukaemia Busters charity.

For their part, Berkovic's advisors could see the fall-out as the catalyst to find a bigger and better club for their client, who was linked with Graeme Souness' Benfica, Liverpool and Manchester United.

Hartson, on the other hand, reportedly considered suing the FA which led cynics to suggest he should contact OJ Simpson's legal team. That the FA could charge a player for an incident that occurred in the perceived privacy of the club's training ground, however, opened a whole new line of debate, while Redknapp insisted that both of his valuable stars would stay at the club.

"They are both terrific players and I'm not getting rid of either of them," he declared. "I cannot condone what Hartson has done – I hate violence and that incident hurt me very much. John has got to get his head right and learn quickly."

Certainly, the club could not afford to sack its £10m-rated goal-getter, while the innovative Israeli was the most creative player at Upton Park.

"You were probably left scratching your head when you read last week's column because I hadn't mentioned the full extent of the incident with Eyal Berkovic," wrote Hartson in his next *Newham Recorder* column. "The reason for this is simple. After it happened Harry sat everybody down and said that it was an internal matter for the club to deal with. We were under strict orders not to discuss the topic but the story then broke in all the national papers.

"I feel I have to keep my head down now and concentrate entirely on my football. With this in mind I have decided not to speak to any of the media for the foreseeable future. Unfortunately, that must take in the *Newham Recorder* so this will be my last column."

But *Recorder* editor Tom Duncan fumed: "West Ham's attempt to cover up the John Hartson affair was at best naïve and at worst deceitful. It calls into question the relationship that has traditionally existed between the club and its supporters.

"Hartson resigned as our columnist and said he had no intention of speaking to the press again until the whole affair was settled. Yet seconds later he told a member of our sports staff that he was considering substantial offers from two national newspapers. There were also reports that an 'exclusive interview' was being hawked around for £20,000.

"Hartson has a lot to learn from this incident and so does West Ham United."

As Iain Dowie took over as caretaker manager at Queens Park Rangers, Ludek Miklosko and Tim Breacker headed on loan to Loftus Road, while another hopeful from Down Under – Michael Ferrante – signed for a nominal fee from the Australian Institute of Sport.

Hartson and Berkovic trained together on the eve of Hammers' game against league leaders Aston Villa, and following the goalless draw in which they both played the full 90 minutes, Harry confessed: "After all that's gone on, I'm glad we got back to playing football today."

But Redknapp was far from happy as Hammers twice surrendered the lead at Charlton Athletic, where poor Dicks was run ragged by Danny Mills, and then substitute John Robinson, on a rain-lashed pitch.

The Hammers' skipper was dropped for the trip to St James's Park, as two-goal

NEARLY REACHED THE SKY

Wright secured a 3-0 win over Newcastle United, who had future Hammer Stuart Pearce dismissed for an awkward aerial challenge on other goalscorer Sinclair.

"Afterwards, I told my players: 'You played an excellent game and 0-3 is no reflection'. We were not beaten by better opposition," claimed arrogant Magpies' boss Ruud Gullit, those dreadlocks no doubt covering his eyes.

Back in London, Dicks insisted: "There's no point in me slogging my guts out and playing well if I'm going to be dropped for the next game. Harry only includes me when he's struggling to put out a side. I want to finish my career at West Ham but if I'm getting used like a dogsbody what's the point of me being here?"

A defiant Harry replied: "I'm not going to guarantee Julian a place every week. Some weeks he might get picked, other weeks he might not. That's the way it is."

Joe Cole marked his 17th birthday by signing a five-year contract on the pitch before a 1-1 draw against Chelsea in which Ruddock scored his first-ever goal for the club and promptly celebrated with another impromptu impression of Frank Lampard senior – rolling his socks down and cruelly squashing his nose.

But there was only pain for Pierliugi Casiraghi whose career was, ultimately, ended by the accidental sandwich with Hislop and Rio Ferdinand that ruptured his knee ligaments.

A 3-2 win over Leicester City lifted Hammers into sixth place before Wright and Ferdinand put in superb performances for England in a 2-0 victory over the Czech Republic at Wembley.

Another 2-0 win at Derby County – in which Keller opened his account with a 65 miles-per-hour screamer – was overshadowed by the furious row that erupted between Redknapp and Storrie following the proposed sale of Andrew Impey (32+2 apps), 24 hours earlier.

"I understand that we've got to sell a player," said H after the board accepted a £1.6m bid from Leicester City. "But we should have been looking to do it tomorrow not last night! I've been working with him on set pieces for two days.

"It's a problem when you get non-footballing people involving themselves."

In reply, Storrie revealed: "Harry and I agreed that we would sell someone by the end of November to balance the books after investing over £3m on five new players in this summer.

"An offer came in for a player who was not always in the team and we accepted it. You can't then play him and risk him breaking a leg.

"There's no financial crisis and we are not intending to sell our best players."

At Upton Park, Sinclair's double secured a 2-1 win over Tottenham Hotspur, who had made an audacious £4.3m, midweek bid to sign Frank Lampard, a player who they released as a schoolboy.

"I don't want to make threats to anyone but I wouldn't want to stick around if players like Frank and Rio were being sold. What kind of future would that hold for the club? I'm looking to build a team here," said Redknapp after a victory that lifted Hammers up into second spot, while the month's unbeaten run also won him Carling Manager of the Month for November 1998. "Anyway, why should Frank want to go to Spurs? We're above them in the league."

As is typical, the curse of the award coupled with the advent of December saw

Redknapp brought crashing back to earth by two future Hammers.

Firstly, Lee Bowyer bagged a double in a 0-4 defeat at Leeds United, where Margas returned to action for the first time since that 3-4 reverse against Wimbledon. And having suffered a reaction to that knee injury, he was on his way back to Chile to see a specialist by the time Brian Deane scored in a 0-1 loss at Middlesbrough.

In an effort to repair some of the damage caused by the Berkovic incident, Hartson agreed to be interviewed by *Hammers News Magazine* on the condition that both he and Storrie could see the article prior to publication.

"I'm deeply sorry that I let my reactions go so far," admitted Hartson in a candid interview. "Eyal's a smashing little fella and I shouldn't have done what I did. We're good friends – we always have been – and it was one of those spur of the moment things. It really does bother me that I'll be remembered for what happened at Chadwell Heath, regardless of what I go on to achieve in the rest of my career.

"I was on *News at Ten* and *Richard and Judy* and there were about 50 cameramen with long lenses sat down at the end of my garden," he added, clearly unsettled by the public outcry over his moment of madness.

"John Hartson doesn't seek forgiveness," concluded the proposed article. "All he asks is that he is given one last chance to get his career back on the road."

Storrie gave the draft an instant thumbs up before Hartson phoned in merely to request that the final closing line should be deleted.

"Everything else is fine," he confirmed. "But would you leave out that bit about me wanting a final chance. After all, *if* I was to do the same thing *again*, everyone would say that Hartson's already asked for one final chance once before!"

Going into Christmas, Bilic, Unsworth and Don Hutchison returned to Upton Park only for Hammers to run out 2-1 winners over Everton as they headed into Christmas in sixth place.

After the Hartson-Berkovic furore, the last thing Redknapp needed was the arrest of Ruddock and goal-scorer Sinclair just 24 hours after the final whistle. Entertainments guru Dale Gordon may have left the club but Christmas parties were clearly still *de rigueur* down Upton Park way.

An altercation had occurred in Romford town centre between a group of men in fancy dress and a woman in a Mini – a small car, not short skirt – that ended up with beauty therapist Belinda Knowles complaining to police that her vehicle had been besieged and vandalised by the drunken crowd leaving Yates's Wine Lodge.

A future England international dressed in pink trousers jumped on the roof of the car and rolled onto the boot before lying in front of the vehicle.

According to the *Daily Mirror*, the 19-year-old victim claimed: "Suddenly we heard a huge thump on the roof and a leg was swinging over the side. There were loads of people in weird costumes all around us. The next thing, the man from the roof rolled over on the bonnet and then the ground, breaking my wing-mirror, aerial and windscreen wiper. I got out and it got nasty. One person told me: 'Get back in the f****** car right now!' As soon as the man got off the bonnet, I drove away and someone threw a glass at the window. It was cowardly and pathetic."

Vociferously protesting mistaken identity, Ruddock was originally charged with affray and was subsequently cleared of the reduced indictment of using threatening, abusive or insulting words, while Sinclair was charged with causing criminal damage to the extent of £225.85.

Both were given unconditional bail by Havering Magistrates.

Understandably, Redknapp was furious. After the juvenile events of years gone by, he now had a team of high-quality, high-paid, high-profile players on the cusp of a UEFA Cup spot who really should have known better than to parade in 1970s fancy dress through a busy high street at Sunday tea-time.

"I told them to enjoy themselves and make sure they were well behaved. They promised there wouldn't be any aggro and then, sure enough, I got a call," he cried after learning that his players had later been arrested in nearby Secrets nightclub. "That's it! There won't be any more Christmas parties. Not while I'm here. I don't think this sort of thing happens at Juventus. The Italians have a glass of wine but they don't go out and get drunk.

"I've done everything I can. I've banned alcohol from the players' bar and can't understand why they have to go out in fancy dress like that. The days are over when they can all go out on the booze together. They've got to set an example."

One man who had been a role model during his time at Upton Park was Ludek Miklosko (373 apps).

But instead of tucking into his Christmas dinner, the goalkeeper was in west London with QPR boss Gerry Francis, hastily turning his loan spell into a permanent move to Loftus Road.

With Hislop now firmly installed as Number One, the 37-year-old, 41-times capped Czech Republic international was firmly out of the first team reckoning.

Sadly, that disastrous performance at Derby, just over a year beforehand, was to be his last outing for the club and after nine years at Upton Park, he left in acrimonious circumstances after Hammers insisted on a fee for their loyal keeper who had been one of the bedrocks of the Boleyn since his bargain £284,000 move from Banik Ostrava in February 1990.

"My understanding was that I could have a free transfer when I reached age 35 but because it was not actually written down on a piece of paper, that never happened," the Czech claimed after finding himself out of pocket and out of the coaching reckoning following Les Sealey's return to the club. "I also said I would like to stay to be West Ham's second keeper and coach but things have happened since then and I have had to move on.

"West Ham also owed me some money and they said that I could only go if they could keep most of it. In the end, I just agreed but it's such a shame that it has ended this way. I have many good memories of my time at Upton Park and I never had any problems with any of the other players or the crowd," he added after removing his gloves and climbing into his Skoda following nearly a decade's dependable and dignified service. Indeed, only Phil Parkes (439), Ernie Gregory (406) and Ted Hufton (401) had played more games in goal for West Ham United.

"I only made those mistakes at Derby because I had suffered problems with my knee and when I decided to have an operation Harry seemed to think that I was just trying to make an excuse for myself.

"By then, communication with Harry was bad and I had to buy a newspaper just to find out what he was thinking about me," he added, his relationship with the manager clearly having broken down.

Redknapp replied: "QPR wanted Ludo and we wanted £75,000, which he's worth any day of the week. They said: 'We can only give you £x' but that was their problem. He had to take a bit of a cut from the money we owed him so they could then afford him. Obviously he felt we should have given him a free transfer. If there had been an agreement he would've got one. Why should we give him away? Nobody gives West Ham anything."

A Boxing Day defeat at Highbury did little to lift spirits as Marc Overmars gave Arsenal a 1-0 win, but Hammers did at least get back on track with a 2-0 victory over Coventry City at Upton Park that sent them into 1999 in sixth place.

Having been knocked out of the Coca-Cola Cup by Northampton Town, Swansea City looked to set to condemn woeful West Ham to another premature FA Cup exit before Dicks popped up to bag an 86th-minute saver in a 1-1 draw at Upton Park.

While the veteran skipper showed that it was just a little bit too early to write him off, at the other end of the scale, substitute Cole made his debut, aged 17 years and 55 days, when the clock on the Bobby Moore Stand ticked onto 4.21pm.

That made him the second youngest outfield player and the third youngest of all-time, behind midfielder Paul Allen (17 years & 32 days) and goalkeeper Neil Finn (17 years & three days) and, as the red and white bulbs on the fourth official's electronic board shone like beacons through the murky Upton Park mist, Cole's impending arrival was about to satisfy the curiosity of an expectant East End who had been enthralled by years of Harry's hype.

"It would have been nice if I'd been able to come on and make my debut as an unknown just like most other young players do," said the starry-eyed England schoolboy international, who arrived amidst a roaring crescendo of 23,000 approving locals. "I was looking around the dressing room and couldn't believe I was sitting there with legends.

"Just because I've now played half-a-game, I'm not going to go knocking on Harry's door demanding to play. That'd be stupid and, anyway, there are players in the side who are twice as good as me. I've got so much time on my side."

Manchester United manager Alex Ferguson had coveted young Cole from an early age and, according to Wembley folklore, had even invited him along with the team to see the Red Devils in an FA Cup final.

"How's Joe Cole?" he would frequently ask whenever he bumped into the Hammers' management. And as Cole stepped off the bench at Old Trafford to become the youngest-ever West Ham outfield player to kick a ball in a top-flight match, Fergie was able to see his progression at first hand.

By then, though, United had already sewn the game up and although Cole helped to conjure up a late conversion for Lampard, it was a mere consolation against the backdrop of a 1-4 defeat inspired by the other Cole – the Reds' two-goal Andrew.

Indeed, injuries had seen Ezomo Iriekpen – aged 16 years & 241 days – named as substitute and, stripped for action on the sidelines in stoppage time, he came within seconds of pipping Cole to the title of youngest-ever Hammer. But referee

NEARLY REACHED THE SKY

Mike Reed blew his whistle before the teenager had the chance to cross the white line. And that was to be the closest 'Izzy' would ever get to playing for the club.

For the second time in three seasons, Hammers found themselves crashing out of the FA Cup to lower division, Welsh opposition as Martin Thomas' goal proved to be difference between two teams standing 72 league places apart.

"Don't ask me why but, in the 35 years that I've been around the club, these giant-killings keep happening to West Ham," said Harry after seeing Swansea expose the frailties of his defence to repeat the previous heroics of Wrexham.

"After losing to such illustrious clubs as Grimsby, Wrexham, Stockport and Northampton, the cup debacle at Vetch Field may have sealed the fate of Harry Redknapp. All that remains is setting his date of execution," announced David McDonnell of the *Daily Mail* who, upon his next visit to Chadwell Heath, was personally escorted out of the training ground by the furious Hammers' boss.

"Redknapp's undignified and foul-mouthed behaviour was a performance that did nothing for his own reputation or that of the club he represents. Shouting in my face, he took my arm and led me from the ground, then roared an abusive farewell and yelled that I would never be allowed back in. I had merely been trying to seek out the truth to pass on to our readers," argued the righteous scribe who had become one of the most unwelcome journalists at the club thanks to a series of stories aimed at destabilising both West Ham United and its manager.

Former Charlton Athletic and Chelsea star Scott Minto had been signed from Benfica for £1m by the time Sheffield Wednesday came to town.

And he made his debut in a humiliating 0-4 home defeat to the Owls that left Redknapp admitting: "No, it's not been a good week but I've had worse and I'll bounce back."

Certainly, the critically injured Redknapp had been given a good perspective on life from the moment he had been pulled from the wreckage of the Italian car crash that claimed the life of his good friend Brian Tiler during the 1990 World Cup.

"Pressure isn't losing a football match," he twitched. "Pressure is when you're lying on a bed in an Italian hospital and the doctor puts a blanket over your head because he thinks you're dead!"

With that in mind, Minto's baptism of boos was mere nettle rash compared to what his boss had endured.

"Don't worry," agreed the new boy. "At Benfica we even used to get jeered off at half-time if we weren't winning."

Hammers' lacklustre start to 1999 was the catalyst for Redknapp to shuffle his pack yet further.

While most commentators had expected Berkovic to be the first of the warring, albeit publicly reconciled, duo to go out through the door, Hartson (72+1 apps 33 gls) was the one to leave following Wimbledon's double your money, club record £7.5m swoop for him.

And having opted against buying Glasgow Rangers' prolific, but unfit, Marco Negri, eyebrows were raised when Redknapp announced to the board the other Italian he wished to sign in his place.

Paolo Di Canio had been a pariah of the Premiership following his shove on the unsteady Paul Alcock at Hillsborough that had earned him that 11-match ban and a £10,000 fine. Taking refuge in Rome, the hot-headed Italian, who had been absent without leave from Yorkshire, had not played for Sheffield Wednesday for four months following a dispute with his employers that had seen them willing to offload him for a mere £1.7m.

"I want people to remember Di Canio for his footballing skills – the dribbling, the passing, the goals – not for what happened last September," declared the nomadic former Lazio, Ternana, Juventus, Napoli, AC Milan and Celtic striker who had cost the Owls £4.5m when they brought him south from Glasgow.

The purchases of Hartson and Kitson may have been a gamble but, following some unsuccessful punts on some temperamental foreigners, Redknapp was putting his reputation firmly on the line with the acquisition of Di Canio.

"Everybody has an opinion about Di Canio. But the only opinion that counts is mine and I have no doubts whatsoever. Yes, he pushed a referee but I can tell you about two other players who have pushed referees who didn't fall over," announced H, clearly making reference to Lomas (Blackburn Rovers) and Abou (Tottenham Hotspur). "It's not a gamble. The fact of the matter is that I wouldn't have been able to buy him under any other circumstances because Wednesday wouldn't have sold him," said Redknapp. "Okay the boy made a mistake, but nobody can dispute his footballing ability. He's very passionate about the game."

Outspoken John Sadler of *The Sun* was in no doubt that this was a wheel 'n deal too far.

"Oi, Harry! Got a new motor? He's chuffed at getting his hands on a real classic at a knockdown price. It's history is, well, history. It's tomorrow what counts. And Redknapp's job will be riding in the back seat with every run that Di Canio makes. West Ham's joy at his arrival is outweighed only by Wednesday's relief at his departure. Harry has decided to trust the untrustable. I fear for him when he describes Di Canio as a genius. This is a player who comes with so many strings attached but carrying a noose for the boss who believed in him. Everyone makes mistakes, Redknapp reminds us. And so they do. If the Alfa Romeo is still cruising without a splutter next season, we'll all be thankful Harry has not just made the biggest one of his career."

And unveiled alongside Di Canio was Marc-Vivien Foe – an African powerhouse who had been heavily courted by Manchester United in the run up to the France 98 World Cup.

But disastrously, the Cameroon international suffered the double-whammy of seeing a broken leg rule him out of the finals and United's interest wane.

Ever the opportunist, Harry splashed out a club record £4.5m for the 23-year-old Racing Club Lens midfielder.

"What is the point of crying about not going to Manchester United? I do not have tears streaming down my cheeks," said the religious, 54-times capped Foe. "I would have liked to have joined them but now all my attention is focused on West Ham. This is God's path for me."

Physio John Green confirmed that there were no problems with Foe's fractured fibula.

NEARLY REACHED THE SKY

"As usual, we X-ray chest, knees and ankles before checking out the heart. The specialist is happy with the way the leg's healed," he confirmed oblivious, like everyone else, to the horrific fate that was to befall the African some four years later. "Marc passed with flying colours."

Fate also dictated that Hammers' next game would be against Hartson's Wimbledon at Selhurst Park.

Having seen his designer track-suit torched by the Crazy Gang at his first training session, the Welshman, himself, was left smoking after being put through his paces by the Dons' fitness coach – Olympic gold medal-winning decathlete Daley Thompson.

And while Wimbledon's new skipper was instantly serenaded by his new supporters, the ones that he had left behind taunted him throughout an unremarkable London derby that saw Foé have a steady game and substitute Di Canio step from the dug-out for a 20-minute run-out.

"I thought the West Ham fans were a bit harsh, to be honest," grimaced the booked Hartson after seeing his stormy love affair with the Hammers supporters flounder on the rocks. "Thirty-three goals and £7.5m, what more could I have done for them? I don't want to get on the wrong side of the fans but what they've got to realise is that I never once asked to leave. It was Harry who accepted the money.

"Obviously, I'm very disappointed with the reception I got because I felt I deserved more after all that I did for the club," said the £3.5m striker after signing off with a balance sheet containing the assets of that record fee and 33 strikes and the liabilities of two red cards, 10 bookings, a brace of FA charges plus lifelong notoriety for booting Berkovic.

Ironically, having left West Ham, Hartson then pleaded guilty to that FA misconduct charge for his scrap with the Israeli and was duly fined £20,000 and suspended from three *Dons'* matches.

Alongside Kitson, the enigmatic Welshman had undoubtedly saved Hammers from the dreaded drop following his move from Arsenal two years earlier. And his propensity to find the net had seen him become a reported £10m target for Manchester United, too. On his day, he was a fearsome proposition for the most accomplished Premiership defender.

But his spell at Upton Park had also been blighted by a cocktail of a constant fight for fitness, laced with an inherent tendency to lapse into the comfort zone as he slid down the slippery slope.

Having left Upton Park the goal-getter's destiny was fairly and squarely in his own hands and after subsequently moving to Coventry City, he bravely overcame knee problems that saw proposed transfers to both Glasgow Rangers and Spurs collapse, to join Celtic, where his efforts were recognised by his fellow professionals, who voted him joint Scottish PFA Player-of-the-Year in 2005.

The Hartson (10 goals) and Kitson (11) partnership had yielded 21 conversions from 27 starts and, but for groin, toe, calf and hip injuries to Kits, it had the makings of being yet more lucrative.

"We were productive," agreed Kitson. "I enjoyed playing with John."

Just like Minto before them, Foe and Di Canio were subjected to a 0-4 defeat on their home debuts as Arsenal's Dutch masters Dennis Bergkamp and Marc Overmars left Redknapp admitting that the wheels had, indeed, come off the West Ham wagon.

Already, Tim Breacker (296 apps 8 gls) knew that derby clash with the Gunners was going to be his final game for the club and, after being tactically substituted at half-time, he followed Miklosko to QPR on a free transfer 48 hours later.

"For most of my career I've been first choice and I want to keep that going for as long as I can," said Billy Bonds' first-ever signing, who had given over eight years solid, dependable and honest service. "I think that only internationals and top Premiership players can benefit from the Bosman ruling and I don't want to wait until the summer when there will be a lot of other players out of work, too."

Another professional's professional, back in the summer, Breacker had put Hartson – 10 years his junior – overwhelmingly to shame during one-on-one tests at the National Sports Medicine Institute, and his final assessment report from St Bart's Medical College remains part of Upton Park folklore.

"I suppose you've got to be realistic and if a manager has spent big money on players then he'll play them," added Breacker, who remained on the Loftus Road coaching staff when he finally retired. "There's been a hell of a lot of change during the past few seasons. It wasn't so long ago that just staying in the Premiership was a great achievement. We were under so much pressure. Nowadays, the overall quality at West Ham is just unbelievable."

Ironically, that defeat against Arsenal was destined see one Upton Park legend replace another.

For as Di Canio made his home debut, Dicks trotted out for what proved to be his final appearance.

"I just felt the whole attitude towards me was different and I sensed that my time was up," said the terminated Terminator. "To come back against Northampton was the best game I could ever have asked for. I could then have said I've played that one match and that's it but I just wanted to carry on. My knee still wasn't right but it had made me realise just how much I missed the game.

"I was played out of position at Charlton and, yes, I had a bad game but I'd played left-back for 10 years and then Harry put me at left wing-back. I could run up and down with the ball all day but without the ball it all becomes very monotonous.

"Harry had said after the Northampton game that I was the legend. As usual the newspapers build you up and up and then after the Charlton match I got slated. It was only one bad game but I thought the writing was on the wall.

"The next week he wanted me to go up to Newcastle and sit on the bench and I knew then that time was running out," continued Julian whose innovative excuse – he needed to warm up in the bath and not on the touchline before playing – meant that, in the absence of a hot tub in the dug-out, it had to be a starting place or nothing. "There was no point going somewhere just to be a substitute."

With his knee in an almost permanent state of swelling, Dicks was no longer able to train regularly and that meant his chances of first-team selection grew slimmer.

With an unquenchable desire to try his hand at golf, Dicks' presence at the training ground diminished as he honed his swing with a view to unleashing himself on the fairways of Great Britain, but his time in the not so beautiful game had left him with an unwanted legacy or two.

"I get no more privacy now than when I was playing," he moaned. "I go out and people want to talk about football and that's fine but there are people who still want to have a pop. There's always somebody who remembers what I was like on a football pitch and thinks I'm the same off it, but I'm not like that at all.

"The surgeon's also told me I'll need a knee replacement at some stage but as long as I don't end up as a cripple and can see my kids grow up, I'll be happy. I've got to live for today. It's no good worrying about tomorrow because you might never, ever see it.

"I'm leaving West Ham with no regrets with either the players or the supporters and I wish them all the best, because they deserve it."

Following those two home hammerings, West Ham finally gave Upton Park something to cheer about with a 2-1 win over Nottingham Forest.

"We used to talk just about staying in the division but now all this talk about Europe puts more pressure on me than anything else," echoed Harry who, having recently signed rookie part-timers Gavin Holligan and Jimmy Bullard, saw his side continue to return to form with a spirited 2-2 draw at Liverpool.

Striker Holligan, a £100,000 capture from Kingstonian, had to make the daily journey across London to training by underground train, while midfielder Bullard – a £35,000 purchase – headed through the Dartford tunnel in the battered H-registration Ford Granada bought with his wages as a painter and decorator and the £60 per game plus £10 per goal bonus he earned at Gravesend & Northfleet.

On a surreal afternoon on Merseyside, the new boys found themselves transcended onto the Anfield bench as Hammers twice came from behind.

And twice the Londoners also went agonisingly close to garnering their first win at Anfield since that one which had come in late September back in '63. But the supporting, unmarked Holligan was ignored by a single-minded Sinclair and then the debutant striker found himself foiled by the outstretched legs of future Hammer, David James.

Ironically, neither rookie would come anywhere as near to being part of the first-team reckoning again, although Bullard would return to the Premiership with Wigan Athletic in 2005.

Back at Upton Park, Di Canio scored his first goal for West Ham in a 2-0 win over Blackburn Rovers while Ian Pearce also netted against his old club.

"Looks like I've wasted my money on Di Canio," jested H after seeing Hammers climb back into sixth spot. "I originally set us a target of 40 points for the season and we've got there today. We're safe with 11 games to go and now I can take the wife on holiday!"

A 0-1 defeat at Southampton saw The Dell dressing rooms come in for yet more re-decoration. After caking Hutchison in the post-match buffet three years earlier, this time it was unused substitute John Moncur's turn to have a 15-round sarnie barney with the boss. According to reports, Moncs booted a tray of food at the manager before storming off to the showers and returning to a £7,500 fine.

"I'd be lying if I said it ain't frustrating but there's nothing I can do about not getting picked," said the tearful clown whose 1998-99 campaign was reduced to just eleven-and-a-half hours in the form of six league starts, eight substitute outings, one red card and eight bookings. "I didn't even get off the bench at Southampton and it was a build up of frustration. It was a situation where it all blew up and 10 minutes later I wished I hadn't done it.

"Harry was as good as gold and it's all forgotten. I took the fine – I usually get two or three a season which I pay by direct debit – and that was it. Neither of us bore a grudge and he put me back in the squad for the Chelsea game. End of story."

That said, Moncur was again only named on the bench at Stamford Bridge where the eccentric substitute wore a Comic Relief red nose during his endless touchline warm-ups. And although he did not manage to make it onto the turf, he did have something else to smile about as Kitson's late goal gave Hammers a 1-0 win.

Victory left the self-effacing Redknapp in good mood.

"Lying in bed last night with the missus – when your husband's as ugly as me you'd only wanna talk football – she said: 'If you're still hanging in there 'Arry, gamble and push Sinclair up with Kitson.' It worked a treat!"

Following three knee operations Richard Hall (7 apps) announced his retirement from the game having originally injured his foot in that pre-season friendly at Carshalton so soon after arriving at the club from Southampton for £1.9m in 1996.

Hall's misfortune had echoes of central defender, Simon Webster's signing, pre-season injury and subsequent enforced retirement about it.

And just for good measure, the Margas soap opera had a familiar ring of the Beauchamp, Boogers and Raducioiu sagas, too. Having returned to Chile on the pretext that he could have his knee problems diagnosed in his native tongue, he had also taken the opportunity to see whether there were any takers for his services down South America way.

Certainly the upcoming prestigious Copa De America would give him an opportunity put himself in the shop window, but there were also conflicting tales emanating from Santiago that Margas was about to quit the game altogether.

Back in the boardroom, Storrie had also reached the end of the line, too.

In another clichéd pre-prepared club statement, so typical of those that usually accompany executive departures, chairman Terence Brown said: *"Following a board decision to restructure the management side of the club, by mutual agreement Director of Football Peter Storrie will leave the club after nine years dedicated service. Peter has made a major contribution to the growth of the club since his appointment in 1990 and I would like to thank him on behalf of West Ham United and its supporters for all he's achieved for us. We wish him every success in the future."*

For many, Storrie had been the fall guy appointed to deliver the ill-fated Bond Scheme, but after seeing the chasm that emerged between West Ham United and its loyal followers, his subsequent legacy was one of developing an openness between the club and its followers.

And in an era when the fanzines had developed a healthy market share, he had certainly given those unofficial publications a free rein and unprecedented access to the club, thus allowing them to compete against the staple programme and official magazine – two publications that actually generated revenue to fill the coffers of West Ham United rather than the purveyors' own pockets.

The *Pravda*-like environment of years gone by had now been replaced with a Green Street *glasnost* where free and frank exchanges of information with all-comers were the norm.

There were similarities with Leeds United's subsequently usurped Peter Ridsdale in Storrie's demeanour and, as many before them had found to their cost, in the minefield that is football administration, it is impossible to be all things to all men.

Having seen Storrie work with him on so many of the transfer deals that had taken place in recent seasons, Harry admitted: "It's a sad week. Only Terence Brown would know the reasons behind the decision, although I think Peter's seen it coming for a while. I told the chairman that I was disappointed and couldn't see any reason for it."

As Sheffield Wednesday's Graham Mackrell prepared to be appointed into an expanded role of Company Secretary, Storrie could have been forgiven for feeling distraught at the prospect of departing his empire.

A life-long Hammers fan, the director of football had enjoyed the high profile that had come with the territory of the West Ham United job. Just who had fed the sports editors the lines was anybody's guess, but he had even been the subject of transfer-gossip-type reports on the back pages linking him with big money moves to other clubs.

The reality, however, was to be much, much different.

Certainly, it was difficult to envisage Storrie being photographed sitting alongside England head coaches and other footballing dignitaries in the directors' boxes of cash-strapped Southend United and Notts County where he ended up, before eventually finding himself re-united with Redknapp at Portsmouth and returning to the Premiership.

Meanwhile, Di Canio scored again in a 2-0 win over Newcastle United in which Kitson also found the net against his former club and, clearly, Redknapp was enjoying the entertainment provided by an Italian revelling in his renaissance.

"I like players who get me off my seat because they can do things that I never could," said the Hammers' boss basking in the heady heights of fifth spot. "We'll give anyone a decent game these days."

But as Hammers headed to Villa Park where they would play out a goalless draw against Euro-rivals Aston Villa, UEFA ridiculously ruled that mid-table Newcastle United – as FA Cup semi-finalists – would be given European qualification priority over the Premiership placings.

Quite simply, fifth place would not be good enough.

Following the scrapping of the European Cup Winners' Cup, England had been awarded just six European places.

The three Champions League spots would be filled by those finishing first (Manchester United), second (Arsenal) and third (Chelsea) in the Premiership.

And with the Worthington Cup winners (Tottenham Hotspur) being awarded a UEFA Cup place alongside the team finishing fourth (Leeds United) in the

Premiership, only one entry remained.

With the FA Cup semi-finalists already comprising European qualifiers Manchester United (champions), Arsenal (runners-up) and Spurs (Worthington Cup winners), the bureaucrats of Zurich insisted that the FA Cup should take precedence over league placing for the third and final UEFA Cup spot. And that meant fourth semi-finalists – 13th-placed Newcastle United – were going to strike lucky in the final reckoning.

"You've got to have ambition," insisted H now raising the bar from fifth spot, too. "I'm still looking for fourth place and will keep plugging away."

Struggling Charlton jolted that dream of a UEFA Cup challenge with a 1-0 win at Upton Park, before Hislop single-handedly kept Leicester City at bay in a goalless draw at Filbert Street.

But following two blanks, West Ham saw off Derby County with a scintillating 5-1 win as Berkovic and Di Canio herded the Rams into a closed East End pen.

"Once again, Di Canio showed what an outstanding talent he is and anyone who thinks otherwise is a fool," repeated Harry, revelling in the fact that he had, indeed, plucked a gleaming, high-performance Ferrari, rather than Sadler's spluttering Alfa Romeo, off soccer's scrapheap. "All in all, we've got a decent team here at West Ham United now."

Former Spurs' midfielder Moncur received a ticking off from the linesman for man-marking him during his touchline warm-up and he was in yet more trouble when he was sent off in a 2-1 win at White Hart Lane, where despised ex-Gunner Wright opened the scoring and eight bookings were dished out.

And there were cards galore in the next match, too, as Wright, Hislop and Lomas were all dismissed against Leeds United. After seeing his side finish well beaten 1-5 and with eight men, H lambasted referee Rob Styles for an inept display.

"The referee lost the plot completely in the end and he was all over the show," roared Redknapp after seeing West Ham fall to the three card trick as they crashed to their biggest home defeat for 32 years.

The equally incensed Wright – having picked up his eighth booking of the season for raising an arm at Alfe-Inge Haaland before being dismissed in the 16th minute for bundling into Ian Harte – vented his anger by reportedly kicking in the door of Harris' dressing room, hurling his clothes on the deck and then smashing the match officials' television set onto the floor.

It did not end there for the Oxford-based referee, who dished out a dozen cards in total. Some 90 minutes after the final whistle, his T-registration Rover 618 was spotted in Green Street and ambushed by an angry tribe of disgusted natives swarming from the Boleyn pub.

That terrifying incident heralded the introduction of a new ruling whereby Premiership match officials would be chauffeured to matches from their hotels.

Not surprisingly, the ranting Wright found himself on an FA misconduct rap that would eventually see him fined £17,500 and banned for the first three games of the following campaign.

The *News of the World* even tried to put the official on an incompetence charge.

"Rob Harris had one of the worst performances ever witnessed at a football match," declared the Sunday tabloid.

"Leeds booked their place in Europe while West Ham simply got booked," added the *Daily Mirror*.

United boss David O'Leary could afford to be generous in victory.

"I thought the referee had an excellent game," he announced. "After all, he was only enforcing the law!"

Just when things could not get any worse, though, Everton annihilated the Hammers in a 6-0 Goodison Park pasting.

The good ship West Ham United may well have been leaking goals like the Titanic let in water but the next generation of youngsters were showing the seniors the way with a convincing 9-0 aggregate FA Youth Cup final victory over Coventry City.

Where the likes of Lampard and Ferdinand had fallen at the last hurdle to Michael Owen's Liverpool in the 1996 final, this time around Cole, Michael Carrick and Bywater cantered to the finish as they saw off the Sky Blues in style.

A 3-0 win at Highfield Road was followed by a simply sensational 6-0 victory in front of an official attendance of 21,500 at a sold-out Upton Park which even appeared to possibly contain a few thousand more. And in an ironic twist, that man Harris was back at the Boleyn Ground as the official in charge!

And the superkids also won the Academy Under-19 Championship thanks to a 1-0 play-off win over Sheffield Wednesday with the final kick of extra-time.

"The test comes over the next two years," cautioned youth team boss Tony Carr. "We'll see how many follow Rio and Frank Lampard into the first team."

Fittingly, Hammer-of-the-Year Hislop kept a clean sheet as Hammers rounded off an incredible season with a 4-0 win over Middlesbrough to secure a fantastic fifth place finish.

Certainly, the Berkovic-Hartson incident, coupled with all those Christmas party shenanigans, had dragged the club's name into the gutter, while embarrassing cup exits at the hands of Northampton Town and Swansea City had further left dark skies over Upton Park.

But in a surreal season that had seen Hammers concede four goals or more on an incredible six occasions, Harry had still steered the club to its second-highest finish in its history.

Redknapp had also balanced the books on the transfer fee front – if not wages-wise – and yet again, Margas apart, he had improved the quality of the squad thanks to more shrewd wheeling and dealing.

Already he looked to have stolen Di Canio, while the £7.5m commanded for the infuriatingly talented yet temperamental Hartson was a trade of the utmost quality.

Only John Lyall had guided the club to a higher position, but in the wake of Heysel, that UEFA ban on English clubs meant that the former manager's 1986, third-place finish prevented a trip to Europe.

And now, ironically, Harry faced the same heartbreak.

Determined not to miss out on a richly deserved cross-Channel sojourn, Hammers therefore entered the much-maligned Intertoto Cup, in a bid to gain back-door access to the UEFA Cup.

"As soon as I told the players that if we finished fifth we'd go in the Intertoto Cup, we lost 0-6 at Everton and 1-5 against Leeds," joked H, knowing that he now faced a July 17 start. "Today I told 'em that we're not going in it and we won 4-0!

"Seriously, Fifth place? Not too bad, is it?" he beamed, having now raised expectation levels down E13 way onwards and upwards towards another sphere. "It's a terrific achievement after a tremendous season. I said all along that we'd do better than last year. We've finished above a lot of so-called big clubs and with the kids winning the FA Youth Cup, too, it just doesn't get much better.

"Now please explain the Intertoto Cup to me, because I haven't got a clue!"

PLAYERS IN

Jimmy Bullard	**Gravesend & Northfleet**	**£35,000**
Paolo Di Canio	**Sheffield Wednesday**	**£1,700,000**
Michael Ferrante	**Australian Inst. of Sport**	**Nominal**
Marc-Vivien Foe	**Racing Club Lens**	**£4,500,000 (Record)**
Shaka Hislop	**Newcastle United**	**Free transfer**
Gavin Holligan	**Kingstonian**	**£100,000**
Javier Margas	**Uni'dad Catolica de Chile**	**£2,000,000**
Scott Minto	**Benfica**	**£1,000,000**
Neil Ruddock	**Liverpool**	**£100,000**
Ian Wright	**Arsenal**	**£750,000**

PLAYERS OUT

Tim Breacker	**Queens Park Rangers**	**Free transfer**
Richard Hall	**Retired**	
John Hartson	**Wimbledon**	**£7,500,000 (Record)**
Andrew Impey	**Leicester City**	**£1,600,000**
Ludek Miklosko	**Queens Park Rangers**	**£75,000**
David Partridge	**Dundee United**	**£30,000**
David Unsworth	**Aston Villa**	**£3,000,000**

Chapter 13
1999-2000

WHAT'S THE STORY? EURO GLORY?

West Ham United had just won £2.76m in Premiership prize-money and, with a return to Europe beckoning via the elongated Intertoto Cup, Harry Redknapp had been offered a new four-year, £2m contract.

As he sat at Peter Storrie's last supper in the Ming Court chinese restaurant in Romford, chop-sticks in hand, H could have been forgiven for choosing Number Five off the menu.

"It's amazing that even when we had Moore, Hurst and Peters the club never reached these heights," he said, comparing the previous season's finish to the best-ever eighth spot achieved by the legendary triumvirate in 1968-69. "The top three pick themselves every year so to end up fifth behind a massive club like Leeds is a big achievement. It's going to be even harder from now on but I know what I need – a right-back, a striker and a central defender. I'll work hard. I'll sign a few."

Liverpool's Rob Jones, Benfica's Gary Charles, the US Soccer Federation's Richard Gough, Derby County's Paulo Wanchope and Real Madrid's Davor Suker topped the list alongside a shameless bid for . . . Everton's Slaven Bilic.

But having steered his over-achievers into the upper echelons of the Premiership, his squad was also coming under the scrutiny of poachers.

Celtic had set their sights on £5m-rated Eyal Berkovic, while Marc-Vivien Foe had already declared his desire to move to Liverpool for a similar fee.

Already on long-term contracts, both Frank Lampard and Rio Ferdinand – who had been linked with a £14m move to Roma – were both stalling on new deals.

According to the *News of the World's* sordid kissing-and-telling 17-year-old Aimee Smith, the two team-mates had reportedly not been so slow to seize the initiative on holiday in Cyprus. After claiming to have crammed into a toilet cubicle with Rio, she then found herself in Lampard's Grecian Bay hotel bedroom where, allegedly, it really was a case of girls on top.

A few months earlier, H had written in *Harry Redknapp – My Autobiography:* "Being the youngest members of the side, Frank and Rio get most of the attention. But even those two recognise the sacrifices they have to make if they are to stay at the top of their profession. Players have to be careful because there's always a bird willing to earn a few bob by selling a story to a newspaper about a famous footballer's prowess and giving him marks out of 10 or some other nonsense. Young players have to be careful about how they behave off the pitch."

His nephew, incidentally, was given 8/10 by 'sex bomb' Miss Smith while Rio's reported quick fumble left him unmarked by the High Wycombe seductress who, seemingly, oozed everything except class.

There were no such shenanigans in Yaoundé, but having returned from his native Cameroon with malaria, Foé's £4.6m move to Anfield collapsed.

Rob Shepherd of the *Daily Express* wrote. "I understand that the main stumbling block was the insistence by Foé's agents that West Ham pay the remainder of his contract. But the club do not feel they are obliged to settle the rest of the three-year deal given the short-term nature of Foé's engagement at Upton Park. Liverpool, on the other hand, do not see why they should take up the obligations of Foé's contract given they were prepared to offer him a new one and a signing-on fee.

"The deadlock highlights the growing chasm between players and clubs."

Ironically, Liverpool's move for Foé signalled Mersey misery for Paul Ince, who was told by Gerard Houllier that his Anfield career was over. Aged 31 – and precluded from training with the first team – Ince had also suffered the double-whammy of being omitted by Kevin Keegan from England's Euro 2000 qualifiers.

Ever the opportunist, Harry announced: "At £1m Paul Ince would be an excellent buy for a club. He is a very, very good player."

For many, it was a ploy to test whether the East End had forgiven the Guv'nor.

The answer was an emphatically, overwhelming: 'No!'

"I don't think the fans would take too kindly to having Paul Ince at West Ham," observed H, now distancing himself from the notion. "I never had any intention of trying to sign him."

One man who would have been accepted back, however, was Bilic, whose career had nosedived from the moment he went to that 'bigger club', Everton.

An injury-punctuated spell at Goodison Park had been compounded by his pathetic play-acting at France 98, where his feigning face-holding in the semi-final had seen the consequently red-carded French skipper Laurent Blanc mugged of the chance to lead his country to their World Cup final victory over Brazil.

Afterwards, it transpired that Bilic, too, expected to receive a sending off that would have precluded him from playing in the final had Croatia prevailed in the last four, and his histrionics were a mere smokescreen to divert the attention onto the luckless Blanc.

Unperturbed by the Croatian's Public Enemy No.1 tag, Redknapp was keen to re-sign him in a bargain-bucket £500,000 deal but, with his hips shot to pieces, Bilic was uninsurable. A pay-as-you-play basis would not have given the player any long-term security compared to the three-year contract he had on Merseyside and he returned to Goodison Park before eventually being paid off out of the Toffees' insurance proceeds and joining his native Hajduk Split.

"Everton have told me that I'm no longer in their plans but if nothing else happens I will see out my time there. I would not have attempted to leave them for any club other than West Ham United," said the dejected Bilic, who had realised long ago that the Goodison grass was not even green, yet alone greener. "West Ham fans still say to me: 'Please come back Slaven.' Harry and I had been talking for weeks. I sort of regret leaving West Ham because it hasn't been a 100% success by any means, but if I hadn't left then I know I would've been sorry, too. I loved it at Upton Park but I couldn't have spent the rest of my days wondering what would've happened if I'd gone to Everton. I had to find out for myself."

One man on the move, however, was Berkovic. Certainly, that disgraceful incident involving John Hartson had done little to prolong his stay at Upton Park. Indeed, with the proactive Pini Zahavi as his agent, many believed that, from the moment the Welshman raked his studs into the Israeli's skull, the manipulative midfielder had the perfect lever to prise himself away from Upton Park.

Having been linked with countless moves, virtually from the day he arrived from Southampton for £1.5m, Berkovic (75+4 appearance 12 gls) expressed his disappointment that neither Liverpool nor Manchester United had entered the fray before he joined Celtic in a £5.75m move.

With Joe Cole having been carefully nurtured along, H knew that he already had a worthy replacement on his books and, indeed, the teenager had been invited to train with the full England squad for their Euro 2000 qualifiers.

"Some of the things Joe did while he was with us were tremendous," enthused England coach Kevin Keegan. "So far he has been rightly nursed along by Harry but I'm looking forward to seeing Joe Cole playing in the Premiership, this year."

Berkovic's transfer also opened the door for the Hammers to be linked with an audacious cut-price bid for striker Hartson, who was finding life difficult at Wimbledon under new Norwegian boss Egil Olsen.

Real Madrid's Suker – winner of the Golden Boot at the France 98 World Cup – had been suspended without pay since May 6 for criticising coach John Toshack. Although he, apparently, announced on Spanish television that he was going to join West Ham United – the move being hailed as Redknapp's greatest ever coup – in reality his wage demands of £40,000 per week made it a non-starter and he headed to Arsenal instead.

Striker Paulo Wanchope was, however, signed from Derby County for £2.5m but he was not available for the opening Intertoto Cup, third round, first leg tie against Finnish outfit FC Jokerit. And the moody Costa Rican was not available to sign autographs, either, as he quickly overlooked the young Hammers' fans at Chadwell Heath who were about to pay his wages.

The new boy was soon reminded of his responsibilities at the 'Academy' by the furious locals.

Throughout the summer, West Ham were hoping that their fifth-place finish would still elevate them straight into the UEFA Cup first round proper, given Yugoslavia was embroiled in the bloody Balkan war.

But those gnomes of Zurich decreed otherwise and so on Saturday, July 17 – just 62 days after the final whistle had blown against Middlesbrough – Hammers were back in action.

The Intertoto Cup had been established several years earlier as a football pools enterprise that would allow tote-style betting to continue throughout the European close-season.

And as the size of the competition increased it also provided basement level entry to Europe, although interest from English clubs had always been limited, given the early summer start and the half-dozen or so ties required just to get to the

UEFA Cup first round proper.

However, if it was now good enough for the likes of Juventus, SV Hamburg and Espanyol, then why should not West Ham chance their hand, too?

As Hammers dipped their toe into the tournament for the first time, a combination of high admission prices, live TV and summer holidays ensured that just 11,098 were at Upton Park to see Paul Kitson give Hammers a slender 1-0 lead to take to Finland.

"This will all be worth it if we get a UEFA Cup place," insisted H, knowing that there were still five games to go. "But while Europe's important, it's come a bit early for us. There are three major domestic competitions for us this year and the Premiership remains our priority."

That European torch was kept burning thanks to Lampard's equaliser as West Ham drew 1-1 in Helsinki's Olympic Stadium, where substitute Ian Wright (23+3 apps 9 gls) – having already announced that he would be quitting the game at the end of the season – played his final game for the club before joining Nottingham Forest on loan and eventually heading to Celtic on a free transfer and thus saving Hammers his £25,000 per week wages.

Lee Hodges (0+6 apps) joined Scunthorpe United for £130,000 while fellow youngster Chris Coyne (0+1 app) was destined to head to Dundee on a free transfer, his only outing having come in that farcical 1-5 defeat against Leeds United the previous season. With his first-team chances equally restricted, striker Lee Boylan (0+1 app) joined Swedish outfit Trelleborgs FF on a free transfer.

A knee injury had ruled 27-year-old Rob Jones (1 app) out of action for 15 months. And having signed on a free transfer from Anfield, the booked former Liverpool and England right-back played his first and last game for the Hammers in Finland before sadly undergoing another operation which subsequently forced him to retire and open a children's nursery.

Stan Lazaridis (68+18 apps 3 gls) had also played his final match for the club as he headed to Birmingham City for £1.5m after Redknapp decided to cash in on the £300,000 Aussie whom he had unleashed on the Premiership back in 1995. "You have to be realistic and look at the size of the squad here now," said the likeable Lazaridis. "I was quite happy to fight for my place but it's up to the manager as to who he wants to let go."

Lampard was also on target in the fourth round, first leg tie against Heerenveen at Upton Park four days later, where just 7,485 witnessed the 1-0 victory.

And there was no sign of Marco Boogers or his fabled caravan as Hammers headed north across the Dutch polderland for the return leg, which they also won 1-0 thanks to Wanchope's strike.

By the time the Premiership campaign started on August 7, Hammers had already played four competitive games while Chilean exile Javier Margas suddenly turned up out of the blue at Chadwell Heath to resume training following a half-decent showing in the Copa America. But he then had to return home to his pregnant wife as the club awaited the renewal of his work permit.

There had also been the added bonus of the capture of 37-year-old Stuart Pearce on a free transfer from Newcastle United.

NEARLY REACHED THE SKY

"Pearcey will be tremendous for us," announced Harry. "There are special people around in football and he's one of them. He wants to play. He'd only just got here and he went off to St Albans to play in a game alongside the kids. Some of them learned more in half-an-hour than they'll learn in half-a-season. Then he went to Dover and did the same thing all over again."

'Psycho' Pearce made his debut in the opener against Tottenham Hotspur when Lampard was again on target but the 1-0 victory was marred by a cruciate ligament injury to Ian Pearce's left knee that would rule him out for the entire season.

Sensing that Hammers were on the brink of the UEFA Cup, the board sensibly cut admission prices to stimulate a full house crowd of 25,372 for the visit of FC Metz in the Intertoto Cup final first-leg. But after Louis Saha gave the Frenchmen the lead, Lampard left West Ham's Euro-hopes teetering on the white cliffs of Dover when he missed from the penalty spot on the hour to leave them chasing a 0-1 deficit in the second leg.

Twice Hammers came from behind in their second Premiership game at Villa Park, as Trevor Sinclair salvaged a 2-2 against Aston Villa with 15 seconds left.

Wanchope and Paolo Di Canio then secured a 2-1 win over Leicester City at Upton Park before Hammers headed to FC Metz, where they needed to overcome that first-leg defeat at the Stade Saint Symphorien.

Backed by a massive following that had headed deep into eastern France, Sinclair and Intertoto expert Lampard put West Ham in the driving seat before Nenad Jestrovic's goal levelled the tie at 2-2 on aggregate.

Although Hammers would still prevail on away goals, the atmosphere both on and off the field threatened to boil over, before Wanchope went some way towards placating a minority of restless, boozed-up Brits amongst the 3,000 travelling Londoners, with what proved to be the winner.

"There appears to be an innate xenophobia carried in the hearts and minds of far too many West Ham fans," wrote fanzine contributor Tim Crane in *Over Land and Sea* after seeing a London element try to tear down the metal fences holding them inside the visitors' enclosure, when a fire-cracker was seemingly hurled into their pen. "The boisterous drunkenness was out of keeping with the sedate surroundings. Very much a case of *The Long Good Friday* meets *Emmerdale Farm*. The majority of Metz fans were family types and young couples. No wonder the terrace practically emptied when the fence-shaking incident occurred. If the Metz goal and the whiff of elimination that came with it served as a contributory factor, then we are faced with an inevitable ugliness in the rounds ahead."

As the French riot police sprayed fire extinguishers into the English fans, club safety officer John Ball told Metz officials: "That will only *inflame* the situation!"

Wanchope's goal ultimately confirmed the 3-2 aggregate victory that allowed skipper Steve Lomas to lift the Intertoto Cup – one of three given to a trio of winners. As Hammers collected their first piece of silverware since they lifted the Division Two Championship trophy in 1981, Juventus also saw off Rennes, while Montpellier beat SV Hamburg in those other 'finals'.

"We've had to do it the hard way," enthused Harry after seeing the name of West Ham United finally enter the draw for a first-class European competition after an

18-year absence. "But we're in the UEFA Cup now, it's a great night and I'm very proud that we've established a good team here. It means a lot to the punters."

There was no champagne hangover as Hammers efficiently beat Bradford City 3-0 at Valley Parade to go fourth in the Premiership.

Stuart Pearce was called into the England squad for their upcoming Euro 2000 qualifiers and the shocked 37-year-old showed that he still had a zest for international football as he took his cap count to 78 in the 6-0 win over Luxembourg and the goalless draw in Poland.

But disaster struck upon his return when he broke his leg in an accidental collision with Watford's Micah Hyde right on the stroke of half-time. Di Canio may have got his name on the score-sheet for the second week running in the 1-0 victory over the Hornets, but that injury was stinging news for Redknapp who could but marvel at his veteran defender's bravery.

"Pearcey tried to put his boot on and go back out there," revealed Harry. "He said: 'I'll give it a go.' But he couldn't even stand on his leg."

According to Upton Park folklore, the club phoned Psycho's wife, Liz.

"Stuart's coming home with a broken leg," warned the medical man.

"Oh dear, whose is it?" came Mrs P's apparent reply.

Back in the summer, chairman Terence Brown had interrupted his holiday in the Seychelles to refute rumours that he was about to sell the club to South African businessmen in a £60m deal.

"There is absolutely no foundation in the rumour," insisted secretary Graham Mackrell. "Terry Brown has big ambitions for this club and it is absolute cobblers to suggest that he is about to sell out."

Now, months later, *The Daily Telegraph* claimed that Carlton Television had been in talks to buy a stake of around 10% in the club. Yet again Brown, apparently, could not agree terms with the broadcaster, which was looking to follow in the footsteps of Granada (Liverpool) and Sky TV (Leeds United), who had bolstered the transfer kitties of both Gerard Houllier and David O'Leary.

An anonymous man, preferring the peaceful sanctuary of the directors' box rather than the media spotlight enjoyed by some of his more egocentric counterparts, Brown broke his silence to tell Ken Dyer of the *Evening Standard*: "When I became chairman the club had four main goals: to be a top-eight club, have the best youth system in the country, play in a big stadium and have no debts. We're not there yet but we're going the right way.

"We are the fastest growing club in the Premiership. We're lucky to have Harry Redknapp here. He's the second longest serving manager in the division behind Alex Ferguson and his future is secure. West Ham is also a club which is prepared to give youngsters their big chance if they're good enough."

West Ham United was certainly in a stronger position than it had been when Michael Tabor had come sniffing a few years earlier and, as they contemplated their UEFA Cup campaign, Redknapp fatefully allowed reserve team winger Manny Omoyinmi to join Gillingham on loan with a view to a £400,000 move.

On the other side of the balance sheet, Harry had rustled up £600,000 to sign Hartson's good friend, Igor Stimac, from Derby County. And, after making his debut in that victory over Watford, the Croatian central defender found himself facing his fellow countrymen from NK Osijek – who were watched by Suker, their most famous son – in the first round, first leg.

Having been missing in action in South America for so long, Margas returned to the fray, too, sporting a claret and blue dyed hairdo in an unashamed bid to win over the sceptical West Ham fans. The Chilean found the East Enders in forgiving mood, as goals from Wanchope, Di Canio and Lampard gave Hammers a comfortable 3-0, first-leg lead to take out to war-torn Croatia.

"I didn't dye my hair just to get the fans on my side," argued Margas. "Only one thing could do that – my football. I've had my problems but things are very different now. This is a chance to repay the club and the fans for their support."

The midweek exploits took their toll, though, as West Ham succumbed to their first Premiership defeat at Everton, where Francis Jeffers gave the Bilic-less Merseysiders a 1-0 win, before John Moncur was dismissed in a 0-1 defeat by Coventry City.

But Hammers got back to winning ways in Osijek's bullet-scarred Gradski Vrt stadium – just 10 minutes from the Serbian border – despite the Croatians' dirty tricks campaign.

"We were originally meant to leave our hotel at 7pm for the 9pm kick-off. But nearly an hour later, the coach still hadn't turned up," revealed Lampard junior, who had just signed an extended contract that was scheduled to keep him at Upton Park until summer 2005. "In the end we had to hijack the press coach. We had the nuttiest ride of our lives, flying down the wrong side of the road in what must have seemed like a runaway double-decker.

"I don't know if Osijek were trying to psyche us out but someone said that when they came to Upton Park for the first leg, the coach was late for *them*. Maybe they were trying to get us back. Very strange."

Unperturbed by that late dash, goals by Kitson, Neil Ruddock and Foé gave West Ham a 3-1 win.

As Hammers flew home to learn that they had been paired with Steaua Bucharest – 1986 European Cup winners – in the second round, Lampard and Sinclair earned richly deserved England call-ups for the friendly with Belgium. While Sinclair would not even make the bench, Lampard was destined to win his first cap at the Stadium of Light, where cousin Jamie Redknapp's winner gave the Three Lions a 2-1 victory.

Over a year had elapsed since Di Canio had been involved in the fracas against Arsenal that saw him banished from the English game. Now for the first time since he had forced referee Paul Alcock to take his theatrical tumble, he faced the Gunners and, in particular, their chief protagonist that day – Martin Keown.

It may have been Sunday, but this was to be no day of rest for referee Mike Reed, who dished out 10 cards as Foe and Patrick Vieira were also dismissed.

After putting Hammers ahead, Di Canio then audaciously lobbed the ball over *agent provocateur* Keown and doubled the lead before Suker pulled one back.

"Paolo's a genius," argued Harry after seeing his ice-cool Italian keep his head while all those around him lost their own in a 2-1 victory. "A master of the football who got slaughtered for making one mistake in his life."

But for all the polish there was also some spit. And grotesquely it came from the mouth of Vieira, who sprayed Ruddock en route to the tunnel after he was red-carded for twice tripping Keown's nemesis, Di Canio.

The Frenchman also came within a whisker of getting arrested for booting the referee's assistant's electronic board and threatening a police officer in the tunnel. But instead the Met decided to report Vieira to the FA – who charged him with misconduct, fined him £45,000 and handed him a six-match ban.

"I was just trying to calm things down," claimed the righteous Razor.

As Arsenal tried to deflect attention from the despicable volley of Vieira spittle, they laughably accused Ruddock of being racist.

But their claims were not based on the differing colours of the players' skin, instead they were furious that the mocking defender had gone on Sky TV's satirical *Soccer AM* programme and accused the French World Cup winner of smelling of garlic.

"Razor's definitely not a racist," argued Marc Keller, who saw his team-mate warned about his future conduct by the FA. "A showman? Yes. A racist? No way."

Quite simply the band-wagon was beginning to roll, as Harry Harris of the *Daily Mirror* obtained a Hebrew translation of Berkovic's autobiography in which he had allegedly accused West Ham both of being a pub side and hating all foreigners.

If the Celtic star was seeking big publicity for his claims he certainly achieved it. But with copies hard to come by in London, and no definitive Hebrew translation available to the common man it was difficult to determine whether Berkovic had actually written just what the tabloid claimed.

"Eyal Berkovic never said what was in the *Daily Mirror*," insisted Redknapp, warning that Harris would be sued by both the club and the player. "He swore to me today and I believe him. He's distraught and can't believe what was written. All Eyal said was that he felt we had a problem – and I've said it myself. Sometimes we bring foreign players here and leave them to their own devices, dump them in Essex and just expect them to get on with it.

"And how can this club be racist? Half my team are coloured lads. I've got players from all over the world.

"My best mate's Jewish! It's absolute nonsense because there's no other club in the country that does more for race relations than West Ham.

"A pub team? We ain't a pub team, either. If we're a pub team, then what must the rest of the country be like, because we finished fifth in the Premiership last season? The kids won the FA Youth Cup. I've got four players in the England side...don't tell me that this club's anything except a fantastic football team now.

"This is the crap we have to put up with now. I think the game's gone with some of the s*** that gets written these days.

"When people come to my training ground telling me their editor's told them to 'make a f***** story up 'if you ain't got one', what is it coming to?

"But I'm f***** bullet-proof, just have a look at my record here. Look what this club's done."

Shaka Hislop – the Hackney-born, Caribbean-raised keeper – who won a PFA merit award in 2005 for his anti-racism work, insisted: "I certainly haven't experienced any racism since I've been at West Ham. I would have been the first out of the door if there had been any hint of prejudice at this club.

"I think Eyal's alleged comments were, well, diabolical. If he did say all those things then, in a sense, they were cowardly. He seems to have waited until he was up at Celtic and able to get out of it all down here. We all seemed to think that he absolutely loved it here at West Ham, and we loved having him here, too."

Eventually, the media-fuelled Anglo-Israeli sniping died down with neither a public statement of apology from Berkovic nor legal action taken by any party.

Ironically, Berkovic, Redknapp and Hislop would later be reunited at Portsmouth some years later.

Meanwhile, Vieira had not been the only Frenchman causing problems.

Following his bright start, Samassi Abou's erratic form and inability to integrate into the Premiership way of life had seen him become surplus to requirements.

The early cult-hero cries of 'Abouooooooo' had receded over time in direct correlation with his lack of appearances, but try as he might to offload his dreadlocked striker, the frustrated Redknapp was finding it impossible to raise precious cash against his unwanted, depreciating asset.

Quite simply, Abou – who had already been on loan at Ipswich and Walsall – would not go, despite some over-zealous attempts to persuade him to depart.

Indeed, 12 months earlier, a delegation of Heart of Midlothian officials had arrived at Southend United's Roots Hall ground to take the Ivory Coast goal-getter back to Scotland following a West Ham reserve match.

But steadfastly he refused to swap the East End for Edinburgh.

And with the pen nib now hovering tantalising above the £900,000 cheque payable to West Ham United Football Club Limited, Abou, this time, had now declined to head to the Granite city's other club, Hibernian.

"I love it when the crowd boo me," he argued, while also delighting in the fact that he would become a Bosman free agent at the end of the season if he could prolong his tenure at Upton Park.

The furious Redknapp subsequently managed to farm out his recalcitrant striker on loan to Kilmarnock, but he knew that his chance of bolstering his war chest had departed across Hadrian's Wall, as he resigned himself to the fact that the scheming Abou (19+12 apps 6 gls) would, indeed, depart a free man in May.

While one striker controversially refused to leave, another had willingly arrived in equally acrimonious circumstances from Charlton Athletic a few months earlier.

As West Ham had started to nurture their next generation of strikers, the Addicks had threatened to report the club to the FA over an alleged illegal approach for their 16-year-old striker, Jermain Defoe.

Charlton MD Peter Varney said: "It makes you think about West Ham's success in youth football when you actually see how they operate. Heaven knows what's gone on. Their behaviour is totally outside the regulations and they know it."

Prior to his departure, Storrie had replied: "We can understand Charlton being upset but we didn't approach the player. It was all legal and above board. Jermain is something special and we could be talking about the next Ian Wright here."

A Football League appeals committee ordered Hammers to pay an initial £400,000 for Defoe, rising to £1.65m if he went on to make 40 senior appearances and ever won an England cap.

Finnish Under-18 striker Daniel Sjolund became the next teenager to be signed when he left Swedish outfit Brommackjaran in a £200,000 deal, while former Lloyds TSB bank clerk Tommy Williams later signed from Walton & Hersham in a £40,000 move, alongside 17-year-old Lucchese striker Emmanuel Cascione.

And Leon Britton, a pint-sized 16-year-old Arsenal midfielder, was also captured after a Football League tribunal set an initial £400,000 fee rising to some £1.5m with appearances and international recognition.

Another Gunners' reserve – Omer Riza – was also signed for £20,000.

"Are we supposed to just sit back and let clubs nick boys off us?" said Harry. "I'm all for getting in there. Good luck if we nick one off Arsenal. I love it."

Hammers' Youth Cup success – and the sight of Lampard, Ferdinand, Cole and Michael Carrick breaking into the first team at an early age – was attracting some of the game's brightest young prospects through its doors.

It was a far cry from 1993 when old boy Geoff Pike found himself compromised in his FA monitoring role that saw the club's Centres of Excellence closed.

"I was employed to go around and make sure that things were being run in accordance with the regulations," said the 1980 FA Cup-winning midfielder. "One day I was at Chadwell Heath when West Ham were playing an Under-11 game against a local representative side who included kids from other clubs, as an 11-a-side trial match. It was completely against the regulations and I ended up having a confrontation with Tony Carr and Jimmy Hampson on the sidelines.

"It was a difficult situation because I'd been at West Ham for over 20 years as a player, the club was in my blood, and to have to say to them that what they were doing was illegal was very hard for me.

"The FA took West Ham to task over it, they were fined and all their Centres of Excellence closed down for one year.

"I was portrayed as the villain and Peter Storrie banned me from the club. But there were lots of other things reported to the FA by other clubs and various other people that had, allegedly, gone on. The FA had a file on West Ham that was four inches thick and my piece was just one sheet of A4 paper. I was just doing my job.

"I subsequently showed Tony and Jimmy my report which was, basically, they played an ineligible fixture – they should only have been playing small-sided matches – and we had a long meeting which was productive and amicable. I'm now welcome back at Chadwell Heath."

Back at senior level, there was even more controversy as NK Osijek sniffed a UEFA Cup lifeline following their resounding, aggregate 1-6 first round defeat. The crafty Croatians sought Hammers' expulsion for playing the technically banned Stimac, who had been red-carded while playing for Hajduk Split against Panathinaikos in the second round of a Champions League qualifier back in 1995.

Mackrell protested: "At the start of the competition UEFA circulates a list of suspended and Igor's name was not on it. We have done nothing wrong."

And after UEFA conceded its own administrative shortcomings and ruled that

NEARLY REACHED THE SKY

West Ham would remain in the tournament, desperate Osijek appealed against the decision. It meant the Hammers' secretary had to attend a further UEFA sitting in Geneva where the Balkan protests were again hurled out of court.

Having been nipped by the minnows during the previous season's cup exits at the hands of Northampton Town and Swansea City, Redknapp was relieved to leave his old side Bournemouth battered in the Worthington Cup.

Keller and Lampard netted in a 2-0 win ahead of a trip to Middlesbrough, where Shaka Hislop was sent off in a 0-2 defeat that left the visitors in 10th place.

Hammers' European adventure continued at Steaua Bucharest's oppressive, rain-lashed Stadionul Ghencea. It was only October 21, yet already this was the club's 19th game of the season.

On the half-hour mark, Foe was sent clear by Wanchope but instead of netting a vital away goal he curiously – albeit unselfishly – fed the offside Di Canio.

The raised flag of the referee's assistant also signalled that Hammers – a Premiership club in the second round of a major European competition – had peaked under Redknapp, for shortly afterwards Laurent Rosu and Sabin Ilie gave the Romanians an insurmountable 2-0 lead to take back to Upton Park. West Ham would never achieve such prominence again under his stewardship.

"The ref told John Moncur to tell me to take Paolo off otherwise he would be sent off," claimed H afterwards as the booked, substituted Di Canio's 55th-minute departure remained shrouded in mystery. "I have never known that before."

But Danish referee Claus Bo Larsen insisted: "I didn't tell West Ham to take him off. I just advised their manager that if they weren't careful and didn't watch him, then he would get a red card. He was trying to get Romanian players sent off."

And the protesting Italian alleged that Larson had, at one stage, roared: "Get the f*** up you bastard!"

But there was still more damage to be done to Anglo-Romanian relations.

For as an English supporters' coach was about to head from Bucharest's Ambassador hotel to the airport the following morning, two not so bright sparks decided to 'hijack' the vehicle – whereupon they promptly crashed it into the bus in front before the eyes of the local police.

As the officers threatened to fingerprint each passenger in a bid to establish whose erratic steering had caused £4,000 damage, the culprit – a Grays man – owned up and returned home two days later after paying a £1,900 fine.

Sinclair bagged a late leveller in a 1-1 draw against Sunderland at Upton Park, before future Hammer Titi Camara – reeling from news of his father's death in Africa just hours earlier – gave Liverpool a 1-0 win at Anfield. And as injuries continued to take their toll on weary West Ham, Ian Harte's strike gave Leeds United a 1-0 win at Elland Road.

"Show me any team in the country who would be just as good without seven of its best players," challenged H, who then saw Hammers huff and puff without blowing the Steaua Bucharest lead away.

A goalless draw signalled the end of the Euro dream as West Ham did everything except score at Upton Park in a game in which Steaua psycho Albert Duro took full advantage of Czech referee Pucek's leniency.

"The Albanian defender committed at least seven bookable offences and must rank as one of the luckiest players to complete a match," observed *The Daily Telegraph*.

"It was one of those nights. It just wasn't going to happen, was it?" sighed Harry after seeing 25 goal attempts – and the rampaging Ruddock's vigilante vendetta on the black-eyed Duro – come to nothing. "That Duro's mad, isn't he? Just how did he stay on the pitch?

"But Europe's been good for us and the future looks fantastic with Rio Ferdinand, Frank Lampard and young Joe Cole around."

And upon being asked by the visiting press delegation whether he would be interested in signing any of the Steaua stars, Redknapp, still scarred by the experiences of Ilie Dumitrescu and Florin Raducioiu, diplomatically and comically replied: "I think I'm alright for Romanians at the moment, thanks!"

Another goalless draw followed at Stamford Bridge where the now auburn Margas was red carded for halting the fleeing Didier Deschamps.

Following weeks of uncertainty, Canning Town-born Gary Charles finally proved his fitness and signed from Benfica in a £1.2m deal.

"I've got great confidence in my ability," crowed the twice-capped international. "I'd like to think that when I'm fit, I'm as good as any Englishman in the right-back or right wing-back position in the country."

Despite their Euro-exit, West Ham's self-belief began to return, too, with a hat-trick of triumphs.

Skipper for the day against bottom-placed Sheffield Wednesday, Di Canio faced his former employers for the first time since *that* shove and predictably became embroiled in more controversy as Hammers won 4-3 in a roller-coaster game. Danny Wilson, his former manager, wrongly accused the innocent Italian – who netted a penalty – of getting Danny Sonner deservedly sent off as his side led 2-1, and 3-2, before Lampard clinched it.

And Sinclair's goal ended Liverpool's eight-match unbeaten run as a 1-0 victory elevated Redknapp's men to ninth place. But it was not a happy day for the subdued, substituted Wanchope who departed to a free and frank discussion with the barracking Upton Park boo boys.

In the Worthington Cup, Kitson bagged an 88th-minute equaliser before Cole netted his first-ever senior goal to give Hammers a 3-2 victory at Birmingham City and set up a home quarter-final with Aston Villa.

Lomas then became the third successive Hammer – following Abou and Moncur – to be dismissed at White Hart Lane as West Ham held on to secure their first goalless draw with Tottenham Hotspur since 1947.

Alarmingly, the Hammers' skipper had become the fifth Hammer – behind Moncur, Foé, Hislop and Margas – to be dismissed before 1999 was over.

But that six-game unbeaten run was brought to a halt in a pre-Christmas FA Cup third round tie at Tranmere Rovers, where Nick Henry's goal gave the Merseysiders a 1-0 win. Outwitted. Outplayed. Out of the Cup.

"For the first time this season I've had to go into the dressing room and have a right go," confessed Harry after seeing Hammers slain by lower division opposition for the second year running.

And with that FA Cup exit came the first murmurings from the dissenting Di Canio, who was substituted midway through the second period.

"Every player passed badly," he moaned after seeing all hopes of a Wembley final drift down the Mersey. "We were badly organised and without anyone running or working hard. Maybe it's me but I can't do magic when I am 50 yards away from the others. Not even Maradona would be able to play well that way!"

The window for cup glory was, however, still open as Villa rolled into town for that Worthington Cup quarter-final and, in an absorbing encounter, goals by Lampard and the reconciled Di Canio set up the 2-2 draw that led to extra-time.

With 114 minutes gone the fresh legs of Omoyinmi entered the fray.

In July 1995 the youngster had poignantly admitted: "My weakness is my lack of concentration. I need to become a bit more aware of what is going on around me on the pitch."

Certainly, he had little time to make any meaningful contribution during those six remaining minutes and a nerve-tingling penalty shoot-out followed.

Although Sinclair had missed, Lampard, Lomas, Di Canio, Ruddock and Keller had each scored. With the score standing at 5-4 to West Ham, Gareth Southgate bravely stepped forward to take a sudden death kick.

Alongside Italia 90 culprits Stuart Pearce and Chris Waddle, the Villa skipper had made a few pounds out of a Pizza Hut advertisement following his own costly and infamous miss against Germany at Euro 96.

However, there was also a certain career-blighting notoriety that had come with England's excruciating semi-final defeat at Wembley to Johnny Foreigner.

And now he had the chance to bury his demons as the whites of Hislop's eyes came into his sights under the Upton Park floodlights.

But again Southgate's laser-guided goalie-glove searchers let him down as he drilled his sudden death spot-kick towards the outstretched hands of the courageous Hislop, correctly diving low to his left.

The Villa skipper's unenviable record now read: Four penalties. Four misses.

As the predictable 'Worthington Cheer' headlines vied for back-page space alongside photographs of the disconsolate Southgate, Hammers celebrated a semi-final appearance against Tony Cottee's Leicester City.

"It's nice to have a semi-final to look forward to in January," beamed Harry, oblivious to the fact that he would soon be crying in his beer. "Give credit to Gareth Southgate for putting himself on offer with the penalty. He showed great character and he didn't hide."

Forget the froth, for there were some bitter dregs about to rear themselves in the slops. As Hammers prepared for their sell-out Premiership clash with Manchester United, news broke that they had fielded an ineligible player against Villa.

The ashen-faced Southgate certainly left Upton Park with his head in his hands but now the entire East End was copying him.

Omoyinmi may have had an anonymous half-dozen minutes against the Midlanders, but it was subsequently discovered that he had earlier played for Gillingham in both legs of their 1-6 aggregate defeat to Bolton Wanderers, in the second round of the competition, back in mid-September.

Redknapp had been keen to put his on-loan, Nigerian-born, youth team product in the shop window in a bid to realise that £400,000 tag. And the Gills had been furnished with a letter allowing him to play in any competition during his stay.

An official statement issued by Mackrell read: *"West Ham United has been advised by the Football League that the player Manny Omoyinmi was not eligible to play when he appeared as substitute in the Worthington Cup quarter-final tie against Aston Villa on 15 December 1999, having previously played in this competition whilst on loan to Gillingham FC. When the player returned form his loan period West Ham believed he had not played for Gillingham in the Worthington Cup competition. West Ham now acknowledges this was not the case but wishes to emphasise that the club acted in good faith. Manny appeared for only six minutes against Aston Villa and had no influence on the result of the tie.*

West Ham United firmly believes that the tie was won fairly, that the result should stand and that no further action is necessary."

Not surprisingly, Aston Villa chairman Doug Ellis had other ideas.

It did not matter that nobody could even recall Omoyinmi touching the ball during his short stint on the Boleyn turf, for here was the potential of a money-spinning, two-legged semi-final, with the added chance of a Wembley showdown and UEFA Cup football for the winners of the ultimate prize.

Quite simply, the stakes were too high for Villa to take the sporting option and accept their elimination with good grace.

Instead, the Midlanders lodged a formal complaint with the Football League seeking, as a minimum, a replay.

In direct contradiction to his opposite number, Villa secretary Steve Stride declared: "We are treating this as a serious breach of rules. We trust the outcome will reflect the seriousness of the matter. I've been in the game for 28 years and have never come across anything like this. It's every secretary's nightmare."

And the bad dream got worse. For immediately following the Premiership clash against Manchester United at Upton Park, the League ordered a January 11 replay. As West Ham saw their first Wembley final for 19 years – plus the potential millions it could reap – disappearing over the horizon, Mackrell and football secretary Alison O'Dowd promptly resigned, to be replaced by Tottenham's respected Peter Barnes.

Never mind the bench, 'ringer' Omoyinmi – now *persona non grata* in the East End – would not even have made the Upton Park stands for the re-match and he was farmed out to Scunthorpe United on loan.

Stimac spoke for the players when he said: "We don't have to sacrifice a young, talented player like Manny. And I believe that's the general feeling amongst all the other players, too. Sure he has to take some responsibility but the players only come to the dressing room to play the game. That's all we can do."

The self-righteous Ellis was less forgiving as he announced that he had done the whole of east London a favour: "After some arbitration between Dave Richards, the Premier League chairman, Terry Brown and myself, quite frankly, I conceded. The alternative was to go to a commission where West Ham would have been thrown out of the competition. I came to the conclusion that I'd bow my head and allow the game to be re-staged at the same venue, despite the fact that I felt West Ham had not been punished. They've admitted their mistake. It's a let-off.

"I don't want to be accused of winning something by default and I'm sure my players feel the same way, too."

For once, Harry had been undone by events played on paper rather than grass. And the Mannygate scandal had hit the boss hard.

"I had driven home from the training ground and was about five minutes away from seeing my grand-daughter in Poole Hospital," said Harry, whose original joy at beating Villa had been heightened by the new arrival of baby Millie – the daughter of son Mark and daughter-in-law Rachel – his first grandchild. "Then I got the phone call from Gillingham's Peter Taylor confirming that Manny had played for them in the cup. It felt like my world had caved in.

"Obviously, none of us knew that Manny had turned out for them. To be fair, when I let him go there on loan, I thought that would be the last I saw of the kid. I never had a clue he'd played in the competition for them otherwise he wouldn't have been anywhere near the place for the Villa game.

"You can't follow every kid, I've had about eight out on loan this year. Let's be truthful, I'm not going to bring him on with six minutes to go when he hasn't kicked a ball for the first team for a year. Am I really gonna take a chance? With respect, we're not talking Paolo Di Canio here. We're talking Manny Omoyinmi.

"Obviously Villa are going to take every opportunity to make the most of it. Ask Doug Ellis and he'll say: 'Kick 'em out!'

"My secretary Alison O'Dowd checked it out with Gillingham and she got a message back that he hadn't played. It never entered my mind that he was cup-tied.

"If the kid knew, then why didn't he say anything to me? I've asked him and he replied: 'I didn't think!' He came on for six minutes and touched the ball twice. We're all involved and, without putting the blame on Manny, I just don't know why he didn't say something to me. I'm not knocking Manny but I don't even know why I changed him with Paulo Wanchope.

"The players are very down, very low. It's a massive disappointment.

"Questions were asked of Gillingham and the wrong answers given. It was a genuine administrative error. Alison was so thorough. Every day I'd get a page of bookings and suspensions. She checked this one, too, but got the wrong answer.

"I'm not just saying this but I don't know if I'd want to go to Wembley having been beaten and then taken advantage of a replay. We got into the semi-finals on merit. In horseracing terms, interference took place but it didn't affect the result."

Already rocked by the shattering news that the previous Wednesday's exertions had, perhaps, all been in vain, Mannygate was hardly motivational for a wearisome West Ham side that found itself trailing 0-3 to United inside 19 minutes.

But it was pure theatre at Upton Park as Di Canio single-handedly put on a superhuman showing to reduce the deficit to 2-3 just after the curtain rose for the second half of an absorbing show. And on the hour he found himself one-on-one with Reds' 'keeper Raimond Van Der Gouw but the Dutchman saved.

As the Italian beat the living daylights out of the sodden turf, Dwight Yorke broke upfield to seal a 4-2 win for the Premiership leaders.

The inconsolable Italian was distraught.

"I've let you down," cried the Roman as he returned to the dressing room to hear confirmation of the Football League's ruling on that replay.

A 2-2 draw at Wimbledon on Boxing Day was followed by a 1-1 stalemate against Derby County in which Di Canio netted a magical equaliser.

"A special goal from a special player," drooled Harry after unwittingly becoming embroiled in the bare-chested maestro's celebrations.

Kicking off the new millennium, the prospects of a third successive draw looked remote as Hammers trailed Newcastle United 0-2 with just six minutes to play. But Lampard and then Stimac struck late to ensure that injury-ravaged West Ham United remained unbeaten in the new century. Fittingly, a new era heralded a St James's Park debut for former Wallsend boy Michael Carrick and fellow teenager Shaun Byrne, while Defoe, Izzy Iriekpen and Adam Newton were on the bench.

The second game of Year 2000 was that re-match with Aston Villa.

And when Lampard put Hammers ahead, it looked like justice would prevail. But Ian Taylor forced extra-time before Julian Joachim swept Villa ahead. And when David James saved Di Canio's lame spot-kick, Taylor sewed up a 3-1 victory to set up a semi-final date with eventual trophy winners, Leicester City.

"This will haunt me forever," announced the deflated H. "Personally, though, I would have found it very difficult to ask for a replay.

"Now I've got to pick the players and myself up. We can't let one bad night ruin all the hard work I've put in since I've been here."

In one of those weird quirks of footballing fate, within a few days Villa were back at Upton Park for a Premiership clash and Taylor was again on the mark to put the visitors in front before Di Canio capitalised on a James' blunder to force a 1-1 draw. By now, there was no love lost between the future Hammers' keeper and the irascible Italian, who pushed a hand into James' face after his offer of a post-match handshake was apparently declined. And having been photographed making a middle finger gesture in the match, Di Canio was also fined £5,000 by the FA.

Out of both domestic cups, Hammers still had a high-ranking Premiership place to aspire to, in the hope that they could qualify for another European adventure.

And the much-maligned Wanchope went some way towards appeasing his detractors with a double in a 3-1 win at Leicester City.

"I can understand the fans having a go at Paulo for putting the ball over from four yards," conceded Harry. "But the boy works his socks off. His finishing is poor, I'll admit that, but he's got to work and improve. I could have sold him at a profit to two Premiership clubs last week. People forget he's only 23-years-old."

Belize's Manul Bilches was a Wanchope fan, too. Incredibly, for reasons best known only to himself, the national coach nominated him in third spot in the FIFA World Player of 1999 poll behind Gabriel Batistuta and Fernando Redondo.

The luckless Charles had sliced his shin open on his debut in the Worthington Cup at Birmingham City and, upon his return to the fold, he netted an 86th-minute own goal to give Southampton a 2-1 win at The Dell.

Four-two down. Five-four up. With thrills and spills galore, Hammers' nine-goal classic with Bradford City had to be Upton Park's wackiest, white-knuckle, roller-coaster ride for years.

"To score four times and yet come away with nothing tells its own story," winced beleaguered Bantams' boss Paul Jewell after failing to find any fun at the fair.

Hislop had soon found himself stretchered away with a broken leg, after he fell awkwardly clearing upfield amidst accidental contact with Dean Saunders, and that saw nervy debutant Stephen Bywater pitched in for his first 86 minutes of Premiership football. The teams walked off at half-time deadlocked at 2-2 before two-goal Jamie Lawrence put City into a seemingly unassailable 4-2 lead.

And when Di Canio's third decent shout for a penalty again fell upon the deaf ears of referee Neale Barry, the infuriated Italian angrily strode over to the dug-out simply demanding to be taken off.

Fortunately, Harry would have none of it and when Hammers did finally win a spot-kick, Di Canio and Lampard wrestled for the ball like playground schoolboys. The Italian's persistence won the moment and the ticking time bomb eventually drove the penalty home. Cole then bagged his first-ever Premiership goal before Lampard gave Hammers a surreal 5-4 win.

While Foé remained away winning the African Nations Cup with Cameroon, and Craig Forrest was in the USA lifting the Concacaf Gold Cup, Hammers conceded four goals at home in their next match, too, as Everton's Nicky Barmby plundered a hat-trick past Charlton's on-loan third-choice keeper Sasa Ilic (1 app).

"I've just told 'em exactly what I thought about today," revealed Redknapp, whose only positive from the game was the return of Stuart Pearce. "And it wasn't a case of 'unlucky chaps!' I'm so disappointed. We were woeful up front, out-run in midfield and all over the place defensively."

A 2-1 win at Watford was followed by a 2-0 victory over Southampton. But disastrously, Pearce caught the sole of Kevin Davies' boot and cruelly broke his leg in the very same spot that he had incurred that fracture back in September.

"I'm sick for Pearcey because he's a special player," said Harry, knowing that any chance his veteran defender had of making it to Euro 2000 had just disappeared. "He's down but he'll be back."

Equally, Omoyinmi came back from Scunthorpe reportedly suffering from depression before again being sent out on loan, this time to Barnet.

Di Canio returned to Sheffield Wednesday for the first time to face the wrath of Hillsborough but, on an afternoon of acrimony, he was more concerned by Hammers' 1-3 defeat and things only slightly improved at Chelsea where Stimac was dismissed in a goalless draw at Stamford Bridge.

As April beckoned, Hammers unveiled £6m-rated, on-loan striker Frederic Kanouté, who had joined from Olympique Lyonnais.

This son of a Mali-immigrant had just had his contract suspended for 15 days by the Lyons' board, following an alleged showdown with coach Bernard Lacombe.

"I had a bad groin injury that kept me out for six months," explained the French Under-21 international. "And although I'm fit, the coach hasn't wanted me in the team for about a year now. I could have gone to Juventus 18 months ago but it was just too early in my career for me. After that, I was linked with a £4.5m transfer to

Monaco but Lyons did not want to sell me. I don't know what I will do at the end of the season but if my time at West Ham is spent well, then why shouldn't I stay? There are too many problems for me in France and they are now compelled towards letting me leave," concluded Lyons' *enfant terrible*. "We will just have to wait to see whether Harry wants to buy me."

Certainly, H could not wait to get the cheque book out as the Frenchman marked his Premiership arrival with the winning goal in a 2-1 victory over Wimbledon at Upton Park. But the real highlight of the game was Di Canio's technically brilliant wonder strike that both lifted the roof off Upton Park and put the lid on the Goal-of-the-Season awarded by BBC TV's *Match of the Day*.

Foe's greatest pass in a claret and blue shirt saw him send a raking eighth-minute cross-field ball out to Sinclair on the right wing. Spotting the Italian at the back of the Dons' box, West Ham's wide boy then whipped over an equally precision waist-high cross that saw the vaulting Di Canio – both feet off the turf – adjust his posture to send an angled, airborne 12-yard volley back beyond the despairing dive of Neil Sullivan.

It remains a goal etched in the memory of everyone privileged enough to see it rip into the Wimbledon net.

"I got a lot of praise for the volley," wrote the scorer of one of the greatest strikes ever witnessed at Upton Park in his book *Paolo Di Canio: The Autobiography*. "Sure, it was a spectacular goal. What I did was extremely difficult because it requires total body control, timing and balance. Compared to a bicycle kick or scissors kick it's much more difficult and when I struck the ball, both feet were in the air, even just making contact was quite an achievement.

"But goals like that don't come out of thin air. I was able to do it because it was something I had practiced for hours and hours in training. I attempted it so many times that it became an instinctive gesture. As the cross came in, I didn't even think about what I was going to do. My brain just decided for me.

"I just wish that my team-mates and some of the younger footballers understood that, without the hard work in training, I would not have pulled that one off."

A breathless Harry exclaimed: "I enjoyed watching us out there today. We played some great stuff. Paolo showed why he's not far away from being Footballer-of-the-Year while Frederic Kanouté had a fantastic debut. Together they made for a frightening pair."

Hammers travelled to Old Trafford in good heart and looked equally scary as they promptly went 1-0 up thanks to Wanchope's early strike.

"We started well and I thought it was going to be our day," said Harry who subsequently found himself sitting with his hands over his eyes as the Theatre of Dreams became the House of Horror thanks to the Reds' goal avalanche that simply overwhelmed his side.

United's eventual 7-1 victory condemned Hammers to their biggest defeat since a 2-8 mauling at Blackburn Rovers on Boxing Day 1963.

Forrest had been in confident mood having been named in the 'All Star' squad following Canada's surprise Concacaf Gold Cup tournament victory but, having once been on the receiving end of a 0-9 defeat while at Ipswich Town, it was a case of *deja-vu* for the poor keeper as United simply ran riot.

Wanchope was on target again in happier circumstances as his late winner secured a 2-1 victory over Newcastle United. Then the in-form Costa Rican headed back to Derby County, where his 15th goal of the season silenced the Pride Park protagonists, who jeered his every touch during Hammers' 2-1 win. Having returned on loan from Cardiff City for a second stint at Upton Park, American keeper Ian Feuer (3 apps) finally made his Premiership debut in the absence of the injured Hislop and Forrest.

That win was, however, overshadowed by an over-zealous challenge by Rory Delap on Cole, whose campaign was brought to a premature end due to a cracked bone in his leg.

Both Carrick and Margas bagged their first goals for the club in a 5-0 victory over Coventry City that also saw two-goal Di Canio and Kanouté hit the target.

"Di Canio, Kanouté and Wanchope looked unplayable," announced Harry, still salivating at the sight of his armed and highly dangerous strike force.

Having retired from football to take up golf, Julian Dicks was also high-scoring in his professional debut on the European Pro Tour, where he endured a scorching baptism of fire at the East Dorset Golf Club. Not even three inches of torrential rain could dampen the enthusiasm of the 70 or so people who had made the trip especially to see him swing his first competitive club in anger.

"Because of all the people who had turned up, they left the course open just for me," he said, reflecting upon 18 horrendous holes of horror that were destined to end in a nervy 92 that left him trailing in last of the 115-strong field. "As I got up to go to the tee, the whole place just went deadly silent. You could hear a pin drop and I thought: 'B*******, I don't need this!' I had one of my mates caddying for me just to calm me down. Without him, you can forget 92, I would have probably gone through the 100-mark! Although I was shaking like a leaf, I somehow managed to hit my first shot straight down the middle.

"It was a nerve-wracking experience compared to taking penalties. No matter how important they were, those spot-kicks weren't pressure as far as I was concerned. I can go out on the course and regularly shoot below par but that's no good when you can only do it against your mates. It's all about going out there and doing it under tournament pressure and that's going to take me a couple of years."

With a record of five red cards and 66 bookings stretching back across his 11-year Hammers' career, it was hardly surprising that Julian had already had a few run-ins with the old farts of the establishment.

"Rules are rules and I stick to them and dress properly. But I've still had it all," he said, reflecting on the odd dust-up at the 19th hole with officious bar stewards. "Once I was at the club minding my own business when some old bloke came up to me and started speaking to me like I was a little kid. At the end of the day I just had to tell him to f*** off!"

Instead of making those infamous trips to disciplinary hearings at the FA's Lancaster Gate HQ, Dicks was now heading to the Secretary's Office at The Warren Golf Club.

"There are people who have been at golf clubs for 40 or 50 years and they really do think they own the place," he fumed. "I just end up telling the old 'uns to clear off and then I usually find myself grassed up to the bloke who runs the club."

In years gone by, entry into the Intertoto Cup was there for virtually any English club mad enough to venture out into the mid-day sun. But having seen Hammers use the competition as a conduit into the UEFA Cup several Premiership takers now prepared to battle until the final kick of the season to qualify.

As one of the holders, Hammers were entitled to automatic Intertoto Cup qualification. But that also meant participating in the first round at the start of June, rather than joining proceedings at the third round stage in July.

The decision was taken to waive the club's right to defend their prize and opt for qualification via its final league position.

But an unexpected late hat-trick of defeats shattered all hopes of another European jaunt.

Brain Deane's penalty gave Middlesbrough a 1-0 win at Upton Park, before the handballing Emmanuel Petit netted a controversial late winner at Highbury after all but removing the lace and firing Gunners to a 2-1 victory.

The frustrated, twice-booked Sinclair was then dismissed, before Moncur and Foé were landed with FA misconduct charges at the final whistle.

And Kevin Phillips drilled home his 30th goal of the season to give Sunderland a 1-0 win at the Stadium of Light, where the furious Di Canio saw a cast iron appeal for a spot-kick waved away.

Going into the final game of the season, Leeds United wanted to get into the Champions League, while West Ham United – with nothing to play for except pride – just wanted to get home.

But they made the Yorkshiremen battle for the point that secured their European place in a gritty goalless draw that saw Foé become the eighth Hammer to receive a red card for half-volleying the grounded Matthew Jones.

"You can't do that," agreed Harry, who also saw the cautioned Moncur (10 bookings + 1 red card) take his card count into double figures to join Wanchope (11 bookings) and Stimac (12 bookings + 1 red card) high on the yellow fever list.

A 302-day, 53-game campaign was finally over.

And what a season it had been for 10th-placed West Ham United.

Intertoto Cup glory from Europe's *hors d'ouvres* menu had given Hammers a taster of the UEFA Cup *entrées*, while Premiership wins over runners-up Arsenal and fourth-placed Liverpool demonstrated just what West Ham could do.

Having netted 17 times, Di Canio's goal-of-the-season – later voted the best-ever in the Premiership's history – had all but completed his reformation while Ferdinand, Stuart Pearce and 13-goal Lampard had all won full England caps and squad man Sinclair was knocking on the door. Wanchope had produced 15 goals, Kanoute looked tailor-made for the Premiership and youngsters Cole and Carrick, while not having replaced the vastly more experienced Berkovic, were in the England Under-21 reckoning.

But weary West Ham had finished five places lower than the previous season and Mannygate had left an indelible blot on the season.

Even so, Redknapp still had plenty to smile about.

"People have got to remember where we've come from in the past four or five years. There's not the aggravation here that there used to be," he observed. "I don't get up in the morning thinking I've got to deal with this player or that one.

"I had to make changes because of the type of people who were here and things are so much better now.

"Di Canio has been fantastic. The stuff he's done on the pitch has been frightening. What a player! But he's a timebomb. In fact he's a hand grenade and we've just gotta make sure that the pin doesn't come out!

"Look at the people we've got here now. Look at the football that's being played. I honestly think that we can entertain as well as any other team in the country.

"The kids are coming through, too, and I think we're in really great shape. We've just pulled off another top 10 finish," he concluded, looking forward to more of the same continuing into the new millennium. "Yeah, the future's looking good."

PLAYERS IN

Leon Britton	Arsenal	£400,000
Emmanuel Cascione	Lucchese	Free transfer
Gary Charles	Benfica	£1,200,000
Jermain Defoe	Charlton Athletic	£1,650,000
Rob Jones	Liverpool	Free transfer
Stuart Pearce	Newcastle United	Free transfer
Omer Riza	Arsenal	£20,000
Daniel Sjolund	Brommaekjaran	£200,000
Igor Stimac	Derby County	£600,000
Paulo Wanchope	Derby County	£2,500,000
Tommy Williams	Walton & Hersham	£40,000

LOANS IN

Ian Feuer	Cardiff City
Sasa Ilic	Charlton Athletic
Frederic Kanouté	Olympique Lyonnais

PLAYERS OUT

Samassi Abou	Gaz Ajaccio	Free transfer
Eyal Berkovic	Celtic	£5,750,000
Lee Boylan	Trelleborgs FF	Free transfer
Chris Coyne	Dundee	Free transfer
Julian Dicks	Retired	
Lee Hodges	Scunthorpe United	£130,000
Rob Jones	Retired	
Stan Lazaridis	Birmingham City	£1,500,000
Scott Mean	Bournemouth	Free transfer
Ian Wright	Celtic	Free transfer

Chapter 14
2000-01

SPEND, SPEND, SPEND

Rio Ferdinand had been a shock inclusion in Glenn Hoddle's France 98 World Cup squad.

And it was a mark of his progression that he was now an equally shock omission from Kevin Keegan's Euro 2000 campaign. With the England coach favouring a three-man defensive axis with wing-backs, rather than a flat back four, alas, there was to be no place for Rio.

Back in 1998, Hoddle had famously faced the wrath of the shell-shocked Paul Gascoigne when he invited him to his room to tell him that there was no place on the plane to France. In his subsequent rage, Gazza left La Manga's light-bulb laden maintenance man working overtime in his quest to get the room ready for the hotel's next guest.

This time around, his successor Keegan was to have no such problem when he headed along the corridor to tell Rio that he was one of the unfortunate half-dozen culled as his squad for Belgium and Holland was cut from 28 to 22.

Ferdinand could not be roused from his deep sleep, forcing the England coach to return later.

"Kevin said that I should be positive," said Rio once he had finally woken from his slumber. "I'm only 21, but I told him that I don't think that I've had a fair crack of the whip. To be fair, he agreed and he said my chance will come."

Former England international, Gary Lineker observed: "It was a pity that our most accomplished ball-playing defender was omitted, but Keegan must have seen something at close quarters that told him he was not ready."

Meanwhile, Frank Lampard went to the European Under-21 Championships admitting that he had not expected to make the full Euro 2000 squad as Sinclair, still looking for that elusive first-cap – despite being named in several squads – also confirmed: "It would have been a bit stupid to have taken somebody like me who is untested at international level."

But while England were crashing out of the tournament following Group A defeats against Portugal and Romania, back home Rio was rarely out of the news.

Ever since he had broken into the first team, he had been linked with all manner of big money transfers to bigger clubs, including Liverpool and Roma.

But having ironically secured their lucrative Champions League place at Upton Park on the final day of the season, Leeds United were now back, sniffing around £8m-rated Frank Lampard and £10m Ferdinand with more determined intent.

NEARLY REACHED THE SKY

"Leeds have come back with another £15m bid for Rio but I've had a long talk with the chairman and we decided to resist it," said Harry, as the offers got both more serious and more sizeable.

"I'm not going to Leeds," insisted Ferdinand, who was also a reported Barcelona target. "I'm perfectly happy here at West Ham. I will only be leaving if the club say that they want to sell me. West Ham gave me my chance in football and I want to repay them for that."

Snubbed Leeds' chairman Peter Ridsdale admitted: "We would love to have Rio but we are told he is not available and we respect that. I have asked the West Ham chairman to inform me immediately that situation changes."

But as the first piles were being driven into the foundations of the new 15,427 capacity, West Stand that would incorporate 72 executive boxes-cum-non-matchday hotel rooms, the stark reality was that this third-phase of the £35m Boleyn Ground redevelopment was going to create severe financial constraints.

With the Bobby Moore (South) stand and Centenary (North) stand having already cost £11.5m, this latest construction would increase the all-seating capacity to 35,595 pending future re-development of the 1960s-built East Stand.

And according to Ken Dyer of the *Evening Standard*, Harry was further hamstrung in the transfer market by the club's annual £30m wage bill that had even seen the likes of youngsters such as Lampard and Ferdinand reportedly earning around £20,000 per week, with Joe Cole not too far behind.

Having already had their previous summer's sexploits highlighted in the Sunday tabloids, Lampard and Ferdinand found the *News of the World* exposing more lurid, debauched tales as they returned to the Grecian Bay resort in Cyprus, clearly having failed to learn their lesson of 12 months earlier.

This time around, the Hammers' duo alongside Newcastle United's Kieron Dyer, were accused of secretly filming each other in a series of lewd acts with various female holidaymakers.

In response to the 'England stars' video orgy shame' Frank Lampard senior told the newspaper that he would be confronting his son, while Ferdinand, whose inner circle allegedly sold the recording to the press, reportedly argued: "I've never degraded a woman in my life."

One year on, another sun, sea and sex scandal involving both his nephew and his prize asset was the last distraction that Harry Redknapp needed in a close season that had seen him busily trying to balance the books.

The sale of Marc-Vivien Foe (47+1 apps 2 gls) to Olympique Lyonnais for £6m had already enabled him to turn Frederic Kanouté's loan move from the French side into a permanent £3.75m transfer.

West Ham had never brought the best out of the likeable Foe, who was consequently fined £8,000 and banned from the first four games in *Le Championnat*, following his full-time dust-up at Highbury and subsequent dismissal in his final Hammers' appearance against Leeds United.

After winning his second French championship title with Lyons in 2002, the Cameroon international duly returned to England for a loan spell at Manchester City. Foe by name but friendly by nature, the powerful midfielder settled far better in the Premiership second time around, scoring nine goals at Maine Road before heading to FIFA's ill-fated end-of-season 2003 Confederations Cup tournament.

And tragically, while playing for Cameroon in the semi-final against Colombia, ironically in Lyons, he collapsed on the pitch with heart problems and, despite the efforts of paramedics, died within an hour, aged just 28.

Elsewhere, it was a tale of two Cities as Manchester and Bradford battled it out for Paulo Wanchope (42+4 apps 15 gls) after Hammers agreed a £3.65m fee with both clubs.

"The Bradford chairman said that Manchester City might be perceived as a bigger club," quipped Maine Road boss Joe Royle after winning the tug-of-war for the Costa Rican. "Thank God for perception!"

But not for the first time, agent Dennis Roach was to come under the FA spotlight for his role in the deal.

Neil Ruddock (50+5 apps 3 gls) was given a free transfer to Crystal Palace ahead of moving to Swindon as player-coach alongside former Anfield boss, Roy Evans.

Comically, Razor almost missed the first game of his Robins' career while waiting for a pair of shorts that would fit him to be especially flown in from the Far East and, after leaving the Wiltshire club, he tried his hand as a reality TV celebrity before undergoing self-help treatment for alcohol-related problems.

Following the Worthington Cup debacle, Emmanuel Omoyinmi (2+10 apps 2 gls) was never going to recover from Mannygate and he duly joined Oxford United on a free transfer before moving to Conference outfit Margate.

Rookie striker Gary Alexander (0 apps) had only ever made it as far as the bench and, with his first-team opportunities looking severely limited, he was sold to Swindon Town for £300,000, while Scott Mean (0+3 apps) returned to Bournemouth on a free transfer.

Despite making just 14 starts for Arsenal during the 1999-2000 campaign, 32-year-old Davor Suker still managed to score 11 goals before moving to Upton Park from Highbury.

"If I am healthy and without injury I will score 20 or 25 goals," promised the 57-times capped Croatian marksman who had netted 42 times for his country.

"Davor is a genuine world-class player," enthused Harry having finally got his man on a free transfer, 12 months on. "And to be fair his wages are not over the top. I've got real competition now with Di Canio and Kanouté, too."

And fellow countryman Igor Stimac predicted: "We can expect a lot of goals from Davor this season, don't worry about that."

Another player on his way from Highbury was veteran left-back Nigel Winterburn who eventually signed in a £250,000 deal after Arsenal – having offered the triple-title winner an extended 12-month contract – reluctantly allowed him to head east in search of first-team football.

Subject to receipt of a work permit, Australian central defender Hayden Foxe was signed on a free-transfer from Japanese J-League side, Sanfrecce Hiroshima.

"I had a few other offers but Harry seemed very keen and I liked the set-up here," said the flame-haired 23-year-old, totally oblivious to an eternal wait ahead for the elusive permit that would, hopefully, allow him to seal a four-year deal.

NEARLY REACHED THE SKY

Christian Bassila, a powerful French Under-21 midfielder, arrived on loan from Rennes to be joined by fellow countryman Kaba Diawara, a bustling striker who had also had spells with both Arsenal and Blackburn Rovers.

Aside from the signing of Kanouté, the club's only other multi-million pound capture was the £2m purchase of 79 lots of Bobby Moore footballing memorabilia put up for auction by his first wife, Tina, including the jewel in the crown – the legend's 1966 World Cup winners' medal.

The haul was purchased for display in the proposed club museum, once the West Stand building works were complete.

Hammers rounded off their pre-season preparations with a 1-2 friendly defeat at Celtic, where Di Canio received a hero's welcome before subsequently scoring upon his return to Parkhead.

And in their final warm-up game, a crowd of 14,424 loyally paid a toppy £25 per head to pay homage to Julian Dicks (326 apps 65 gls), as he pulled down the curtain on his controversial West Ham United career with a testimonial against Athletic Bilbao, before heading off to the golf course and then taking over the Shepherd & Dog pub near Colchester.

Fittingly, the Hammers' hard man saw the 'friendly' do as much for Anglo-Spanish relations as Sir Francis Drake's armada sinking exploits of centuries gone by and, following a 17-man brawl, Di Canio and Josebe Etxeberria were told to leave the field in an enforced substitution.

All eyes were on Suker as Hammers kicked off their 2000-01 campaign at Stamford Bridge. But it was another Croatian – Chelsea's £5.6m Mario Stanic – who stole the headlines with a wonder 35-yard goal in the Blues' 4-2 victory.

And four days later, another Croat – Stimac – was occupying the column inches following his sending off in the 0-1 defeat against Leicester City as the Foxes recorded their first victory at Upton Park since 1966.

"The referee was just booking people and laughing," argued the central defender who – alongside Di Canio, Suker, Ferdinand and Michael Carrick – was accused of harassing official Rob Styles after the Croatian was dismissed for felling the theatrical, long-haired Robbie Savage.

"I hate players like Savage with his hair and style of playing," steamed Stimac. "They should be models and go on catwalks. I never tried to hurt anybody and, believe me, if I had elbowed him he still would not be up off the floor today."

Having made his entrance as an interval substitute, it was to prove six and out for Gary Charles as he made what was, ultimately, his final appearance for the club, before being sent out on loan to Birmingham City where he was quickly returned to sender.

According to Tom Bower in *Broken Dreams*, Terence Brown was shocked to have seen his purchase from Benfica make just three starts, plus a trio of substitute outings, before being farmed out to St. Andrews within a year of making that £1.2m move from Portugal.

"Is he no good?" the chairman asked his manager.

"What do you expect for £1.2m?" replied Redknapp.

"Why buy him then?" asked Brown. "We're paying him £1m per year in wages."

"Yeah, but they're all getting that," came the apparent, throw-away riposte.

Following the disappointment of the Leicester defeat, it also looked all over for West Ham when Manchester United led 2-0 at Upton Park with just five minutes to go, but a foul on the electrifying Cole gave Di Canio the chance to pull one back from the spot, before Suker headed home a last-gasp leveller to make it 2-2.

Cole had been simply inspirational and, after initially seeing his request declined, the star-struck Hammer had impressed David Beckham sufficiently to persuade him to breach United rules and swap shirts in the tunnel an hour later.

With Cole in the full England squad, and Carrick having made the breakthrough at Under-21 level, both youngsters paid credit to coach Glenn Roeder.

"It's good to have Glenn here because he isn't involved in all the decision-making," enthused Carrick. "He can sit back and see what's happening and win, lose or draw, he's always there with good advice for us young lads."

And Cole concurred: "Glenn's been brilliant. When I was left out of the side he made a lot of sense out of my situation and told me that I would end up going back to him as a first-team regular and, hopefully, he's now been proved right. I just wouldn't like to have to go around collecting as many balls as he does after training, though. He needs to sort that out!"

Bassila, a 68th-minute substitute, also needed to rectify his foot that required an operation following an injury sustained on his Hammers' debut.

There was nothing wrong with Suker's left peg, though, as he looked set to honour his promise when he struck the equaliser in a 1-1 draw at the Sunderland.

But Sol Campbell then gave Tottenham Hotspur a 1-0 victory at White Hart Lane and, going into mid-September, win-less West Ham were bottom of the table.

Although Di Canio's penalty secured a point in a 1-1 draw against Liverpool at Upton Park, it did little to help their plight.

"This ain't a crisis," insisted Harry, who was also angered by the decline of Foxe's work permit. "We're creating chances and a win'll come. It's only a matter of time because this is the best team they've had at West Ham for 20 years, since Brooking and Devonshire were here. It's tough at the top but it's even tougher at the bottom!"

For his part, Di Canio had been a £4m target for desperate Gianluca Vialli just days before he was sacked as Chelsea boss.

"It was a big opportunity," admitted Di Canio. "But I saw the chairman and he said: 'I love you.' And I said: 'I love you, too!' West Ham is my second family. That was it. In 10 years I want to see my statistics: Paolo Di Canio – UEFA Cup with Juventus, *Scudetto* with AC Milan, European Super Cup with AC Milan and . . . FA Cup with West Ham.

That elusive first victory finally arrived at Walsall in the Worthington Cup second round, first leg, where debutant substitute Jermain Defoe's first-ever goal for the club gave a West Ham side containing – unlike the previous year – 11 eligible players, a 1-0 victory.

While the match-winner prepared to head to Bournemouth for a prolific loan spell, Hammers were back in the Midlands at the weekend, where they also returned to winning ways in the Premiership, with a 3-0 victory at Coventry City.

NEARLY REACHED THE SKY

"I've only ever told the truth when I've said that it's just a matter of time before we got a league win," announced H. "All along we've been playing well – not crap – and my confidence has never waned. Looking at the players around me, I'd have been an absolute idiot to have thought otherwise."

A lack-lustre 1-1 draw against Walsall in the Worthington Cup return was nowhere near as disappointing as the following Saturday's result.

"This has f****** ruined my weekend," roared Redknapp after Dan Petrescu's injury-time leveller earned bottom-placed Bradford City a fortunate 1-1 draw at Upton Park. "It makes me really angry to read all this stuff about me being an easy-going bloke, it's a load of b*******. People who say that don't work with me and they don't know me!"

And H would not have been pleased as the 'threatening and insulting' Sinclair found himself back in the familiar surroundings of Havering Magistrates Court after he was involved in yet another incident in Romford's South Street, just 48 hours before playing in the 1-1 draw at Ipswich Town.

West Ham, in 18th-place, had won just one Premiership match by mid-October, before Arsenal strode out 2-1 victors at Upton Park.

"The situation's not that bad," argued Harry. "I'm still confident that we'll finish in the top half. Nothing will change my mind about that. I'm not often wrong."

But the *News of the World* enquired: "Redknapp is forever telling us that West Ham will finish in the top half but when will he achieve lift-off?"

Match-winner Kanouté – the subject of a spurned £11m bid from Glasgow Rangers and interest from Chelsea and Liverpool – had the answer when he launched Hammers to their first home victory of the season, a 1-0 win over Newcastle United.

And goals from Suker and Di Canio then gave Hammers a 2-0 victory over first division Blackburn Rovers in the Worthington Cup third round, to set up a comfortable looking fourth round tie against Sheffield Wednesday.

A dire goalless draw against Derby County was followed by a 4-1 win over Manchester City that lifted Hammers into 13th spot to leave Redknapp declaring: "We'll keep going onwards but whether we go upwards only time will tell."

Di Canio's audaciously chipped, back-spinning penalty had stitched up the grounded Luke Weaver to seal Hammers' 100th Premiership victory.

But as they prepared for their next match at Leeds United – where Ferdinand was still being linked with a £15m move – the mischievous tabloids had enjoyed a field day following the publication of the ice-cool Italian's autobiography that contained everything from his views on Mussolini to a recipe for tiramisu.

For with England heading to Italy for a Turin friendly, Di Canio announced at the launch of *Paolo Di Canio – The Autobiography* at Bertorelli's restaurant in London's West End: "Joe Cole and Rio Ferdinand are very talented but if I am going to be honest, then I must say that I don't think that they are ready for England just yet. It's too easy just to say that they are ready. They must prove themselves, match after match, for a long time, not just in a few games. It's not just about talent when you come up against countries like Italy, France and Germany."

But, conveniently, the column inches did not extend as far as adding his counterbalancing observation: "Rio reminds me of a young Alessandro Nesta who's at Lazio. He's one of the best in the world with a good mix of incredible skill and defensive qualities. I've told Rio that he can play much better, but he needs to carry on working hard if he is to play at a different level for his national team."

By the time Ferdinand had returned from Italy having earned rave reviews despite England's 0-1 defeat in Juventus' Stadio Delle Alpi, all hell had broken loose after Redknapp had castigated Di Canio for his so-called outburst.

"Enough is enough," said Harry who had only recently turned down a £3m bid from the Italian's former club – and boyhood heroes – Lazio. "I can't allow this to go on. Paolo is upsetting people and shouldn't be surprised if no-one wants to talk to him. I've got a wonderful team spirit here and won't stand by and watch somebody wreck it. He's entitled to his opinion, but when it involves people he works with and threatens to undermine everything, he should keep it to himself."

Di Canio replied: "I said a lot of positive things about Rio and Joe because I want to help them. And I would rather my team-mates hate me and we finish in the top five, than everyone love me and we finish bottom."

Curiously, Winterburn had confronted Di Canio when he was dismissed for shoving referee Alcock at Hillsborough in September 1998 and, in his book, the Italian had painstakingly recalled how the Gunner had been yapping like a hyperactive dog before retreating, 'wetting his pants in fear.'

"Nigel knows that I was talking about one game two years ago and not now," said Di Canio as he embarked on a peace-keeping mission of which Henry Kissenger would have been proud. "We've spoken since the story was printed and we don't have any problems. He's intelligent and he understands the situation."

Winterburn replied: "The book had been written before I signed. I knew Paolo was here and if I thought that there were going to be problems I would have walked away. It might surprise a few people but I do get on very well with him."

While Winterburn scored his one and only Hammers' goal to give West Ham a rare 1-0 win at Elland Road, Di Canio was a notable absentee at Leeds United.

"Paolo told me on Friday that he had an upset stomach and that if he got on the coach he thought he might have been sick, so we had to leave him behind," said Harry in the knowledge that victory had strengthened his hand in the argument with his AWOL star. "But this was a very effective performance from 11 very hard working and honest players. Today was a big result. We don't come here often and get something and not everyone in your team wants to come to Leeds, anyway!"

And as speculation mounted over £15m-rated Ferdinand's future, the Hammers' boss added: "I don't want to sell Rio. We've got to build a team around him, Frank Lampard, Joe Cole and Michael Carrick. They're the future of this football club."

But money talks.

And having seen Ferdinand put in a solid performance against his side, David O'Leary returned to the table with a mouth-watering, increased, British record bid of £18m that would also make the 22-year-old the world's most expensive defender, ahead of Roma's £13m Walter Samuel.

All in all, the entire package was projected to cost the Yorkshiremen around £33m over five years.

NEARLY REACHED THE SKY

But there was a 72-hour impasse as his agent Pini Zahavi reportedly sought a £1,300,000 settlement under his player's West Ham United contract that still had five years left to run.

Mihir Bose, of *The Daily Telegraph*, had other ideas, though.

"Could it have been that Zahavi had a contract with West Ham which only lasted as long as Rio was at the club?" he wrote. "So once Rio moved, the agreement would come to an end and there would be the question of compensating Zahavi for his loss of income."

Following the delay, Ferdinand finally signed on the dotted line to eclipse the £15m that Newcastle United paid for Blackburn Rovers' Alan Shearer, in 1996.

"West Ham accepting the bid came as a big surprise to me," admitted Rio after he finally signed a five-and-a-half-year contract that would reportedly increase his wages from a weekly £21,000 to £32,000 per week. "Harry told me that he didn't want me to leave but I felt that the club's decision to accept the fee showed that they were ready to let me go. I said all along that the only way I would go was if West Ham wanted to sell me."

Award-winning Paul Hayward, of *The Daily Telegraph*, cynically observed: "The £18m price on Rio's head confirms the death of 'The Stopper', whose job it was to smear the centre-forward onto the advertising hoardings."

With FIFA reviewing a transfer system that was perceived by many to be on the point of collapse, given the proposal that all players over 24 should be allowed to move on free transfers at the end of their contracts, Redknapp added: "Rio was special to us and he was happy here. But £18m was just an amazing offer. What can you say to that? We couldn't turn it down.

"The chairman said he wanted £15m for Rio. He said: 'Look, Harry, the transfer system's falling apart, we'll never get this offer again.' I said: 'Listen, they'll come back with more and if it's not them then Barcelona will buy him because he's the best.' He said: 'I can't see that.' Sure enough Leeds came back with £18m so West Ham made £3m there. The chairman said: 'Harry, we've got to take it.' And I said: 'Yeah, I see that.' Now the fans are waiting to see how much money I'm going to be given to spend – that will decide whether or not they accept Rio leaving.

"If I end up asking to sign a player who is going to cost £8m, and the chairman says that we can't afford it, then I'll know we're gonna be struggling!"

Certainly, the cash-rich Hammers' boss resisted the temptation to get the cheque book out ahead of the trip to Southampton, where West Ham won 3-2 in their first game without Ferdinand (151+6 apps 2 gls).

Despite that victory, however, Harry was determined to call for reinforcements and it turned out to be more of a supermarket sweep than a discerning shop for designer goods, as he bought them cheap and piled them high . . . and higher.

First up was Liverpool's Cameroon international Rigobert 'Song' Bahanag. The athletic 62-times capped defender had represented his country as a 17-year-old at the USA 94 World Cup, but after moving to Anfield in a £2.7m transfer from *Serie A* side Salernitana in January 1999, he soon fell out of favour with Reds' boss Gerard Houllier after missing swathes of the season due to international call-ups.

With the 2002 World Cup qualifiers beckoning, Hammers would be faced with a similar problem but, never one to miss out on a cut-price bargain, Harry duly acquired the dreadlocked defender for £2.5m as Finnish youngster, Daniel Sjolund, headed to Merseyside for £1m without ever making a first-team outing.

"People are looking at me because I am the new one," observed Song. "But please don't look at Rio and then look at me, because I don't want any comparisons made between the two of us."

But West Ham fans soon had him under the microscope as first division Sheffield Wednesday twice exposed the African's defensive frailties to notch a shock 2-1 win at Upton Park and progress into the Worthington Cup quarter-finals.

Redknapp's annoyance at that defeat was compounded by yet another refusal to award Foxe the work permit that would allow him to make the move from Japan.

After seeing his proposed acquisition black-balled, yet again, the manager patriotically climbed onto his soapbox and threatened to take the case all the way.

"It's a scandal and a total disgrace," he declared. "Something's crooked. Hayden Foxe is an Australian and they fought in the war with us. What about the Commonwealth? What about the Queen? It's not as though we're trying to bring in a foreigner who has no allegiance to this country."

But for many at the tribunal, Hammers had over-egged the Aussie's case by comparing him to Bobby Moore.

Having called a truce with Di Canio, Redknapp was relieved to see the Italian's 20-yarder secure a 1-0 win over Middlesbrough. That lifted Hammers into the top six, five places above Leeds, for whom Rio made his debut in a 1-3 defeat at third-place Leicester City.

A 1-1 draw against Aston Villa followed, before Di Canio was involved in amazing scenes at Goodison Park.

After Kanouté wiped out Danny Cadamarteri's opener, the Frenchman then sprinted onto Lampard's injury time through-pass. But, racing out of his area to intercept, Everton keeper Paul Gerrard was left incapacitated on the touchline after skidding awkwardly and twisting his knee.

And when the supporting Sinclair crossed to the edge of the penalty box – where only outfield players David Weir and Michael Ball were guarding the Toffees' goal – Di Canio, 18 yards out, looked all set to beat Niclas Alexandersson and Steve Watson to the centre.

But Christmas came early for Everton, as the Italian ignored any chance of glory and sportingly caught the ball to spontaneous, generous Goodison applause.

"It was unusual, wasn't it?" observed an incredulous Harry trying to disguise his anger beneath a thin veil of sporting appreciation, after settling for a 1-1 draw at the end of his 250th game in charge of the Hammers. "I've never seen anything like it. Ever! I thought Paolo was going to catch the ball on his chest and roll it in. Very unusual! Obviously you'd like to get three points but what you never know in football, or in life, is whether anyone else would do the same thing for you.

"If their keeper's seriously injured you want him to get treatment but, in fairness, he'd missed the ball and would've got it just as quickly if we'd scored. I've not had a go at Paolo, nobody has. It's a difficult situation but it was good sportsmanship. Paolo's done what he's done and that's it. Anyway, if you still get a point away from home it's never the end of the world," he concluded. "Now you'll have to excuse me, I'm just going to get Paolo's stretcher!"

Once the Goodison gratitude had subsided, the cynics rightly suggested that, even for a striker of Di Canio's calibre, there was still much to do – 18 yards out – to turn one point into three.

"It is, it seems, essential to the story that Di Canio turned down a certain goal," wrote Simon Barnes of *The Times*. "Not a half-chance. It has to be a certainty. He would, however, have required at least two touches. But the overriding point is that Di Canio didn't hesitate, the notion of trying to score didn't occur to him."

Following *that* push on referee Alcock, the redeemed Roman now had a half-decent chance of being remembered in the British game for *that* catch.

And when Sepp Blatter awarded the Italian the FIFA Fair Play award, unlike, say, Hartson, his salvation in the English game was complete.

Like shoeaholic Imelda Marcos in Freeman Hardy & Willis, Redknapp continued to shop till he dropped.

Next on his list was towering Finnish international defender Hannu Tihinen, who joined on a three-month loan spell from Norwegian side, Racing Stavanger.

"Rio is a very good player," said the £2m-rated stopper who, ironically, had been watching from the stands of Helsinki's Olympic Stadium when Hammers knocked FC Jokerit out of the Intertoto Cup, 18 months earlier. "It's going to be difficult but I hope that I can go some way towards replacing him."

And Harry also came close to signing Inter Milan's Robbie Keane, too, but having already seen the aggressively acquisitive Leeds United seize his prize asset – Ferdinand – the Hammers' boss could only look on helplessly as the striker headed to Elland Road, and the Champions League, in a £10m deal.

In the Irish international's place came the lesser-rated Aboubaca Camara. Liverpool's Guinean striker – like Song – had found everything going Titi up with Houllier for putting country before club, once too often.

"There's a s*** gaffer at Liverpool," said the 28-year-old goal-getter in his broken English after signing a three-and-a-half-year contract and making a £1.5m move from Anfield. "I had no problem with the football club, all my troubles were with Houllier. He has no respect for African players. But I spoke to Jamie Redknapp before I came here to West Ham and he said I'd have no problems. Harry's a good gaffer!"

Those sentiments were no doubt echoed by Houllier, who had just recouped £4m on two players who would, inevitably, be increasingly away on international duty deep in darkest Africa as the World Cup 2002 qualifiers loomed.

According to Tom Bower's *Broken Dreams*, Redknapp had received a £300,000 share of the Ferdinand fee on condition that he did not initiate a buying frenzy, although Harry later insisted it was a gift in recognition of the way that he had been running the club.

Taking to his manager's suggestion that the club should buy both Song and Camara, Brown was led to believe that the agent would be Pape Diouf. But his English associate was Willie McKay, a close pal of the Hammers' manager, whose friendship was even reflected in the name of a racehorse – When Harry Met Willie.

Unaware that West Ham had, apparently, agreed to pay McKay a commission to seek out the Africans, Liverpool's chief executive was delighted when the agent approached him, allegedly, offering to place the players for a fee.

Making his debut in a 1-3 defeat at Leicester City, £30,000 per week 'Titi' Camara – as nicknamed by a baby sister – posed more threat to BBC TV's *Match of the Day* cameraman perched on the roof of the Filbert Street stadium than he did to Tim Flowers in the Foxes' goal.

"So far, the West Ham supporters have only seen 40% of me," promised the man who scored 10 goals for Liverpool following his £2.6m move from Marseilles in the summer of 1999.

While Camara also drew a familiar blank on his home debut against Charlton Athletic on Boxing Day, a 5-0 victory at least got Hammers back to winning ways.

But after seeing their next scheduled match with Chelsea postponed, West Ham were brought back to reality with a 1-3 defeat at Manchester United, where Song endured a nightmare return to the north-west.

Having again been linked with moves to Lazio and Liverpool, Di Canio's presence at away matches was becoming selective at best. And his absence from the New Year's Day visit to Old Trafford again left Harry fuming: "Paolo Di Canio had a cold…I think? He was going to play against Chelsea and even then he said he didn't think he would be fit to play against Manchester United. Sometimes Paolo's not well, just like last year when we came here!

"But United are different class and they gave an absolute object lesson on how to play the game. I just wish that I hadn't been f****** well tonight either!"

In the FA Cup third round at Walsall, Lampard's early opener eased any jitters before a Kanouté double – including a long-range thunderbolt – secured a 3-2 win.

"Fredi was absolutely magnificent on the day," quipped future Hammers' keeper James Walker, who had been put up for target practice in the Saddlers' goal. "The ball stayed about four inches off floor for the entire 20 yards. That has to be the crispest shot that I have ever had to face. My defence and the crowd thought I was diving at full stretch but, really, I was just clapping it into the net!"

The nation's new England coach, Sven-Goran Eriksson, was at Upton Park to see his first game as the country's main man, but he learned little about any of his Three Lions as Scottish international Don Hutchison scored against his former club, before Slovakian Stanislav Varga rounded off Sunderland's 2-0 victory.

Ironmongers Robert Dyas were struggling to keep up with demand as a new clothes hook went up in the dressing room with the passing of virtually every day.

Svetoslav Todorov, an unknown Bulgarian international striker, joined from Liteks Lovech for £500,000 and, having been in pursuit of Scottish international defender Christian Dailly for several weeks, Redknapp finally got his man when he saw off late challenges from Leicester City and Everton to sign him in a £1.75m deal from Blackburn Rovers.

Dundee-born Dailly had cost a sensational £5.3m when, pressured by Rovers' owner Jack Walker, Roy Hodgson hurriedly bought him from Derby County ahead of the Champions League registration deadline back in August 1998.

But when fellow Scot Graeme Souness took over he wasted no time in deciding that Dailly was not for him and promptly set about getting rid of the utility man.

Fortunately for Dailly, a changing room peg immediately became free after Javier Margas (25+4 apps 1gl) finally retired and headed home to Chile, whereupon he duly opened a new hotel with the offer of free bed and board to any Hammers' fans looking for a room at the inn.

Norwegian defender, Ragnvald Soma, returned from a trial with Italian side Perugia to join West Ham at the second attempt.

The sober Scandinavian had first made headlines after the *Evening Standard* splashed a mischievous story claiming that the yobbish drinking culture associated with the English game was the reason why he had not wanted to sign for the Hammers in the first place.

"I didn't like to hear that because it was just a journalist taking what I had actually said out of context," protested the £800,000 capture from FC Bryne, who subsequently ensured that the newspaper printed an apology. "Yes, I admit I said I don't like the English alcohol habits but, no, I didn't say anything about West Ham. Back home in Norway we'd all read about Leicester City being sent home from La Manga and Liverpool players getting up to things at their Christmas party. Incidents like those had given English football a bad reputation."

FC Metz defender Sebastien Schemmel had caught the eye of watching Hammers' scout Glenn Roeder when Harry sent him to assess the club's Intertoto Cup final opponents back in summer 1999.

And following a fall-out with his club for allegedly assaulting a reporter who had criticised him in print, the right-sided defender headed to Upton Park on loan until the end of the season with a view to a £3m move.

The Nancy-born, 25-year-old was reportedly described as 'phenomenally unstable' by the French club's president.

By now, if they had a pair of football boots they were linked with West Ham.

The list was endless: Daniel Kenedy (Estrela Amadora), Henning Berg (Manchester United), Ermin Siljak (Servette), Gareth Southgate (Aston Villa), Dani (Barcelona), Andres D'Alessandro (River Plate) and Lorenzo Amoruso (Glasgow Rangers) to name but a few.

Indeed, even Gamba Osaka's Japanese international Tsunejasu Miyamoto was said to be heading from the Far East to the East End.

"Ah, Billy Bonsai?" acknowledged Redknapp, acutely aware that this was more of a marketing-driven deal primarily aimed at selling the Hammers' brand in the Land of the Rising Sun and beyond. "I just hope that he can play football!"

There were debuts for both Schemmel and Dailly in a 1-1 draw at Charlton Athletic, where Eriksson was again in attendance.

And had satellite navigation been fitted as standard in Soma's car, there would have been a third bow, too.

"Although I'd only been to Upton Park once before, I felt I knew the road from the hotel but, suddenly, I found myself heading to Cambridge." confessed the red-faced Raggy, who missed the team coach after speeding the wrong way up the M11 with neither map, nor compass. "When I finally got into the dressing room at Charlton, my shirt was still hanging up and I knew that I could have been sitting out there on the bench. I was a bit stressed and it wasn't a great experience. I felt bad but Harry understood and I learnt my lesson."

Another Hammers' defender reportedly experiencing road traffic problems was Gary Charles. Following his £1m move from Benfica, he had managed just those three starts. And there was no sign of him, either, when a Mercedes reportedly registered in his name was found abandoned in Hornchurch, Essex with its lights on and the keys still in the ignition. Police found a half-bottle of whisky and a pair of trainers on the front seat following a collision.

After being chased by the driver of the consequently damaged H-registration Ford Sierra and then refusing to exchange insurance details, the Mercedes driver apparently said: "I'm a bank robber and I'm on the run. Just take my car."

According to *The Sun*, the Mercedes was not reported stolen and after failing to appear for training, Charles ended a mystery two-day disappearance by arriving at Hornchurch police station with his solicitor.

Following a 30-minute interview, he was released without charge.

A Scotland Yard source said: "If someone is suspected of drink-driving, it is impossible to prove two days after the event. It is an offence to leave the scene of an accident but not serious enough to warrant an arrest. Inquiries are continuing."

For his part, Redknapp added: "I opened my newspaper today and saw a picture of Gary Charles in a West Ham shirt. Blimey, how rare is that?"

Having rode the potential FA Cup banana skin that was Walsall, Hammers travelled to Manchester United for a fourth round tie as underdogs.

But after defending for their lives, West Ham turned the form book upside down with another Di Canio classic that immediately entered the Hammers' hall of fame.

With just a quarter-of-an-hour remaining in a goalless encounter, an Upton Park replay was beckoning. But the irresistible Italian had other ideas when Kanouté threaded an inch-perfect ball between Jaap Stam and Nicky Butt. Timing his run to perfection, Di Canio ghosted onto the Frenchman's pass, sensibly ignored the raised arm of Barthez bluffing that he was offside, and coolly slotted the winner past the appealing keeper from eight-yards out.

Throughout, the referee's assistant had so rightly kept his flag down by his side.

"It's been difficult to come here and get results over the years because Manchester United are a fantastic team. I've taken it on the chin and had a few beltings here," announced happy Harry. "I think Barthez was trying to psyche Paolo out – 'you're offside' – waiting for him to pick the ball up, but he's such a clinical finisher I wouldn't have wanted anyone else in that position.

"Today we had a bit of belief about us and had a right go. We couldn't stand back admiring United, getting played to death. We were 10/1 to win but I never had a bet because we would've lost!"

After seeing the odds upset by Hammers' shock 1-0 win, the beetroot-faced Sir Alex Ferguson duly cancelled May's scheduled FA Cup final weekend break in Cardiff and opened his weighty excuse book.

"There's a 40-yard patch out on the pitch and I just can't believe that Manchester United – the biggest club in the world – allows rugby to be played on its pitch," he bellowed after receiving a reality check in the Theatre of Dreams. "It's a disgrace!

Also, we should have had a penalty in the first half, it was a clear handball. Then the referee only added four minutes on, there should have been a lot more.

"West Ham may have put in a good, determined performance but if we'd have taken our first chance we'd have won comfortably. Maybe it's West Ham's year? Look at their team and they've got every chance of winning the FA Cup."

The Daily Telegraph gushed: "The measure of any triumph is dependent on the form of the defeated. What made West Ham's day especially sweet was that United had played well."

With the influx of bodies, Marc Keller (46+10 apps 6gls) was allowed to join Blackburn Rovers on a free transfer. Far better in attack than defence, he undoubtedly had touch, talent and a thunderbolt shot, but his durability to withstand the rigours of the English game had frequently been called into question.

Indeed, he had even been known to refuse media interviews on the basis that it was too cold for him or that his hair was still wet from the post-match shower.

Having captured the frail Frenchman, Rovers then found themselves battling it out for Steve Lomas with his former club, Manchester City, only for the Hammers' skipper's proposed £3.65m move to either club to fall by the wayside.

At Cambridge United, on-loan Defoe scored in his 10th consecutive match for Bournemouth to equal the post-war record but, alas, he could not go one better on the Cherries' trip to leaders Millwall, where he finally failed to find the net for an 11th successive game.

Hammers also drew a blank in a goalless draw against Tottenham Hotspur and, ever-mindful of Fergie's FA Cup excuses, Harry joked: "The pitch was bumpy and the referee didn't play enough injury time!"

Flu apparently ruled Di Canio out of another long, arduous trip north to Anfield, where Hammers lost 0-3 to Liverpool.

John Hartson – Coventry's new signing from Wimbledon – had a goal wrongly disallowed on his Sky Blues' debut at Upton Park, but he still had something to smile about when Dailly's own goal wiped out Cole's 82nd-minute opener.

By now, European qualification was looking an increasingly difficult goal.

But having seen off the might of Manchester United in their own back yard, Hammers were full of confidence as they headed to Sunderland for the next instalment of their FA Cup adventure.

And Kanouté's 76th-minute strike secured a quarter-final meeting with Tottenham Hotspur at Upton Park.

Since his New Year arrival, Eriksson had seen several West Ham matches and he duly named Carrick, Cole and Lampard in his first England squad to face Spain in a friendly at Villa Park.

Lampard, whose double at Bradford City at the weekend had given Hammers a 2-1 victory, made a second half appearance, but there were no caps for Carrick (hamstring) and Cole (ankle) as injuries, unfortunately, kept them out of the 3-0 win over the Spaniards.

Come the following Saturday, however, it was Lampard who was on the end of a 0-3 hiding as Arsenal's Sylvain Wiltord grabbed the matchball at Highbury.

And in the absence of Di Canio, having just played for England, Lampard was suddenly the highest profile Hammer in north London where he came in for merciless baiting from the gloating Gunners fans questioning his weight.

'Big Fat Frank' insisted: "I took it as a compliment because it's testament to the fact that you're doing all right. Anyway, a lot of players who are bigger than me have taken a lot more stick from fans."

Whether he was talking about profile or physical size remained unclear.

The derby disappointment continued when Chelsea secured their first away win for 11 months with a 2-0 success at Upton Park, where goals by Eidur Gudjohnsen and Jimmy Floyd Hasselbaink gave the Blues an awayday victory at the 17th time of asking. Such was the highly-paid Suker's impotency that, when he was booked for fouling Graeme Le Saux, the restless Hammers' fans chanted: "Off! Off!"

Despite having done the spade work for the rest of the FA Cup survivors by eliminating Manchester United and Sunderland, many in E13 thought that the name of West Ham United was already on the trophy.

In an unashamed fervour of partisan East End expectancy, Upton Park was whipped into a pre-match cauldron of frenzy, as injury-hit Tottenham Hotspur came across town for the sixth round showdown.

Confidence was high. So high, in fact, that PA announcer Jeremy Nicholas bullishly announced before kick-off that the Hammers would be playing Arsenal – earlier victors over Blackburn Rovers – in the semi-finals.

As Spurs' boss George Graham later remarked: "I did'nae have to bother carrying on with the team talk after that!"

Indeed. Two goals by £11m striker – and another future Hammer – Sergei Rebrov eased Tottenham into those semis with a 3-2 win.

"It's disappointing when you give people jobs to do and then they don't do them," said Harry, singling out Cole for his first public caning. "Joey walked off the post for their third goal, but I'm not having a pop because a lot of them are young and it's still a learning process."

Despite joining Todorov on the scoresheet, there was little consolation for Stuart Pearce in defeat.

"Maybe we believed our own publicity a bit too much," he admitted. "We were still only in the quarter finals but we thought we'd already done all the hard work."

The hangover dragged into further home defeats at the hands of Ipswich Town (0-1) and Everton (0-2) and that left former Arsenal striker, Alan Smith, observing: "Public naming and shaming does nothing for player-manager relations and it had clearly hit the sensitive Joe Cole hard. For days after the cup exit it is said that he was stricken with remorse. You can see that he is still nursing deep wounds. Cole must be feeling lower than at any time during his short professional career."

Di Canio, on the other hand, received a framed momento from Everton keeper Gerrard following his act of sportsmanship at Goodison Park back in December and, following a 240-day wait, Foxe, having finally secured a protracted work permit, made his debut wearing the Number Six shirt reserved for him all season.

"I like West Ham and I love it here but I'm not going to go and marry some bird just to join a football club!" roared Foxe, clearly not giving a XXXX for those cynics who had reckoned he only tied the knot with his French girlfriend in Las

Vegas in order to unravel the red tape snagging that permit. "I've got a lot more decency than that and, anyway, if that was my motive then I'd have married Fabienne on Day One. It's very hurtful for both of us to hear these suggestions because the situation wasn't like that at all.

"West Ham always had first option to sign me and they've stuck by me while I've stuck by them. It was a very difficult time and there were occasions when I felt like giving it all up and trying my luck elsewhere."

While Redknapp was putting the finishing touches to an extended contract that was scheduled to keep him at Upton Park until 2005, Hammers were still not totally safe from relegation.

Frank Lampard – again a renewed £10m target for Leeds – netted a late equaliser in a 2-2 draw at Aston Villa.

But still West Ham had won just one league game – at lowly Bradford – in a dozen attempts during 2001.

A 3-1 triumph over Derby County at Upton Park eased the jitters before Newcastle's 2-1 victory at St James's Park left Hammers in 14th place just two wins clear of the Premiership drop-zone.

And Ferdinand's scoring return to Upton Park helped Leeds United to a 2-0 win before struggling Manchester City bagged a 1-0 victory at Maine Road, too.

Quite simply, in the euphoria of those quick-fix FA Cup victories at Manchester United and Sunderland, the free-falling Hammers had merely papered over the cracks of crisis.

Redknapp's annual end-of-season interview with the Gary Firmager-edited fanzine *Over Land and Sea* had just been published, too.

It would be hard to imagine another Premiership manager such as, say, Ferguson or Arsene Wenger, giving an unpaid warts 'n all exclusive to a pirate publication.

But away from the sanitisation of the matchday programme, club website and official magazine, the fanzine article did, at least, provide the manager with a convenient conduit with which to put over his more controversial views on all things West Ham.

Indeed, his honest off-the-cuff words proved manna from heaven for the tabloids as they habitually took the raw material of Redknapp's ramblings and cooked up some simply sensational scoops.

The past couple of seasons had seen that fifth-place finish followed by a European sojourn but, this time around, the fans had every right to be disappointed with the endeavours of the 2000-01 term.

That historic FA Cup victory at Old Trafford had proved scant consolation against the backdrop of the sale of home-grown Ferdinand, a 15th-place, 42-point finish and, fundamentally, the £7.5m purchase of seven waifs and strays rather than two or three star names.

An *Over Land and Sea* reader had posted a letter from chairman, Terence Brown, onto a website which stated that the club had already spent £15.2m of the Rio proceeds on Harry's purchases and loan players.

According to the fanzine, Redknapp read the document at the interview and replied: "I can't see it. Not £15m, that's for sure. There's seven-and-a-half million quid there, you know? Song was £2m, Todorov was £500,000 if he starts 200 games or so. Tihinen was only a couple of hundred grand to loan. One hundred and fifty grand or something we paid...a hundred grand. Schemmel was nothing, we paid about £30,000 or something. Camara doesn't go up and I think Dailly's is what it is.

"I think we're talking about £8m there. Yeah, it's £8m pounds. I can't see anything else there. But I'm not going to get into a situation where I'm going to start arguing with people. I'm not in a position to start at the moment."

Clearly Redknapp believed that there was more than half of the Ferdinand kitty remaining, while the chairman, with a main stand to finish building too, equally believed that the well was all but dry.

At least a 3-0 win over Southampton at Upton Park in Hammers' last home game meant that they could head into their final game of the season, at Middlesbrough, with their Premiership status still intact.

"It's not been a bundle of fun lately," admitted Harry. "Can I wait for the new season? If you asked my wife whether she's looking forward to the new season, she'd send you to see a psychiatrist!"

Before that, though, there was a week's break for the FA Cup final between Tottenham's conquerors Arsenal and Liverpool.

The gulf in their calculation of the amount of cash still remaining in the transfer chest, however, was set to put Redknapp on a collision course with his chairman.

But as he drove to the Boleyn Ground from his luxurious pad on the exclusive Sandbanks peninsula in Dorset for a meeting with Brown, the unsuspecting Harry – expecting to put pen to paper on that unsigned four-year contract worth a reported £1.6m plus bonuses per annum – was on his in-car phone sounding out his contacts over the feasibility of making a move for Arsenal's Ray Parlour.

By the time he returned, shell-shocked, to his Mercedes a couple of hours later, though, the former Hammers' winger was now a former Hammers' boss, too.

Only Manchester United's Ferguson had managed his Premiership club longer and 54-year-old Redknapp – departing under the all too familiar 'mutual consent' banner – told the *Evening Standard*: "I've had a chat with the chairman and feel it's been a tough season. The last eight weeks or so haven't been particularly enjoyable and I feel that maybe it's time for a change."

But on the dole and clutching the unsigned £6.4m-plus contract and his P45, in reality Redknapp could not believe that he had been ousted from the Upton Park hotseat after a seven-year stint.

Indeed, John Barnwell, Chief Executive of the League Managers' Association, added: "I've spoken to Harry and it would be inappropriate to say too much. But you can assume a manager of a Premiership side with two years to go on his contract is unlikely to have resigned. If he's resigned I'd be extremely surprised.

"He has been at West Ham for a long time and is steeped in their history. Harry has been a player, coach and manager under the 'academy' philosophy. He will be a hard act to follow."

Indeed.

"To depart makes no sense at all, unless his employers were muddying the water," wrote David Miller of *The Daily Telegraph*.

Only the manager and his chairman know what was said in the heated debate that led to Harry's departure but nearly all observers agreed it centred upon their differing perceptions of the 2001-02 transfer budget.

A few months later, Harry told Brian Viner in an *Independent on Sunday* newspaper interview: "I'd agreed a new four-year contract with the club, but then I did a thing with a fanzine that the chairman didn't like. Four lads came in one Friday morning and I sat there chatting to them. They said: 'The chairman says you've spent £15m of Rio's money.' I said: 'He can't f****** add up, it's only £8m.' Anyway, the chairman read it; he reads all the fanzines and looks at everything on the internet. And he took the hump. So the following week after we'd beaten Southampton, I walked in to see about my contract and he says: 'I'm not happy with you, Harry, I'm going to call it a day.' I said: 'Okay, if that's the way you feel but I've got two years left on my contract. You'd better make sure that you sort me out.' And that was it. Shame. I got on well with Terry Brown. I hold no grudges and I never felt sorry for myself either."

Brown, who saw Redknapp go on to steer Portsmouth into the Premiership with the help of several ex-Hammers before he controversially took over at neighbouring – and subsequently relegated – Southampton early in 2005, argued in *Hammers News Magazine*: "I have often been amused by the comment that the board were affected by an interview that Harry gave to the *Over Land and Sea* fanzine. I am not a spin doctor. I suspect that if I was one then I would have thought of that myself. On the whole we had a good working relationship, although we are, of course, different personalities. It would be fair to say that we were concerned at the beginning of the 2000-01 season with Harry's approach to the coming year, which was pessimistic.

"We only managed to stay up by beating Southampton on our last home game of the season and the decision to sack Harry was agreed unanimously by the board."

Certainly, Redknapp had enjoyed a colourful tenure during his seven years on the Boleyn bridge.

While he may not have been a tactical genius or the greatest coach, he certainly knew how to play the market.

Having bought an extraordinary 67 players for around £56m and sold an equally extraordinary 66 players for some £68m, no-one could ever accuse him of having stood still in the transfer market.

His profit – including the £18m proceeds from the home grown Rio – equated to £31m, while he left behind a playing squad assembled at a cost of £25m.

According to Bower's *Broken Dreams*, Brown had been aware of the rumours – and mere rumours they were – about Redknapp's extraordinary trade in players.

Add Harry's close relationships with agents and the alleged involvement of son, Mark, on the periphery of some deals, and there was certainly rumoured to be more than a puff of smoke, notwithstanding the absence of a raging fire.

"We've never found any evidence of anything untoward but we've never investigated Harry," said the chairman.

A few years earlier, amidst a wave of allegations against George Graham, Terry

Venables and Brian Clough, Brown had previously asked former managing director Peter Storrie for an explanation of his manager's dealings with agents.

"Harry likes the turnover of players because he always wants to freshen up the dressing room," vouchsafed Storrie, who would eventually be reunited with H at Portsmouth.

"But does Harry take money?" enquired Brown – a qualified accountant.

"Absolutely not," replied Storrie.

And Redknapp himself told the *News of the World* in an unpaid interview: "The claims made in *Broken Dreams* are absolute rubbish. It's been written by a man who knows nothing about football, who's dropped in on Terry Brown and got an easy interview. It's as if he's saying that I did all the deals. Doesn't he understand that it's the club that signs the cheques!"

Curiously, in the industry that was football, any suspicion of financial indiscretions were habitually ignored by clubs as long as managers were successful and the transfer budget was being balanced.

Indeed, boards only ever seemed to take the drains up if they began to sniff the stench of failure while, for his part, Redknapp had always insisted that he had never taken a 'bung' in his life.

The manager was, however, never afraid to air his views on his wages.

"While players' salaries have rocketed, managers' pay has nowhere near kept pace," he had previously argued. "The influx of foreign players has led to an increase in wages but as bosses we could never book a ticket on the gravy train.

"If you're the manager of a Premiership club, you've got massive responsibilities. If things don't go well you're out and that can be the end of your career. Established managers find their wages static while the foreign coaches come in getting vast salaries.

"When you're managing a Premiership club you're in the Top 20 of your profession. It's criminal that we should be earning less than a player not even guaranteed a place in the first team.

"Our lot has improved and I make a good living managing West Ham but it still has much further to go before I'm completely happy.

"Surely my pay should be on a par with my top players?"

While he had wrested his backside into the Hammers' hotseat via, allegedly, Machiavellian means, Redknapp had gone on to give the West Ham United supporters the modern day time of their lives, despite the fact the club had never finished with a positive goal difference in any of his seven seasons in charge.

It had, however, come at the cost of what was once a treasured friendship with Billy Bonds.

Harry had delivered a fifth-place Premiership finish, an Intertoto/UEFA Cup run and more hope than glory in the cups.

Like any prospector, he unearthed his fair share of gleaming, golden nuggets while also panning more than enough mud and silt of mediocrity.

For every Berkovic or Bilic there had been a Boogers.

For every Di Canio there had been a Dumitrescu.

Sure, in some cases it had been more of a morsel from the tasting menu rather than a full-blown feast.

But at least he had tried to supplement the skilful staples of Berkovic, Di Canio and Kanouté with the cosmopolitan Paulo Futre, Dani, Hugo Porfirio, Ilie Dumitrescu, Florin Raducioiu and Suker.

Redknapp had also overseen the renaissance of a youth academy that spawned Ferdinand, Lampard, Cole and Carrick together with the Charlton-reared Defoe.

Assets such as Bilic, Berkovic, Di Canio, Hartson, Kanouté and Sinclair had also greatly appreciated in value under Harry's tutelage.

However, many meals are best remembered for the dessert and having received that irresistible £18m for Rio – the jewel in Hammers' crown – there was little cream around when it came to the likes of journeymen such as Dailly and the sour leftovers of Song, Camara, Soma, Todorov, Minto and Charles.

"The club is now sitting on a fortune in terms of players and if they want to sell them they could make mega-money," announced the departing Redknapp. "We took some chances in the transfer market and made some great signings. Of course, some of them didn't come off but that's football. We were always dabbling at the cheap end of the market.

"But where will you find four young kids like Ferdinand, Lampard, Cole and Carrick? It might be a long time before another bunch like that comes along."

Chairman Brown acknowledged: "Harry contributed an enormous amount to West Ham United. His knowledge of football is second to none. At his best he can wheel and deal with anyone in the game. He did love the club, signed some great players and gave us some very exciting seasons and, of course, kept us in the Premier League. It was right to accept Leeds' offer for Rio Ferdinand but I wish we had then avoided the financial commitments we made in the transfer market and with the players' long-term contracts.

"It was an indication that merely spending money in the transfer market does not automatically guarantee success on the pitch."

Harry Redknapp's Managerial Record:

League:	P-269	W-94	D-71	L-104	F-324	A-359
FA Cup:	P-20	W-7	D-6	L-7	F-23	A-22
League Cup:	P-26	W-14	D-3	L-9	F-41	A-26
UEFA Cup:	P-4	W-2	D-1	L-1	F-6	A-3
Intertoto Cup:	P-6	W-4	D-1	L-1	F-7	A-3
TOTALS:	P-325	W-121	D-82	L-122	F-401	A-413

With Frank Lampard senior departing alongside Harry, Glenn Roeder – a man of immense integrity – was put in temporary charge as West Ham headed down by the Riverside for their final game of the season.

"The players have been very professional since Harry and Frank left. Even though they were disappointed for a few days, they haven't caused any problems and they've worked hard all week," said the entrusted caretaker following the 1-2 defeat at Middlesbrough. "I haven't officially been told who the club will be interviewing and am only reading about all the speculation in the newspapers.

"While the board can't give any of us any assurances, hopefully we can all still stay but a new manager could bring his own team and then we'd have to leave.

"Football management is like a packet of cigarettes. There's a health warning printed on the side but people are still stupid enough to smoke and we're still stupid enough to want to stay in the game."

PLAYERS IN

'Titi' Camara	Liverpool	£1,500,000
Christian Dailly	Blackburn Rovers	£1,750,000
Hayden Foxe	Sanfrecce Hirishima	Free transfer
Frederic Kanouté	Olympic Lyonnais	£3,750,000
Ragnvald Soma	FC Bryne	£800,000
Rigobert Song	Liverpool	£2,500,000
Davor Suker	Arsenal	Free
Svetoslav Todorov	Liteks Lovech	£500,000
Nigel Winterburn	Arsenal	£250,000

LOANS IN

Christian Bassila	Rennes
Kaba Diawara	Paris Saint-Germain
Darren Peacock	Blackburn Rovers
Sebastien Schemmel	FC Metz
Hannu Tihinen	Racing Stavanger

Transfers Out

Gary Alexander	Swindon Town	£300,000
Jimmy Bullard	Peterborough United	Free transfer
Rio Ferdinand	Leeds United	£18,000,000 (Record)
Marc-Vivien Foe	Olympic Lyonnais	£6,000,000 (Record)
Marc Keller	Blackburn Rovers	Free transfer
Javier Margas	Retired	
Emmanuel Omoyinmi	Oxford United	Free transfer
Neil Ruddock	Crystal Palace	Free transfer
Daniel Sjolund	Liverpool	£1,000,000
Paulo Wanchope	Manchester City	£3,650,000
Tommy Williams	Peterborough United	Free transfer

Chapter 15
2001-02

LAST MAN STANDING

Harry Redknapp's silver Mercedes had barely passed through the gaudy claret gates of the Green Street forecourt for the final time before the speculation over his successor began.

While the tearful H – who had been at the club for 37 years – just wanted to get back home to Dorset for a cuppa with his missus, Sandra, it was another former Hammer, Alan Curbishley, who looked most likely to be the board's cup of tea.

After the Macari debacle, the stability that Billy Bonds and then Harry had given meant that any CV containing Upton Park playing experience was always going to be well received.

Forest Gate-born Curbs had made 95 appearances – scoring five goals – between 1975 and 1979, before finding his first-team opportunities limited in a midfield containing Trevor Brooking and Alan Devonshire.

Having disconsolately voiced his opinion and headed to Birmingham City, Aston Villa, Charlton Athletic and Brighton & Hove Albion, he became the Addicks' boss in 1991.

Reportedly, there was an 'escape' clause in the "flattered" Curbishley's contract that would release him for £2m.

Having spent four years in The Valley dug-out alongside Steve Gritt, and six further solo years, Curbishley's decade of managerial experience made him the truly outstanding candidate.

"Any top job is interesting," observed the man who enjoyed a Sir Alex Ferguson-like grip in south London, where he was revered by the fans, respected by the players and regarded highly by a board that virtually gave him a free rein.

West Ham might have been a bigger club but it was not going to be a straightforward decision for him.

And Charlton's defensive tactics in heading off any would-be poachers did not make it any easier.

With the lure of a reported, new £1m per annum contract, Curbishley's inclination to head through the Blackwall Tunnel receded.

"Alan was always our first choice," admitted managing director Paul Aldridge. "But Charlton were adamant that he wouldn't be leaving so we looked elsewhere."

Stuart Pearce, who had briefly managed Nottingham Forest and had 50 Hammers' appearances on his CV, threw his shinpads into the ring stating: "If West

Ham fancy taking a gamble, they know my number."

Sacked Tottenham Hotspur boss George Graham – his reputation forever tarnished by the infamous Highbury bung scandal – hopefully put his name forward, offering to show that he could still win silverware with the right club.

For Redknapp's part, with an estimated £3.5m house overlooking Poole Harbour and reports of his imminent move to a £5m pad just along the road – where only New York, Tokyo and London land prices were dearer in square-footage terms – he was certainly not going to be reduced to selling the *Big Issue*.

Indeed, according to Tom Bower's *Broken Dreams*, Redknapp received £1.6m compensation payable over 20 months after the PFA helped to thrash out a severance deal for the former Hammers' boss and his assistant, Frank Lampard.

"We were always confident that we would reach a settlement agreeable to all concerned without any problem," announced Aldridge.

"I'm very pleased with the way the club have handled this situation," confirmed Harry. "I wish West Ham well. Life moves on and the most important thing is that I know I've done a good job. I was only an employee at the end of the day. I think people respect what I've done – you've only got to read the papers to see that."

And his number two added: "I've had a few offers but I'm not going to rush into it. Thankfully, I'm in a position where I don't have to and I can wait until something comes along that suits me. We'll just wait and see what happens."

Going into the 2005-06 season, Harry's sidekick – fabled for an 'only at West Ham' habit of taking on-pitch mobile phone calls while putting the first team through their pre-match paces – had still not returned to the game.

As the Premier League's second longest-serving manager and his assistant, Lampard, walked away a little happier, the father of the Premiership house – Ferguson – prematurely announced that he would quit Old Trafford at the end of the 2001-02 season.

And with United openly admitting that Fergie's Number Two, Steve McClaren, would not be succeeding him, Sven-Goran Eriksson's part-time coach was given a glowing reference by the Swede as he arranged for his representatives to open talks with the West Ham board.

"I'll make my decision in the next few weeks," he said as he contemplated leaving the Premier League champions with the reluctant – albeit full – blessing of Fergie. "I'm open minded."

At his subsequent Upton Park interview, McClaren had proved impressive as he outlined his proposals to bring a more scientific approach to the East End via nutrition and fitness, while the board had also received further positive soundings about the man who was now the only serious contender for the job.

But just as United declared that they did not want Ferguson's right-hand man to leave just yet, manager-less Middlesbrough also entered the fray following the departure of Terry Venables.

And as a three-way tug-of-war developed, Aldridge admitted: "It looks like Steve won't be coming. We were due to meet him again but he's now going back to talk to Middlesbrough. That's disappointing but a factor must be that he doesn't have to move his family down to London."

NEARLY REACHED THE SKY

Out of the claret and blue, Hibernian boss Alex McLeish and Preston North End's David Moyes also emerged as surprise candidates.

But in the end, the club appointed from within, handing Glenn Roeder the job.

"Neither Alan Curbishley nor Steve McClaren were in a position to join us," chairman Brown later told *Hammers News Magazine*. "The rest is history."

Certainly, the former Gillingham and Watford manager had sneaked up unnoticed on the stands-side rails as all the favourites fell by the wayside.

"I didn't chase the job," declared Roeder after being handed a contract with such a short 'best before' date – widely speculated to be June 2002 – that the board declined to announce its precise term. "The people who have turned it down will have their own reasons, but I'm pleased they did. I feel a bit like Foinavon in the 1967 Grand National. I'm the only one left standing!

"This isn't the easy option for the club – that would have been to wait and find a so-called higher profile manager.

"I'm very excited about being given this chance. If someone had said a few months ago that I would have been in this position, I would have just laughed. As a nine-year-old, I used to stand on a beer crate in the Chicken Run to watch West Ham play. I never dreamed that I would end up being manager of the club.

"I'm honoured. I understand what a huge responsibility it is and I can only say that I will give it my very best in the hope that I can move the club forwards.

"Talk is cheap, many people can speak a good game, but all that matters is results on the pitch and that is what I will be judged on."

As the overlooked Pearce (50 apps 3 gls) headed to Maine Road to link up with – and eventually take over from – Kevin Keegan, Roeder made ex-Hammer Paul Goddard his Number Two after missing out on Watford's Ray Lewington.

"I know that Glenn Roeder was seen as the cheap option," admitted Brown, who welcomed Hammers' legend Trevor Brooking onto the board as a non-executive director. "But that was never the case. He was paid a good salary. When we appointed him, we wanted an experienced coach who could retain and develop our young players. His work with the England squad, and the feedback we received, confirmed his coaching skills."

With the main stand still in the throes of construction, Roeder – who had even been known to spend winter afternoons at Chadwell Heath washing footballs – was, fittingly, pictured wearing a hard hat.

And how he would need it during the 12 months ahead as he set about finishing the house that Harry had started to rebuild.

One unfortunate by-product of Redknapp's dismissal was the Lampard situation.

While likeable, old Frank had received the financial settlement that would enable him to continue to concentrate fully upon his long-standing, property-investment activities, young Frank now found his position at Upton Park untenable.

Even before Hammers had played their final game of the previous season at Middlesbrough, under caretaker boss Roeder, the England international had already made it perfectly clear that he would not play for the club again.

Having been constantly linked with a host of clubs, his father's departure from Upton Park certainly provided the perfect window for young Frank to leave, too.

And on the day that Roeder was unveiled as his uncle's successor, Lampard (169+17 apps 38 gls) was making an £11m move to Chelsea after snubbing Aston Villa, Leeds United and Liverpool.

"There are big names everywhere you look and the squad's bigger than West Ham's," he said upon his arrival at Stamford Bridge. "There are no bacon sandwiches at the training ground. Chelsea are very on the ball with diet, coaching and fitness training."

An incredible statement, given his own father had resisted all attempts to install a chef at the training ground, while it was his uncle who had sanctioned the very bacon rolls that he was now decrying. "Frank's been through a lot as a young lad and it's made him both physically and mentally tougher," revealed Frank senior. "Hopefully this move will now bring his own game on a bit."

Chairman Brown said: "We should never forget that Frank senior brought his son to the club and was responsible for collecting Rio in the early days for training when he worked, unpaid, with the youth academy. I am often sorry to see his contribution to the club during Harry's period overlooked."

Like Paul Ince and Rio Ferdinand before him, Frank Lampard junior found the move the making of him.

Only myopic cynics could claim that the midfielder was in the West Ham side because of those nepotistic family ties.

And only fantasising conspiracy theorists could argue that he had made it into the England team via such flimsy bloodlines, too.

Certainly, the intelligent, articulate, media-friendly Lampard had ability, talent and energy, but like many that had walked across those white lines before him, he had also slipped perilously into the Upton Park comfort zone.

But while many Chelsea fans moaned that Claudio Ranieri had overpaid, time would prove that they had bagged a bargain later described as the 'best midfielder in the world' by Brazilian World Cup-winning legend, Carlos Alberto.

Indeed, when the curtain had dropped on the 2004-05 campaign, the 30-times capped Lampard had helped the Blues to their first Championship in 50 years.

"As a 17 or 18-year-old it wasn't nice to be warming up on the touchline at Upton Park," he told the assembled audience of the Football Writers' Association as he collected his 2005 Footballer-of-the-Year award. "I'd often be told to get back in the dug-out with my uncle and my dad because I just wasn't good enough to play for West Ham."

Clearly the pain of those early years had not subsided.

Ranieri's arrival at Chelsea had seen his predecessor Gianluca Vialli take over at Watford.

After failing to sign Di Canio while in charge at Stamford Bridge, Vialli made another attempt to prise his pal away from Upton Park.

With Manchester United also said to be monitoring the situation, a transfer to Vicarage Road was not the ideal option for Di Canio.

But having seen Redknapp rescue his career, the irate Italian was still fuming at the double-whammy of Harry's dismissal and Roeder's inside-job ascension to the Upton Park throne.

NEARLY REACHED THE SKY

Indeed, the Italian believed that aspiring youngsters such as Joe Cole, Michael Carrick and Jermain Defoe had made representations to the board supporting the man who had once mentored them between the youth team and the first eleven.

Cole told the *Daily Express*: "Glenn is probably in the top three coaches I have worked with. Being a manager is different but if there is anyone who I know that can do the job, he can."

Carrick was equally enthusiastic about Roeder's appointment, adding: "A lot of us were saying how much we respect him. It's easy for people to jump on the bandwagon and give a new manager some stick when things don't go right but the players have never doubted him for one minute. The thing that has impressed me is his professionalism and organisation. From day one he has made changes that have helped players. Things like watching videos of our opponents and making the training ground more private might not seem a lot but they have made a big difference. It's all geared towards making us stronger as a team."

But recuperating from a sinus operation back home in Rome, Di Canio fumed: "Glenn is a great coach but our young players should learn to sit back, work hard and keep their mouths shut. They have no business deciding who the next manager is going to be. West Ham are a talented club but we need a strong, expert manager to bring everything together. If you are going to make a change you need a plan."

Roeder replied: "It's up to me to change Paolo's mind over how he feels."

Around 100 season ticket holders had a change of heart, too, as they took up the club's offer of a refund.

Certainly, the new manager's first signing was impressive, as he persuaded David James to make a £3.5m move from Aston Villa and leapfrog the immensely disappointed Shaka Hislop into pole position between the Upton Park goalposts.

"When was the last time West Ham signed a current England international with his best years ahead of him?" asked Roeder, who was no stranger to the goalkeeper given he was previously his manager at Watford. "David James is the first piece of my jigsaw."

In reply, the four-times capped James observed: "Glenn is talking about building the squad, but he's already got at least half-a-dozen players here who would easily grace 99 per cent of Premiership sides. I want to become England's No.1 'keeper and play in the 2002 World Cup finals and I need the right vehicle to do that."

But with Hammers having made a pre-tax loss of nearly £5m it was clear that there would be more departures than arrivals.

The disappointing, goalless Kaba Diawara (6+5 apps) headed to Spanish second division side RC Ferrol, before returning to France where he topped the scoring charts for Nice and subsequently headed to Al-Ittihad in Qatar.

Christian Bassila (0+4 apps) came in for special criticism from Brown, who revealed that the Frenchman had cost Hammers £720,000 for his 85 minutes.

Davor Suker (8+5 apps 3 gls) looked more like a lead boot holder than a golden one and he headed to TSV Munich 1860 on a free transfer, having hugely disappointed everyone except his bank manager. Indeed, in his annual report, chairman Brown revealed that this 'free' transfer had cost almost as much as the club had earned from the whole of the East Stand for the season.

While he had drawn a blank up front, Redknapp had certainly done better in the defensive market.

Hannu Tihinen (7+3 apps) had proved solid and reliable during his brief loan spell but, priced at £2m-plus, he left during the summer impasse and, by the time Roeder took permanent charge, the Finn had bolted, only to end up in Belgium with Hammers' 1976 European Cup Winners' Cup conquerors Anderlecht.

Sebastien Schemmel (13+2 apps) had performed well at right-back, too.

Certainly, he had shown no signs, as yet, of being phenomenally unstable, but citing a multi-million transfer fee as the obstacle, Redknapp had already decided that he would let him to return to France.

Igor Stimac (52 apps 1 gl) still had one year of his contract left to run but with his three-year-old daughter suffering from chronic asthma, he decided to move back to Hajduk Split, in order that she could benefit from the healthier Dalmation coast air. According to *The Sunday Telegraph*, the club gave the defender a £50,000 settlement as he headed home to his chain of 100 betting shops and two nightclubs, to play for his cash-strapped first club for just £125 per week. That represented an annual pay-cut of £750,000. And closer to home, Gavin Holligan (0+1 app) joined Wycombe Wanderers on a free transfer.

Again, Roeder showed encouraging signs in the transfer market as he returned to FC Metz to recapture Schemmel for a bargain £465,000, from under the noses of both Middlesbrough and Manchester City.

"The chairman of Metz said that I wasn't going to West Ham," said the French Under-21 international. "Carlo Molinari said I hadn't played well, but when Glenn Roeder called me I said: 'I am coming. I will get on a bicycle now and ride to London.' I don't know why I was only sold for that amount, though, because when Bordeaux wanted to sign me last year, Metz said I would cost £4m."

Piece-by-piece the jigsaw puzzle was coming together.

Chairman Brown endorsed Roeder's early dealings stating: "Some of our previous expenditure cannot be justified and we will make no apologies for approaching future transfer negotiations in a far more structured and considered way. In this context I have been greatly encouraged by Glenn Roeder's diligent approach to current negotiations.

"The danger in failing to control costs should be obvious to everyone. We do wish to win trophies and appear in European competitions but we will not pursue those ambitions recklessly at the expense of future generations of supporters nor, indeed, at the expense of the club itself.

"If we show the determination to retain some of the money which passes through our hands, rather than simply acting as a conduit for passing large sums to players and agents, then I believe everything is in place to ensure an exciting future for this great institution and I believe we can look ahead with considerable optimism."

But sadly for Brown, he could not possibly have envisaged what was in store when he concluded his annual report: "The last 10 years represent an amazing journey for the club and, whilst history is unlikely to repeat itself, I am sure we have many more twists and turns ahead of us during the next decade."

As a consequence of those principles, Barcelona veteran Josep Guardiola's £2m per annum (net) wage demands priced him out of the market. And Manchester United duo Jonathan Greening and Mark Wilson opted to join their former coach McClaren at his new club, Middlesbrough, after Ferguson allegedly intervened to steer them strongly towards to the Riverside Stadium.

"I need to make signings that will make a difference," said Roeder. "But there are also an awful lot of ordinary players being pushed our way by agents. I'm confident that if I get the chance to speak to the right players it would be a good move to come to West Ham. The problem I have is getting clubs to agree to sell."

The instability created by Harry's departure and the loss of England internationals Rio Ferdinand and Lampard had also created the potential for further meltdown as Aston Villa's John Gregory and Jean Tigana's Fulham considered £10m-plus bids for Frederic Kanouté, while Newcastle United made a £5m approach for the now unsettled Trevor Sinclair who, according to the *Sunday Mirror*, was looking for a move.

"I wanted to go to Fulham because I knew their manager and thought it would be a good opportunity," conceded Kanouté. "Harry Redknapp had left and others were going too, but in the end I felt I owed it to Glenn to listen to what he had to say about his plans. I was very impressed. When I saw how determined he was and how important he said I was for the team, I made my mind up that I would help West Ham achieve their ambitions."

Sinclair also insisted: "My future's definitely at West Ham. It was just sour grapes from my old agent who wasn't happy that I'd found a new one. I went back to pre-season training one day early just to tell Glenn that I was looking forward to working with him. We're all playing for West Ham, not Harry Redknapp. All the boys know Glenn and we're well happy that he's the one who's got the job."

Before the autumn departure of Rio, Hammers – with adequate central defensive cover – had been just two full-backs away from making the likes of Hislop, Ferdinand, Lampard, Cole, Carrick, Sinclair, Di Canio and Kanouté a virtually nailed-on top six side.

And while Carrick and Cole had made their England debuts in a 4-0 win over Mexico at Pride Park and Jermain Defoe had, predictably, scored on his Under-21 debut, Roeder desperately needed to retain the experience that would complement the club's blossoming youth stars.

Having criticised his predecessor for over-exposing Cole at a young age, Roeder was determined to keep Defoe in the shadows.

"I will hold Jermain back," he said. "There's no question about that. He is all about next year and the year after that."

Having previously undertaken several scouting missions for Harry, Roeder had found himself in many a foreign field and was soon linked with Oliver Bierhoff, Pascal Cygan, Ludovic Asuar, Hakan Sukur, Julien Rodriguez and Sylvain Legwinski, as the national press tried to spend his £10m transfer fund.

After making peace with Di Canio and heading off all hostile approaches for his senior stars, Roeder started to stamp his mark on the club.

Having already been privy to the day-to-day workings of the club by virtue of his in-house coaching role, he had witnessed long-standing Spanish customs that he would simply not have tolerated had he been in charge.

Now the new broom had a chance to sweep away such bad old habits.

Firstly, he controversially closed Chadwell Heath to the public.

The bunker mentality had already seen most clubs turn their training HQs into fan-free zones, but for West Ham, that had never been an option.

Originally working out of an old, dilapidated cricket pavilion that had been good enough for Bobby Moore, Geoff Hurst and Martin Peters, West Ham United now inhabited a modern all-purpose set-up with further plans to develop it into a state-of-the-art complex.

For as long as anyone could recall, Chadwell Heath had opened its doors to all.

But with the more sinister proliferation of agents, ticket touts, tabloid scribes and general hangers-on infiltrating a manor hitherto occupied solely by starry-eyed fans and autograph hunters, Roeder – who had worked at both Fortresses Tottenham and England – padlocked the gates.

Entry was now by invitation only.

"All fans will be welcome during the school holidays on Tuesdays and Thursdays," he declared. "West Ham has got a tradition of being a family club and having a warm atmosphere and no-one wants to kill that at all. But we can't have it open house as it was before."

Redknapp had once argued: "The most important people at the football club are the punters. I opened the doors at Chadwell Heath to everyone because I thought it was important that everybody could watch training. It's their club. If you haven't got time to talk and sign autographs then you shouldn't be in this game. You are only in football because of the people who pay your wages."

And it was not only McClaren who had thought about the wider implications of sports science, either.

With John Green also a keen student of dietary and fitness techniques, the physiotherapist was no longer shouted down by the steak, chips and a pint of lager brigade convinced that ability, and ability alone, won football matches.

"You can't coach Beckham to cross a ball," Harry would often claim, missing the point that nutrition and health were only meant to complement ability rather than replace it. "And Mooro just used to eat and drink whatever he wanted to."

Certainly, a bowl of pasta and a quick stretch was not going to turn Lenny Henry into Thierry Henry anymore than a pre-match fry-up would transform Paolo Di Canio into Luciano Pavarotti.

But as Arsenal's Arsene Wenger and a whole host of his continental counterparts had proved, emphasis on general, healthy living not only gave players an edge but also prolonged their careers, too.

Just ask reformed alcoholic Tony Adams, who benefited from the Euro-culture subsequently imbibed into him at Highbury.

And now with the old 'bacon sarnie' regime departed, the new-found freedom afforded to Green ensured that the players did, indeed, enjoy their greens.

Sports scientist John McCarthy had worked one-on-one with certain Hammers during their rehabilitation and, for the cost of one player's monthly salary, he was taken on full-time alongside a chef and various other medical back-up staff.

NEARLY REACHED THE SKY

"We're going to be trying to keep footballers working on top of their game," said the former Lancaster University lecturer. "We need to get top sportsmen training like elite performers and behaving like them, too. It's about fitness, smart diet and optimal performance. After all, you can't put diesel in a Ferrari."

With millions tied up in playing stock, it made sense to look after the goods and, alongside assistant Russell Holman, McCarthy took responsibility for all warm-ups and warm-downs – a far cry from the old school, ad-hoc preparations.

If nothing else, Roeder was meticulous.

Next up, he introduced a video studio as part of his pre-match focus and post-game debrief.

But for all the behind-the-scenes organisation, he certainly could not have had a more daunting fixture list ahead.

After sending 25-year-old trialist Aliou Cissé back to Paris St Germain with his grainy promotional video following a 3-1 friendly win at Rushden & Diamonds, Hammers set off to Jersey, where they beat FC Utrecht in a penalty shoot-out in the first-ever football match staged on the Channel Islands by two top-flight sides.

As the curtain rose on the 2001-02 campaign, Hammers went to Liverpool still looking for that elusive first victory since September 1963.

Former Reds' keeper James had made double-Dutch spot-kick saves in St Helier and, as he prepared to return to Anfield, he boldly announced: "I've got to make my Premiership debut for West Ham at some time and we've got to play Liverpool at some time, too. Let's deal with both events together."

Before that though, he had another midweek meeting with the Dutch.

This time around he appeared as a second half substitute in England's 0-2 friendly defeat against Holland at White Hart Lane. And just seconds after taking his stance between the posts, he injured his knee ligaments in an accidental collision with Martin Keown.

With his £3.5m signing now disastrously out of action until Christmas, Roeder had an early chance to use his man-management skills to lift the reinstated Hislop.

Relegated to second-choice, cast away with the Number 17 shirt and destined for a long season on the bench, 32-year-old Hislop could have cut up rough.

But fortunately for the new manager, the tried and trusted Trinidadian was the consummate professional who, while acknowledging that he was only a stop-gap pending James' return, also realised that it was an opportunity to put himself back in the shop window ahead of an end-of-season Bosman free transfer.

"It's been a difficult summer for me and it's never a nice situation to see your place threatened," said Hislop. "But you have to remain positive. This is why you need to have at least two top-notch goalkeepers on your books. Glenn Roeder has been up front and honest with me, though, and that's a quality I like. Even though I didn't like the news, I did respect the way in which it was presented to me."

Certainly, Shaka was not to blame as Michael Owen put Liverpool ahead, before Di Canio again produced a party piece of a penalty, as he chipped an audacious spot kick straight down the middle and over the diving Pegguy Arphexad, right in front of The Kop.

Ironically, as Hammers' Merseyside-bound plane taxied along the Stansted runway, Di Canio had gone into panic mode, necessitating his removal from the aircraft.

Having subsequently been driven north, the Italian could not have given clearer confirmation that he had kissed and made up with Roeder as he sprinted to the halfway line and embraced his delighted manager.

But their joy was short-lived as Owen's second goal gave the Reds a 2-1 opening day win ahead of a goalless draw against Leeds United at Upton Park, where the new main Dr Martens Stand was opened.

Since leaving Upton Park in January 1996, Don Hutchison had gone some way towards fulfilling the potential that had once persuaded Redknapp to splash out a club record £1.5m fee for the former fork-lift driver back in September 1994.

Following his £800,000 move to Sheffield United in February 1996, Hutch then moved to Everton for £1.2m prior to joining Sunderland for £2.5m in 1998. Along the way, he had garnered 16 Scotland caps and had memorably scored the only goal of the game as the Scots – trailing 0-2 from the first-leg – beat England at Wembley in the return match of the Euro 2000 play-off qualifiers in autumn 1999.

During the 2000-2001 season, Harry's nemesis had also scored for the Black Cats at Upton Park on his way to netting 10 goals at the Stadium of Light that term.

Now aged 30, and tagged at an inflated £5m, Hutchison was always going to be a costly, depreciating asset for any takers, but with Lampard – who netted nine times in his final year – now departed, Roeder needed a goal-scoring midfielder.

"Don is the perfect replacement for Frank and I'm a firm believer that players don't fully mature until they reach the age of 29," insisted the Hammers' boss.

"I think I could have done a lot better for West Ham last time I was here," admitted Hutch after signing a bumper contract and becoming the only player to have broken the club record transfer fee twice. "I can assure the fans that I am a better, more mature person than I was when I was here before.

"I wouldn't have left Sunderland, who finished seventh, if I thought I was joining a team that didn't have the potential to be up there."

Hutch made his debut in a second successive goalless draw at Derby County.

And Hammers made it a hat-trick of 0-0 draws in the Worthington Cup second round at Reading, where penalty shoot-out misses by Defoe and Scott Minto enabled Alan Pardew's Royals to win 6-5 on spot-kicks.

"I've got no sympathy for West Ham," barked Reading's assistant manager, Martin Allen. "We won. They lost. That's professional football."

But the game had paled into insignificance against the backdrop of the far more catastrophic events taking place in the world on September 11, 2001.

Two planes had surreally reduced the twin towers of New York's World Trade Centre into a double, tragic heap of rubble while the Pentagon in Washington had also come under terrorist attack and United Airlines flight 93 had been downed in Johnstown, Pennsylvania.

In Hutchison, Roeder had found his midfielder and he now had his eyes on a defender, as he set about the impossible task of replacing Rio Ferdinand.

It was Fiorentina's £4.5m-rated Alessandro Pierini who looked most likely to sign, before the move was scuppered by medical complications and his wife's reluctance to move to England.

But the Italian's team-mate – Tomas Repka – had previously caught Roeder's attention, too, and all focus now switched to the Czech Republic international.

Following a government investigation, cash-strapped Fiorentina were under orders to sell and, while the 40-times capped central defender had been reluctant to move to England, a few impassioned words were required from fellow-countryman Ludek Miklosko to persuade him to head to the Hammers.

Let down by what he considered to be false Redknapp promises, Miklosko had, of course, left Upton Park in acrimonious circumstances back in 1999.

But when Roeder also dispensed with goalkeeping coach Les Sealey (2+2 apps) in the wake of Harry's departure, the door had been opened in mid-June for the immensely likeable Czech to return to the fold.

"It's great for me," confirmed Ludo as he drove his Skoda back to the East End. "I didn't want to leave here in the first place, but I had to."

Roeder added: "Like Paul Goddard and Roger Cross, Ludo is happily married and part of a steady and stable family, which is important to me, because I like people with steady, balanced lives."

That goalkeeping merry-go-round was, however, overshadowed by Sealey's subsequent, untimely, death following a heart attack in mid-August at the age of 43. The self-styled 'Cat' left sons Joe and George, who were goalkeeping trainees at Upton Park.

"The worst thing West Ham did was to get rid of Les," insisted Redknapp in a Sunday newspaper interview a few months later. "He was the life and soul of the dressing room. They didn't realise what they were losing. And it hurt him so bad I could've cried for him. He was the most enthusiastic character I've ever seen."

And there was further bad news for another Hammers' keeper when Craig Forrest (34+4 apps) was diagnosed with testicular cancer.

"The thing that concerns us now is that Craig gets over his illness and has a full and healthy life," said Roeder after naturally agreeing to release the Canadian.

Failing twice to pull out of his transfer to England, Repka told the *News of the World*: "I'm really very angry. I didn't want to go but Fiorentina forced me to leave. They sold me to pay the other players' wages but after another few months they'll be back where they started."

Just like Jeroen Boere and Marco Boogers before him, Repka endured a fiery Premiership baptism. Indeed, at Middlesbrough he was booked for kicking the ball away before collecting a second caution for tugging Dean Windass.

"I now understand that the English game is very different to *Serie A* in Italy," confessed red carded Repka following Hammers' 0-2 defeat up at Boro.

Five games into the season, only Di Canio's Anfield penalty had registered in West Ham United's 'Goals For' column.

Financial irregularities had spelt double demotion for French side Toulouse and their 22-year-old left-sided winger Laurent Courtois had arrived on a free transfer, after Kanouté handed Roeder a highlights video of his friend in action. Alongside Hutchison and Repka, he made his home debut against a Newcastle United side that, dauntingly, had just beaten Manchester United.

First time around, Hutch had marked his home debut with a goal against the Magpies and he also opened the scoring on his second coming, too, as West Ham romped to a 3-0 win over Bobby Robson's side, who had not won on their last 25 trips to London.

Skipper Di Canio wore a stars and stripes armband out of respect for the victims of the 9/11 atrocities but, across London, Lampard was involved in more drunken, disrespectful antics alongside John Terry, Jody Morris and Eidur Gudjohnsen at Heathrow's Posthouse hotel, where passengers were stranded as a result of the grounding of trans-Atlantic flights.

While Chelsea claimed that the *News of the World* reporting was over the top, the players were still fined two weeks wages – which meant that some £130,000 was donated to the Twin Towers' disaster fund – for their part in an alleged pub crawl that eventually led to them being asked to leave the hotel.

"We went out and had a drink," admitted Lampard, who was consequently dropped from Eriksson's squad to face Greece in a 2002 World Cup qualifier at Old Trafford. "But, yes, we went too far."

After calling unsettled, transfer-seeking Sinclair into the fold instead, the England coach said: "We have to conduct ourselves well. We have a big responsibility because many millions of young people look at us as heroes."

Ironically, as the Blues prepared to fly to Bulgaria to face Levski Sofia in the UEFA Cup a few weeks later, Lampard could be seen in the Heathrow departure lounge engrossed in George Best's autobiography, *Blessed*.

The events of September 11 were pivotal in world history.

And on a significantly lesser scale they also proved to be the turning point for Lampard who, no doubt guided by his level-headed father, concentrated upon staying on the back pages rather than the front ones on his way to becoming one of the top midfielders in the world.

Alongside Best, Paul Gascoigne had seen his career destroyed by the demon drink, and at Goodison Park the injured Gazza left the field in tears after just eight minutes. But it was Roeder who was crying his eyes out following a 0-5 defeat, as Hutchison scored an own goal on his return to Merseyside.

"It's been a Jekyll and Hyde week," fumed Roeder. "I'm not going to say what was said in the dressing room because we've got to keep ourselves tight as a unit."

Christian Dailly insisted: "It doesn't mean that the roof's caved in just because we conceded five goals in one game."

But there was more travel sickness in store when West Ham headed to Blackburn Rovers, where Eriksson witnessed complete capitulation as Rovers ran out 7-1 winners to equal Hammers' heaviest Premiership hiding.

Youngster Grant McCann unfortunately sliced a clearance into his own net and Repka received his second red card in his first three Premiership games, for fouling David Dunn and Corrado Grabi.

"If we had only lost 1-3 we could have made a few excuses and brushed it under the carpet as an away defeat," said Hayden Foxe. "But that's impossible now."

And Roeder, seeing his side in 19th-place with a goal difference of minus 11, fumed: "If we carry on defending like that, we're going to have serious trouble.

"We had players out there who can do better and players who did their best but just can't do any better.

"This squad is four or five players short of the class we need and it's a massive job to rebuild and restructure the team.

"It can't be done overnight. I hope I'll be given time, but whether it's me or someone else, there's no magic wand. Patience is the key and results are critical."

And as Roeder chauffeured Di Canio back down the M6, his ears ringing from the manic mutterings of the irate Italian, his misery was compounded by the flash of a speed camera, as he got within just a few minutes of the refuge of his home.

"That was an interesting six hours," admitted the Hammers' boss. "Some managers had warned me that Paolo was 'unhandleable' but I haven't found him to be a monster. He is just so passionate about his football and doing well. What drives him mad is when players' standards do not match his own."

Amidst tight security at Chadwell Heath, an extended team meeting was held on the eve of Hammers' crunch clash with struggling Southampton. As Roeder played back a recording of the match in the new television faculty, unfortunately, it would not be the only video nasty to be beamed onto the screen during his tenure.

That said, there was to be a feel-good factor to the following week's showing after Kanouté's double secured a 2-0 win that lifted West Ham out of the bottom three and cost Saints' boss Stuart Gray his job.

"I asked the lads to show some good old fashioned East End bottle," announced Roeder, knowing that he, too, had come perilously close to the axe.

Having been made director of football at Portsmouth, where he insisted that he had no intention of taking over from manager Graham Rix at the coalface, Redknapp had also turned down the chance to manage Leicester City after discovering that, while there would be an awkward commute to the Midlands, there was no role available for his proposed assistant, Lampard.

As an element of bitterness began to creep in, Redknapp told Sunday newspaper journalist Brian Viner: "Cole? Carrick? Sinclair? Kanouté? West Ham have got fantastic assets. When I read that the players West Ham have got now aren't good enough, I think: 'What a load of rubbish.' I don't know how to explain their present predicament. With respect, if you were the manager of Torquay or Rochdale you wouldn't expect to get beat seven and five, so West Ham either aren't defending, or they're not working hard enough. It's for Roeder to work out.

"Glenn's ended up with a great job that he never in his wildest dreams saw coming. I met him at a dinner one night and felt sorry for him. He was out of work, a nice fella, with a family so I said: 'Come in for a couple of days a week'. He helped out with the reserves and did a lot of scouting for me. So it's a dream to come from where he was, to being manager."

Roeder responded: "Of the 22-24 players in our squad, between six and eight are sub-Premiership standard. And for Harry to whinge through the media was pretty low. I saw Harry as being a bigger person than that."

Way out west, Reading's Pardew was in the throes of sacking his assistant Allen.

"The manager decided that he didn't require his services any longer," revealed Royals' chairman John Madejski.

"They called me Mad Dog as a player and I've had to carry that tag around my neck," replied Allen, who claimed that he had been made the sacrificial lamb. "But, yes, I do expect players to work hard, improve themselves and to both expect and take criticism."

As Newcastle United, Sunderland and Liverpool all chased Sinclair, Lampard made his first return to Upton Park, where Hammers defeated unbeaten Chelsea 2-1, and then made it a hat-trick of victories as Defoe, in injury time, netted his first-ever Premiership goal to snatch a 3-2 win at Ipswich Town.

That trio of victories lifted West Ham into a very respectable 11th place, just three points away from a coveted, albeit unlikely looking, top six spot.

But all hopes of a four-timer were destroyed by newly-promoted Fulham, who grabbed a 2-0 win at Upton Park.

After leaving AC Milan, Nigerian defender Taribo West opened talks with the club, which, according to the *News of the World*, was more than Di Canio had managed. Indeed, the Italian claimed that West Ham were refusing to offer him a new contract given he still had 18 months left on his £25,000 per week deal.

"This is very strange, I've proved my worth to this club time and time again. Now it's time West Ham told me whether I'm part of their future plans or not."

Scarlet fever continued to haunt Repka, too, as he picked up his third red card of the season for elbowing Belgium's Bart Goor in the Czech Republic's World Cup play-off defeat. It was to prove the end of his international career.

In an Old Trafford friendly, Sinclair finally made his full England debut in a 1-1 draw with Sweden. And he had an eventful game, winning the dubious penalty that allowed David Beckham to put the Three Lions ahead, before conceding the free-kick that allowed Hakan Mild to equalise.

"I was delighted because it was a dream come true for me," enthused the new cap. "I thought that I did alright and it was a relief to finally play because I've been on the fringe for so many years. I thought: 'I've got nothing to lose here.' I knew that if I played s*** then I wouldn't play again so I might as well go out there, enjoy it, give it everything and try and put in a decent performance.

"It was a penalty. Don't even suggest it wasn't! Their player clipped me."

Forgotten striker Paul Kitson made his first start for 21 months as Hammers made the short trip to Charlton Athletic, and he promptly left with the matchball, after hitting a sensational hat-trick in a thrilling 4-4 draw that also saw his subsequent replacement, Defoe, find the net upon his return to The Valley.

Despite the point, those four goals conceded meant that gentleman goalkeeper Hislop (131 apps) had, effectively, played his last game for the club ahead of an end-of-season move to Redknapp's Portsmouth, where he would remain for three seasons before returning to Upton Park on yet another free transfer in the summer of 2005 as understudy to Roy Carroll.

"It's always difficult when you have been a Number One," conceded Roeder. "And it was obviously hard for him to be a Number Two, but Shaka was no problem to me. He never complained and never caused me any problems. I always knew that if I had to call upon him he would have come in and done a good job."

Indeed, the fit-again David James was provided with the perfect window to finally make his Hammers' debut, although it proved to be a point-less afternoon as Les Ferdinand gave Tottenham Hotspur a 1-0 win at Upton Park.

And as Roeder found his old club, Newcastle United, holding out for an ambitious £1m fee for 35-year-old Robert Lee, he again found no joy in the north-east as Kevin Phillips – a player he had once signed for Watford from non-league Baldock Town – gave Sunderland a 1-0 win at the Stadium of Light, where skipper Hutchison came in for merciless jeering.

Dion Dublin's first-minute goal was wiped out by Defoe's last-gasp equaliser as Hammers salvaged a 1-1 draw against Aston Villa after Di Canio's penalty-cum-backpass was easily claimed by Peter Enckelman.

By now, West Ham had slipped into 16th-place following a win-less four-game streak and the last place they wanted to be visiting was Old Trafford.

While Hammers had pulled off that Di Canio-inspired FA Cup fourth round victory back in January, the chances of lightning striking twice looked remote.

But, incredibly, West Ham produced an even better display against Ferguson's team, who had taken only four points from their last half-dozen games, and when Defoe met Di Canio's deep cross with a far post header, it gave Roeder his first-ever victory at Old Trafford as both player and boss, in what would prove to be the highlight of his tenure.

"To come here as a manager and go away with a victory is special," said Roeder as the press declared that United's title hopes were at an end. "I told the lads not to be fearful and to enjoy the game. This is definitely my best day as a manager."

Having helped to engineer that second successive victory at Old Trafford, Di Canio was then booked for diving in a 1-1 draw with Arsenal before heading to Zurich to collect his FIFA Fair Play award for catching that ball at Everton.

After taking four points off the top two sides in the country, the France-bound Roeder had simply told his Di Canio-less squad – complete with Upton Park bodyguards in tow – to stay out of trouble as they headed off to Piccadilly's Sugar Reef for their Tuesday night Christmas party in high spirits.

And when he returned from his cross-Channel scouting mission, he was relieved to hear that the night in London's West End had passed off without incident, unlike the unruly parties at Leeds, Leicester, Blackburn and Oldham.

Thorough to the last, Roeder had even told West End Central police where his players would be but, when he picked up his Thursday newspaper, he saw that the evening had not been as low-key as he had first been led to believe.

For Hayden Foxe had reportedly dropped his trousers and urinated onto the bar.

Leaping to his defence, the Aussie's agent, Peter Smiley, helpfully declared: "It was actually in a pot-plant. But we're not condoning it. Hayden's disappointed. If he could turn the clock back he wouldn't do it again. He'd walk whatever distance it was to the toilet."

An Italian waiter at the club revealed: "The players were like a bunch of animals. I don't think anyone who saw them could quite believe how bad they were."

Witnesses said another player vomited over tables while a third led a barman around in a headlock. After running amok in their cordoned-off VIP area and ringing up a reported £1,800 bar bill, the remaining players were asked to leave.

The venue's marketing manager John Jonyantin admitted: "A group of guests were asked to leave as their behaviour was not conducive to other guests."

Roeder, who took swift action by fining his Australian defender two weeks wages, announced: "I was disappointed because, as I had understood it, there hadn't been a problem, but there was an incident with one player whom I have spoken to and dealt with strongly.

"It's sad because of the 24 or 25 boys that went out, it was just the one player who let everyone down. But, unfortunately, we all get tarred with the same brush. When the incident happened 60% of the players were already long gone and home in bed, but it was portrayed as if everyone was involved and that's not the truth.

"There's a responsibility for footballers to keep their heads down. I don't think it's asking too much for them to behave in the manner we want them to.

"Fortunately, no one was physically injured or hurt and the player has absolutely guaranteed that it won't happen again. That is the end of the matter.

"He was very apologetic, not just to me but to the club, his team-mates, the supporters and his family," concluded Roeder, signing off with a poor choice of words after reportedly making the flame-haired stopper pay £14,000 for spending that bad penny. "He hopes it doesn't run and run."

As Di Canio's appeals for a new, improved, extended contract continued to fall on the deaf ears of the Hammers' board, his advisors began to engineer a move to long-term admirers Manchester United.

After all, the inventive Italian had been the chief architect of the East Enders' two recent Old Trafford victories, and with United's season faltering, another Red Devil was now needed.

Certainly, Ferguson had tamed the loose Gallic cannon that was Eric Cantona, and there was no reason why he should not be able to replicate more of the same with that unexploded grenade, Di Canio.

Indeed, the 33-year-old Hammers' playmaker looked every inch the short-term fix needed to repair United's stuttering Champions League challenge, too.

But there was one stumbling block.

The PLC board of Manchester United demanded that books had to be balanced.

With Dwight Yorke looking set to tread what was now becoming a well-worn pathway between Old Trafford and Steve McClaren's Middlesbrough, however, Di Canio's days in a divided East End looked well and truly numbered.

Certainly, 15th-place West Ham could ill-afford to be without their star player, but £3.5m was a significant fee for a thirty-something cocktail of mischief.

Indeed, Roeder knew that his off-the-pitch life would be easier without the disruptive Di Canio constantly undermining his every move.

Having watched from afar as Di Canio's prima donna antics frequently led his predecessor a merry dance, the Hammers' boss had, no doubt, resolved not to allow such behaviour should he ever take charge.

But now that he was in the hot-seat, he gradually realised that the Italian was, perhaps, not so easy to tame.

And notwithstanding a propensity to jet home to Italy at any opportunity, Di Canio's selective fear of flying contributed to him missing 40 of the 100 away matches contested by the Hammers during his time at the club.

A move looked assured and, after netting another audacious equalising penalty in an ill-tempered 1-1 draw at 10-man Leicester City, Di Canio left the pitch for what many perceived was the final time, in a flood of tears.

Matt Elliott's dismissal for butting Sinclair had raised the temperature all round, and the distraught Di Canio was involved in a heated Filbert Street fracas with a steward who complained to Leicestershire police.

The Italian's former Sheffield Wednesday compatriot Benito Carbone was then dismissed for Derby County as Hammers won 4-0 in a Boxing Day clash in which Di Canio again starred.

The highlight of the morning was the want-away Sinclair's spectacular volley after the Italian and Cole had combined at a short corner to ensure that the ball found the net without ever touching the floor.

"Trevor scored a great goal but he still said: 'Boss, I can do better.' I told him that he'd just worked his socks off but that just goes to show how committed he still is," observed Roeder after seeing the transfer-seeking Sinclair bag the Goal-of-the-Month. "We won't break our promise to him and, if someone comes in with a bid matching his valuation, we'd let him talk to that particular club.

"Obviously I don't want him to go but only Trevor can decide whether or not he wants to withdraw his transfer request."

Sinclair was on target again as Hammers dominated against an over-confident Liverpool side, too. Indeed, the Merseysiders had to drag Michael Owen off the bench to make up a four-man forward line that also included Jari Litmanen, Emile Heskey plus Nicolas Anelka, and the England striker duly obliged with his 100th goal for the Reds to salvage a late 1-1 draw.

Having finished 2001 with a fine six-match unbeaten run, West Ham – minus the dubiously injured, but certainly unsettled, Di Canio – could not have kicked-off 2002 in worse style as Mark Viduka's double sent Leeds racing into a two-goal lead inside the opening seven minutes. And by the time £11m Robbie Fowler added a third, Leeds were assured of Premiership top-spot.

With a January 31 Champions League transfer deadline looming, Di Canio's move to Old Trafford – alongside Independiente's £7.5m-rated Uruguayan striker Diego Forlan – appeared imminent even though Hammers' £3.5m valuation was considered to be too high.

"Paolo loves West Ham but imagine being at the end of your career and a big club like Manchester United wants you," said the Italian's agent Matteo Roggi.

"Di Canio's a natural entertainer who also produces the goods," enthused Ryan Giggs as he prepared to lead the welcome party. "There's no doubt that on his day he's one of the best players in the Premier League to watch."

Between dreams of Premiership titles and Champions League trophies, Paolo retreated to his personal website.

"I am going to have to ask you to be patient," he told cyberspace, knowing that there would be many, many hits coming his way. "I don't feel this is quite the right moment for me to speak yet. But you can rest assured that in the next few days I'm going to have a lot to say. I'll be saying it all here on my personal website."

Macclesfield Town's 6,000-capacity Moss Rose ground was sold out for the visit of West Ham, who found themselves lining up against the third division side's player-coach Kevin Keen.

But a Defoe double and a Cole effort ensured that there would be no giant-killing by a team in 88th place in the league, while Moncur somehow managed to collect two yellow cards inside the space of 30 seconds after fouling Chris Byrne and then forcibly trying to lift him up.

This time around, a heavy cold conveniently ensured that Di Canio had not been cup-tied and, after the match, Roeder revealed that United had faxed the club an unacceptable offer, thought to be in the region of £2m.

And by the time Leicester City arrived at Upton Park, the recovered Di Canio fittingly netted the winner in a 1-0 victory.

Following wild goal celebrations, the East End was left in no doubt that they had seen the last of their Roman god when he took an age to depart down the tunnel.

"It wouldn't be the first time that Paolo has been the last one off the pitch and as far as I'm concerned he's still very much a West Ham player," insisted Roeder. "I love having him in my team because he's a God-given talent. Any manager would want to keep him, but Manchester United have come calling. There's been no increased offer, though, so you'll have to ask United what's happening next."

Despite being sent off for stamping on Jody Morris in a 1-5 defeat at Chelsea, Di Canio still managed to quip: "Maybe this will end all the speculation. Maybe United will not want to buy me even for one pound. At least it shows that I am thinking only about West Ham, otherwise I would not have acted so passionately."

And as United concentrated upon tying up the South American signing of Forlan, the canny Italian – not having officially asked to go – craftily began to play that loyalty card in what many believed to be a calculated bid to see whether there was any chance of extracting an Upton Park pay-off from the deal, too.

Meanwhile, sensing that he held the key that would, ultimately, unlock the transfer merry-go-round, Yorke – who was seemingly on £24,000 per week at United – stalled over a £6.2m transfer to Boro after reportedly seeking £58,000 per week and refusing to settle for a take-it-or-leave-it £37,000 per week.

While Yorke and Di Canio dallied, two men on the move were Vladimir Labant and David Forde.

Enshrined in expectancy, left-sided, 17-times capped Slovakian defender Labant was signed from Sparta Prague in a £900,000 deal that would almost certainly spell the end of Nigel Winterburn's days at Upton Park.

"Everyone says he is the best left-back in the Czech and Slovak Republics," insisted Miklosko.

"His pedigree is decent," observed Roeder, who also bought Republic of Ireland Under-21 goalkeeper, Forde, from Barry Town in a £50,000 transfer.

Returning to Stamford Bridge in the FA Cup fourth round just seven days later, Kanouté forced a 1-1 draw and an Upton Park replay.

Hammers then lost 0-2 at Southampton to slip into 15th place, before Boro pulled out of any deal for the avaricious Yorke, clearly looking to cover the upcoming Pampers account about to be run up by his pregnant girlfriend, Jordan.

NEARLY REACHED THE SKY

Suddenly, Di Canio looked vulnerable and, as that January 31 Champions League deadline passed, the curtain fell on his move to the Theatre of Dreams.

The long-running episode had involved more twists and turns than *The Italian Job* and more real-life soap than *Eastenders*.

Like estranged lovers, Di Canio and West Ham United were reconciled again.

But only hopeless romantics would have bet upon the union running its course.

Instead of making his Old Trafford debut against Sunderland, the Italian was back at Upton Park helping Hammers to a 2-0 win over Blackburn Rovers as the club went some way to avenging their 1-7 defeat at Ewood Park.

"We're just glad that the deadline came and went," announced a relieved Roeder, who had been looking for the situation to be resolved one way or another for an entire month. "The saga's been laid to rest and now we can get on with our season. Paolo was last off the pitch against Leicester when everybody assumed he was leaving and he was last off the pitch again today. That just proves he hadn't been saying farewell to us. Like all players, he really enjoys his victories."

But many could claim he would equally have found himself milking the acclaim from Old Trafford's Stretford End.

For in the end, it was only exasperated Middlesbrough's reluctance to bow to father-to-be Yorke's unrealistic, idealistic demands that prevented United's PLC board from transforming Di Canio from East End darling to Red Devil.

Greed had got the better of all in a high-rolling round of Premiership poker.

One-by-one, the players, their agents and their clubs had each upped the ante before stacking their hands in frustration as the sands of time slipped by.

With the clock ticking down to that European D-Day West Ham United had sat patiently waiting for the fax to start whirring with a more realistic, increased offer.

Di Canio, himself, had apparently been made a financial offer he could not refuse by Old Trafford godfather Ferguson, but it was tempered by the cautious length of the contract offered by the PLC board.

But for a man about to blow out 34 candles in July, the move represented the perfect opportunity to bring the curtain down on a controversial career with some glistening late silverware.

Having publicly kept his distance from the negotiations, back in London, he had, indeed, been free to insist that he had not asked Hammers for a transfer. By implication, with a double-edged sword, the Italian was entitled to a golden handshake from the club that had saved him from soccer's scrapheap following *that* push, while he could also try to hold out for a longer deal up north.

"These things happen and it's disappointing because I thought that by bringing in Di Canio I was going to get someone who could change the course of a game," confessed a curt, frustrated Sir Alex after coolly retiring from the table in the solemn knowledge that United's £360m stock market valuation meant that the £3.5m sought by West Ham could surely have been raised from matchday pie sales alone. "I've always been an admirer of Paolo but Dwight Yorke's agent wouldn't make the move so it's finished."

As Fergie prepared to banish Yorke to the obscurity of the reserves, the weary Roeder was just grateful that those weeks of uncertainty had passed.

While he would have welcomed the cash for his ageing star, the Hammers' boss also knew that it would have taken yet more wise spending to find a ready-made, goal-making, goal-getting replacement for just £3.5m.

Indeed, during the three years and 114 games since his £1.7m arrival from Sheffield Wednesday, Di Canio had been responsible for some 40% of his team's goals either by netting 38 times himself or helping out by way of direct assists.

But in Defoe and Kanouté, Roeder also knew that he had a younger, more placid, geographically mobile, strike partnership which – injuries permitting – was ripe and ready to be unleashed on the Premiership.

"Alex Ferguson is one of the shrewdest judges in the business and if he wanted Paolo then there must have been a good reason why," concluded Roeder. "He's one of those players who can be the difference. No one can be special all the time but while he's on the pitch there's always that possibility that he might just do something. This is the longest he's stayed at any one club and that must show that he likes east London and he likes working for the people who employ him."

Now after seeing his move to the Theatre of Dreams fade and die, the chameleon-like Di Canio was, predictably, embarking upon an all-out damage limitation exercise, pledging his allegiance to the other United – West Ham United.

"Manchester United wasn't for me," he insisted making a dramatic U-turn that simply insulted the intelligence of the entire East End population. "I know that in order to stay at West Ham, I have turned my back on Champions League football, playing in front of crowds of 67,000 people each week and possibly even a little, little chance of going to the World Cup with Italy.

"As a professional it would have been fantastic to have played with the likes of Beckham and Giggs but as a person I am happy in this one place.

"For me, West Ham is more important. Even if I went to the top club in the world, I could not have found better supporters than the ones here at West Ham.

"Yes, it was a big opportunity and my team-mates all said: 'Are you sure, Paolo? Why don't you go, Paolo?' They were telling me that I was crazy. That's normal and I'm not surprised because even Tottenham and Chelsea players would say that I was crazy not to go to Manchester United. If it had happened to any of them, then I'm sure they would have gone very quickly.

"I read that I was asking for a £500,000 golden handshake," Di Canio then told Gabriele Marcotti of the *Daily Mail*. "I have also read that I wanted United to give me an extra year on my contract.

"Neither is true," he pleaded. "I never asked for an extra penny or an extra day. I never spoke to either club about this. Nor is it true that only Dwight Yorke's refusal to move to Middlesbrough killed the deal.

"Had I wanted a move, I could've been a United player by Christmas."

Fortunately for Roeder, Sven Andersson (0 apps) did not have the same quandary leaving Sweden as he signed the veteran keeper on loan from Helsingborgs.

In the FA Cup fourth-round replay, Chelsea's Terry put Hammers in the driving seat at Upton Park with an early own goal, but the Blues fought back to make it 2-2 before the former West Ham schoolboy atoned for his early error by heading the Stamford Bridge outfit into the last 16 with a late winner.

And another defeat followed at Bolton as Ricardo Gardner gave Bolton Wanderers a 1-0 victory. Kitson's 77th-minute substitute appearance at the Reebok Stadium was to prove his last for the club.

There was no doubt that, alongside John Hartson, the striker's eight goals had been pivotal in saving Hammers from relegation following his £2.3m transfer from Newcastle United in January 1997, but the moody Kitson (55+25 apps 22gls) had endured an injury-ravaged five years at Upton Park.

Finding first-team opportunities limited, 1999 FA Youth Cup winner – and man of the match in that final against Coventry City – Adam Newton (0+3 apps) joined Peterborough United on a free transfer, where he linked up with Jimmy Bullard (0 apps) and Tommy Williams (0 apps) who had been released a few months earlier. Discovering himself in a similar situation, Omer Riza moved to Cambridge United on the same basis, while Michael Ferrante (0 apps) was also released.

Meanwhile, having come off the transfer list at his own behest, Sinclair announced: "I've changed my mind and I want to stay. Basically, it all boils down to the fact that I've seen all the good work that Glenn Roeder's done. He's settled the ship and made some very good signings. Glenn's shown his quality with the way he's dealt with everything that's happened with certain players at the club and, indeed, with me all through my transfer saga.

"Back in the summer I thought the club had gone totally against what they'd originally said about selling their best players, but maybe I should have looked at the bigger picture and the longer-term issues that needed to be addressed.

"The club's heading in the right direction again. If they show that they're equally ambitious and want to hold onto their best players then I'll happily finish my career here," announced the 29-year-old who had attracted interest from Newcastle United, Sunderland and Liverpool during his time in the shop window.

"Glenn Roeder is as honest as the day is long and he told me about the interest of those clubs, but to be honest, I was disappointed that West Ham put such a huge price on my head. I knew that the club weren't going to back down on their price and I still knew that nobody was going to pay £10m for me.

"But by not lowering my fee West Ham showed that they have now applied a different policy. They've shown that they don't just want to cash in and take the money for their key players," continued Sinclair, who knew that he needed to be settled and on top of his game if he was to have any hope of filling Eriksson's left-sided void in time for the 2002 World Cup.

"And I've decided to knock the beer on the head," he claimed. "Before, I kept getting involved in silly little incidents and it was all down to the booze. I was always the fool who got himself into bother and a few scrapes and that just wasn't me because I'm not a troublemaker. Basically, I couldn't handle alcohol. It didn't mix with me. I go out now and again but these days it's more for meals and whenever I see the lads, I just stay on the Coca-Cola and drive them around.

"When you look at the way in which Paolo Di Canio trains he's a model pro. I've watched him and learned how to conduct myself on the training ground and how to turn up every day and give 100%.

"I've got one England cap and there's possibly even a World Cup ahead of me. I could be involved, who knows?"

Despite missing a crucial spot-kick in a penalty decider, one Hammer, Rigobert Song (26+1 apps), was already claiming international honours by helping Cameroon to retain the African Nations Cup. But he had already played his last game for the club after being farmed out on loan to FC Cologne with a view to a £3m move, before eventually joining French side RC Lens for a discounted £1m.

And Roeder had also decided that there was no Upton Park future for another former Anfield star either, but when Sheffield United came knocking to take Titi Camara on loan, they simply could not afford the reserve striker's wages.

Having taken on the very job that he always said he did not want, newly-installed Portsmouth boss Redknapp won the tug-of-war with Nottingham Forest to sign Svetoslav Todorov (5+12 apps 2 gls) – the striker he originally brought from Bulgaria to Upton Park – in a £750,000 deal.

A 1-0 win over Middlesbrough was marred by injury to Hutchison. Having lost James with a knee injury at the start of the season, a ruptured anterior cruciate ligament now ruled joint-record signing Hutch out of action for the rest of 2002.

At Villa Park, Di Canio's penalty put Hammers ahead before Angel equalised and Vassell snatched an injury-time winner for Aston Villa.

As Roeder supposedly contemplated bringing former Newcastle United team-mate Gascoigne to Upton Park, Sinclair's deflected goal was enough to sink Everton at Upton Park to leave Hammers in 10th spot with nine games to play.

Manchester United arrived at Upton Park seeking to avenge the previous autumn's defeat at Old Trafford. Twice Hammers took the lead through Steve Lomas and Kanouté, only for Beckham and Nicky Butt to conjure up equalisers. And although Defoe set up a frantic finale after Paul Scholes and Ole-Gunnar Solskjaer had put United well in front, Beckham's penalty sealed United's 5-3 win.

A 3-1 victory at Ipswich Town was followed by a 1-0 win at Fulham, but after Kanouté headed Hammers ahead, all hell broke loose when, in order to preserve West Ham's slender advantage, Roeder replaced Di Canio with Moncur.

With his brother watching from the Craven Cottage terraces, the embarrassed and agitated Italian vented his anger at his boss before theatrically trudging around the touchline and disappearing down the tunnel, whereupon his sibling climbed the perimeter wall and headed for the dressing rooms, too.

"If West Ham don't want me around then they have only got one thing to do – give me a free transfer," declared Di Canio angling for another lucrative East End exit. "I won't be treated like a kid. Roeder is at the beginning of his managerial career and young managers have to learn the same way that young players do.

"The manager should appreciate he will not go far if he cannot find the courage to substitute the players who need to be substituted.

"His decision to take me off left everyone amazed. I gave my all for the team and, although my colleague scored a goal, apart from that, his contribution, defensively, wasn't as intense."

Kanouté replied: "I was surprised to read Paolo suggesting I should've been replaced. If he has a problem, he should talk to me in person. And if the West Ham fans have a problem with me, too, then it could be the end of our journey."

NEARLY REACHED THE SKY

Di Canio and Kanouté were both on the score-sheet as Hammers coasted to a 2-0 win over Charlton Athletic, but all hopes Di Canio had of engineering an early departure collapsed when he was stretchered away with knee ligament damage.

That hat-trick of victories saw Hammers hit the heady heights of seventh place, before Ian Pearce salvaged a 1-1 draw at Tottenham Hotspur to leave them 13 points behind Leeds United in sixth-spot with just four to play.

While possessed with a laser-guided left-foot, the white-booted Labant had not proved as defensively durable to the English game as Roeder had first believed.

Indeed, having announced that Winterburn would be released at the end of the season, the Hammers' boss had to replace the Slovakian with the veteran Gunner for his own protection after an hour's torment at White Hart Lane.

A 3-0 win over Sunderland at Upton Park consolidated Hammers' hopes of finishing seventh and, having steadied the ship, Roeder's reward was set to come via a new, three-year contract that would replace his probationary 12-month deal.

With World Cup 2002 looming, Eriksson's selection problems were not confined to the England team for he also had to choose between Swedish mistress Ulrika Jonsson and Nancy Dell'Olio.

And as all eyes focused on the England coach and his long-standing Italian girlfriend in the Highbury directors box, both referee Steve Dunn and his assistant Mark Canadine failed to see that Kanouté's shot had clearly crossed the line before Ashley Cole slid in to clear.

Just to add insult to injury, Freddie Ljungberg and then Nwankwo Kanu gave leaders Arsenal a record-breaking 10th consecutive win, to put them four points clear of Liverpool in the title race, with just three games remaining.

"I didn't think it was a goal, I *know* it was a goal," fumed Roeder. "The ball more than crossed the line. The linesman may have made an honest mistake but it was a bad error and it's his job to spot things like that. Championships are won and lost on those decisions. Like us, he should be held accountable rather than just be allowed to scurry off into the night."

Defoe put Hammers ahead at Newcastle with his 14th goal of the season, before the Magpies hit back to win 3-1, leaving West Ham in eighth place – level on points with Tottenham Hotspur – going into the final match of the campaign.

Thursday, May 9, 2002 represented a momentous day for Cole. For not only was he presented to HM The Queen as she formally opened the £20m, 15,427-seater Dr Martens Stand but, alongside James, at high noon he was also named in Eriksson's World Cup squad.

But when the disappointed Sinclair played back his answerphone, he had found himself listening to a message from the England coach telling him that he had not made the 23-man cut.

Going into the final minute of the final game, Hammers were drawing 1-1 with Bolton Wanderers while Tottenham were losing 1-2 at relegated Leicester City.

The East End crowd had been calling for Steve Potts (463+43 apps 1 gl) to step from the dug-out and make his 400th, and final, league appearance for the club.

However, with the Filbert Street and Upton Park outcomes still in the balance, the cautious Roeder was simply not prepared to let his heart rule his head in the quest for seventh spot.

But when Pearce popped up to score the 89th-minute goal that would guarantee West Ham United both victory and seventh-place, Potts – who had been warming up for an eternity – looked certain to make an emotional entrance.

Incredibly, though, he was overlooked in Roeder's injury-time double substitution as rookie Richard Garcia and Moncur replaced Carrick and Kanouté, to the consternation of the crowd, whose disappointment was only tempered by the immediate blowing of a full-time whistle that confirmed, against all odds, West Ham had, indeed, mustered a top-half finish.

"Steve understands and I don't even think it's a point of discussion," insisted the ruthless Roeder. "He's a terrific professional who has been brought up in the right manner, under the influence of John Lyall. Steve wouldn't want to be put on just for the sake of it. We needed to win the game."

With the diplomacy that had been the trademark of almost two decades service, the Dagenham & Redbridge-bound Potts – the ninth highest appearance-maker in the club's history – replied: "Glenn's entitled to his opinion and I don't want to let that last afternoon take away everything that I enjoyed and achieved at the club.

"Anyway, I could still be the last player to stay at West Ham for 19 years and play over 500 games. I was very disappointed but worse things are happening on the planet and a last appearance for West Ham just wasn't to be, was it?"

Only champions Arsenal, runners-up Liverpool plus Manchester United, Newcastle United, Leeds United and Chelsea had finished higher than the Hammers, who ended the season with a goal difference of minus nine.

As the predictable seventh heaven headlines rolled from the presses, this Number Seven was a far cry from the basement days of the previous October, where a 1-7 hammering at Blackburn and cruel chants of: 'Are you Burnley in disguise?' had been ringing around Ewood Park.

"The doubters have been left licking their wounds," cried the *News of the World* papering over the cracks. "Roeder is firmly in control after a solid seventh-place finish in the Premiership cauldron."

Following a long season that had seen major signings James and Hutchison crocked, top-scorer Di Canio star in his very own soap opera, 14-goal Defoe cut the Premiership mustard and several Hammers achieve international recognition, Roeder observed: "It's difficult to finish in the top half of the Premiership, but all credit must go to the players within this small squad. Looking ahead, we need more strength in depth and I want to add three or four quality players in the summer. But they're going to have to be low budget buys or Bosman signings.

"In Defoe, Carrick and Cole we are very lucky to have three such talented young players. The most important thing is that we keep them here. That's not going to be a case of fighting the board because they want to keep these boys as much as I do. It will be a case of fighting any clubs trying to prise them away.

"I understand that, after finishing in seventh place, the expectations amongst supporters are going to rise. We have to be realistic, though, and the bottom line is that for at least a dozen clubs, getting to the 40-point mark is the first objective.

"You have to be aware of the downside and none of us can afford to be that blasé or stupid enough to think that we have a divine right to be in the Premiership. It has to be earned.

"We must never lose sight of the fact that, with the way football is slipping in the lower leagues, retaining Premiership status is everything."

PLAYERS IN

Laurent Courtois	Toulouse	Free transfer
Don Hutchison	Sunderland	£5,000,000 (Record)
David James	Aston Villa	£3,500,000
Vladimir Labant	Sparta Prague	£900,000
Tomas Repka	Fiorentina	£5,000,000 (Record)
Sebastien Schemmel	FC Metz	£465,000

LOANS IN

Sven Andersson	Helsingborgs

PLAYERS OUT

Christian Bassila	Rennes	Released
Kaba Diawara	RC Ferrol	Released
Michael Ferrante	Released	
Craig Forrest	Retired	
Shaka Hislop	Portsmouth	Free transfer
Gavin Holligan	Wycombe Wanderers	Free transfer
Paul Kitson	Brighton & Hove Albion	Free transfer
Frank Lampard	Chelsea	£11,000,000
Adam Newton	Peterborough United	Free transfer
Stuart Pearce	Manchester City	Free transfer
Steve Potts	Dagenham & Redbridge	Free transfer
Omer Riza	Cambridge United	Free transfer
Rigobert Song	Racing Club Lens	£1,000,000
Igor Stimac	Hajduk Split	Free transfer
Davor Suker	TSV Munich 1860	Free transfer
Hannu Tihinen	Anderlecht	Released
Svetoslav Todorov	Portsmouth	£750,000

Chapter 16
2002-03

THE ROED TO RUIN

As Glenn Roeder sat down to scheme how he was going to hit that 40 point landmark, David James and Joe Cole carried the claret and blue flag to the 2002 World Cup in Japan and South Korea.

And there was an added bonus for Trevor Sinclair, too, when a round of golf was interrupted by a call from Sven-Goran Eriksson asking him to join up with the squad on standby.

"When do you want me? What time?" begged Sinclair as he cancelled his holiday in St. Lucia to fly to meet the squad in Dubai, where the Swede waited to see if injured Steven Gerrard and Kieron Dyer would be fit in time for the finals.

"I'm not going just to make up the numbers," insisted the hopeful Hammer. "I'll be training as hard as I can to get into the team. It would mean everything to me as it's the highlight of any player's career."

With Gerrard succumbing to groin surgery, team-mate Danny Murphy was promoted to the full squad while Sinclair waited anxiously to see if Dyer could overcome a knee injury.

But after appearing as an unconvincing half-time substitute in the 1-1 friendly draw with World Cup hosts South Korea, the heartbroken Sinclair found himself put back on standby as Eriksson decided to gamble on Dyer's recovery.

"I had a bit of a nightmare and I know I haven't done myself any favours," admitted the 24th man. "It's not as if I've set the world alight."

After talking to the England coach, Sinclair checked out of Seogwipo's Paradise Hotel, on Jeju Island, on the shores of the South China Sea and returned to his pregnant wife Natalie in London.

As the FA diplomatically thanked him for his professionalism, understanding and commitment to Team England, the dejected Hammer planned to train at Chadwell Heath in case Dyer failed to make it.

"It would be difficult for me to wait there," he said, taking some consolation from the fact that the players' committee had shown a degree of sympathy by agreeing that he would still share in their bonus pool worth a reported £75,000-plus. "If they need me to come back I will, but to stay here on standby I'd be hanging on a string. It's not nice just waiting for someone to get injured."

With the media questioning Sinclair's temperament in jetting away from an already acclimatised England camp, Eriksson defended his man on standby.

"He has not turned his back on his country," insisted the Swede. "It is the opposite. He is not going on holiday and is going to work until the beginning of June, perhaps, for nothing. Everything in life is not black and white and as long as he is happy it is better for him, better for England and better for me. Yes it was the second best solution, but I understand his wishes.

"As far as I'm concerned he has been very professional. His number was 24 which says everything, but if he is happy we can gain from that."

However, just as a jet-lagged Sinclair arrived back at Chadwell Heath for a solo training session, news filtered through from the Far East that the luckless Murphy had broken his foot in training.

It meant that Sinclair had to jet 8,000 miles back to Jeju where he was handed the ill-fated No.4 shirt vacated by both the luckless Gerrard and Murphy.

But while there was to be no place for Sinclair when the tournament proper started, substitute Cole became the first English Hammer to play in a World Cup finals since Alvin Martin at Mexico 86, in the Group F opener against Sweden.

Following that 1-1 draw versus Eriksson's countrymen, however, it was substitute Sinclair's turn to step from the bench to help England to an epic 1-0 win over Argentina.

"In the end, the World Cup unfolded very well for me," he enthused. "It was an amazing experience. When Sven told me that I was going on I had a whole mixture of feelings. Excitement, fear, expectation. You name it, I felt it. I looked around at Crespo, Zanetti, Veron and all of the other Argentinians and knew that I must not be afraid. I wanted to get stuck in and perform."

And Sinclair deservedly kept his place as England qualified for the last 16 with a goalless draw against Nigeria.

Making the left midfield berth his own, Sinclair then helped England to qualify for the quarter-finals with a 3-0 win over Denmark, before being replaced by Dyer as the Three Lions crashed out of the tournament with a 1-2 defeat against eventual winners, Brazil.

While Cole and Sinclair both featured, James had been confined to the bench.

But Ronaldinho's speculative long-range winner that clinched victory for Brazil spelt the beginning of the end for first-choice keeper David Seaman and that would open the door for the Hammer to show that he could take over the gloves as England's Number One.

With Shaka Hislop having departed to Fratton Park, Roeder snapped up Raimond Van Der Gouw on a free transfer from Manchester United, who had just signed Rio Ferdinand – England's star of the 2002 World Cup – from Leeds United for a whopping £29m.

"There's always a time to come and a time to go," said the 39-year-old Dutch keeper who was, however, destined never to make a first-team appearance for the club. "The time to leave Manchester United had arrived. I know that I'm only going to be number two but whenever Glenn needs me, I'll do my best for him."

The Republic of Ireland's World Cup exit on penalties to Spain in Suwon meant that Gary Breen could finally set about looking for a new club.

After turning down a new contract at Coventry City – whom he had once cost £3m – the central defender was available on an all too familiar free transfer.

Inter Milan, Parma, Real Mallorca, Celtic and five other Premiership clubs were said to be hot on the trail of Breen, although stories of interest from the mighty Barcelona were grossly exaggerated.

But with a wages offer reported to be in the region of £30,000 per week, Breen signed a one-year contract that re-united him with Roeder, for whom he had played under at Gillingham.

"Glenn is the main reason why I have signed for West Ham. His coaching pedigree is there for all to see. Everything bodes well for this club. I had a lot of fantastic offers but I put everything else to one side and concentrated on the World Cup," said the 47-times capped central defender who had overcome a tumour on his spine as a 12-year-old. "I expect to be playing the best football of my career in the next four to five years.

"And we want to build on last year's seventh-place finish. We've definitely got the players here to do that."

Upon the recommendation of Thierry Henry, French Under-21 international midfielder Edouard Cissé joined on loan from Paris Saint-Germain until the end of the season with a view to a permanent move.

And teenage French striker, Youssef Sofiane joined from Auxerre alongside Trinidad & Tobago midfielder Brent Rahim.

Having been tipped off to apply for the job by former team-mates Steve Potts and Paul Goddard, Kevin Keen was appointed as Under-17 coach in place of the retiring Peter Brabrook.

"I feel like I've returned to my family," enthused the keen ex-Hammer, who set straight to work, weeks before his contract officially started.

John Moncur was equally happy to still find himself at Upton Park.

Indeed, he even took a pay reduction to stay at the club for one final season.

"It's gonna be a big wage cut but I've had to do that for the past couple of years, too," said the grateful 35-year-old midfielder after being handed an eleventh-hour reprieve. "I've had more cuts than Sweeney Todd so it's nothing new to me. It's a good job that I've only got one year otherwise I'd be paying West Ham to play for them next season!

"I'm desperate to play as many games as I can in my final year but the likes of the talented youngsters in front of me such as Joe Cole and Michael Carrick don't come along every day, do they?"

And it was business as usual for Moncur on the practical jokes front, too.

"A few of the lads were in a bar looking out over Covent Garden one night," revealed Moncs. "There was a fire-eater bloke doing his stuff in front of a load of people on the Piazza in front of Punch & Judy's. I just grabbed the extinguisher off the wall of the bar and ran out across the square and doused out the flames. Despite what the crowd thought, I definitely wasn't meant to be the other half of his act!"

With those question marks hanging over Vladimir Labant, Winterburn was grateful of his new one-year contract, too.

"I had a better offer elsewhere but I didn't want to move," said Winterburn after seeing his wages slashed, too. "It wasn't about money, I just want to play."

Heading for the exit, Hayden Foxe (7+5 apps) rejoined Redknapp at Portsmouth in a £500,000 deal, knowing that he would be remembered more for his Christmas party antics in the Sugar Reef than his performances at Upton Park in the hallowed Number Six jersey.

And another defender, Ragnvald Soma (4+5 apps) returned to FC Bryne in Norway after failing to establish himself in the Premiership. Having originally cost £800,000 in January 2001, the *Newham Recorder* reported that Hammers were believed to have accepted a 'substantial loss' on their sober investment.

The Lord Lucan-like Gary Charles (3+3 apps) decided to retire after making more headlines off the pitch than on it during his controversial three-year stay.

"He has cost the club £4.4m on salary and transfer fee during the period of his contract," announced Terence Brown.

Even after he had left the club, the player who had managed just 212 league appearances during his 17 seasons in England was still making headlines.

First there was reported confusion over his transfer fee as Benfica's President Joao e Azevedo – who was subsequently jailed for fraud after allegedly pocketing the fee from the sale of Russian keeper Sergei Ovchinikv – apparently suggested that Charles had moved to Upton Park on a free transfer rather than for £1.2m.

And while there was nothing to suggest any impropriety on the English side of the equation, the player also found himself behind bars and doing a four-month stretch in Nottingham prison after driving off from a Long Eaton pub in his Mercedes, flattening a wall and mounting the pavement before being found asleep on the floor of the vehicle. That came four months after he was discovered apparently drunk in his girlfriend's car, surrounded by torn-up banknotes and his own excrement. On both occasions he had refused a breath-test.

In summer 2004, Charles was jailed for five months after cutting off his electronic curfew tag and flying to Spain, where he was spotted on the Costa Del Sol by a probation officer.

Judge Andrew Hamilton told him: "You are a silly young man who ought to grow up. You have no future in the bottle. You flagrantly breached the curfew order and it is clear that any effort to deal with you in the community has totally failed."

Newcastle's on-loan defender Olivier Bernard reportedly stayed away from pre-season training on Tyneside to sign a pre-contract agreement with West Ham.

But with the Magpies protesting that they had an option to buy the Frenchman, St James's Park chief Freddy Shepherd told the *News of the World*: "What West Ham have done is disgraceful and I will fight this to the bitter end."

Hammers argued they were under the impression that Bernard was a free agent.

However, a Premier League hearing dismissed the player's appeal against the decision that stopped him quitting Newcastle United and moving to Upton Park.

In the fickle world of football, Bernard duly returned to the North East and signed a three-year contract and, ironically, found himself lining up against West Ham as the curtain rose on the 2002-03 campaign.

Fredi Kanouté – a summer target for Liverpool – pulled out at the eleventh-hour with a stiff neck and with Cole hastily pushed up front to partner Jermain Defoe, Hammers crashed to a humiliating 0-4 defeat on Tyneside live on Sky TV.

"We protected David James for the first hour and then showed a lack of resilience just like we did at times last year," observed Roeder after seeing his side's defences collapse to two-goal Lomana Lua Lua, Alan Shearer and Nolberto Solano inside the final 30 minutes.

Arsenal came to Upton Park looking for a record-breaking 15th consecutive win.

But West Ham were in no mood to roll over to the previous season's Premiership champions and FA Cup holders, as Cole and the fit-again Kanouté sent them into a 2-0 lead. And although Henry pulled one back, Kanouté then had the perfect chance to seal victory, but Seaman could have thrown his cap onto the Frenchman's weak backpass of a penalty and with two minutes remaining, Sylvain Wiltord snatched a 2-2 draw for the Gunners.

"We've got to be as motivated as that every time we play," urged the disappointed Roeder. "We had individuals outperforming Arsenal's internationals but we've only taken a point from a game we should've won."

For many, Kanouté's miss, just two games into the new season, was to prove one of the most pivotal moments of a campaign eternally layered in false security.

Indeed, after that stunning performance, few would have backed Charlton Athletic to get anything out of their visit to Upton Park, but with the Hammers' youngsters trying too hard in front of the watching Eriksson, Claus Jensen and Jon Fortune secured an unlikely 2-0 win for Alan Curbishley's side.

Having recovered from knee ligament damage, Chievo and Lazio target Paolo Di Canio returned to the side for the visit of West Bromwich Albion.

"I've another two great seasons in front of me," he declared as he prepared to see out the final year of his Hammers' contract. "One at West Ham and the other with whoever wants to sign me."

But the Italian was powerless to prevent the newly-promoted Baggies from leaving with a 1-0 victory on a night when Tomas Repka had a serious and damaging altercation with his own fans at the final whistle, while the biggest cheer of the evening had been reserved for Carrick's substitution.

And Di Canio was then embroiled in a bust-up with Roeder at White Hart Lane when his manager tried to substitute him with 10-man Hammers trailing 1-2. But after setting up Sinclair to make it 2-2, he was all smiles as he willingly retired, only for Anthony Gardner to steal a late winner with a deflected long-ranger.

"Paolo is a very passionate man," argued Roeder. "In our position we need that sort of person."

A goalless draw against Manchester City at Upton Park left Hammers bottom of the table after six games, the only Premiership side without a victory.

But even though two-goal Di Canio teed up a 25-yard wonder strike for himself at Stamford Bridge to give West Ham a 3-2 victory over Chelsea, the club still remained at the foot of the table.

"Paolo hit it well and the ball kept moving unbelievably," said shell-shocked fellow countryman Carlo Cudicini after picking the ball out of the Blues' net. "First it went right, then it went left and I couldn't do anything."

Di Canio's prolonged 'Mama Mia' celebrations earned him a strong FA censure.

Defoe then put Hammers ahead in the Worthington Cup at Chesterfield, before Chris Brandon equalised for the Division Two side. As frustration flared, Repka and Di Canio had a stand-up row before extra-time and penalties.

"That's nothing unusual," argued the former Czech Republic international. "It was just two players who care about the team wanting to make things better."

Fittingly, courageous Carrick hit the deciding spot-kick to give Hammers a 5-4 victory in the subsequent shoot-out.

"It wasn't a big deal for me," said the scarred Geordie, who went a long way towards repairing his relationship with the boo-boy minority. "I've just tried to keep my head down. It's been the worst two or three weeks since I've been here at West Ham, but it certainly wasn't as bad as the press made it out to be.

"The spirit is still good," he added. "And we're all behind the manager. The ability is here and it's only the players who can turn things around. There's no point settling for a mid-table finish because our ambitions are higher than that. It's still early in the season and we're confident that we can turn it around."

But a Stern John double then gave Birmingham City a 2-1 victory at Upton Park.

"They were basic errors which you wouldn't expect to see at this level," fumed Roeder. "Unacceptable defending left us with a mountain to climb. If you play like that you've then got to score three goals and you won't do that every week."

Repka leapt to the defence of the Hammers' boss.

"It's not Glenn's fault, it's the players' fault," he confessed. "We know that we should be playing better than we are. It's up to us to make things better."

A 1-0 win at Sunderland, on the day that Howard Wilkinson and Steve Cotterill took charge of the Black Cats for the first time, led Roeder to declare: "We're out of the bottom three for the first time and must make sure that we don't go back."

Di Canio's late penalty then gave Hammers a 1-0 triumph at Fulham, which made it a hat-trick of successive away victories for the first time since 1995.

As the Roman sought an answer to the eternal question over his future, the club remained non-committal as to whether his contract would be extended.

"We don't feel it's an appropriate time to start talking," explained Roeder. "I can understand that Paolo wants to know what his future holds, but we need to be in safer waters before we can sit down and have any positive discussions."

Still Hammers had not won at home and with just two points from five matches at the Boleyn, Roeder switched training to Upton Park.

But Lee Carsley's goal still gave Everton a 1-0 win and just a week after becoming the Premiership's youngest-ever goalscorer, substitute Wayne Rooney – having just turned 17 – almost added a late second.

And there was more Mersey misery as a Michael Owen double gave Liverpool a 2-0 win at Anfield.

After being felled by the England goal-getter, it was the turn of two former Hammers' strikers to inflict further damage as Iain Dowie and his assistant, David Cross, brought second division Oldham Athletic to Upton Park for a Worthington Cup third round tie.

Yet again, West Ham – who had won 12 and drawn four of their 20 home games the previous season – could not muster that elusive Upton Park victory as Carlo Corazzin gave the Latics what was, perhaps, not such a shock victory after all.

"I'm hugely disappointed and I hope that the players feel just the same as me," admitted the dejected Roeder, trying to reconcile the performance he had just witnessed, with the one that had seen Hammers run Arsenal off Upton Park back in August. "I'm preparing them and sending them out down the tunnel but it just isn't happening. We can't run away from the situation and I can certainly understand the crowd – it's a natural reaction – but I feel exactly the same way."

The following day's headlines heaped yet more pressure on the beleaguered Hammers' boss.

"How many times have West Ham's disgruntled fans witnessed a similar scenario this season?" asked the *Evening Standard*. "The longer this awful home run goes on, the more clamour there will be for Roeder's head."

And *The Sun* added: "Roeder was jeered off to chants of 'What a load of rubbish.' Right now, the harsh truth is that West Ham are exactly that."

It would not get any better when Leeds United rolled into town.

Calamitous defending had seen Hammers trailing 1-4 at the interval, before Di Canio and Sinclair added some second half respectability to the scoreline.

"With the transfer window closed I've got no choice other than to say that the current group have got to stop defending so poorly," fumed Roeder after seeing his one-time QPR mentor Terry Venables send him back into the bottom three. "To score three times against Leeds and take nothing just makes me so angry."

As ineptitude reigned, again the newspapers had their say.

"If Glenn Roeder eventually loses his job, his players should hang their heads in shame. The Hammers were intent on firmly banging the nails into his coffin themselves with an appalling first half display in which they went 1-4 down – and it could have been eight," declared *The Sun*, once more.

"Roeder has six days to work out how the worst back four in the Premiership can hold off Manchester United," added *The Times*.

It looked like going to form when Ruud Van Nistelrooy put the Reds ahead but Hammers finally discovered a slice of luck when the clearly offside Defoe netted a late equaliser to force a morale-boosting 1-1 draw against United at Upton Park.

But it was a short-lived upturn.

A 1-4 defeat followed at Aston Villa, where James emerged to face the music with typical honesty.

"Last weekend I said that things couldn't get any worse than they had been and that after drawing 1-1 with Manchester United it could only get better.

"Yet six days later we're back to square one. The fans are upset and they've got every right to be angry. This result hasn't helped the manager or any of the players and, as a team, we all know that we've let West Ham United down badly.

"Things aren't good right now," agreed the no-nonsense 32-year-old as the tabloid head-hunters started sharpening their quills in an attempt, no doubt, to stimulate another spin of the managerial merry-go-round. "Today's defeat was not the manager's fault and as players we've certainly got to look at ourselves. It's not just the boss, the defence, the midfield or the attack, this is about all of us.

"We win, we draw and we lose as a team. One defeat is unlucky but after two, three or more, it becomes an issue and we've got to start turning things around.

"We've got international players here yet we're bottom of the Premiership. For me, somehow the two just don't go hand in hand."

With fragile Kanouté – having been injured for two months – abandoning a comeback on the eve of the crucial game, Ian Pearce was a shock choice to partner Defoe up front against Southampton at Upton Park where the 'Brown Out' banners were soon unfurled in force.

And the 33/1 shot almost left the bookies facing a bleak Christmas as he found himself with several chances to bag the first goal and land an extraordinary East End betting coup for those quick enough to see the team-sheets ahead of the cashiers in Ladbrokes' on-site booths.

But in the end, the makeshift striker drew a blank before James Beattie's 91st-minute goal gave the Saints a 1-0 win and left the desperate Hammers bottom of the Premiership, once more, to the fury of the hundreds who called for Brown to stand down in a post-match demonstration.

"We're in a hole, but half-a-dozen players ran themselves into the ground for me tonight, and while they do that, we've still got a chance to turn it around," insisted Roeder after taking just one point from a possible 18. "This is hurting me as much as our die-hard supporters but I'll fight on because I don't know any other way."

Whereas his predecessor had been able to wheel and deal his way to safety intra-season, the restrictions of UEFA's newly-imposed transfer window left Roeder willing the New Year to arrive.

But while the Hammers' boss was pinning his hopes on a refreshing re-shuffle following the opening of the January window, Brown had to decide whether to sack or back the hard-working, honest, Roeder.

"Glenn is a top-class coach," declared Brown, clearly looking to give the dreaded vote of confidence. "I have to be aware that he's manager during a time when we need to show financial caution and that he does not have the funds that have been made available to previous managers. These factors are not always immediately obvious to the supporters but they are very apparent to me."

With Di Canio forced out of action by a knee injury, Cole was named captain for the trip to Middlesbrough.

"Like many of the best players, he's already had so many amazing footballing experiences so age didn't really come into it," said Roeder, after handing the 21-year-old the armband. "I took him to one side and asked him if he wanted to take on the responsibility that comes with the job. His eyes literally lit up as though I'd given him a present. He's exactly the sort of character who should be captaining this club because he's a West Ham boy through and through. Joe's come up through the ranks here at Upton Park and he knows what wearing the West Ham United shirt really means."

And the goalscoring Cole responded with a captain's innings, while Pearce also finally found the net, too, but twice Hammers surrendered the lead as Ugo Ehiogu made it 2-2 with a late leveller.

Vladimir Labant (7+8 apps) had been a major disappointment following his £900,000 move from Sparta Prague and he went back to the capital of the Czech Republic on a one-year loan deal with a view to a permanent return home.

A 0-3 defeat at Manchester United, left Hammers bottom of the Premiership as they headed into their final game before Christmas, all too aware of the fact that history could soon be against them, too.

There is never a good time to be bottom of the table but none of the 10 teams previously in that perilous position on Christmas Day had ever escaped relegation from the Premiership.

When the in-form Pearce put Hammers ahead against Bolton Wanderers at Upton Park, West Bromwich Albion looked set to be the turkeys, but Michael Ricketts forced a 1-1 draw to condemn Hammers to bottom spot as they sat down for their Christmas lunch.

"Pardon my English but that statistic is s***!" announced Sebastien Schemmel following a familiar theme. "We have too many fantastic footballers here at Upton Park for us to go down. It just isn't possible to have four England internationals and all the other talented players for us stay at the bottom of the table."

And Breen agreed, adding: "The records may say that you'll be relegated but all I'd say to that is if you start thinking about the past you'll struggle. That's history and I know we're going to break that trend, I've got no doubts about that at all."

After seeing Hammers make it 11 league matches and one cup tie without a win at Upton Park, Roeder – insisting the initials 'GR' on his bench coat did not stand for Getting Relegated – argued: "What better motivation is there for my players than to prove history wrong by staying up after being bottom on Christmas Day."

Martin Samuel wrote in the *News of the World*: "And so this is Christmas and West Ham are done. No team finding itself bottom of the Premiership on December 25 has ever avoided relegation and frankly no team that has reached that date without winning a home game deserves to."

Certainly, having abandoned any East End xenophobia, the life-long Hammers' fan had a valid point.

Indeed, the last survivors were Sheffield United, back in the old Division One in 1990-91, and that made Hammers 8/11 shots with the bookmakers to be relegated.

Repka's senseless dismissal – his 25th card in 53 games – in the Boxing Day clash with Fulham, left Hammers walking off at Upton Park just thankful for their 1-1 draw. But after making just seven starts all season, Kanouté hobbled away with a recurrence of his groin injury and flew with physio John Green to Vancouver for specialist one-on-one treatment with Alex McKechnie.

And as West Ham pulled down the curtain on 2002, Defoe's late equaliser bagged an unlikely 2-2 draw at Blackburn Rovers after James let in a soft Damien Duff effort.

Forget Shrewsbury Town's 2-1 win over Everton, the shock of the FA Cup third round was Hammers' 3-2 win over first division Nottingham Forest at Upton Park. That hard-fought home win which finally came at the 13th time of asking – on January 4 – secured a daunting fourth round tie at Old Trafford.

And Hammers almost followed up the feat against Newcastle United, but Jermaine Jenas' first-ever Premiership goal earned the Magpies a 2-2 draw.

"We may be off the bottom but I'd rather be another place further up the table," said Roeder after seeing his side leapfrog West Bromwich Albion.

"The one nugget of hope is that – bad as they are – West Ham might just be a little bit better than some of the others," suggested the *News of the World*.

But the real issue of the day had been the pre-match protests at the arrival of Lee Bowyer from Leeds United on a short-term contract for a fee estimated at around £100,000, until the end of the season.

Only a few months earlier, Liverpool boss Gerard Houllier had pulled out of a £9m deal for the once-capped England player stating that he was unconvinced of his desire to play for the Merseysiders.

On a surreal Saturday lunchtime in Green Street, in the London Borough of Newham – where some 56% of the population were ethnic – a line of mounted police kept the divide between those dishing out leaflets proclaiming "West Ham fans United against racism" and those chanting *Rule Britannia*.

However, the confrontational, 26-year-old midfielder was carrying more baggage than Louis Vuitton.

After failing a drugs test at Charlton Athletic, he had smashed up a McDonald's before being cleared at his Hull Crown Court re-trial of being involved in his pals' drunken attack upon Sarfraz Najeib as they belatedly celebrated Bowyer's 23rd birthday. But he had also been refused the award of his estimated £1m costs by Mr Justice Henriques who considered that his police interviews, following the savage beating of the Leeds' student, were 'littered with lies'.

And just for good measure, on the day he signed for West Ham he also received a six-match ban from UEFA for stamping on the head of Malaga midfielder Gerardo during Leeds United's UEFA Cup campaign.

After refusing to sign a new contract at Elland Road, where he still reportedly owed the club legal fees of around £1m payable at £5,000 per week, Bowyer was rumoured to be on a seven-figure bonus if he could help West Ham – the team he claimed to support – avoid the dreaded drop, come May.

Indeed, after apparently attracting the interest of eight other clubs, his arrival back in the East End was shrouded in controversy from the moment he ignored official lens man Steve Bacon to be exclusively photographed holding a Hammers' shirt by Tony Hampson – the son of youth development manager, Jimmy.

But with the club seemingly under the naive impression that the image was to be used solely for the player's personal website, a bizarre misunderstanding led to the subsequently sold snapshot being splashed all over the back pages of *The Sun*.

Having seen its thunder stolen, the embarrassed club's proposed unveiling of Bowyer was consequently abandoned.

Roeder's predecessor had famously declared that 'desperate times call for desperate measures' and the present incumbent could not have been more needy as the controversial, curious deviation from his hitherto admirable mantra of only signing steady, stable, family men demonstrated.

"In different circumstances, we would not normally have been able to afford him," announced Roeder after seeing Bowyer – who was raised in an end-of-terrace council house in Poplar – receive the most mixed of mixed Upton Park receptions. "I will only be talking about Lee's football ability and the qualities he can bring to our team and that is all he wants to do, too.

"Everyone under the sun has got their own opinion on him but already he's shown that he doesn't want to play in the comfort zone and has come to West Ham because he wants to be involved in a pressure situation."

A far less controversial acquisition was veteran striker Les Ferdinand, who signed from Tottenham Hotspur for £200,000 following a reported spat with White Hart Lane boss, Glenn Hoddle, who insisted he had to buy before he could sell.

The 36-year-old former Queens Park Rangers and Newcastle United goal-getter had previously been linked with West Ham on numerous occasions and, while injuries had punctuated the twilight of his career, 17-times capped 'Sir Les' – who had netted 168 league goals in 376 appearances – was to prove a good influence.

One striker who had not made the grade at Upton Park was Titi Camara. Appearing overweight and lethargic, he had even failed to set reserve team games alight and with no future in E13, he headed yet further eastwards to the lucrative footballing fields of the Gulf States.

No longer were the ageing stars and misfits of the game put out to grass.

With oil-rich sheikhs looking for their kicks, seasoned internationals such as Steffen Effenburg and Bebeto were invited to ignore the sands of time and try their luck amongst the dunes of the Sahara desert.

Departing on loan, never to return, the exit of £1.5m Camara (7+7 apps) alongside Song (£2.5m) Soma (£800,000) and Todorov (£500,000) meant that just over two years on, the lone survivor of Redknapp's Rio spree was his only British acquisition, Christian Dailly (£1.75m).

Adding on the loan signings, wage costs, bonuses, agents fees and a sprinkling of associated 'extras', Brown knew that the club was not that much better off than if it had let the £18m Ferdinand depart on a free transfer.

"Glenn Roeder said my fitness was not good," Camara told the *Sunday Telegraph*. "Why did he play Ian Pearce, a defender, up front? Why didn't he give me a chance? I just don't think that he understands football."

And after scoring a 16-minute hat-trick in his second game in Qatar, the striker was lavished with cash and gifts including three luxury cars. Add a presidential hotel suite, a private villa, servants and security staff and the Upton Park flop was doing very nicely in the Middle East, thank you very much.

"I was going through a difficult time at West Ham," he later told *The Sun*. "But when I feel sorry for myself I just count my money – I'm loaded!"

And the greedy Guinean's *piece de resistance* was a subsequently fruitless attempt to sue the club in the High Court for breach of contract.

"From the details that we have so far been given, the club believes the action to be wholly without merit and we will vigorously defend any proceedings that are ultimately served," said company secretary, Scott Duxbury.

Following his own goal in the previous season's defeat at Blackburn Rovers, Grant McCann (0+4 apps) never kicked a ball for the Hammers again and joined Bobby Gould's Cheltenham Town in a £50,000 deal, while Frenchman Laurent Courtois (5+3 apps) returned home to FC Istres after failing to make any impact.

At Highbury, the unlucky Steve Lomas was red carded in the 13th-minute and, although Defoe wiped out Thierry Henry's consequent penalty, the Frenchman's hat-trick gave Arsenal a 3-1 win. West Ham's plight was summed up by the fact that Henry scored his first-ever headed Premiership goal . . . in his 122nd game for the Gunners.

There was more derby misery at Charlton Athletic, too, where a re-scheduled game – following a New Year's Day wash-out – ended in an embarrassing 2-4 defeat as the Addicks scored all six, both Hammers' efforts coming in the shape of Richard Rufus and Mark Fish own goals.

"There are four teams at the bottom, three are going to pay the biggest price and one will survive," observed Roeder, whose job was dangling by a thread. "We've got to make sure that one is us."

Quite frankly, too many players were underperforming. While Cole was giving his all in every game, players such as World Cup quarter-finalist Sinclair were living off past glories.

Indeed, following his return from a loan spell at Millwall, enthusiastic, energetic, 18-year-old, England U-20 defender Glen Johnson was thrown into the mix as Roeder desperately looked for that elusive winning formula.

"It is still hard to believe a team with such talent is in so much trouble," declared the *Daily Mirror*.

But too many players believed everything would simply be alright on the night.

And following an FA Cup fourth round humiliation at Old Trafford, where a live Sunday lunchtime television audience saw the red tide of Manchester United brush Breen – on his last-ever start for the club – and his fellow defenders aside, ex-Hammers' boss, Lou Macari, delivered his own damming verdict.

"The players have got to realise that they're earning big money at West Ham – probably more than the club has ever paid – and they've got to go out there and earn it by playing 90 minutes of hard-working football," insisted the no-nonsense Scot after witnessing the 6-0 slaughter. "There were 9,000 supporters here from Upton Park and the majority of those stayed until the end of the game, which was a lot longer than I would have done to be honest! The work rate was poor today. The penny's got to drop that ability, alone, is just not going to be good enough.

"Glenn Roeder's got to ask them to pull their fingers out, earn their wages and show some real fighting spirit for both the fans and himself between now and May. They've got to work harder otherwise I can't see a way out of trouble for them."

Before his counterpart prepared to make the long, thought-provoking journey south, Sir Alex Ferguson took Roeder to one side.

"Stick at it," the sorcerer urged the beleaguered apprentice, who had never been afraid to listen to advice or seek guidance from his elders.

Notwithstanding their spats over both Sinclair and Bernard, Bobby Robson's counsel had often been sought, and there were even rumours circulating that he had made tentative enquiries to see whether John Lyall would be interested in putting down his fishing rod to return to Upton Park as a part-time consultant.

Despite that drubbing, just three days later, rock-bottom Hammers incredibly recorded their first home Premiership victory, when Defoe's late strike gave them a 2-1 win over Blackburn Rovers in front of 34,743 loyal, long-suffering fans.

"We embarrassed our football club at Old Trafford," admitted Roeder after finally breaking his Upton Park duck. "But I now hope this is a turning point in our season. There's still a lot of hard work to do but this result really makes us believe that we can survive."

But sadly it was business as usual when Liverpool rolled into town, four days later, and went 2-0 up inside nine minutes before leaving with a 3-0 win.

It proved a baptism of fire for substitute Rufus Brevett, who with the January transfer window about to slam shut, made a last-gasp dash from Fulham.

As he signed autographs through the Colditz-like railings surrounding the Upton Park players' car park, the icy stare said it all.

For following that crushing debut defeat, one cheeky teenager in the small throng of post-match stragglers had the audacity to ask the new-boy whether he was looking forward to playing Nationwide League football the following season.

Shaking his dreadlocks in the chill, East End night, the puzzled defender fixed his gaze and answered with two clinical questions that left his interrogator somewhat thankful for the presence of the metal barrier.

"Do you think I would have come here if I thought we were going to get relegated?" he asked. "And do you really call yourself a West Ham fan, mate?

"We've all got to believe that we're going to get out of this situation.

"As soon as you lose that faith then you're in trouble and that applies to the manager, the players, the supporters and everyone connected with the club."

With the continental invasion limiting the midfielder's opportunities at Highbury, Arsenal's 21-year-old former England youth international, David Noble also signed on a short-term contract until the end of the season, alongside University College Dublin defender, Clive Delaney.

Kanouté's sending off for his attack on Seth Johnson did not help Hammers' cause on Bowyer's return to Elland Road, where Leeds United won 1-0.

As international week arrived, the Boleyn Ground hosted its first full international – a friendly between England and Australia.

While James and Cole were named in the squad, there was to be no place for the out-of-form Sinclair.

Certainly, it was nothing new when the Hammers' keeper found himself picking the ball out of the Upton Park net after Tony Popovic and Harry Kewell sent the Aussies racing into a 2-0 interval lead, against a Three Lions' side containing the returning Rio Ferdinand and Frank Lampard.

And the game turned to farce after the break when Eriksson, having changed his entire XI at half-time – still leaving Cole rooted to the bench – saw Francis Jeffers pull one back, only for Brett Emerton to secure a 3-1 victory for the Socceroos.

Away on international duty with the Republic of Ireland, Breen was quick to distance himself from Hammers' defensive crisis.

"I love being in a team that's organised as opposed to what's at home," he said. "I don't know if everyone at West Ham knows what they're supposed to be doing. I look at the squad and it's very talented – just as I thought when I made my decision to join them – but for some reason…"

There was anarchy at The Hawthorns as Hammers took on West Bromwich Albion in a must-win encounter.

A full-blown row between Repka and James proved mere undercard fodder, for the main event saw Di Canio explode at Roeder when his manager substituted him, two minutes into the second half.

The Italian had pulled up like a thoroughbred racehorse just before the break and, despite insisting he was fit to continue, it was patently obvious to everyone in the 27,042 crowd that he was not.

When Roeder decided to pull rank just after the restart with Hammers leading through Sinclair's opener, Di Canio went ballistic. Danny Dichio's equaliser did little to placate the irate Italian, but in the end Roeder was vindicated as Sinclair secured a priceless 2-1 victory with his second goal of the game.

Just a month earlier, Sinclair found himself dropped for the first time in a decade. And with Hammers trawling the depths of the Premiership, he had now lost his international place, too.

"It was only right that I was left out and if I couldn't get into the West Ham side then I wasn't going to get into the England squad, was I?" he admitted. "I've got a reputation now because I played in the World Cup and there's a lot more expectation surrounding me these days.

"I was facing my 30th birthday thinking: 'Bloody hell, is this the shape of things to come?' I looked at myself in the mirror and told myself that I had to be hungrier.

"Looking back I'd probably got myself into a comfort zone and lost my edge but I realise that the ball's in my court to go and win my England place back. That's my goal and hopefully I'll succeed.

"At West Ham we've totally underachieved this year but it's definitely in our own hands to make sure that we get ourselves out of trouble.

"We'll survive because there's too much spirit and confidence around the place for us to get relegated, but you can also understand the fans getting a bit panicky."

That spirit was not everywhere, though.

If Breen's outburst had created tension, then the decision not to renew Di Canio's contract just poured more rocket fuel on the flames of discontent.

"Glenn Roeder is still a young manager and he makes mistakes," argued the Italian. "Just because we won at West Bromwich, it doesn't mean that his decisions were all good ones."

The Hammers' boss refused to rise to the bait.

"I have no need to respond to personal criticism, all I'm interested in is the team, not individuals," he replied.

"It's not meant to be about one player, it's about the club," agreed Defoe who often found himself 'rested' to make way for the Italian. "You can't pick one player just to keep him happy. You have to pick the best side to get you the result. There were a lot of times when I should've been playing. Who wants to be rested?"

The injured Di Canio was absent as Ferdinand produced the perfect moment to score his first Hammers' goal when he found the net against former club Spurs in a 2-0 win at Upton Park.

"At the final whistle the PA system played the theme from *The Great Escape*," wrote David Lacey of *The Guardian*. "Roeder's team has shown a sudden willingness to dig in for survival even if they may still end up in the commandant's office rather than outside the perimeter fence."

A goalless draw followed at Everton, while Alan Pardew apologised for attempting to lure Di Canio – by now cast aside by Roeder and receiving treatment in Bologna – on loan to Reading.

Going into April, both Sunderland and West Bromwich Albion had demonstrated that they were by far and away the worst two sides in the Premiership.

Indeed, a 2-0 win over the Black Cats at Upton Park lifted Hammers out of the bottom three at Bolton's expense. With just 19 points on the board from 31 games – compared to West Ham's haul of 30 points – the Wearsiders were all but down.

While that victory secured the Barclaycard Manager-of-the-Month award for Roeder, his wry counterpart Mick McCarthy found little to cheer.

"Do we score in training?" replied 19-goal Wearsiders' boss McCarthy to a post-match question. "Occasionally!"

Following a 1-1 draw at Southampton, it also finished all-square at 2-2 against Aston Villa at Upton Park.

"There are 15 points to play for and we're going to be playing for every single one," said Roeder after Hammers' poor finishing resulted in a slip back into the bottom three. "There's a massive belief here that, come May, we'll be okay."

Still, Hammer-of-the-Year elect Cole was shining like a beacon in a sea of negligence as he desperately tried to lead West Ham to safety.

"It has only been in the past couple of months that we've shown the kind of strength and belief needed. Hopefully, it has come in the nick of time," he said.

Going to the Reebok Stadium, Hammers – who had just signed a four-year sponsorship deal with the same kit manufacturers – stood in 18th-place with 32 points from 33 games, compared to Bolton Wanderers, whose 35 points left them in the comparative safety of 17th place.

The stakes were high and frustration thresholds low and, after Jay-Jay Okocha netted what proved to be the winner, Pearce was dismissed while Cole and Brevett were charged by the FA – at the behest of Greater Manchester Police – following a full-time skirmish with Bernard Mendy and anyone brave enough to come near the angry duo. Cole was eventually fined £15,000 and banned for two matches some 227 days later, while Brevett's punishment amounted to a £1,000 fine.

"I'd rather run around Bolton in an England shirt," said unused substitute Dailly, whose misery was compounded by the victories for Aston Villa, Fulham and Birmingham City that still left West Ham six points adrift of safety, when asked to offer some post-match comment.

"It should never have come to this but the writing has been on the wall for the past couple of months," said Tony Gale putting down his Capital Gold Sport microphone following an eventful 90 minutes commentating. "You've got to examine the start of the season and the middle of it, too. At times it was useless but ever since West Ham have got themselves into serious trouble they've played with the opinion that: 'We're too good to go down, it'll be alright next week. We're too good to go down, it'll be alright next week...' Everyone has tried to warn them that nobody's too good to be relegated but they just haven't listened.

"It's only a slim chance but something might still happen to save them," continued the hopeful, if not convinced, Galey. "Whatever happens, though, West

NEARLY REACHED THE SKY

Ham have got to win all their remaining games if they're going to survive. Nobody knows the ramifications of going down at the moment. Who'll go? Who'll stay? If West Ham have to sell one or two, then so be it, but if I was a player I'd have to say that I owed it to the club to stay for another season.

"Players have to be honest enough to accept responsibility for this. They certainly should not be looking around the dressing room blaming the player sitting next to them or opposite them. After all, it's time for the team to stand up and be counted. If they are honest, then the players have got to realise that it's themselves – and no-one else – who have put West Ham United into this situation."

After climbing the stairs of his Essex home on Easter Sunday, Roeder lay awake preparing for the following Bank Holiday afternoon's visit of Middlesbrough. But his thoughts were disturbed by a mindless, drunken yob who hurled a full bottle of beer through the bedroom window of his teenage daughter Holly.

It was hardly the ideal preparation for a must-win game, and with the match goalless with just 15 minutes left, boos rang out as he emerged from the dug-out.

"I wasn't sure whether it was Don Hutchison or me getting the stick!" he quipped after curiously spending most of the match on the bench rather than in his more familiar arms-crossed pose on the edge of the technical area.

But his post-match relief was tangible, thanks to Sinclair's subsequent 77th-minute winner that had given 18th-place Hammers (Played 35/Points 35) a lifeline as they kept in touch with Leeds United (P-34 Pts-38) and Bolton (P-35 Pts-39).

His post-match media duties over, Roeder sat on the sofa in his office sipping a glass of white wine with coaches Roger Cross and Ludek Miklosko plus the trusted Ken Dyer of the *Evening Standard*.

Suddenly, a so-called life-and-death victory was about to find itself put firmly into perspective when the Hammers' collapsing manager slipped sideways across the sofa before falling in and out of consciousness.

Fortunately, club doctor, Ges Steinbergs was on hand until the ambulance arrived to rush Roeder to the Royal London Hospital in Whitechapel, where he was kept heavily sedated for five, long days as the medics diagnosed that he had an operable brain tumour causing the blockage of a minor blood vessel in his brain.

In grave danger with just three games left to go, worryingly, the club had now lost its critically ill manager, too.

Chapter 17
2002-03

CRITICAL CONDITION

Forgetting points targets, forgetting fellow strugglers and forgetting the fact that Hammers were about to enter the most telling three games of their recent history, goalkeeper David James was single-mindedly focused on one thing.

"The only issue that matters here is that West Ham United have got to go out there and win each of their three remaining matches," he said.

"It's as simple as this: Manchester City, Chelsea and Birmingham City represent three games where we've got to get three victories.

"People fall down trying to distinguish between differing levels of cruciality. You mustn't say one period of a season or even your career is more vital than another.

"If you look at the top players in any sport, they just go out there and try to play their best all the time. They treat each and every game as importantly as the next – no matter how big or small it may be."

But even if now manager-less West Ham United played their best, they were still reliant upon Bolton Wanderers or Leeds United slipping up.

Cometh the hour, cometh the man.

And the Upton Park board were fortunate to have a figurehead in the shape of Trevor Brooking to step into the breach alongside Roger Cross and Paul Goddard.

"It certainly wasn't my idea that I should take charge but what are the options?" asked the Hammers' director as – Superman-like – he slipped out of his boardroom business suit and into a training ground tracksuit. "It would have been unfair and totally insensitive to bring someone in from outside the club and the feeling was that this will keep everyone solid and together during the weeks ahead."

The 47-times capped Hammers' idol turned media pundit may have possessed a soft-looking outer layer, but inside there was a hard centre.

Beyond that gentlemanly exterior, Brooking, a well-educated, Barking-born son of a policeman, was no happy-go-lucky, laid-back pushover.

Certainly, nobody playing nearly 700 first-class matches could be.

A man of immense integrity, he did not suffer fools gladly and was often visibly frustrated when other people's standards fell below those of his own.

Indeed, many under-estimating politicians had discovered that to their cost when he had been chairman of Sport England battling for grass-roots causes.

Likewise, at the other end of the scale, while trying to ply their amateur trade for Havering Nalgo, many Brentwood Sunday League kickers and hackers had incurred the wrath of a man who had played at the Spain 82 World Cup.

Indeed, the myth that Brooking never cursed had been dispelled on many Essex pitches, too.

"I want to talk to you at half-time about your first touch," he once instructed a less than competent left-back who would have made a saint swear.

Upon eagerly approaching the international midfielder for some interval coaching advice, the hapless defender was promptly told: "First touch? You just haven't got one, have you?"

And as he prepared the side for the trip to Manchester City, Brooking – who had no real hands-on coaching experience – would also have found many of the club's high-earning players falling well below his own high standards, too.

"Am I being paid?" replied Brooking, who had seen more Premiership football than most in his roving commentary role. "I really don't know. We haven't discussed it because it's not even an issue. Someone will pipe up at some stage."

Ironically, in the opposing Maine Road dug-out was his former international team-mate and friend, Kevin Keegan – the other half of England's famous late 70s Trev 'n Kev double act.

After seeing his counterpart censured by the fourth official for his countless, animated, illegal forays out of the technical area, the City boss later observed: "Trevor's new to management, he doesn't know what to do!"

With the game goalless at half-time, Brooking bravely went for a 4-3-3 formation throwing on Kanouté. And even though the brave Les Ferdinand was soon stretchered off, Hutchison stepped from the bench to keep up the pressure.

That attacking strategy paid off, for with just nine minutes remaining, Kanouté bagged a precious winner.

"It's been a tough week!" announced Brooking after the 1-0 win. "One point was never going to be enough to keep the pressure on our fellow teams at the bottom of the table and that's why we had to push on. We were desperate for three points.

"Glenn Roeder already had everything mapped out for the week, so the players and the staff also deserve a pat on the back. This is a huge boost, because although it's out of our hands now, this win keeps us bubbling along."

The following day, the great and the good of West Ham United were gathered at another main road. This time, they were at the junction of Green Street and Barking Road, just a goal kick from the main gates, where the 'Champions' sculpture was unveiled by Prince Andrew, HRH, The Duke of York.

Philip Jackson's £750,000, four-tonne, bronze celebration of England's 1966 World Cup triumph depicted Bobby Moore holding the Jules Rimet trophy aloft perched upon the shoulders of Hammers' team-mates Geoff Hurst and Martin Peters . . . and Everton's Ray Wilson.

It might have mirrored the lasting pose of that famous day but, amazingly, all thoughts of artistic licence had gone out of the window for the joint venture between the club and the London Borough of Newham.

Saturday, July 30, 1966 witnessed the country's finest two sporting hours.

And never have three players given so much for their country than the West Ham United triumvirate of Moore, hat-trick hero Hurst and second goalscorer, Peters.

Certainly, it would be hard to imagine Manchester United allowing the

Evertonian to gatecrash a monument to their own 1966 winners, Bobby Charlton and Nobby Stiles, while none of the legendary Hammers would have expected to be cuckoos at Wilson's Goodison Park, either.

Forget the image of the day, as much as the Blues' defender was every part of the 4-2 triumph over West Germany, the East End would have preferred an exclusive three-man monument solely depicting their very own trio of Hammers' heroes.

Another modern day idol, Paolo Di Canio, returned for his last-ever game at Upton Park against Chelsea and, while he had not seen eye-to-eye with Roeder, the fit-again Italian started with a clean slate as far as Brooking was concerned.

Football-wise, Di Canio was what Brooking would have prescribed for any team.

Yet again, the caretaker went for a three-pronged attack and, in a bid to end a goalless stalemate, he launched the Italian into action 10 minutes after the break.

Typically, it was pure theatre as Di Canio pulled down the curtain on the Upton Park stage he had made his own, with a 70th-minute winner.

"The players have come up with the goods," said the modest Brooking after masterminding a second successive 1-0 victory. "I went with three strikers while I also had Paolo waiting in the wings. I had no doubt that I'd be using him and he got the winner on his last appearance here at Upton Park. It had to be!

"This result means a lot to everyone but for many weeks now I've always thought that the final trip to Birmingham City will be the hardest game of the lot."

Incredibly, the win moved Hammers onto 41 points – one more than Roeder's pre-season safety target.

But if 18th-placed West Ham (goal difference minus 17) were to retain their Premiership status, they would need even more going into their final match.

For Bolton, still in 17th spot, level on 41 points (goal difference minus 11) faced Middlesbrough at home.

Although Ferdinand gave Hammers a glimmer of hope by putting Hammers ahead at Birmingham, fate was always conspiring against them at the Reebok Stadium where 10-man Boro fell 0-2 behind.

In the end, Wanderers won 2-1, while West Ham subsequently found themselves trailing by the same scoreline.

And Di Canio's last-gasp equaliser at St Andrew's proved fruitless as the crestfallen Hammers surrendered their top-flight status.

Unbeaten Trevor Brooking's treble chance had not paid a winning dividend.

But at least his undefeated three-game reign had seen Hammers go down kicking and screaming with a determination that had so sadly been missing for so long.

"It was only a three-week burst for me but I'm pleased with the quality and character demonstrated by the lads," said the caretaker as he prepared to put his head back below the parapet and hang up his overalls following the 2-2 draw.

"As far as management is concerned, that's it for me," continued Trevor, no doubt taking heed of fellow pundit Gary Lineker's text-message to him: 'Quit now while you're a genius!'

"Apart from, perhaps, putting the ball into the net a few more times, though, I couldn't have asked for any more. We've played really well and the supporters have seen us give our all. We've restored a bit of pride and have seen in recent weeks that there is enough talent here to do okay in the Premiership. We've shown the fans that we still feel for this club and they've been fantastic, but we're going to have to ask them to be loyal to us now that we find ourselves relegated.

"We were in trouble at Christmas but it's a strange situation to go down with a record 42 points. Now we've got to look to repay them by bouncing straight back.

"The players have certainly found their belief, confidence and spirit and I said to them at St. Andrew's before the Birmingham game: 'I know which dressing room I'd rather be managing' That's the real frustration for me.

"Relegation will take time to sink in but it's been at the back of my mind that this would happen. We just wanted to keep things going for as long as we could.

"We also need to look back upon what happened in the first half of the season," he continued after seeing Hammers win 22 points out of a possible 33 during a battling 11-game run-in.

Brooking might well have been in a no-lose situation.

But as a man of immense pride, he had put his unblemished reputation within the game on the line and risked succumbing to some sorry three-match capitulation.

From the moment he had sat in the Upton Park hot-seat, his collective band of under-achievers had instantly oozed respect for their stand-in leader.

Playing with pride and passion, they had come so close to engineering an escape that would have demoted the late, great Harry Houdini to the supporting cast.

Equally, Brooking had raised eyebrows, too, as he quickly became engulfed in a frantic fervour that saw him kick every ball, from the first whistle to the last.

And he celebrated the Hammers' goals with more rapture than he ever did as a player, when he struck on 102 occasions for West Ham and five times for England.

"We've got to let relegation and all its implications sink in," he added. "There certainly won't be any rash decisions as we start to think about putting the right structure in place that can give us an opportunity to bounce straight back.

"We're despondent but we can't afford to feel sorry for ourselves for too long.

"We'll sit around as a group and look at the decisions that need to be taken.

"Hopefully, we'll also be able to see how Glenn's recuperation goes. We want to see where one or two of the players want to go, too!

"By the same token we also need to be left with a nucleus that can try and give us a bit of hope that we can return straight back to the Premiership next season.

"We'll see what develops but we want to be in a position where we've still got a squad that can give us a decent chance.

"But to say who's staying and who's going is just impossible at the moment and there's bound to be a lot of speculation. I can't see us having the same squad at the start of next season, though, compared to what we've got now.

"In any event, there's a £15m-plus gap and we've got to reduce the wage bill. It's reckoned you should try and half your salary burden but you also need a squad that can cope with 46 Nationwide league games rather than 38 in the Premiership. It's not going to be an easy balancing act.

"No-one has indicated a desire to stay or go so far and, while a lot depends upon what happens to the squad during the summer, we're certainly confident and upbeat enough to believe that we can come straight back at the first attempt.

PLAYERS IN

Lee Bowyer	Leeds United	£100,000
Gary Breen	Coventry City	Free transfer
Rufus Drevett	Fulham	Undisclosed
Les Ferdinand	Tottenham Hotspur	£200,000
David Noble	Arsenal	Free transfer
Youssef Sofiane	Auxerre	Free transfer
Raimond Van Der Gouw	Manchester United	Free transfer

LOANS IN

Edouard Cissé	Paris Saint-Germain
Clive Delaney	University College Dublin
Brent Rahim	Levski Sofia

PLAYERS OUT

'Titi' Camara	Al-Ittihad	Free transfer
Leon Britton	Swansea City	Free transfer
Gary Charles		Retired
Laurent Courtois	FC Istres	Released
Hayden Foxe	Portsmouth	£500,000.
Vladimir Labant	Sparta Prague	Undisclosed
Grant McCann	Cheltenham Town	£50,000
Brent Rahim	Luton Town	Released
Ragnvald Soma	FC Bryne	Undisclosed.

Chapter 18
2003-04

GREEN STREET CLEARANCE SALE

Billy Bonds had been relegated both as a West Ham player and manager.

And as the club started looking to unlock the door back to the Premiership, the Upton Park legend called upon the players to demonstrate similar loyalty to that which he, alongside one-club men such as Trevor Brooking, Frank Lampard, Alvin Martin and Alan Devonshire, had shown in years gone by.

"Talk of a £15m-£20m loss has been bandied around and that's a lot of money to forfeit," he said as he surveyed the wreckage of relegation. "And while the club has to make cutbacks, there are also individuals who will want to jump ship.

"I think the players are all entitled to give it one more year. They owe it to the club, the fans and themselves to see whether they can bounce straight back to the Premiership, but we'll just have to see whether or not that turns out to be the case.

"There was a certain loyalty in my days but the game's a bit different now."

No kidding.

For less than 24 hours after the bell had tolled to signal that West Ham had arrived kicking and screaming in the Nationwide League, Jermain Defoe was the first player to hand in a transfer request.

It was declined.

"The timing was absolutely terrible," confirmed Bonds, whose own proud playing career had been characterised by both honour and integrity. "The kid's had bad advice. You would certainly expect things to have been handled a bit more delicately and sensibly just a day after the club had been relegated.

"I know that his request has been turned down and you can only hope that he accepts the situation and that the club ends up keeping him.

"There are teams out there aware of the fact that there are some good, young players at a club that has just seen its financial situation change dramatically.

"But the younger lads need to be here next season. If you're going to sell, then let the older players leave, because the kids are the ones to build your team around.

"Joe Cole's just had a fantastic season, Jermain Defoe's now firmly established himself on the scene and we all know what a great player Michael Carrick is. Glen Johnson has also brought commitment to the team, too.

"People are asking whether relegation to the Nationwide League will affect international careers but, personally, I think everyone knows what the West Ham boys can do and, most importantly, Sven-Goran Eriksson realises that they've already cut it in the Premiership, too.

"At the end of the Birmingham City game, I was sitting there watching the players coming off and thinking: 'Why are we going down?' When you look at the talent out there you have to ask whether West Ham were any worse than Blackburn Rovers and Everton, who ended up battling it out for that final UEFA Cup spot.

"West Ham probably had the best squad the club has ever assembled. It's certainly better than the teams that went down in my time here, so for me it all has to boil down to the individual commitment of the players.

"When you think about some of the stuff we saw around Christmas time, and when you also look back and remember that they didn't win at home until January, suddenly it isn't so hard to believe that West Ham have been relegated.

"To be honest, it was on the cards all year, wasn't it?

"The players have got to take a good look at themselves. Glenn Roeder is a very honest bloke and he will certainly have asked himself what he's done wrong."

With the tumour successfully removed from the right lobal side of his brain and a reducing daily dose of 14 tablets in his pocket, Roeder pencilled in July 1 as the day he would return to work.

"This experience has taught me so much," Roeder told Ken Dyer of the *Evening Standard* after they were reunited in far happier circumstances than that fateful Easter Monday. "The doctors and nurses who cared for me are the real stars, not footballers. They don't seek the limelight but every day they are saving lives.

"Anyone can have a brain tumour and stress didn't cause this. I blacked out because it had reached a certain size.

"But this whole affair has made me more determined to keep going because, as far as I'm concerned, there is unfinished business."

Working as hard as ever from the moment he brushed the dust off his desk at Chadwell Heath, Roeder was determined to make up for lost time.

"I've come back simply for one reason. I want to be given a fair opportunity to lead the club back to the Premier League at the first attempt."

Despite releasing eight players, Roeder knew the phone would soon start to ring as the Premiership colleagues he had left behind prepared to pillage the academy.

Having been linked to his beloved Lazio, Paolo Di Canio (136+4 apps 50 gls), his 35th birthday now passed, took a reported £25,000 per week pay cut to join Charlton Athletic in a £15,000 per week deal.

"The West Ham United supporters are incredible and they gave me so much strength," he declared as he said *arrivederci* to the East End before making the short trip through the Blackwall Tunnel. "You will not find fans like those in any other country. They are incredible and you just cannot put a price on that.

"The board decided that I must go and that is not a problem. When you get relegated, though, it's not only the players' fault. Yes, we go out on the pitch and I take my responsibility, not just when we win but also when we lose.

"But when you go down you have to share the blame with the coaches and the board, too. If you are at the bottom for one year, and you have the power to alter something and stop it from happening, then you must try and change it," he added, his post-mortem clearly establishing that Roeder's retention had been the cause of West Ham's demise. "That's only my opinion but it's about planning and changing things. It's not just about what happens out there on the pitch.

"My life at West Ham United is now finished and all I will say is that I just hope that this club can maintain a good team that will come back straight away.

"They have to do that for their supporters, because they deserve it. I can't imagine West Ham spending more than one year outside the Premiership. It won't be fair upon the fans if they're in the Nationwide League for any longer.

"I won't be here, but I will still be able to look back at the people and the supporters. Forget all of my goals, for me the best memory that I can take away from West Ham United will be the fans," said the prima donna after drinking up time was called on an explosive cocktail of tantrums, tears and thrills.

The rocky roller-coasting marriage might well have finally ended in an acrimonious divorce, but in the eyes of the fans, the inventive Italian had certainly repaid the club for salvaging his career by leaving an enthralled Upton Park audience on the edge of its seat more times that it could remember.

One man who had under-delivered, however, was Lee Bowyer (11 apps).

And his departure to Newcastle United on a free transfer following a non-descript spell was a far more subdued affair than his controversial arrival.

"I am saddened that Sir Bobby Robson has chosen to harbour such a disreputable man," observed *The Daily Telegraph's* Michael Parkinson.

Gary Breen (13+5 apps) headed for Sunderland, leaving the East End wondering how his name and that of Milan's mighty Internazionale had ever been mentioned in the same breath.

Edouard Cissé (21+7 apps) returned to France, where he joined AS Monaco, whom he helped into the 2004 Champions League final against FC Porto.

Scott Minto (55+7 apps) joined Rotherham United as Clive Delaney (0 apps) returned home to Ireland and Izzy Iriekpen (0 apps) headed to Swansea City, where he linked up with former Arsenal starlet Leon Britton (0 apps).

The lure of Premiership football tempted Les Ferdinand (12+2 apps 2 gls) to Leicester City before he headed to both Bolton Wanderers and then Reading, where he duly collected an MBE in HM The Queen's 2005 Birthday Honours' list.

Dutchman Raimond Van Der Gouw (0 apps) went to Stoke City on trial before returning home to RKC Waalwijk, while Nigel Winterburn (89+5 apps 1gl) simply retired alongside John Moncur (156+47 apps 9 gls)

Moncs had arrived at the same time as misfit Joey Beauchamp.

And while the homesick winger stayed for just 58 farcical days, the manic midfielder remained at Upton Park for nine eventful, remarkable years.

"It was such a privilege to be at West Ham for so long," said Moncur. "I feel so proud. These days players seem to get fed up after being somewhere for just two years but I've enjoyed every single day of my time here. I'm still only just getting over being told that I'm out of work. I could have left three times. Arsenal, Queens Park Rangers and Bolton Wanderers each wanted to sign me at one stage or another but I was always very happy at West Ham."

Certainly, his zany sense of humour, silky touches, never-say-die commitment and X-rated tackling made him a cult-hero on the terraces, during a double-century of appearances, nine goals, 66 bookings and three red cards.

"It was just so disappointing for me that we ended up getting relegated in my last season at the club. I just didn't think it was ever going to happen to us. We'd been involved in a couple of scrapes before and managed to get out of them and I always thought we were going to escape again.

"I couldn't believe it when we didn't," added Moncur shortly after making the surprise revelation that he was a committed Christian.

"I am what I am. People think that Christians are wimps but it doesn't mean you can't tackle, play pranks or have the odd drink. Football was my job and out on the pitch I was very competitive and always doing my best to win while trying to have a laugh at the same time."

Indeed, in a candid confession that suggested he was once out of control and treading the path towards self-destruction in a dangerous cocktail of alcohol, violence and even drugs. Moncs told *Observer Sport Monthly*: "There's a real stigma attached to being a Christian, both in football and in society. Look at the story of Jesus. He hadn't done a thing wrong yet he got battered; he walked with a cross on his back and got mullahed, and he knew he was going to die, but that through his dying the rest of us could have hope. To me that's the strongest geezer I've ever known. How many of us who think we're hard would do that?

"I suppose people will say that I'm the most unlikely Christian. As a young man I used to binge drink and that led to all sorts of aggravation. My temper has also always been a nightmare and I reached the point where I had to change. I'm definitely a better person for having found God. I'm a lot more at peace now."

According to *The Daily Telegraph*, the Hammers' board agreed to take a 50 per cent salary cut in the wake of the club's relegation.

The directors' emoluments of chairman Terence Brown had amounted to £540,822 in salary, benefits-in-kind and pension contributions during the year ended May 2003. Those of managing director Paul Aldridge totalled £249,662 while finance director Nick Igoe earned £179,651 and Charles Warner's remuneration was £50,000.

Consequently, during the year to May 2004, the executives' remuneration was, indeed, considerably less as Messrs Brown (£276,406), Aldridge (£132,727), Igoe (£94,921) and Warner (£25,000) kept to their word, agreeing that those higher numbers would only be reinstated if the club ever returned to the Premiership.

But having slashed their salaries and offloaded nine players already, ongoing cash generation remained vital.

And across London a slice of fortune came the club's way.

Roman Abramovich's takeover at Chelsea led to the rouble-rich Russian oligarch immediately making available £6m to Claudio Ranieri for the shock purchase of 18-year-old Johnson (14+2 apps).

In many ways, that surprise acquisition looked set to save the sale of another more established player.

But, alas, the squad still continued to dismantle, thick and fast.

Trevor Sinclair (202+3 apps 38 gls) was sold to Manchester City for £2.5m after resting on his international laurels and totally underperforming following his return from the 2002 World Cup finals.

NEARLY REACHED THE SKY

And Frederic Kanouté (87+5 apps 33 gls) was the next to leave in a £4m move to Tottenham Hotspur that saw £500,000-rated Matthew Etherington head to Upton Park in the opposite direction.

Like several other of the fragile French to have passed through the gates of Upton Park, the enigmatic and, at times, precious Kanouté had endured an injury-ravaged spell at West Ham.

A devout Muslim, his cause had not always been helped by his religious observance of Ramadan and other self-sacrificial festivals that had sometimes drained him of strength and, ironically, immediately upon arriving at White Hart Lane, he injured his groin.

Privately, Roeder was pinning the blame on Kanouté's limited dozen-game, five-goal season as the major factor in the club's relegation.

"We lost Fredi for six months," he rued. "Without another striker of his physical presence at the top end of the team we couldn't cope. From the moment he arrived at the club he was a major influence on us winning games, and the small size of our squad was exposed. And how can you expect to pick up points with a centre-half like Ian Pearce playing at centre-forward? My hands were tied with the transfer window closed and it wasn't until after Christmas, when Les Ferdinand, Rufus Brevett and Lee Bowyer came in, that we proved what we could achieve with a fully fit squad. We took 25 points from our last 14 games, which is Championship-winning form. It's not an excuse, it's a fact."

Following a pre-season tour of Sweden that had seen Hammers beat Atvidabergs 5-2 and share a goalless draw with Djurgardens IF, they rounded off their preparations with a visit from PSV Eindhoven.

An ill-advised interview with Sky Sports saw Sebastien Schemmel fined two weeks' wages for criticising Roeder and claiming that the club was trying to force him out after he reportedly turned down a £1m move to Glasgow Rangers.

And when the Frenchman turned up at Upton Park for the friendly against the Dutch, Roeder reportedly called for security to remove him from the dressing room, ahead of the 1-2 defeat.

Alerted to the availability of Schemmel (70+3 apps 1 gl), whose position was now untenable, Portsmouth's Harry Redknapp swooped to take yet another ex-Hammer to Fratton Park.

And before the season had even kicked off, the playing staff reduced yet further.

For Ranieri got Ambramovich's cheque book out once more to take his spending to £58.6m as he lured Joe Cole (126+23apps 13 gls) to Stamford Bridge for £6.6m after it was revealed that the England midfielder had told Hammers a year earlier that he would not be renewing his contract at the end of the 2003-04 season.

Nobody had tried harder than Cole to retain Hammers' Premiership status but while Carrick and Manchester United-target Defoe remained at the club, psychologically, his departure in the wake of the previous exits of Rio Ferdinand and Frank Lampard, now meant that the last pillar of the academy had toppled.

"I felt I'd gone as far as I could as a West Ham player," he said after insisting that he still would have left even if Hammers had stayed in the Premiership. "More than a year ago I was asked to sign an extension of my contract. The club had just finished seventh but I felt that to further my international career I would need to move on to a team that was playing regularly in Europe. For all my belief in West Ham United, I could not honestly see them competing at that level."

As the East Enders came to terms with the loss of their favourite son, Brooking, now back in the boardroom, admitted: "If we hadn't had 17,000 season ticket holders coming back we would have had to go into administration. I knew the implications of relegation and this is the harsh reality."

And chairman Brown told those season ticket holders: "During the last 18 months we had discussions with both the player and his father in an attempt to persuade Joe to extend his contract beyond summer 2004. Had financial terms been the issue, I am sure we would have reached agreement but, unfortunately, he wanted to play in the Champions League and felt that his future lay elsewhere. His preferred route was to fight to keep us in the Premier League and then leave to join a team playing in the Champions League, ensuring his place in England's Euro 2004 squad and delivering a large cheque for us to assist with team-building.

"His alternative route was to see out his contract and leave at the end of the current season under Bosman rules. Under those circumstances Joe was free to commence negotiations with foreign clubs on January 1, 2004 (five months' time) and we could not afford to find ourselves in a Sol Campbell or Lee Bowyer situation and, therefore, had to accept an offer during the close season.

"No club in the Nationwide League and few in the Premier League could invest nearly £8m in the services of one player, no matter how talented, to play a maximum of 46 league games at a cost of £200,000 per match.

"Joe is possibly the best all round product of the Academy in my time as chairman. He has a great deal of affection for the club and I would not be in the least bit surprised if, one day, we see him back here in a claret and blue shirt."

While that was an ambitious, hopeful ask, with so many vacant coat pegs in the dressing room, Roeder knew that he needed some low-budget, cheap bodies.

Moving the other way, David Connolly, a 37-times capped, Republic of Ireland striker was signed from Wimbledon for £285,000, while midfielder Kevin Horlock returned to Upton Park in a £300,000 transfer from Manchester City, having left Hammers for Swindon Town in 1992 without ever kicking a ball for the first team.

Leeds United's 19-year-old central defender Matthew Kilgallon headed south on three-months loan, while at the other end of the scale, 37-year-old Robert Lee finally achieved a lifelong ambition to sign for West Ham when he joined on a free transfer from Newcastle United.

In his quest to join his beloved West Ham United, the Plaistow-born Lee had experienced more false alarms than the London Fire Brigade, but as he prepared to extinguish the flames on an epic 750-game career, he had finally realised a burning ambition.

"It's no secret that I've always wanted to play for this club. I've been linked with transfers here so many times, but having been so near, and yet so far, on so many occasions, I must admit that I thought the opportunity had passed me by," said the 21-times capped England midfielder. "This is my last season so I'm very pleased to be here at last. You don't always get what you want in football. I'm very lucky."

NEARLY REACHED THE SKY

As Hammers travelled to Preston North End for the opening game of the season, the team-coach picked up Liverpool's on-loan Neil Mellor at a motorway service station on the way to Deepdale.

With new-signing Connolly controversially relegated to the bench in favour of Mellor, the visitors could not have got off to a worst start after Eddie Lewis put the Lilywhites ahead after just two minutes.

The £10m-rated Defoe – who had reportedly been dating David Beckham's sister Joanne – may have seen his chances of moving to Manchester United diminish following Becks' departure to Real Madrid and the Reds' acquisition of Cristiano Ronaldo, but he was certainly too good for the Nationwide League.

"Relegation was a step back and all of my mates have gone but, yes, the transfer request was bad timing," he admitted, seemingly pointing the finger at his advisors. "It should never have happened, but it wasn't me. That said, the club told me that they were going to try and keep us together, especially the youngsters like Cole, Carrick and Johnson. The England coach doesn't watch the first division. If he doesn't come to see us, how is he going to know who is playing well?"

Indeed, by the fifth minute, Defoe had bagged his first goal of the campaign and then Connolly stepped from the dug-out to secure a 2-1 victory.

But the striker – had previously played under Roeder at Watford – was not happy.

"I had been part of the starting line-up in training all week and then we picked up Neil Mellor and I was told he was playing instead of me," said the irate Irishman. "It's mind-boggling, a real kick in the teeth. I was very disappointed with the manager and I told him so. How can he pick someone who has only trained with us for an hour? I don't know if Mellor is going to play all the time but if he is, then I'm going to look for another club."

The *Sunday Mirror* cried: "Goal-scoring debutant slags off the manager and tells the world he'll be looking for a new club after a mere 30 minutes on the pitch. Welcome to the shambolic world of West Ham United."

After Di Canio's shenanigans the Irishman's outburst posed Roeder no problem.

"Connolly's an angry ant," he replied. "I gave him his debut at Watford when he was 16-years-old and he hasn't changed much. Am I going to get upset and let this take the gloss off the win? Not a chance."

The team that kicked off at Upton Park against Rushden & Diamonds in the Carling Cup was a shadow of the side that had beaten Chelsea in the final home Premiership game of the previous campaign.

Already the natives were restless.

Predictable cries of 'Brown Out' had filled the air at Deepdale.

And by the time the likes of lifelong supporter Dave Grant and thousands of his fellow season-ticket holders had filed their way through the Upton Park turnstiles to see two-goal Connolly and Defoe fire Hammers to the 3-1 win that would set up a second round tie at Cardiff City, they had each found the following letter from the chairman nestling on their doormats: *"During the forthcoming season the club will have to repay £8m of loans to its banks and our income will be reduced by £20m following relegation. As a result we had to find £28m cost savings in order to avoid very serious financial consequences. We have found that sum by reducing the wage cost of the playing squad by £10m and raising £18m net in transfer fees.*

Those who say we should have shown more ambition and kept the whole squad together – with £30m at stake if we are promoted – need to understand that by November we would have run out of cash and cheques would then have bounced.

I have been told by supporters that I should have been more open with them and explained to the whole football world that we needed to raise £20m. Had I done so my former Premier League colleagues would have smelt blood in the water.

Prior to the sale of Glen Johnson I received several telephone calls with offers for Trevor Sinclair (£500,000), Jermain Defoe (£1.5m), Glen Johnson (£1.5m) and Joe Cole (£2m) on the basis that we could save the wages. I was sorry to see Glen leave but the £6m received from Chelsea was the turning point and I received no further frivolous calls after he left.

I am also told that our problems have been caused by financial mismanagement but this is simply not the case. On 11 May 2003, our income was suddenly reduced by £20m per annum. No small business in the world could sustain such a blow without embarking upon a major financial reconstruction – bearing in mind we had the seventh highest wage bill in the Premier League in 2001-02 – and that is what has taken place at West Ham United, both on and off the pitch.

The only issue is whether the Board were best placed to carry out that financial reconstruction or whether an Administrator would have been better placed.

Before we all become submerged in the doom and gloom currently surrounding West Ham United, may I remind you of some good news:

1- We are now in a sound financial position and have delivered everything we promised to our banks.

2- Even after all the cutbacks we can still afford a player wage bill of £17m p.a.

3- We have no need to sell any more players for financial reasons and that includes Jermain Defoe.

4- We will be bringing in new players in the near future.

5- We have not reduced expenditure on The Academy. It remains in good shape.

6- Contrary to press reports, we have not sought to defer the players' salaries.

7- We have negotiated 25% sell-on fees in respect of Cole and Johnson,

Had we remained in the Premier League we would have made substantial profits and, with the wage bill reduced by £8m per annum, would have been in an excellent position to strengthen the squad and move forward.

I am sorry that last season went so horribly wrong for all of us and I thank every one of our supporters who have remained with us.

Sadly it did not work out in the way we all wished but the time has now come to stop looking back at what might have been and to start looking forward."

A goalless draw against Sheffield United at Upton Park in front of a respectable crowd of 28,792 continued an unbeaten start to the campaign, ahead of an ill-fated trip to Yorkshire.

After checking out the miniscule Millmoor dressing rooms, it was decided that the squad would start to get changed at their hotel before heading to the stadium to face Rotherham United.

But upon arriving at the ground, their 'southern softy' approach was misconstrued by local folk.

"Because of the size of the travelling squad and the amount of staff here, it made sense to get *partly* ready at our hotel and then come here and get fully prepared," insisted Glenn Roeder, denying the Big-Time Charlie accusations.

But they were the least of his worries, for Darren Byfield's 14th-minute goal had seen the Millers grind out a 1-0 victory.

"We've spoken lots of times about what to expect in this division," fumed Roeder. "And there are lessons to be learned from today. Rotherham competed in all areas of the pitch much better us, and consequently we conceded an early goal from which we never recovered. We should've recovered but we didn't."

While Christian Dailly had literally given blood after having his front tooth knocked clean out in an accidental collision with Richie Barker, Roeder had every right to be angry at an acute lack of Cockney commitment.

For with rookie right-back Anton Ferdinand playing only his second league game for the club, the manager was entitled to expect a senior professional, such as £5m Don Hutchison, to put in some effort, help protect the teenager and earn the level of wages that undoubtedly accompany a record transfer.

"The only surprise was that we were surprised," observed director Martin Cearns after seeing Hammers caught like startled rabbits in the headlights of Rotherham's bright early start.

And within 24 hours, the board had made the following announcement on its official website: *"West Ham United wish to announce that Glenn Roeder's contract has been terminated with immediate effect and he has been relieved of his duties as team manager.*

The Board would like to place on record their gratitude to Glenn for his hard work and commitment since his permanent appointment in June 2001. This was demonstrated by his desire to return to active duty so quickly after his recent illness and I am sure all supporters recognise how dedicated he was to the Club.

The Board, however, feel that the Club's best chance of returning to the Premiership at the first attempt would be enhanced by a change of manager."

Ironically, with Jobserve now the club's main sponsors, the recruitment agency's on-line, internet advertisement was placed under the luckless Roeder's photograph: 'Looking for a job? Jobserve have thousands of vacancies now!'

The disappointed Lee said: "I was totally shocked and very disappointed to see Glenn go. I'm finding it difficult to come to terms with the situation. Why did they let him bring in new players? I think he's been used a bit and the timing is unbelievable, too. Glenn certainly couldn't have gone on the basis of this season's four results – two wins, a draw and just one defeat."

For many, though, the writing had been on the wall from the day he took over.

And while the respectable seventh-place finish during his first season earned him the right to a second term, it was debatable as to just how long he should have been allowed to steer sinking West Ham towards the rocks of relegation.

After all, a dozen defeats without a home victory before Christmas were the vital statistics of failure.

In the end, off the pitch events were overtaken by his illness, and it would have been wholly lacking in compassion to have sacked their hospitalised manager in the wake of the calamitous drop to the Nationwide League.

But a carefully, stage-managed move to the sidelines on health grounds would have represented a far more dignified exit for a manager who was asked to oversee the £19m sale of the family silver before being given the heave-ho just those four games into the new season.

And the jinxed Roeder will forever argue that in his predecessor Redknapp's last season, Hammers had finished 15th in the Premiership with the self-same 42 points that had seen himself relegated.

Glenn Roeder's Managerial Record:

League:	**P-80**	**W-26**	**D-21**	**L-33**	**F-89**	**A-93**
FA Cup:	**P-5**	**W-2**	**D-1**	**L-2**	**F-9**	**A-12**
League Cup:	**P-4**	**W-1**	**D-1**	**L-2**	**F-4**	**A-3**
TOTALS:	**P-89**	**W-29**	**D-23**	**L-37**	**F-102**	**A-108**

Rob Shepherd, football editor of the *Daily Express*, announced: "The timing might seem insensitive, even cruel, but the brutal fact is Glenn Roeder had to go. That might sound harsh about a man who, four months ago, was on a life-support machine. But football is a harsh world and, awful as this sounds, he kept his job after West Ham were relegated only because of his illness. One has to admire the way he overcame his health problems but football-wise he was on borrowed time.

"There have been clear signs that Roeder has lost key figures in an already dispirited dressing room.

"And while there is a strong element of chairman Brown wielding the axe to deflect criticism of himself, Roeder is more suited as a No.2 than the boss."

In an *Evening Standard* interview, managing director Paul Aldridge later admitted: "I am sure most people would say our biggest mistake in the last five years was to appoint Glenn Roeder and, looking at the outcome of his second season, it would be hard to disagree.

"However, this only tells half the story: people forget that he took a team, which only narrowly missed relegation under Harry Redknapp, to seventh in the Premier League the following season.

"A combination of injuries to key players, and the effects of the first year of the transfer window, mask the fantastic effort put in by the squad after January when we strengthened the team, although ultimately our 42 points were not enough."

NEARLY REACHED THE SKY

PLAYERS IN

David Connolly	Wimbledon	£285,000
Matthew Etherington	Tottenham Hotspur	£500,000
Kevin Horlock	Manchester City	£300,000
Robert Lee	Newcastle United	Free transfer

LOANS IN

Matthew Kilgallon	Leeds United
Neil Mellor	Liverpool

PLAYERS OUT

Lee Bowyer	Newcastle United	Released
Gary Breen	Sunderland	Released
Edouard Cissé	AS Monaco	Released
Joe Cole	Chelsea	£6,600,000
Clive Delaney	UCD Dublin	Released
Paolo Di Canio	Charlton Athletic	Released
Les Ferdinand	Leicester City	Released
Glen Johnson	Chelsea	£6,000,000
Ezomo Iriekpen	Swansea City	Released
Frederic Kanouté	Tottenham Hotspur	£4,000,000
Scott Minto	Rotherham United	Released
John Moncur	Retired	
Sebastien Schemmel	Portsmouth	Free transfer
Trevor Sinclair	Manchester City	£2,500,000
Raimond Van Der Gouw	Stoke City	Released
Nigel Winterburn	Retired	

Chapter 19
2003-04

THE CARETAKER RETURNS

In Glenn Roeder's absence, once again, Hammers had a ready made stand-in.

An official club statement read: *"Trevor Brooking CBE will once again act as caretaker manager. Interviews will begin immediately and Glenn Roeder's successor will be appointed in due course. Until that time the Board has complete confidence in Trevor's ability to manage the team."*

And as Brooking dusted down the overalls that had seen him steer the club through last season's, unbeaten, three-game run-in, there was never any chance of him taking over the role full time.

Indeed, former team-mate and fellow Hammers' legend Billy Bonds knew more than most that a permanent post simply was not an option.

"Trevor's tasted management," he said. "And I wouldn't think he'll be tempted to take up the role full-time. He enjoyed his three games and did great – he certainly didn't surprise me – with two wins and a draw but he's very level-headed.

"He may have shown passion but he's been involved in the game long enough to know there's another side to the coin, too. He certainly won't be fooled by the results of that three-game spell."

Typically, Roeder left a 'Good Luck' message on his friend Brooking's mobile phone prior to his first game against Bradford City.

"This is an uncomfortable period for me," admitted the still unbeaten Brooking after Jermain Defoe got him off to a winning start with a brilliant individual strike in a 1-0 victory. "It's been a difficult summer and we've had some traumatic times. We're down and we're in Division One. We've got to accept that and move on."

The bookmakers prepared a short-list of Brooking (5/4 favourite), Paul Goddard (5/2), Alan Pardew (5/1), Iain Dowie (6/1), Steve Cotterill (12/1), Joe Kinnear (12/1), Stuart Pearce (12/1), Paul Hart (12/1) and Steve Coppell (33/1).

He may have been the bookies' favourite and the club's first choice, but Brooking simply did not want the job. Astute and intelligent, he knew that honeymoons did not last forever.

As the East End thumbed their way through the runners and riders, it had also been rumoured that Roeder had seemingly been unimpressed by Goddard.

And that all but ruled the assistant manager out of the running, too.

Pardew and Coppell had proven records in Division One, while ex-Hammer Dowie had worked wonders at Oldham Athletic and Hart was well-regarded.

A short-list of four had begun to emerge.

And as West Ham won 2-1 at Ipswich Town thanks to strikes from Defoe and David Connolly, an appointment looked imminent.

"This should be my last game as a manager, so it's been good to keep my unbeaten run going!" said Brooking, who had suggested to the board that Reading's Pardew – with the best track record in the division – was their man.

But the Royals' chairman, John Madejski, had no intention of letting his manager move to a promotion rival.

"I was approached by West Ham United asking for permission to speak to our manager about the vacant managerial position and I said no," he announced.

Following a second, declined, official approach, Pardew admitted he was "flattered" to be linked with the job and, ahead of Reading's visit to Upton Park, he tendered his resignation, which was rejected by the Madejski Stadium board following a two-hour meeting in which the Royals insisted he must honour his three-year contract.

In limbo, the Royals' boss was not at Upton Park as his assistant Kevin Dillon sat through a 0-1 defeat in which Christian Dailly gave Hammers a third successive win.

"It was always going to be an extremely sensitive day given the Alan Pardew situation but all we can do is focus on our matches," said Brooking after winning the battle of the caretakers. "I don't know how the situation moves on from here but I just hope we can resolve it. While we're winning games we won't push the panic button, but I do hope I'm not still sitting here next April!"

With his position at Reading now untenable, Pardew was in an uneasy situation.

For if the stubborn Madejski decided that the point of principle was worth more than Hammers' compensation, then the East Enders would have to look elsewhere while the former Crystal Palace and Charlton Athletic defender would find himself in the wilderness of no-man's land.

West Ham – who had made the loan signings of Everton's Swedish international Niclas Alexandersson and Newcastle United's Wayne Quinn – went 3-0 up inside 25 minutes before easing off the gas at Crewe Alexandra, as Brooking steered them into second place in the table, level on points with leaders Wigan Athletic after seven games.

Now on gardening leave, Pardew found himself stranded in the Strand as Madejski headed to the High Court to seek an injunction for breach of contract.

"I am darned if I will let him go to one of our major competitors. I cannot agree to that and I never will," declared the Royals' owner as he headed into London.

But money talks. And with the clubs settling on a figure of £380,000 compensation and costs, the case was settled and it was agreed that Pardew could take control of West Ham United on October 18.

"We reached a stage where we had made our point," said Madejski, who had also insisted that no Reading player or member of staff could move to Upton Park until the end of the season. "It's a vindication that we have done the right thing, but we had to fight hard for it. When contracts are signed they should be adhered to, not just ripped up every time something better comes along.

"We had an agreement that Alan could talk to Premiership clubs but not first division clubs and that has been ignored."

Pardew – who had reportedly tripled his salary from the £150,000 per annum he was earning at Reading – would spend the next four weeks making his garden the best in Royal Berkshire.

"I've left behind a legacy that can continue to grow but I'm delighted I'm going to be the new manager of West Ham United Football Club," he smiled. "It's a challenge and I'm looking forward to it.

"I know the pressure is on but that doesn't faze me. At some point I must accept a big challenge like this and that's what I've decided to do."

Meanwhile, Brooking remained at the helm as he endured a 0-2 defeat at Gillingham, his first – and ultimately – only loss as Hammers' boss.

The frustrated Defoe had been sent off at Priestfield Stadium for launching into a volley of abuse at the officials.

But with Hammers trailing 0-2 at Ninian Park, he went from villain to hero when he bagged a Carling Cup hat-trick to give West Ham an unlikely 3-2 win and a third round tie at Tottenham Hotspur.

As Hammers awaited Pardew's arrival, a 1-1 draw against Millwall was followed by a 3-0 win over Crystal Palace in which the awkward, lumbering, green-looking Neil Mellor finally found the net with a double, alongside Defoe. With limited collective goal celebrations, rumours abounded that Connolly, Defoe and Mellor were embroiled in a triangle of acrimony that had led to them refusing to pass to each other.

The winner at Pride Park came from midfield as Don Hutchison's goal handed West Ham a last-minute victory at Derby County, before Peter Crouch's leveller gave Norwich City a 1-1 draw at Upton Park.

"We're still within touching distance of the top two but that kind of performance won't get us into the automatic promotion spots," conceded Brooking, acutely aware of the uphill struggle about to face his successor.

And as he took charge for his 14th, and final, game, he was relieved to see Pardew paraded before the Upton Park crowd ahead of a 2-2 draw against Burnley in which Hutchison conjured up a late equaliser.

"It was good that Alan Pardew was here today to see our frailties," preferred Brooking as he prepared to swap the dug-out for the boardroom once more. "It's going to be a tough start for him. Already we can see that there's still a lot of work to be done if we're going to be in the reckoning come next May."

Trevor Brooking's Managerial Record:

	P	W	D	L	F	A
League:	P-13	W-8	D-4	L-1	F-19	A-9
League Cup:	P-1	W-1	D-0	L-0	F-3	A-2
TOTALS:	P-14	W-9	D-4	L-1	F-22	A-11

Chapter 20
2003-04

A LONG PARD SEASON

A window-fitter by trade, Alan Pardew had once found himself perched precariously up the 42-storey, NatWest Tower in London's Old Broad Street.

And now it was his task to take West Ham United Football Club back to the heady heights of the Premiership, too.

Born in Wimbledon on July 18, 1961, Pardew had combined his 6am starts in the City with run-outs for Dulwich Hamlet, Corinthian Casuals and Yeovil until he was given his chance as a 25-year-old, in March 1987, by Crystal Palace manager Steve Coppell – the man who, ironically, was now about to step into his shoes at Reading.

After making 170 appearances at Selhurst Park and appearing in the 1990 FA Cup final, he then moved on a free transfer to Charlton Athletic where he had another 124 outings before playing 79 games for Barnet.

Following a spell as reserve-team manager at Reading, the subsequently redundant Pardew then found himself reunited with his glass-cutter and the putty, before being invited back to the Madejski Stadium where he took over as caretaker manager prior to easing himself onto the Royals' throne.

Like his predecessor Glenn Roeder, despite enjoying a steady, if unspectacular, career as a central defender/midfielder, he had graduated as a keen student of the science of football.

"I had a classroom built for the players at Reading with a lot of good books and videos and information about fitness and diet. I wanted them to understand what I wanted to achieve," he revealed. "I'll explain the same things to the West Ham players. If they understand what you're trying to achieve and they've got good spirit, you've got a chance."

And upon arriving at Upton Park, one of his first tasks was to hammer as many doctrines as possible onto the vacant surfaces of his new workplace.

"Luck is what happens when preparation meets opportunity" bellowed the missive of Seneca – a first-century Roman philosopher – from a new plaque affixed to the wall of the players' canteen, in which the wearing of studded footwear and use of mobile phones had also been banned with immediate effect.

And if good fortune had never embraced Roeder, the opportunistic and prepared Pardew would ultimately find luck coming his way in abundance.

The thoughts of Phil Jackson – the legendary basketball coach who had led the Chicago Bulls to half-a-dozen NBA titles in nine years – were the bedrock of the beliefs that had served him so well on the way to the play-offs with Reading.

"Having a clearly defined set of principles to work with reduces conflict because it de-personalises criticism," declared Jackson. "The players understand that the coach isn't attacking them personally when he corrects a mistake, simply trying to improve their understanding."

And as he tried to offer the seasoned players of West Ham United this blueprint for a new era at Upton Park, one Scottish international quickly pointed out to his team-mates that Jackson also had enjoyed the overwhelming services of basketball's slamdunking legend Michael Jordan in his team.

Pardew also introduced a series of rules and a credit card-sized missive of that month's personalised objectives, which he had specially produced for each member of the squad and management targeting, for example, how many victories, points or even goals he expected to be garnered from the weeks ahead.

"Gaining the respect of players is what I need to do quickly," Pardew told *Hammers News Magazine*. "I don't suffer fools and I expect people to pull their weight. I work hard and I expect everybody around me to work hard, too.

"But managing people is the same whether they are worth fifty-grand or £10m – it really is. Of course there are egos in the Premiership but there are big egos in the Nationwide League, too, don't worry about that."

And in his first team meeting Pardew boldly set down the rules and regulations expected under his very own code of conduct.

"There are two types of people in football," he told his gathering of players. "There are winners and there are losers. I'M A WINNER!"

As his assembled squad exchanged glances, no words were necessary.

And a few days after digesting the law according to Pards, skipper Christian Dailly observed: "The rules are very strict but they are just what we need. Everybody is now in no doubt where they stand because the fines cover absolutely everything from indiscipline to dress code. If the manager says do something, then you must do it. If you don't, you pay the price. No argument.

"But all the players have accepted the new rules with no problem. The fines have helped the manager stamp his authority straight away."

Pardew quickly set about shaping his team, signing Hayden Mullins on loan from Crystal Palace in time for him to make his debut in the 1-1 draw with Nottingham Forest.

"Forest represented a tricky first game for me," said the 10th manager in Hammers' history after seeing West Ham make it six points dropped in seven days following a third successive home draw. "It was clear to see that there were things going on out there that haven't been nailed down yet, but there are not just negatives, there were a lot of positives, too."

Mullins' move was made permanent in a £600,000 deal, while Robbie Stockdale joined on loan from Middlesbrough after Niclas Alexandersson (5+3 apps) returned to Everton.

As Pardew banished non-essential backroom staff and officials from the team-coach, those who still made the long trip to Wales must have wondered if the £4.80 Severn Bridge toll was worth it after a goalless draw at Cardiff City.

NEARLY REACHED THE SKY

Back in London, West Ham made the short trip to White Hart Lane for the Carling Cup third round tie against Tottenham Hotspur, for whom lifelong Hammers' fan Bobby Zamora scored his first – and what would prove to be his only – goal since his £1.5m summer arrival from Brighton & Hove Albion.

"I want to create a winning culture here but at the moment we lack a bit of quality at times and that showed up against a Premiership side," insisted Pardew.

By the time West Ham travelled to Highfield Road, veteran striker Brian Deane had joined the ranks on a free transfer from Leicester City, after helping the Foxes to automatic promotion the previous season.

"There are times in the first division when you just have to go out there and grind out results for yourselves and, hopefully, I can help West Ham United back to the Premiership," said the nomadic 35-year-old, who had amassed 181 goals in 583 outings. "We've got a very good chance of going straight back up."

And Deane got his home debut off to a flyer with two goals as Hammers raced into a 3-0 lead over shell-shocked West Bromwich Albion. But Defoe's second sending off of the season was the catalyst for a remarkable Baggies' recovery in which Deano volleyed home a surreal own-goal as the Midlanders fought back to win 4-3 and go top of the table.

"We were cheap in possession when we should've seen the game out," fumed Pardew, still looking for his first win in the knowledge that Defoe now faced a five-match ban. "The players are paid good money and I expect better from them. I shall not forget today in a hurry and I won't let the players forget it either. Without doubt this has been my most frustrating day as a manager."

Defoe was also in further trouble with the boss after failing to carry his personal objective card for inspection on demand.

Following that surreal defeat against the Baggies, it was equally frustrating to see the line-up for England's friendly against Denmark at Old Trafford, where David James was joined by ex-Hammers Frank Lampard, goalscorer Joe Cole and debutant Glen Johnson in a 3-2 win. And only Rio Ferdinand's unavailability – for missing the drugs test that would lead to an eight-month ban – prevented him from joining his former Upton Park team-mates, too.

On the day when England's rugby players won the World Cup in Australia, Hammers were held to a less spectacular goalless draw at Watford, while the suspended Defoe was, bizarrely, asked to coach the Under-10s before heading to Milton Keynes to do a scouting report on forthcoming opponents Wimbledon.

By the time they arrived at the National Hockey Stadium to play the Dons, Marlon Harewood had signed from cash-strapped Nottingham Forest for a cut-price £500,000. The 24-year-old had already netted 15 goals at the City Ground.

"I may have been in the last year of my contract there, but I was already in talks with them and expected to sign a new deal," he said. "I was really surprised that Forest even let me talk to West Ham in the first place but I've joined a bigger club which shouldn't even be in the Nationwide League."

Harewood drew a debut blank against the Dons, for whom Jobi McAnuff wiped out Deane's opener to make it five draws and two defeats for Pardew.

But Pards' duck was finally broken in the 4-0 demolition of nine-man Wigan

Athletic at Upton Park, where Harewood got off the mark with two goals.

"I'm not going to get ecstatic," said the Hammers' boss. "Everyone can see that there's still a lot of work to do."

Trevor Brooking was appointed Director of Football Development at the Football Association in Soho Square, with a three-point mandate:

1-*Coaching and the future of the National Football Centre at Burton-on-Trent.*

2-*Grass-roots football.*

3-*Improving relations between England's top players and the FA.*

And how his former chairman Terence Brown could have done with Brooking's relationship skills after he was forced to clarify comments he had made about Defoe's 'state of mind' at the club's Annual General Meeting.

An official statement read: *"Terence Brown is keen to point out that the club are looking to keep Jermain Defoe beyond next summer and hope he can be persuaded to sign a contract extension. He is aware that an 'off-the-cuff' comment made at the AGM may have given the impression that he was resigned to losing his services before his current contract expires in 18 months' time. He says: "I would like to clarify my earlier comment regarding Jermain Defoe as I would not like it to be misconstrued. While I referred to Jermain's state of mind, I would like to make it clear that I was referring to a time prior to Alan Pardew's arrival, in the aftermath of the bitter disappointment of relegation - a blow that Jermain felt as keenly as the rest of us. Every time Jermain has stepped out for us he has never given less than total commitment to West Ham United. It is not a foregone conclusion that he will be leaving us. Nothing would give us more pleasure than if he did sign a contract extension in the course of this season and that is something the club is actively seeking to encourage."*

Despite his Defoe *faux pas*, the meeting had been a success for the chairman, who had looked set to face a vote of no confidence from a group of rebel shareholders calling themselves Whistle. But time was blown on their motion as they had not given the requisite six weeks' notice.

Generously, Brown agreed that the dissenters, with a one per cent shareholding, could put their proposal to a later, extraordinary general meeting notwithstanding the requirement that such calls need the support of at least 10 per cent – a decision partly helped, perhaps, by the fact that the four items on the AGM agenda had already been unanimously carried by 16million to 50,000 votes.

A 1-1 draw at West Bromwich Albion was the prelude for Hammers' worst performance in the living memory of all 24,365 unfortunate enough to be at Upton Park to witness a 0-1 defeat at the hands of 22nd-placed Stoke City, who had lost their last eight away games.

"I'm scratching my head with some of the displays I'm watching out there and this team is now on a knife-edge," said Pardew, arms folded, typically refusing a chair as he took to the raised podium at the post-match press conference.

Standing upright to gain a psychological air of superiority – and with just one win to show from his 10 games in charge – he was in no mood to field questions from his inquisitors.

Instead, there were to be no excuses and most definitely no spin, as he fed the scribes the lines that he desperately wanted his players to read in the following morning's newspapers. "I need to get this club promoted and the players need to show me that they want to stay here and play. If they don't, then I'm gonna have to make changes. I'm fed up with all this talking, it's time to see some action!"

And when Hammers went 0-2 behind to Sunderland four days later, an on-pitch, into-the-locker-room dust-up between Dailly and Tomas Repka left West Ham with all the hallmarks of a club in crisis.

But in a stirring second half recovery, two-goal Defoe was the architect behind a thrilling 3-2 win that sent the punters home happy.

"Tomas Repka and Christian Dailly clashed on the pitch and in the dressing room but I'll have that," gritted Pardew, forsaking his sports scientist's coat for the rough and tumble of his window-fitting days. "And the supporters want to see that, too. At half-time the fans were drinking their tea thinking: 'We don't know about this team.' But they went away at the end having seen our fight."

That battling spirit was also taken to Walsall by Defoe, who quickly collected his third red card of the season. And although Harewood put 10-man Hammers ahead, the Saddlers forced a 1-1 draw going into Christmas.

Twelve months earlier, Hammers had been marooned to the foot of the Premiership and, this time around, they found themselves eight points behind Nationwide leaders Norwich City. Sadly for Pardew, there were no statistics that said the team in sixth place on Christmas Day had never failed to get promoted.

The *News of the World* claimed Hammers had conceded defeat in their bid to keep Defoe, who interested Manchester United, Arsenal, Chelsea and Liverpool.

But the prolific striker scored in a 1-2 defeat at home to Ipswich Town on Boxing Day and, as speculation grew over his Hammers' future, he also scored in a 2-0 win at Nottingham Forest, where Harewood netted upon his return.

West Ham again proved Wigan's nemesis with a 2-1 win over the Latics at the JJB Stadium in the FA Cup third round. But following those back-to-back away victories, Hammers lost 1-2 to Preston North End at Upton Park, where Pardew was already coming under pressure from the home fans.

"I'm seeing two different sides out there," he said, knowing that the re-opened January transfer window now made every player in the country available for sale or purchase. "We look like promotion contenders away from home but at Upton Park we're nervous and we suffer from indecision. We've made Upton Park a hostile stage by the manner of our recent performances. It's a mystery to me. This is a tough job and the players have either got to show character and come with me on this journey or they'll fall by the wayside."

One player shunted into the sidings was Manchester City's former England goalkeeper David Seaman, who was forced to hang up his gloves as a result of a shoulder injury. With a thirst for spending matched only by Wayne Rooney's girlfriend, Coleen McLoughlin, City manager Kevin Keegan set his sights on the current England stopper, James, to fill the void.

It was a move that suited all parties. Admirably, notwithstanding his Upton Park salary package, unlike some of his relegated team-mates, James had insisted throughout that he would stay and fight to get West Ham back into the Premier

League. But the 33-year-old also had international ambitions to fulfil and he needed to be back on the Premiership stage.

Add an apparently acrimonious split from his wife that had seen the *News of the World* report that he had fled the family nest to re-unite himself with a former girlfriend he had found on the Friends Reunited website, and a change would be as good as a rest both on and off the field.

Never forgetting who paid his wages, the effusive James had been both fan-friendly and media aware.

But his outspoken nature, at a time when the new Hammers' boss was finding it hard to find his feet, meant that Pardew could remove a potentially disruptive influence from the dressing room, win any ego-battle, generate a reported £1.5m in transfer revenue and slash the squad's wage bill yet further.

And for a relatively modest fee that might, perhaps, rise to £2m with add-ons, City had an experienced, ready-made replacement for the retiring Seaman.

"It's a fantastic move and I'm back in the Premiership but it wasn't just a case of me wanting to get back at all costs," said James, who reportedly called Pardew a 'pedant' in his weekly newspaper column because of his insistence on ordering his players to follow petty instructions, which even included precise, blackboard-written details on how to walk out and wave to supporters before the kick-off. "Everything I had built up over 10-11 years could have been ruined in one season, though. I have a position to uphold.

"At West Ham it got frustrating because I was led to believe we did not have to sell anyone but the squad majorly changed. Glen Johnson's sale was the hardest to take. Aged 18, you anticipated that the future of the club was around him."

When he arrived from Aston Villa, James (102 apps) had joined a team that was on the cusp of Europe. Now, 18 months on, not even a Nationwide League play-off place was certain.

Pardew, himself, was holding a double-edged sword.

Firstly, he had to deliver Hammers back to the Premiership.

And, secondly, his mandate was to cut costs – a feat that could only realistically be achieved by exchanging the remainder of the so-called Premiership squad that he had inherited with cheaper Nationwide players.

After a proposed loan move for Bolton Wanderers' left-back Anthony Barness was scuppered, Fulham's Welsh international defender Andy Melville – plus a cash-adjustment – headed to Upton Park in exchange for Ian Pearce.

While Fulham boss Chris Coleman was seemingly delighted that he had signed a central defender with pace, the ex-Blackburn Rovers utility man had clearly not seen his equally versatile, former Ewood Park team-mate in recent action.

For knee injuries had ravaged the career of the shy Pearce (154+9apps 10 gls), reducing him to a shadow of the player whose Hammers' performances of the late 90s had even led to calls for international recognition in some press quarters.

And as The Cottagers reportedly saw their £5m bid for Defoe turned aside following the sale of Louis Saha to Manchester United, they did at least allow another of their defenders, left-back Jon Harley, to move to Upton Park on loan, alongside Arsenal reserve goalie Rami Shaaban.

NEARLY REACHED THE SKY

Harley responded with a stunning debut goal as Hammers raced into a 3-1 lead at Sheffield United and, after keeper Stephen Bywater brilliantly saved Michael Tonge's penalty at 3-2, they looked to be heading for victory before Phil Jagielka made it 3-3 with an injury time equaliser.

"We're trying to build but we're also trying to get promotion at the same time and that ain't easy," grimaced Pardew, who still was not finished in the transfer market as he raided cash-strapped, rock-bottom Wimbledon to sign England Under-21 international Nigel Reo-Coker and fellow midfielder Adam Nowland, for a combined fee believed to be in the region of £500,000.

Having given his staff a chance to prove themselves, he opted to 'change the chemistry' by replacing assistant, Paul Goddard, with Bournemouth's Peter Grant, who was conveniently able to step instantly into his predecessor's monogrammed 'PG' tracksuit.

With Matthew Kilgallon (2+2 apps) having gone back to Leeds United, Neil Mellor (9+12 apps 2 gls) also returned to Liverpool after finding himself slipping further down the Upton Park pecking order.

A 3-1 victory over Premiership Wolverhampton Wanderers in the FA Cup fourth round was followed by a 2-1 win over Rotherham United at Upton Park, where the Millers had no concerns over the size of the dressing rooms.

"I looked around in awe – we're playing Rotherham and we've got 35,000 here," said Pardew after enjoying more success against the Yorkshiremen than the ill-fated Roeder had done back in August. "I've got my principles, my ethics and now I can see them finally coming into the team."

With Manchester United having now signed Saha, Chelsea remaining silent and Arsenal thought to be formulating a derisory £5m bid, Defoe's chances of a big move were receding as January's transfer window started to close.

But Tottenham kept in the hunt and, having been the first to table a post-relegation transfer request, Defoe (72+33 apps 41 gls) was finally one of the last to leave in a £7m transfer to White Hart Lane, as Zamora – with just that Carling Cup goal against the Hammers to his name – moved to Upton Park for £750,000.

"We have offered Jermain a new contract on several occasions, which he has turned down," said chairman Brown. "So we felt it was in the best interests of West Ham to maximise the potential transfer income."

Under *The Times* headline – 'West Ham: an idiot's guide to the destruction of a football club' Martin Samuel wrote: "West Ham were given six of the most promising young players in the country over a period of five years for nothing. Ferdinand, Defoe [sic], Lampard, Cole, Johnson and Carrick each came through the ranks. To end up skint, having sold five of them, takes some doing. There was no imperative for West Ham to sell Defoe. He was 17 months away from leaving for free under the Bosman ruling and that is a long time in football. Who would have imagined in September 2002, that the team with Di Canio, Kanouté and Defoe up front, England's keeper and a midfield featuring Cole, Carrick and Sinclair would be outside the play-off places in the first division?

"The reward for promotion is estimated at £30m but Brown would rather collect £7m by selling and risk another season in the first division than keep the players who could win promotion at the first attempt.

"It is a first division club with a first division squad, a first division manager and, sadly, a Sunday league chairman," he added. "What is the point of bringing in the so-called stars of the future by plundering Tottenham's reserves and the first XI at Wimbledon? If Reo-Coker is the next Lampard, he will surely be sold anyway. Brown's legacy will be the systematic frittering away of natural resources until all that is left in east London is barren landscape and dust."

Following the recent signings of Reo-Coker and Nowland, McAnuff became the third player to move from Milton Keynes to Upton Park for an undisclosed fee, again thought to be in the region of £500,000.

Pardew may have been doing well to cherry-pick the Dons off the administrators for a song, but there was no escaping the fact that the trio had been part of an all but relegated side.

As Stockdale (7+2 apps) and Shaaban (0 apps) returned to Middlesbrough and Arsenal, they were replaced by AS Monaco's right-sided midfielder, Sebastien Carole, and Portsmouth's out-of-favour keeper, Pavel Srnicek.

Hammers' fan Zamora kicked off his claret and blue career with the winner in a 2-1 victory at Bradford City after the team's driver got lost on a 10-hour drive from London. But Pardew was in a forgiving mood given the pilot had yet to deliver a losing team to an away Nationwide or FA Cup fixture under his tenure.

And that good fortune continued at Loftus Road, too, where Dutch keeper Edwin van Der Sar was in unbeatable form as West Ham drew 0-0 with Fulham in the FA Cup fifth round, in front of the watching Sven-Goran Eriksson.

"After West Ham, I want to be England manager," the bullish Pardew told Pat Sheehan of *The Sun*. "If you don't have that ambition, what's the point?"

Carrick, who put in highly-polished performance against the Premiership side in front of the Swede, just wanted to get back into the England side.

"Seeing all those players leave has certainly made things hard for me," admitted the marooned Geordie after doing his international chances no harm.

A 1-1 draw followed at leaders Norwich City, where Etherington was sent off for petulantly time-wasting by placing the ball outside the corner kick quadrant.

Hopes were high in the FA Cup fifth round replay as Hammers again outplayed Fulham, before conceding three goals in the final quarter-hour to give the Cottagers a flattering 3-0 win and a daunting quarter-final trip to eventual competition winners, Manchester United.

With just the league to concentrate upon now, Zamora marked his home debut with the winner in a 1-0 victory over Cardiff City and that left West Ham in fifth place with 13 games to play.

A 1-1 draw at Burnley was followed by a goalless draw against Walsall, with Saddlers' keeper James Walker in fantastic form.

Etherington's hat-trick set Hammers on the way to a 5-0 win over Wimbledon, for whom goalkeeper Steve Banks had a busy night also picking further efforts from Zamora and embarrassed ex-Don, Reo-Coker, out of his net.

But it was back to basics at Sunderland, where Pardew insisted that automatic promotion was still a realistic prospect despite a 0-2 defeat.

NEARLY REACHED THE SKY

After racing into a 4-0 interval lead, the showboating Hammers then saw Crewe add some respectability to the scoreline with a two second half strikes.

"We've got to be in a winning groove to get into the play-offs and beyond," observed Pardew. "The top two – Norwich City and West Bromwich Albion – are still facing some tough hurdles and the hardest part for them is that they've still got to get over the line."

West Ham then succumbed to a second successive away defeat against Millwall at an oppressive New Den, where Dailly scored an own goal and Bywater was sent-off amidst crowd unrest that saw the West Ham fans attempt to break through security cordons. The Lions roared to comfortable 4-1 win and it would have been far worse had they not failed to convert the two penalties that came their way, too.

"We've let our fans down against our nearest rivals. Millwall wanted it more than us today and I offer no excuses, we were second best," said Pardew after a jolting reality check. "We were well beaten and really had our collars felt. My team simply wasn't good enough. All the good work of recent weeks has been undone in one game. We're nowhere near as bad as we've shown ourselves to be today, but I do fear for our play-off place."

Having left Wimbledon, ex-Hammer Steve Banks arrived at Upton Park with Gillingham and duly found himself on the end of another defeat as Etherington's late solo effort gave West Ham a 2-1 victory.

But there was to be a third, successive away defeat in store, too, as Pardew returned to Reading for the first time. The predictable 'Pardwho?' and 'Parjudas!' banners were unfurled as the Royals' fans wasted no time reminding him that he had broken his contract to join West Ham.

And in the hostile atmosphere of the Madejski Stadium that was once his home, the Hammers' boss hastily substituted the bewildered 22-goal Harewood for rookie Nowland after a mere 29 minutes, before Dave Kitson's double gave Reading a 2-0 victory.

"There have got to be a lot of question marks against us," admitted Pards who, upon making a torrid return to Royal Berkshire, also had similar question marks raised against himself following Harewood's humiliation. "You won't get into the play-offs just by wearing a West Ham United shirt and we've got to be more aggressive. We're disappointed with the way we played. That's the third away game on the trot where we've been caught out by the passion and the furore. They're like play-off games but we're not showing enough ability. It's a good day for Reading – I knew it'd be hostile for me – but I'm not pleased with us."

With Euro 2004 looming, Defoe became the seventh ex-Hammer to play for England since September 2002 as he put in an encouraging show in the 0-1 friendly defeat in Sweden.

And despite earning a reported £500,000 transfer add-on from Tottenham, how Hammers could have done with their former striker as they huffed and puffed their way to the goalless draw against relegation-threatened Derby County that led to them leaving the pitch to chants of 'What a load of rubbish'.

Following that ill-tempered clash at Millwall, Hammers were involved in another south London scrap that saw Connolly sent off in a 0-1 defeat at in-form Crystal Palace. While that was eighth-placed West Ham's fourth successive away collapse, for Palace boss Iain Dowie victory was another leap towards the play-offs as his side moved within one point of Pardew's men with a game in hand.

Indeed, when the former Hammers' striker took over on December 22, 2003, Palace were in 19th spot on 28 points. Now, with five games to go, they were in ninth place on 63 points, having won 11 games, drawn two and lost four of Dowie's 17 matches in charge.

Following a 2-0 win over Coventry City at Upton Park, the awayday blues were banished with a 2-0 victory at Stoke City.

Chairman Brown then dispelled all claims by the Whistle rebels that Hammers had serious money matters to contend with, declaring: "I wish to make the position absolutely clear, we do not have a financial crisis at West Ham United and have not had one at any time since our relegation."

A 4-0 win over Watford left Hammers in third place, on 74 points, going into their final match of the season at seventh-placed Wigan Athletic.

"We're within touching distance now, and with three wins and three clean sheets, we're putting the statistics together to achieve what we want to achieve – promotion," enthused Pardew, safe in the knowledge that his side was assured a play-off place provided they did not lose by 0-4 or worse at the JJB Stadium.

Having gone into the game on 70 points, Wigan looked to be in the play-offs, too, as they took a 1-0 lead over the Hammers, while Coventry led Palace 2-0 at Highfield Road.

Dougie Freedman could only pull one back for Palace and that meant that the Eagles were still merely destined to end up with 73 points and an inferior goal difference to the Latics.

However, just 49 seconds of the season remained when Deane outjumped Jason De Vos to nod Carrick's free-kick beyond John Filan to force a 1-1 draw.

Certainly, the eerie vacuum of silence created by Wigan's biggest-ever JJB Stadium crowd of 20,669 unerringly signalled the fact that they were now back on 71 points and in seventh place behind Palace.

"We've finished fourth and, regardless of what anyone says, that means that we were the fourth best team in the division this season," insisted Pardew, clearly relieved that Hammers would now be facing Ipswich Town in the play-offs rather than Wigan. "Mentally, it was a tough game for us because, barring a sending off and a few freak results we were there. But we still had to be fair to all the other sides and go for the win. I can't pay Wigan any bigger compliment than to say that I didn't want to come back here at the weekend."

And while Darren Bent gave Ipswich Town a 1-0 win in the first-leg at Portman Road, Hammers had home advantage going into the return fixture.

"It will be different on Tuesday night, though, because Upton Park will be hostile and jumping," announced Pardew as he prepared for the make-or-break game with some early psychological shots. "Ipswich will be on the back foot defending their lead but I still make them favourites to go through. Let's see how they cope at our stadium."

NEARLY REACHED THE SKY

Even the Chicago Bulls' Phil Jackson had to start somewhere.

And Pardew went to desperate lengths to recreate the atmosphere generated at Upton Park on the floodlit, European glory nights of days gone by.

Cleverly, he insisted that all the televisions on the concourse were switched off a quarter-of-an-hour before kick-off in a bid to get the East End backsides onto their seats well before the start.

The ploy worked, for the punters responded by replicating those barnstorming Boleyn Ground nights of yesteryear and the pandemonium generated by an attendance of 34,002 was, indeed, the most intimidating since the mid-70s when Brooking and company ensured that mud-splattered Johnny Foreigner returned back across the English Channel empty-handed.

Add the teams entering to the 1960s-style bugled fanfare of the *Post Horn Gallop* and Pardew had all the ingredients of a winning formula.

Wearing a commercially exploitive t-shirt emblazoned with the slogan: 'Moore than just a football team', the West Ham boss was relieved to see Bent miss a very good early chance before Hammer-of-the-Year, Matthew Etherington, thundered home the 50th-minute goal that put Hammers level on aggregate.

Twenty minutes later, Christian Dailly bundled home the winner to set up a Millennium Stadium showdown with Crystal Palace, who had beaten Sunderland on penalties in the other play-off semi-final.

"It's been a magical evening for us," beamed Pardew after getting to within 90 minutes of hitting the target detailed in the job description that had first been handed to him by chairman Brown, back in the autumn. "The players responded to the fans and the fans responded to the players. We've had some horrible nights here and some horrible Saturday afternoons, too. Criticism has been levelled at a lot of players this year, alongside our staff, our manager and our chairman.

"Throughout, we've had to keep tight as a unit, hold onto our philosophy and try to win games. That has been the bottom line for us.

"Tonight, I knew that the noise levels would have to rise to get a performance like that, but I also knew that the atmosphere would be electrifying.

"All the cogs turned for us and we played the kind of football that shows exactly what I'm about. It was fast and it was quick.

"We showed that the work ethic here is strong and we won the match in the right way. It wasn't just bash-ball stuff, we really thought about our game.

"Trevor Brooking told me afterwards that while it had been great to win, the highlight for him had been the actual performance.

"Sometimes as a fan, you have to keep turning up to finally get your reward and hopefully they can all now go and have a great day out.

"But there's no great day out and no point going to Cardiff unless you win. We'll be aiming to do that and, hopefully, it'll be the re-birth of this great club."

The play-off final between Hammers and Palace was riddled with sub-plots.

Dowie had played for West Ham, while Pardew had turned out for Palace.

Michael Hughes and Mullins were also lining up against their former clubs.

Both sides had chairmen who were in the public and tabloid firing line.

And, most importantly, each cash-depleted team desperately needed the £25m-plus prize for winning the most valuable game in British football.

Again Pards went for the psychological edge, but in Dowie he was up against a fellow management disciple and scholar of team ethics and sports science.

"You make a living by what you get," said the ex-Hammer. "You make a life by what you give."

And while his side were the firm underdogs, all he asked was that Palace gave their all for the final 90 minutes of a surreal season.

After training behind closed doors at Cardiff City's Ninian Park ground, Pardew, for his part, took his side off to the Celtic Manor resort, where his meticulous preparations were disrupted by a shortage of claret and blue club ties.

His order for invincible-looking white track suit tops had, however, been fulfilled – his idea being that West Ham would, psychologically, appear visibly superior to Palace as they stood side-by-side in the Millennium Stadium tunnel.

But with the line-ups splitting to go their separate ways upon emerging into the Cardiff cacophony of noise, the effect was lost, just like the mouthful of a training top slogan that read: 'It's amazing what can be accomplished if no one cares who gets the credit.'

As it happened, it was Palace's 29-year-old, journeyman striker Neil Shipperley who got the praise when he gobbled up Bywater's parry on 62 minutes to give his side victory.

"There was nothing more that I could have done," insisted the West Ham keeper. "I couldn't really see Andy Johnson's low cross coming through Tomas Repka and, anyway, I was already at full stretch."

On a day when the Hammers' fans had turned up but the players were conspicuous by their absence, West Ham managed just three attempts on target, their cause not helped by a string of curious, hasty, panicky substitutions that gradually saw their fire-power diminish.

Midway through the second half, 26-goal Harewood was replaced by seven-goal Deane, while six-goal Zamora saw his place taken by two-goal Reo-Coker. And then 14-goal Connolly made way for three-goal Hutchison.

With a 46-goal strikeforce replaced by a 12-goal attacking midfield mix, West Ham's only real chance came with just eight minutes remaining when Mikele Leigertwood sent Carrick tumbling in the penalty area.

Referee Graham Poll admitted afterwards that West Ham had a justifiable claim for a spot-kick.

"I thought: 'Hello, I'm interested here,' but no-one, not even Michael Carrick, appealed, so on the basis that no-one at West Ham was interested, I reckoned that they did not think it was a penalty and the play just moved on," revealed the man in the middle, whose final whistle signalled Palace's return to the top-flight.

"We went into the final full of confidence and really thought that we we'd win the match," said skipper Dailly. "Although it was a pretty even game, it's fair to say that in most areas of the park we had players who could've done a bit better.

"While motivation's a word that doesn't come into the equation, we're upset that we didn't have enough to break them down and create problems.

"You have to give credit to Crystal Palace because they fought hard and got the vital break with the goal, but they didn't exactly hammer us. Over the past few weeks, Iain Dowie and his men managed to bring a bit of luck with them into these play-offs, and it looked like Johnson's shot deflected off Tomas Repka just before Shipperley scored the winner. But as for the trip on Michael Carrick, from where I was I couldn't see whether or not it was a penalty.

"We can't make excuses, though, because we simply didn't create enough goal-scoring opportunities."

Ironically, West Ham had been edged out of a £25m passage to the Premiership by the team that they had let into the play-offs in the first place, courtesy of Deane's last day, stoppage time leveller at Wigan.

"We didn't perform today," admitted the nomadic striker. "All credit must go to Crystal Palace, because they got their tactics right and they're in the Premier League now. They were the better side on the day, they were stronger than us and I don't want to start making excuses because we can't argue with the result."

The Sunday Telegraph observed: "Shipperley's goal was a tap-in, but it decided an annual game of ecstasy and broken dreams and at the final whistle two convoys were heading along the M4, one of celebration and one of sorrow."

With the winning line in sight, a West Ham United side totally unrecognisable from the team that had been relegated 12 months earlier had fallen at the final hurdle.

In the Upton Park dressing room there hangs another Pardew placard.

In life there are so many opportunities; they are always around and about us.

However, there are too many people who never see the opportunities.

Then there are people who see those opportunities but do not do anything about them.

But then you get people who are generally life's winners, for not only do they see the opportunities but they go searching for them.

And when they find them, they grasp them and wring every little bit out of them.

Sadly it was Palace who had grabbed the day and extracted every last drop from their Millennium experience.

"We peaked one game too early and we'll never get away from the disappointing display we put on – we have to take that on the chin and the players and myself won't ever forget it. It's tough for the team that gets left behind but we'll be brave, we'll face it and we'll move forward," insisted the luckless Pardew who, in accordance with that ancient doctrine of Seneca, had got his team prepared only for them to spurn the opportunity.

PLAYERS IN

Brian Deane	Leicester City	Free transfer
Marlon Harewood	Nottingham Forest	£500,000
Jobi McAnuff	Wimbledon	£200,000 (estimated)
Andy Melville*	Fulham	
	Swap for Pearce + undisclosed cash (in)	
Hayden Mullins	Crystal Palace	£600,000
Adam Nowland$	Wimbledon	£500,000
		(including Reo-Coker)
Nigel Reo-Coker$	Wimbledon	£500,000
		(including Nowland)
Bobby Zamora	Tottenham Hotspur	£750,000

LOANS IN

Niclas Alexandersson	Everton
Sebastien Carole	AS Monaco
Jon Harley	Fulham
Wayne Quinn	Newcastle United
Rami Shaaban	Arsenal
Pavel Srnicek	Portsmouth
Robbie Stockdale	Middlesbrough

PLAYERS OUT

Jermain Defoe	Tottenham Hotspur	£7,000,000
David James	Manchester City	£1,500,000
David Noble	Boston United	Free transfer
Ian Pearce*	Fulham	
	Swap for Melville + undisclosed cash (in)	

Chapter 21
2004-05

BACK TO THE PROMISED LAND

If the actual defeat at Cardiff had left a bad taste in the mouth, then the underlying financial ramifications of play-off failure were an even more bitter pill to swallow.

Neil Shipperley's winner meant that Hammers had lost out on £12m from the Premiership, together with the extra television revenues, final-placing prize money and associated income derived from a sold-out stadium where supporters would pay top-notch prices for tickets, merchandise and food.

And having already received a £6m parachute payment during their first season in the Nationwide League, the second sum due during the 2004-05 campaign would now be their last.

"There's a massive difference between the Premiership and the first division," insisted goalkeeper Stephen Bywater. "There's a big, big prize waiting for the promoted teams and you soon realise that even more when you don't get up at the end of it all. In Cardiff, the best side won on the day and I don't ever want to find myself in that position again. I'll always remember that feeling of losing at the Millennium Stadium. We've all been taught a huge lesson but if we all pull together, then I'm certain we can get promoted automatically."

Skipper Christian Dailly was also determined to stay and battle it out once more.

"During the past 12 months we've obviously sold plenty of players and there's a new longer-term plan here at Upton Park now," he said. "There are still Premiership players in this squad and I'd like to think that they'll want to stay at West Ham and fight for another season, too. The experience gained during this past year can only help us get back into the Premier League."

Yet again, there was another clear-out at Camp West Ham.

Loan signings Jon Harley (16 apps 1 gl) and Sebastien Carole (0+1 apps) had already returned to Fulham and AS Monaco, while club-less Wayne Quinn (26+1 apps) soon followed them out of the door.

Injury had punctuated the dream Indian summer that Robert Lee (14+5 apps) had hoped to enjoy at his beloved Hammers, and he was released to try his luck at Oldham Athletic and Wycombe Wanderers.

In August 2005, Lee's father Reg went to Adams Park to see his son kick off the new season only to return to find his Hornchurch home ransacked by thieves.

A Newcastle United number seven shirt together with England and Norway jerseys had been stolen alongside his son's Derby County top.

But curiously Rob's framed Hammers' jersey was still hanging on the wall.

"They've *even* taken the Derby shirt so I don't know why the West Ham one's been left behind," said the distraught dad, putting up a £1,000 reward for the items.

Youngster Shaun Byrne (0+3 apps) looked set for a glittering career when he was handed his debut by Harry Redknapp at St James's Park in Hammers' first game of the new millennium on January 3, 2000. But it was not to be and he was duly released alongside Brian Deane (12+20 apps 7 gls).

The veteran striker had left the Millennium Stadium knowing that, while he had played his last game for the club, he was already guaranteed a permanent place in Upton Park folklore.

For in yet another one of those ironic shot-in-the-foot scenarios that, sadly, had all too often been woven into the fabric of Hammers' history, the nomadic goal-getter would always be remembered for his last-gasp equaliser at Wigan Athletic that allowed Cardiff conquerors Crystal Palace into the play-offs via the back door.

"It's sad that everything all turned out that way," he said. "It wouldn't have mattered what game I was playing in. I simply wanted to come on and do my best against Wigan, no matter what effect it was going to have on the play-off positions.

"Already, it's been made plain to me that I won't be staying," continued the three-times capped England international, who had scored 223 goals in 714 league and cup outings for Doncaster Rovers, Sheffield United, Leeds United, Benfica, Middlesbrough, Leicester City and, finally, West Ham United. "Alan Pardew may have brought in a lot of young players who are on their way up, but sometimes you also have to remember that it's equally important to get the blend right with some older, more experienced professionals.

"Can I keep on playing?" he frowned, throwing the enquiry back to his inquisitor with his sharp Yorkshire tongue. "Just look at me and you'll see that it's a question that shouldn't even be asked.

"I'm in good shape and, somewhere, there will be another good side out there who wants me," he insisted, ahead of rejoining former club Leeds United and then gaining promotion with Sunderland before heading down under to Australia.

Pavel Srnicek (2+1 apps) was also released and in his place came the equally experienced James Walker, from newly-relegated Walsall.

"I'm determined to work hard to make sure we get this team up where it belongs," said the jovial keeper who had made 476 appearances for the Saddlers over 11 seasons. "This is a big year for the manager, the players and the supporters because there are some very exciting days ahead. Sure, there'll be some hard times, too, but hopefully we can get to the promised land come next May.

"Having spent my entire career in the three Football League divisions, I'm crossing my fingers that I can finally play in the Premiership."

And Walker's rival for the Number One shirt, Bywater, signed a new three-year contract after Hammers re-negotiated his 1998 transfer terms with Rochdale, given the underlying, expensive add-ons were now looming large on the horizon.

Dale chairman David Kilpatrick was no doubt mindful of the fact that, if West Ham could no longer afford the deal they had agreed as a Premiership club, they might then have to let the England under-21 keeper go altogether.

NEARLY REACHED THE SKY

Conscious that something was better than nothing, he declared: "Following lengthy discussions between our two clubs, we are delighted to have come to an arrangement that allows Stephen to continue his career at West Ham United. We appreciate that in recent years the value of the transfer market has dipped and that it was only fair that a new deal, satisfactory to both parties, was reached."

Bywater added: "Apparently, we weren't talking about 10-grand, I think it was nearer to £200,000. It meant that the club couldn't afford to keep me if they then had to pay more money after I'd gone on to make so many more appearances. In the end, Rochdale had to settle for less because if I'd have left the club and gone abroad, they wouldn't have had any money at all coming to them."

Following the previous autumn's free transfer from Manchester City, Kevin Horlock (29+4 apps 1 gl) rejoined his old Maine Road boss, Joe Royle, at Ipswich Town, on another free transfer, while David Noble (1+3 apps) moved to Boston United on the same basis.

And Hammers also agreed to sell David Connolly (46+2 apps 14 gls) to promotion rivals Leicester City for £500,000. While considered moody and aloof in some quarters, the Republic of Ireland international was undoubtedly the hardest working, most intelligent striker in Pardew's front line and, unless the manager had a ready-made replacement, it was a surprising disposal even if he had only cost £285,000 from Wimbledon.

Those fears were soon allayed, though, as Pardew found another intelligent, international striker to lead the front line. Teddy Sheringham had been linked with moves to West Ham on several occasions but the former Millwall, Nottingham Forest, Tottenham Hotspur, Manchester United and Portsmouth goal ace had never quite made it to the team he claimed to have supported as a boy.

Having been released by Harry Redknapp's Pompey, the 51-times capped England star looked all set to sign for Coventry City before Pards – who shared the same agent, Barry Neville, as the player – swooped to sign him on a free transfer.

"I still enjoy playing football and I think that I can do a job, so I'll carry on," said the 38-year-old. "Anyway, you're always under pressure to produce the goods no matter how old you are. I know that I've got to perform week-in, week-out but I do still want to score goals and win games."

And hot on the heels of Sheringham came Sergei Rebrov. At Dinamo Kiev he had once forged a prolific partnership with Andriy Shevchenko who had, apparently, previously been on trial at the club before being sent packing by Harry after "failing to pull up any trees" at Chadwell Heath.

Now it was the turn of Rebrov – who had once cost George Graham £11m – to finally be shown the door at White Hart Lane after Glenn Hoddle had sent him on a year-long loan spell to Turkish club, Fenerbahce.

"Money is not a problem," said the Ukrainian international. "This is not a financial decision, it's a football one. I am very proud to play for this big club and to help them get back to the Premiership."

With ex-Spurs' stars Sheringham, Bobby Zamora and Matthew Etherington already at Upton Park, Rebrov's stuttering journey from the former Soviet bloc continued as he came in from the cold to become the fourth man.

"You don't want to lose good players like David Connolly but by bringing in Teddy and Sergei I feel we are stronger," insisted Pardew.

And Manchester United winger Luke Chadwick was signed on a one-year contract after previously impressing Pards during a loan spell at Reading.

A pre-season tour of Sweden saw Zamora net a hat-trick in a 5-0 triumph over second division outfit FC Umea, and he followed that up with a double in a 3-1 victory over Gif Sundsvall before Hammers rounded off the trip with a 3-1 win over Friska Viljor FC.

The flagship friendly came in the form of a 4-4 draw with Anderlecht at Upton Park, where Sheringham netted before the Belgians won a penalty shoot-out.

With Michael Carrick's contract due to expire at the end of the season, the last nugget of the exhausted Hammers goldmine was about to be put up for sale following his refusal to sign an extended deal.

Having claimed their Premiership prize, Crystal Palace added insult to injury by making a £2.5m bid for the 23-year-old midfielder, while Harry Redknapp harboured hopes of taking him to Portsmouth. And as Everton, Charlton Athletic and West Bromwich Albion looked on, Arsenal – apparently braced to lose Patrick Vieira to Real Madrid – showed interest in signing Carrick for £3m.

The highly-paid Don Hutchison was told by Pardew that he could continue to have Saturdays off from now on.

"The salary that he is on warrants him playing in the first team and if that's not the case, then perhaps it would be better if he sorted himself out with another club," said the Hammers' boss, cursing the legacy of a club record £5m signing, on huge Premiership wages, left to him by his predecessor, Roeder.

Indeed, a few weeks later, the *News of the World* announced that Hutchison would be left kicking his heels in the reserves on £30,000 per week after reportedly enduring a messy divorce and failing to turn up for a one-month loan spell at Nottingham Forest.

With the new season about to kick off at Connolly's Leicester City, neither Hutchison nor Carrick would be involved.

"Hopefully, the play-off defeat will fuel us all for the challenge ahead this year," said Pardew. "I don't want to be in the position of putting ourselves at risk in the play-offs again, because one bad 45 minutes can cost you your whole season. Over the next 46 games we've got to be one of the two best teams in the league. That's what we've got to aim for.

"I believe we have a very good team for the budget I've been given. The parachute payment finishes now and we have to be on guard for that. The bottom line for me is that I've got a responsibility to make sure this club doesn't die a death and follow the likes of Sheffield Wednesday and Nottingham Forest.

"That's what I'm trying to avoid as I attempt to take the team forward and add better players. I have to keep one eye on the finances and make sure that this club doesn't end up in a position it can't get out of.

"There will always be a section of unhappy fans who believe that we should have the best players at the club, but the reality is that relegation has left us in a situation that means we can't compete when it comes to signing the top stars."

NEARLY REACHED THE SKY

With the Nationwide League being curiously re-christened the Coca-Cola Championship and the old Division Two becoming League One with the former third division being re-named League Two, teams in the Premiership were left desperately hoping that they would not be relegated to . . . the Championship.

An opening day goalless draw at Leicester City's Walkers Stadium was remembered more for the dismissals of Dion Dublin and Rufus Brevett.

And Sheringham marked his home debut by showing a little bit of quality to claim a late winner in the 1-0 victory over Reading, before Hammers were given a sharp reality check by Wigan Athletic, who raced into a 3-0 lead at Upton Park, before Zamora claimed a late consolation.

At Gresty Road, it was Hammers' turn to take a three-goal advantage within the opening half-hour, and although Dean Ashton pulled two goals back, Sheringham's double – and Brevett's first and last goal for the club – was still enough to give West Ham a 3-2 win.

Norwich City target Marlon Harewood also struck twice as Hammers knocked Southend United out of the Carling Cup in a tie that brought full debuts for Elliott Ward and Aussie Trent McClenahan, while promising 17-year-old Mark Noble also stepped from the bench.

Tomas Repka – who had been booked 17 times during the 2003-04 campaign – picked up his first yellow card of the season. But more worryingly for the former Czech Republic international, he had also been arrested following allegations that he had harassed a 46-year-old man from the Hornchurch area. Word on Green Street was that the reported feud had allegedly escalated once insurers had failed to fully cover all the costs when the player's high-performance sports car was damaged in a minor collision in the training ground car park, after being washed and polished by the self-employed, on-site valeting team.

"It was a minor incident," managing director Paul Aldridge told the *Evening Standard*. "A non-football related matter which took place some time ago."

After showing several flashes of promise, Jobi McAnuff (4+10 apps 1 gl) made a surprise £500,000 transfer to Cardiff City.

"I've had to sacrifice him for the good of the team," said Pardew, who needed to raise cash to strengthen his defence after Dailly underwent a knee operation.

McAnuff's former Wimbledon team-mate, Adam Nowland, gave West Ham a 1-0 victory over Burnley at Upton Park with his first goal for the club before young Chris Cohen's raw tackle saw him red-carded in injury time.

And two days later, Steve Lomas became the third Hammer to be dismissed when he was sent off for berating and then making an obscene gesture to a linesman, in the 1-2 defeat at a Calum Davenport-inspired Coventry City, after Sheringham had given the Londoners the lead.

"It was out of character but we should be beating teams like Coventry. We were losing and having come on as a substitute when it was only 1-1, I guess I stupidly started to feel a bit responsible for everything," admitted Lomas.

But as soon as the final whistle had blown, the Sky Blues' joy was tempered by the news that Davenport had been sold to Tottenham Hotspur for an initial fee of £1.1m, rising to £3m with those ubiquitous add-ons.

The White Hart Lane club had been busy for, after weeks of speculation, Carrick moved there, too, in a £3.5m deal after Arsenal withdrew from the race following the collapse of Vieira's transfer to Spain.

Upon signing his four-year contract and linking up with ex-Hammers Frederic Kanouté and Jermain Defoe, Carrick did little to endear himself to his new fans.

"If you get the chance to go to Arsenal, you go to Arsenal," he said. "It's as simple as that. I was disappointed when Arsenal pulled out. I'd be lying if I said I wasn't. But this is still an ideal move for me."

For many, the assured, focused Carrick (150+9 apps 6 gls) had looked set to progress further than the enigmatic Joe Cole. Indeed, with his economical, searching, passing ability he had, at times, looked the closest anyone had come to replacing the irreplaceable Trevor Brooking.

But following a niggling, confidence-sapping groin injury, he had failed to consistently display the form that had earned him two full England caps. While short-changing himself in the goal scoring department, Carrick had been perfectly capable of standing toe-to-toe with the Premiership's finest midfielders. Indeed, he had imposed himself on many high profile games but, equally, far too many matches had simply passed him by and, when his equally talented peers left, a once bright light had disappointingly dimmed.

In an ironic twist, as Defoe scored his first goal for England in their opening World Cup qualifier in Austria, debutant Carrick also found the net for Tottenham reserves in their 2-0 win over . . . West Ham's second string.

Having seen Coventry take three points and Spurs take his best midfielder, there was some consolation for Pardew when he signed Davenport on a three-month loan deal from White Hart Lane. Understandably, the sight of their star defender joining their promotion rivals just 11 days later, left the Sky Blues fuming.

"It sounds really stupid but I don't feel like a Spurs' player yet. I'm here at Upton Park and, as far as I'm concerned, totally 100% committed to West Ham," said the towering, blond central defender. "I know that if I can do well here then I'll be able to go back to Spurs with a realistic chance of playing in the Premiership. I wasn't going to be playing at Tottenham straight away and I wasn't surprised that they were prepared to let me go out on loan, because I'm only 21 and still learning."

Following months of speculation, Welsh-international midfielder Carl Fletcher joined Hammers in a £275,000 transfer from Bournemouth, while Malky Mackay moved from newly-promoted Norwich City in a £300,000 deal.

"Alan Pardew wants me to bring some experience and leadership," said the 32-year-old, Scottish international central defender after declining a move to Coventry City.

Five-times capped England defender Chris Powell joined on loan from Charlton Athletic with a view to a permanent move, while Aussie Richard Garcia (4+18 apps) went to Colchester United for an undisclosed fee after enduring an injury-ravaged end to his short-lived Hammers' career.

Powell, who had briefly played with Pardew at Crystal Palace, observed: "From my very first day here I realised that West Ham have got the quality to get promoted. There's a good mix between experienced players and good youngsters and everyone is working hard both on and off the field. There's a Premier League mentality and we're under pressure from our supporters, but it's now got to be all about the future, because both the club and its fans need Premiership football.

"It's up to each and every player who wears the shirt to make promotion a reality and, preferably, that can come via the top two places. But if we have to go through the play-offs, then we want a happier ending than the one at Cardiff, last season."

Sheringham made it five goals from seven starts when he plundered a late winner in a 2-1 victory at Sheffield United and Etherington's midweek strike gave Hammers a 1-0 win over Rotherham United, who brought a mere 155 followers to Upton Park.

"I'd be foolish to say that the title's there for the taking – we're already seeing what a tough division this is – but we've definitely got a squad that is capable of winning promotion," enthused Pardew as Hammers moved into fourth spot, one point behind leaders Stoke City, with eight games gone.

At Norwich City, Mackay had often been the scourge of local rivals Ipswich and his run continued when he headed Hammers ahead at Upton Park. But after Sheringham missed a penalty, the Tractor Boys levelled to snatch a 1-1 draw.

When Zamora scored after just 18 seconds, 92nd-placed Notts County looked all set to be buried under a Carling Cup goals avalanche, but Hammers did not have it all their own way as the Magpies battled back to 2-2 before Rebrov claimed his first goal for the club with a 30-yard free-kick that squirmed through the red-faced Saul Deeney's grasp. That 3-2 win set up a tantalising third-round tie at Chelsea.

Hammers then travelled to County's neighbours Nottingham Forest, who were mourning the death of Brian Clough. And after Harewood helped fellow former Forest star Sheringham to pin a signed West Ham United shirt to the City Ground gates, he then opened the scoring against his old club before Paul Evans levelled and Marlon King netted an injury-time winner.

"The City Ground was packed to the rafters with fans more concerned with paying their respects to Cloughie than seeing who would claim the points," observed *The Sun*. "But it was fitting – and, of course, scripted – that it would be Clough's old team who emerged with the glory."

Ironically, Hammers then drew 1-1 at Derby County who were also in mourning following the loss of Old Big 'Ead.

Sheringham bagged a late winner against Wolves at Upton Park and, after Hammers lost 0-1 at Queens Park Rangers, the veteran striker had the East End on its feet with a cheeky back-heel that sealed a 2-0 win over Stoke City.

"I told Teddy in training that they only come off once every three years but, yet again, he's walked off the pitch and given me one of his knowing smiles!" said Pardew – in fifth place, six points off leaders Wigan – before delivering the verdict on his first year in charge.

"One wag said to me before the game: 'You've been here for a year now, what have you done?' Well, I'll tell you what's happened in those 12 months – we've got a team of players who aren't looking over their shoulders at the Premiership. There are 11 players out there every week looking to do well. There's a good work ethic here now and while there's no abundance of riches here at Upton Park, there is a bunch of good players just trying to do their best."

As Spurs' old boy Zamora set Hammers on the way to a 3-1 victory over Gillingham, Carrick – still to start a first-team game at White Hart Lane – was told by Jacques Santini that he had to improve to get into the Tottenham side.

There were no such problems for his best friend Joe Cole, though, as he lined up at Stamford Bridge to face his former team for the first time, while the rested Frank Lampard reluctantly sat on the bench and Glen Johnson sat in the stands.

The eventual Premiership champions rotated their expensively assembled, star-studded squad but they still had sufficient strength for Mateja Kezman to score his first goal for the club after 557 barren minutes to put them ahead on the hour-mark.

And things looked like getting yet worse for West Ham when Repka halted Arjen Robben's run into the box at the cost of a penalty. Walker might have been restricted to Carling Cup games thus far, but already the keeper had shown that he was first-team material with a string of assured stops.

Indeed, after Kezman received treatment for a cut sustained by a volley of missiles hurled from the crowd, Lampard's low spot-kick was blocked by Walker, to the elation of the 7,000 West Ham fans packed behind his goal.

Referee Andy D'Urso received an electronic signal from his assistant referee advising him that Walker had moved before the kick was taken but, with no appeal from Lampard or any other Chelsea player, he sensibly allowed play to continue, fearing that, with 16 arrests having been made already, a retake would cause a riot.

Following that 0-1 cup exit at the hands of the Blues, it was a bit quieter down in the West Country, where Hammers were held to a 1-1 draw at Plymouth Argyle after Lomas opened the scoring.

"The most important thing for me is to end up being part of a team that gets itself into the Premiership come next May and, hopefully, I will now be able to get a lot of games under my belt, stay in the team and have a positive influence on this West Ham side," said the combative, fit-again 32-year-old midfielder after returning to the fold. "Many of us had a very difficult summer because the play-off final at Cardiff was a massive let-down for everybody but, believe me, if we don't succeed in getting promotion this season, then it definitely won't be for want of effort."

But as Hammers again headed west to Ninian Park three days later, they found themselves on the end of a McAnuff-inspired 1-4 defeat at Cardiff City.

"It wasn't the performance I had in mind. I need to look at my side because I'm going to have to shuffle the pack," said Pardew, who sold Nowland (7+10 apps 1 gl) to Nottingham Forest for £250,000 before recalling both Powell and Hutchison as Hammers avenged their Loftus Road defeat with a 2-1 win over QPR.

Sitting in 21st place, Brighton & Hove Albion won 1-0 at Upton Park thanks to Guy Butters' header – their only effort on target – and it was all change again by the time Hammers headed to Millwall.

For following Santini's resignation, Davenport (10 apps) was recalled to Spurs, who allowed Argentinian Mauricio Taricco to head the other way on a free transfer.

Upon hanging up his boots, the greying Alan Pardew had turned out on Sunday mornings for Morden Nomads back in the mid-90s, where he once played with Darren Powell. The bulky centre-half had subsequently turned professional and gone on to join Crystal Palace, who had now allowed him to link-up on-loan with Pards once more, in a bid to regain his fitness.

Both Powell and Taricco lined up for a hostile high noon kick-off at the New Den, where Danny Dichio's late goal gave the Lions a 1-0 victory after Harewood had been harshly sent-off for an apparent dive despite Darren Ward – brother of Hammers' Elliott – having clearly made contact.

"I don't expect the fans to be happy with a 0-1 defeat at Millwall," said Pardew after enduring a second successive defeat, a gauntlet of boos and chants of 'You don't know what you're doing,' after substituting the in-form Chadwick. "This is the last year of the Premiership parachute money and the pressure's on to get promoted. I can understand their frustration. I'm trying to do this job to the best of my ability but I also know that I'll stand or fall by my decisions."

Clutching his hamstring, Taricco (1 app) limped away after just 27 minutes and offered to rip up his contract given he was likely to be sidelined for eight weeks.

"I came to West Ham United to be of service to the club," said the South American. "Obviously I won't be able to contribute if I'm having treatment and, when I discovered the extent of the injury, I was very unhappy about the situation. I cancelled the contract so the club would not suffer a serious financial loss by paying wages to a player who had only played for them for less than half-an-hour. This will now give them the opportunity to spend the money on a fit player rather than on someone sitting around in the treatment room."

And a grateful Pardew added: "He didn't have to make that decision, which shows that his character and personality off the pitch is far removed from the image sometimes portrayed. This is one of the most honest acts from a player that I have experienced in all of my years in the game."

Terence Brown – following more than a year on those reduced Nationwide League wages – also announced the club's results for 2003-04. His upbeat Chairman's Statement announced: "Following the devastating financial effects of relegation, the group's financial results are little short of extraordinary. The group generated a pre-tax profit of £11.8m and our net bank borrowings fell by approximately £10m to £33.8m. A remarkable achievement under the circumstances. We continue to contend with the financial consequences of relegation. If it were not a fact of football life, no one would believe that 20 businesses would sign up to a round of Russian roulette that consigns three of their number each year to penury at best or administration at worst.

"We're now faced with the challenge of achieving success on the pitch whilst ensuring sustainability of the business off it. This is no easy task but we have acted correctly in ensuring the survival of the club. We should be proud of what we achieved during the last decade whilst recognising the mistakes that were made.

"We all share the disappointment of relegation and our subsequent failure in Cardiff but we need to channel that frustration towards ensuring that we maintain our unique football club for future generations and return to the Premier League.

"I understand, of course, that in footballing terms the club has fallen a long way in a short time and I realise how disappointing this is for the fans but our situation can change quickly. When that happens and we return to the Premier League, we will be in better financial shape than when we left, with greatly reduced debts."

With automatic promotion looking beyond Hammers just 20 games into the campaign, Paul Aldridge announced: "I understand the fans' frustrations but changing manager isn't an option at the moment."

The calls for Pardew's head intensified after Watford took a 2-0 lead inside 20 minutes at Upton Park before Nigel Reo-Coker, Darren Powell and Rebrov netted in a remarkable comeback that prevented a damaging hat-trick of defeats.

An unlikely 2-0 win at Sunderland gave the Hammers' boss more breathing space, while his counterpart Mick McCarthy launched into a post-match rant after spotting referee Graham Salisbury asking Sheringham to sign his autobiography.

"We've had a season of frustration," said Pardew after booking back-to-back victories. "I'm frustrated, the chairman's frustrated and the supporters are frustrated. I try to accept the criticism. When you are a club of this size, it's frustrating if you're not successful. We've got quality players, and if we can get a run of them staying fit, then I think we'll still be in there as promotion contenders."

Strengthening his squad, Pards then bought Gavin Williams from Yeovil Town in a £250,000 deal while Spurs' rookie keeper Robert Burch (0 apps) was also signed on loan as cover for the injured Walker.

A controversial stoppage-time penalty earned Leeds United a 1-1 draw at Upton Park, before Hammers slumped to a 1-2 defeat at Preston North End in what was to prove to be the final game for Darren Powell (5 apps 1 gl).

Going into Christmas in sixth place – eight points off second-placed Ipswich – for a second successive year, Pardew's festive lunch did not taste too good with a *Daily Mail* report that former Southampton boss Gordon Strachan had been earmarked to take over in the Hammers' hotseat.

Two goals from Sheringham in a 3-2, Boxing Day win over Nottingham Forest turned down the heat, but as Hammers went to Rotherham two days later, there were echoes of Glenn Roeder's Millmoor nightmare when the Millers went 2-0 up.

The portents did not look good for an equally under pressure Pardew.

After all, successive defeats against Millwall and Brighton had been followed by a hard-fought recovery over a Watford side that had gone 2-0 ahead. And while Hammers had returned to form with that win at Sunderland, Leeds had then snatched a late point before Preston had claimed all three. A 2-0 lead had been surrendered against Forest ahead of Sheringham sparing Hammers' blushes. Now, shivering in the northern freeze, the board was looking pitch-wards at an ordinary, wholly inconsistent, West Ham United side trailing to the Championship's bedraggled, bottom team.

Two penalties inside six second half minutes, however, earned Hammers a fortuitous 2-2 draw.

Roeder had found nothing but ill-fortune on the Yorkshire moors but, once again, his successor had proved himself to be a lucky general with that Rotherham rescue.

Goals in the first and last minutes secured a 2-0 win at Ipswich Town on New Year's Day and that left Joe Royle smarting: "I've just asked my team if they had a party last night without inviting me!"

But all that festive work was undone when Sheffield United left Upton Park with a 2-0 victory.

"I can't keep defending our inconsistency," fumed Pardew as the pressure intensified. "Like me, the supporters who travelled to Ipswich will be scratching their heads. The fans were far from happy as they left the stadium today and we're very disappointed with our display. Sheffield United were better than us in every area and we just didn't have any answers. Our individual performances simply weren't good enough. The creativity and zest just wasn't there.

"On Saturday evening, I wasn't feeling under pressure but after today I'm not going to say that's not going to be the case now, because this is a results business.

"It's going to be a big test to stay in touch with the leaders from now, and one or two are going to have to convince me that they're worthy of the West Ham shirt."

According to the *News of the World*, Pardew had until the end of January to save his job.

One of those ubiquitous 'insiders', so often associated with such quotes, said: "The fans are losing patience. There must be a run of results to push us nearer to the automatic places. Another year out of the Premiership isn't an option."

With the transfer window open, Pardew spurned Blackburn's advances for Sheringham.

"The manager told me that Mark Hughes enquired about me going to Ewood Park in a swap deal," said the striker. "Alan Pardew said that I was going nowhere and I was quite happy about that. I like the fact that the manager wants me to stay."

Long-standing Canaries' target, Harewood, netted the winner in a 1-0 victory over Norwich City in the FA Cup third round, as youngster Mark Noble was handed his first senior start.

But that 'giant-killing' only gave Pardew brief respite as Hammers lost 2-4 at Molineux, where Paul Ince scored in Glenn Hoddle's first-ever victory as Wolverhampton Wanderers' boss.

And even more questions were being asked of the Hammers' manager with a January 23 loss to Derby County at Upton Park.

"We can't hide from the fact that we've now got ourselves into a hole," he said after the 1-2 defeat that left Hammers in ninth place, their lowest mid-season position since being relegated. "We've left ourselves with a mountain to climb for automatic promotion, but you make your bed and you have to lie in it.

"The pressure's increasing on both the team and myself but, as for my future here at the club, I haven't even asked that question of the board."

The *Daily Mirror* headline said it all: 'Pard reign's gonna fall – That'll be Al folks as Hammers get ready to fire angry boss.'

"The expectation upon West Ham United as a Championship side is far greater than anything I ever experienced while I was at United," revealed Chadwick, who had even played half-a-dozen Champions League ties for the Reds. "There's massive pressure on us to get promoted. It's a job that we simply have to do."

A 1-1 draw with Sheffield United in the FA Cup fourth round set up a Bramall Lane replay that also ended 1-1, before the 10-man Blades won the penalty shoot-out after Sheringham, Fletcher and Harewood all missed from the spot.

A week earlier, there had been a happier ending for Fletcher after he headed home an 89th-minute winner to snatch an unlikely 1-0 victory over Cardiff City at Upton Park and take some of the heat off the beleaguered Pardew.

Two-goal Sheringham then steered Hammers to a 5-0 win over powder puff Plymouth Argyle at Upton Park, before Harewood secured a 1-0 victory at Gillingham. That hat-trick of league wins had suddenly elevated West Ham into fifth place and slackened the noose around the relieved Pards' neck, yet further.

"People have to accept that it's a time of contrast and that Alan Pardew's had a tough job," said Sheringham after seeing his manager emerge from stormy waters. "Ever since he arrived here, he's had to let players go, rebuild and still keep the club moving in a forward direction. He's doing that and long may it continue."

With Southampton's teenagers due at Upton Park to contest an FA Youth Cup quarter-final, Redknapp set about returning to the Boleyn Ground for the first time since his shock May 2001 departure.

And as the Saints' boss negotiated the East End traffic congestion with sidekicks Jim Smith and Kevin Bond, he took a surreal call from his brother-in-law.

"Ain't it funny how it's turned out?" said a wistful Frank Lampard senior as he, equally, crawled through the heavy West End traffic. "You're on your way to West Ham to see your kids play and I'm going to Stamford Bridge to see young Frank, Joey Cole and Glen Johnson take on Barcelona in the Champions League!"

As it happened, both men went home happy as Harry's boys beat the Hammers' colts 4-1 and Chelsea saw off the Spaniards in a thrilling 4-2 victory.

But back at West Ham, Williams' first goal for the club was not enough to prevent a 1-2 defeat at Leeds United and, following that trio of victories, Pardew was now about to endure a hat-trick of reverses.

For after an ill-tempered 1-2 home defeat to Preston North End, in which Repka was senselessly dismissed ahead of an alleged full-time tunnel brawl, the manager then suffered another embarrassing return to Reading, where Dave Kitson followed up his previous season's double with a treble in the Royals' 3-1 win.

"Automatic promotion is beyond us now," conceded Pardew after seeing his side slip into seventh spot, 15 points off the leaders with just 11 games to play. "We've got to regroup and digest matters but we're still in contention for the play-offs."

Costly successive home draws against Crewe Alexandra (1-1) and Leicester City (2-2) also led *The Guardian* to claim that Strachan had, indeed, been offered the opportunity to replace the Hammers' boss.

"West Ham discussed Pardew's position at a board meeting yesterday and have agreed to sack the 43-year-old provided Strachan accepts their offer," claimed Matt Scott in his story. "They have lost patience with Pardew after a stuttering attempt to win promotion. Strachan is mulling over the offer."

Before the Leicester City game, Tony Cottee also revealed that he was heading a consortium with a view towards taking over West Ham United Football Club.

"I've spoken to some potential investors who are Hammers fans," he said. "But the last thing I want to do is upset what everyone at West Ham is trying to do – get promotion via the play-offs."

But he had offended distraught chairman Brown and the club promptly relieved him of his duties as matchday host and banned him from writing his popular, long-running monthly column in *Hammers News Magazine*.

With no offers tabled, however, Aldridge said: "Much has been written about potential takeovers. I would like to place on record that we have not received any serious offer or even an expression of interest. The board has a duty under the Takeover Code to make shareholders aware of any serious offer for the company; it would then be the decision of the shareholders if it is acceptable to them. The Chairman has stated on numerous occasions that he would welcome discussions with any potential serious buyer that could ensure major investment into the team."

And as speculation now loomed over Pardew's fate, the managing director was clearly taking a neutral stance as far as any vote of confidence was concerned.

"West Ham United has always tried to be supportive of its managers and give them security to make decisions that are in the best long-term interests of the club," he told the *Evening Standard*. "The constant speculation concerning Alan Pardew's position is not helpful but I am sure he is strong enough to cope and not be distracted from his goal. Alan is well aware that expectations are extremely high and everyone demands a return to the Premiership as quickly as possible.

"Being linked by the media with possible replacements for a vacancy that does not exist is not helpful, but it's beyond our control. I believe Alan is comfortable with the relationship he enjoys with the Board and understands the pressure."

But, again, in adversity Pardew drew the right cards to come up trumps.

An unlikely 2-1 win at second-placed Wigan Athletic was followed by a 1-0 victory at Burnley and a 3-0 success over Coventry City. The top six had been winning, too, but seventh-placed West Ham were still in touch with the pack.

A disappointing 1-1 draw with Millwall at Upton Park, however, then left Hammers with a must-win midweek game at Stoke City.

"We've now gone six games undefeated and have still got Stoke, Brighton, Sunderland and Watford left to play. I'll take those," said Pardew, trying to remain upbeat following the disappointing loss of two precious points. It's important to stay positive because this team is certainly capable of getting into the play-offs."

Zamora duly obliged with the winner in a 1-0 victory at Stoke, before Hammers twice let Brighton & Hove Albion back into the game at the tiny Withdean Stadium as Dean Hammond helped himself to carbon copy headers in a 2-2 draw.

And having seen the Seagulls dump on his side with a last minute equaliser, Pardew's agony was compounded by the loss of top-scorer Sheringham with a hamstring injury that would rule him out of the run-in.

Hammers were still undeafeted in eight games, a run that had coincided with the fledgling partnership of Ward and Ferdinand in the centre of defence.

The penultimate game of the season was a televised Friday night match at Upton Park against an already promoted Sunderland side who came to London knowing that they would claim the title with a victory.

Things were going well for West Ham when Harewood gave them an interval lead, but Julio Arca then levelled before substitute Stephen Elliott again exposed the soft underbelly of the Hammers' defence with just three minutes remaining.

As the Black Cats purred home with a 2-1 win and the Championship trophy, Pardew could only survey the wreckage.

Having garnered 70 points and a goal-difference of plus-nine after 45 games, seventh-placed Hammers were seriously struggling to catch Reading in sixth-spot.

Indeed, the Royals, with 70 points and a goal-difference of plus 10, had only played 44 matches. Victory over Wolverhampton Wanderers at the Madejski Stadium the following afternoon would, therefore, leave the East Enders with mere mathematical chances of play-off qualification.

"It's no longer in our hands," conceded Pardew as he prepared to see his former club cement sixth spot at his expense. "We need to put maximum effort into our last game at Vicarage Road and remain focused. It ain't over yet!"

Pards was so right.

Incredibly, despite taking an eighth minute lead, Reading somehow blew their chance as Wolves fought back to win 2-1.

And that meant Hammers and the Royals were now level both on points and goal difference with one game to play.

But having netted 64 goals to Reading's 50, just 19 hours after the full-time whistle had blown at Upton Park, West Ham – without even kicking a ball – had crept back into the top six by virtue of their superior scoring record.

That put the pressure on the Wigan-bound Royals, who would willingly have swapped their final day fixture with a West Ham United side travelling to Watford, where the Hornets had nothing to play for except pride.

With Ipswich facing lowly Brighton & Hove Albion, too, the Latics needed to beat Reading to ensure automatic promotion at the expense of the Tractor Boys.

And with Paul Jewell's side flying out of the traps and into the lead against Reading, down south Ferdinand's first-ever goal for the club all but guaranteed Hammers their place in the play-offs.

Harewood's penalty doubled the advantage and, while Watford also scored from the spot, with Wigan beating Reading 3-1, West Ham's 2-1 victory confirmed a play-off semi-final encounter with third-placed Ipswich, at the Royals' expense.

With Sunderland and second-placed Wigan Athletic duly promoted, Derby County and Preston North End were left to battle out the other play-off semi-final.

This time around, Hammers' play-off challenge was a far more subdued affair as Pardew and, indeed, his players distanced themselves from the media spotlight.

Certainly, with the first leg at Upton Park kicking off on a Saturday lunchtime, it was always going to be difficult to replicate the floodlit frenzy of the previous campaign's second-leg victory over Ipswich.

But two goals inside the opening 13 minutes, by Harewood and then Zamora, raised the East End decibel levels, as rampant West Ham looked set to plough the Tractor Boys into the Upton Park turf.

Just before the break, though, Tommy Miller's low, 18-yard free-kick found the net with deflections off both the reckless Repka and then a helpless Walker.

The Czech Republic international had already announced that, by mutual consent, he would be leaving the club, one year early, at the end of the season.

And having committed a seemingly innocuous foul on Shefki Kuqi, the furious Repka had then been hit by the double-whammy of a 53rd yellow card of his Hammers' career and that consequently deflected Miller goal.

Passions were running high on the pitch, and they were boiling and bubbling in the technical area, too, where Town boss Joe Royle even invited the declining home manager down the tunnel to discuss matters following a touchline row.

"Play-offs are tense situations," proffered a regretful Pardew. "I was really upset because Joe's a gentleman and a person I respect immensely. It was disappointing that he was upset over my actions, because I didn't think that I did anything wrong. Sure, things are perhaps said on the sidelines which you don't mean and I publicly apologise to him for whatever I may have done."

When the interval arrived, super-heavyweight Royle mixed it back in the locker room, too, where he schemed a match-saving double substitution and, as West Ham's first half momentum evaporated, a misunderstanding between Walker and Ferdinand, ultimately enabled Kuqi to level and leave everything to play for in the Portman Road return.

Having seen his side surrender a two-goal lead, the battered Pardew had every right to be furious and frustrated.

But he knew that he could not afford to show his disappointment at that 2-2 draw.

Instead, he calmly gathered his thoughts and launched a psychological broadside ahead of the midweek trip to Suffolk.

"I'm still confident that we can get to Cardiff," he insisted, putting the onus on Ipswich to come out of their shells in what promised to be a rumbustious return. "The pressure is now on them and that definitely favours us. We're ready, we've shown that we can score, and I can certainly sense that we'll get a goal at their place. They're going to have to score two or three times."

Royle, on the other hand, saw the Millennium Stadium looming on the skyline.

"We probably have a very slight advantage going into the second leg under the floodlights at Portman Road," he said, playing down the fact that he held the stronger hand. "It'll certainly be pretty exciting."

But Hammers suffocated the Town midfield and, going it all alone up front, Zamora could not have asked for a better time to have rediscovered the shooting boots that had been left on the peg so often during the season.

For after putting Hammers ahead, he then volleyed his side into the final with the goal of his life.

"If you look at the two matches overall, then it would be fair to say that we had the edge and that the best team won," announced Pardew, trying to mask his delight at an epic victory. "Make no mistake, Bobby has had a tough ride this season. In fact, he's had as much criticism as me and he's had to deal with the lot.

"Over these two play-off games he's been a different class and while I think that Teddy Sheringham will be fit in time for the final, I don't think he'll start because Bobby has come into the side and taken his chance."

Once bitten, twice shy, Pards was determined not to let history repeat itself at Cardiff, second time around.

"We've still got this one game to go," he warned. "And we go into the final still carrying some hurt from the defeat against Crystal Palace. We had played so well against Ipswich in the semi-final, second leg last year and everyone was jumping up and down but, remember, we ended up losing the final.

"Believe me, that hurt and we won't be going mad tonight because, as a team, we have to make sure that we're not like that again."

Certainly, there was a notably more reticent, subdued approach to the final against Preston North End.

Gone was all the psycho-babble.

And out went the confusingly, cryptic T-shirt slogans understood only by Oxbridge's smartest philosophers.

There was no sign of those ill-conceived white track-suit tops, either, as the teams lined up for what – with an estimated £30m jackpot at stake – was again billed as the richest game in British football.

Two points and one place in the table had separated the teams over 46 Championship matches.

And while Preston – semi-final conquerors of Derby County – may well have won both ill-tempered Championship matches by the same 2-1 score-line on their way to fifth spot, man-for-man, Hammers had the edge over Billy Davies' side.

Indeed, in what looked like being his last game for the club, Repka came the closest he had ever done to scoring when he rapped a post after five minutes.

Certainly, that set the tone and, although Cresswell had an early second half header pricelessly cleared off the line by midfielder Shaun Newton – a £10,000 spring signing from Wolves – West Ham looked the most likely to score.

And as the hour mark approached, the in-form Zamora repaid Pardew's faith in sticking by him, when he took advantage of slips by Claude Davis and Matt Hill to sidefoot home Etherington's low cross from just six yards out.

Not even Walker's sickening cruciate ligament injury could prevent Hammers from holding out to book their return to the Premiership.

This time around, it was the Lilywhites who had not turned up in the cut-throat cauldron that is Cardiff.

"It feels good to be a Premiership manager," grinned Pardew after seeing his side, all present and correct, do the business at the second time of asking. "It's been a long, sticky road but it's a vindication of everyone here that we've got there.

"We've had a lot of criticism thrown at us and it's been hard to take but we all stood together. Everybody kept telling us that we had to win, but it still could've been another failure.

"During our preparations for the game, we hardly mentioned last season's final. Instead, we just put the reasons why we wanted to win on the board – some were publishable, some weren't – and then we went out there and put in a great team effort. Now we're back where we belong.

"In adversity, when it mattered, we won and now we can all go and do ourselves justice in the Premiership. There's no reason why we can't stay there.

"We've given the fans some heartache during the last couple of years and I'm chuffed for the supporters because we've done the business for them. It's job done!

"Last year, we lost and everyone dug us out. Today, we proved a lot of people wrong. Whenever the press have gone on about me losing my job, the chairman has stayed solid with me and I'm very pleased for him. He head-hunted me to bring me to this club and it's a vindication for him, too.

"Terry Brown never gets a good press, he isn't particularly good with the media and doesn't like to say too much. The fans hammer him, too, but to be fair to him, he's held his hand up to some of those criticisms."

And as he stood pitchside watching skipper Reo-Coker parading the play-off trophy that was the club's passport back to the top flight, chairman Brown insisted: "It wasn't win or bust for Alan Pardew. He had a plan for staying in the Championship and a plan for going into the Premier League.

"And now we're in a strong position because we've got about £20m and have also got some great kids coming through, too."

In reply, Pardew candidly admitted: "It's been my job to take criticism but we've all learned from our mistakes. Personally, I got a bit carried away last year when, perhaps, I needed to keep myself in check.

"But if you don't learn from things like that, then you just won't progress.

"My failures have put me into check and made me a better person.

"I don't want to lose my confidence or my arrogance but I'm not so exuberant these days.

"As we've all seen, though, Jose Mourinho has shown that you need a bit of that and, hopefully, as I grow as a manager, I'll get that balance right."

The very sizeable matter of Pards' fulsome ego was something that had not been lost on the press pack either, as they looked ahead to the manager's mountainous task of surviving in the rarefied atmosphere of the Premiership.

"Pardew possesses a reputation among his peers for self-confidence," wrote *The Times*. "He must fear that the next campaign will bring more lessons in humility."

Heading into the Premiership, still clinging the hilt of the double-edged sword that demanded he slashed the wage bill while thrusting his way to the top-flight, Pardew had succeeded in completing a task that had proved far more difficult than he could ever have imagined.

The much-maligned manager had every right to savour the moment and hit back at his detractors.

Job done – for now at least.

Alan Pardew's Managerial Record (as at August 12, 2005):

League:	P-79	W-33	D-23	L-23	F-117	A-93
Play-Offs:	P-6	W-3	D-1	L-2	F-7	A-4
FA Cup:	P-7	W-3	D-2	L-2	F-8	A-7
League Cup:	P-4	W-2	D-0	L-2	F-5	A-4
TOTALS:	P-96	W-41	D-26	L-29	F-137	A-108

Pards had fielded 47 of the 56 squad players he had named for his 96 matches while in charge at Upton Park.

PLAYERS IN

Luke Chadwick	Manchester United	Free transfer
Carl Fletcher	Bournemouth	£275,000
Malky Mackay	Norwich City	£300,000
Shaun Newton	Wolverhampton W.	£10,000
Chris Powell	Charlton Athletic	Free transfer
Sergei Rebrov	Tottenham Hotspur	Free transfer
Teddy Sheringham	Portsmouth	Free transfer
Mauricio Taricco	Tottenham Hotspur	Free transfer
James Walker	Walsall	Free transfer
Gavin Williams	Yeovil Town	£250,000

Loans In

Robert Burch	Tottenham Hotspur
Calum Davenport	Tottenham Hotspur
Dusan Kuciak	MSK Zilina
Darren Powell	Crystal Palace

Players Out

Rufus Brevett	Plymouth Argyle	Free transfer
Shaun Byrne		Released
Michael Carrick	Tottenham Hotspur	£3,500,000
Brian Deane	Leeds United	Free transfer
Richard Garcia	Colchester United	Undisclosed
Kevin Horlock	Ipswich Town	Free transfer
Don Hutchison	Released	
Steve Lomas	Released	
Jobi McAnuff	Cardiff City	£500,000
Adam Nowland	Nottingham Forest	£250,000
Chris Powell	Charlton Athletic	Free transfer
Sergei Rebrov	Dynamo Kiev	Free transfer
Pavel Srnicek	Released	
Mauricio Taricco	Tottenham Hotspur	Released

During his time at the club, Pardew had also carried on from where his predecessor had left off by presiding over the stock clearance operation that had seen Defoe, Carrick and David James further depart.

And with West Ham installed as 1,000/1 shots to win the 2005-06 title – and an odds-on 8/15 to be relegated – Pards made an ambitious, tongue-in-cheek shout: "I've got a little message for the likes of Joe Cole, Michael Carrick and Jermain Defoe. Come back, because we still love you. It was a blow to lose them but, who knows, maybe one day we'll get those guys back?"

Meanwhile, he was left to offer renewed contracts to Sheringham, Dailly, Newton and the U-turning Repka. Released by Manchester United and Portsmouth respectively, goalkeepers Roy Carroll and Shaka Hislop would be joining the club alongside Charlton Athletic defender Paul Konchesky and long-time Cardiff City targets Danny Gabbidon and James Collins.

Israeli international midfielder Yossi Benayoun would also sign from Racing Santander together with Stoke City defender Clive Clarke and Viktor Zizkov's Czech striker, Petr Mikolanda. Manchester United's David Bellion and Arsenal's Jeremie Aliadiere would follow on-loan, too.

Having cost what many observers reckoned to be the best part of £10m, the burden of the Millwall-bound Hutchison (74+36apps 18 gls) was finally relieved from the wage bill. Despite claiming to have returned a better, more mature player, the costly, underperforming Geordie had, again, done himself little justice at Upton Park with just five goals from 41 starts, second time around.

The equally disappointing Rebrov (15+17 apps 2 gls) was also allowed to return to his native Dinamo Kiev, while Plymouth Argyle snapped up the massively out-of-favour Brevett (28+1 apps 1 gl).

The arrival of Konchesky saw model-pro Powell (41+1 apps) make a shock return to Charlton on a free transfer, claiming that West Ham had offered him a wage *cut* despite his previous season's endeavours.

Having fallen out of favour with Pardew following the disastrous defeat at Reading, the honest and hard-working Lomas (215+10 apps 13 gls) was so far down the pecking order that he had even been on holiday in Florida as his team-mates strolled down Cardiff's red carpet.

And it was no surprise when the Northern Ireland international was relieved of his number 11 squad number and told that he could be released from his contract.

Across London, the confident, 23-times capped Cole polished the 2005 Premiership winners' medal that he had won at Chelsea. Having finally established himself as a genuine contender for a place in Sven-Goran Eriksson's starting XI, domestically he had also played a key role in helping the Blues to their first league title for 50 years. It was hard to picture Cole ever heading back east.

Likewise, having been experimental England's brightest midfielder on their end-of-season USA tour, it was equally difficult to see Tottenham's four-times capped Carrick returning from north London, where he had started to blend in well with former team-mates Defoe and Kanouté who would soon head to Seville.

Indeed, after neting 29 goals for Spurs in 49 starts and one for England, Defoe had also been on that tour of the States, where he had taken his full cap count to 12. And upon his return, he again became subject to the transfer speculation that has habitually accompanied him throughout his career, when he was linked with big money moves to both Chelsea and Manchester United.

Glen Johnson (4 caps) had been on that American trip, too, and, like Cole, he was also looking forward to another Champions League challenge following Chelsea's Premiership triumph.

Stamford Bridge team-mate Frank Lampard (32 caps) was now one of the hottest properties in the world game and, as the Football Writers' Player-of-the-Year lounged with his pregnant Spanish girlfriend, Elen Rives, on Roman Abramovich's luxury yacht – the mature midfielder's reward for a stellar season – it was a far cry from those heady lads holidays at the Grecian Bay resort in Cyprus.

Back to the promised land

And up in Manchester, led by agent Pini Zahavi, the forgetful Rio Ferdinand (38 caps) – overlooking the fact that United had still paid him throughout his eight-month FA ban – would eventually agree to a new contract approaching a reported £100,000 per week following weeks of haggling.

Back at FA headquarters in Soho Square, following in the footsteps of Sir Geoff Hurst, Sir Trevor Brooking's knighthood meant that West Ham United were the first club to have seen two ex-players cross swords with HM The Queen.

And having witnessed Pardew's eternal struggle to win promotion with a squad ever-diminishing in quality, reluctant manager Sir Trevor knew that his decision to let his head rule his heart had largely been vindicated.

Elsewhere, Glenn Roeder had not worked full-time since leaving those woefully cramped changing rooms at Rotherham United, but the summer of 2005 would give him the opportunity to return to Newcastle United as Academy Manager, where he would be allowed to influence the Magpies' youngsters using his undoubted coaching skills without enduring the pressures of club management.

"Youth development has always interested me most and my job is to find players good enough for the first team so that the manager won't have to spread himself too thinly in the transfer market," Roeder told *The Sunday Telegraph*. "Look at Sir Alex Ferguson's success. A core of home-grown talent means that if he gets £20m he can spend it on a Rooney or a Van Nistelrooy rather than four £5m players. If that happens, you're flying and it's something West Ham came very close to doing.

"No matter what anyone says to try and cover up, the absolute truth is that once Rio was sold, Frank, Joe, Michael, Jermain and Glen were all going.

"I was with those lads every day and they were all leaving, not because they didn't like the club but because they didn't like its lack of ambition."

Having just been relegated with Southampton, Harry Redknapp was privately admitting regret over his acrimonious departure from Portsmouth who, in turn, were still ruing the fact that the Pompey wage bill had been ramped up from £13.8m to £25.5m by the 2003-04 campaign.

Still Redknapp had no contact with Billy Bonds – a frequent visitor to Upon Park as a radio pundit with BBC Radio London/Radio Essex.

"I'm glad to see that certain people are gone from the club now," Bonzo told *EX*. "But I don't feel any bitterness towards West Ham United. It's my club again."

Having fallen off the managerial merry-go-round that had subsequently seen him have spells with Birmingham City, Stoke City, Celtic and Huddersfield Town, Lou Macari now enjoyed a less stressful life as a television and radio pundit.

At home in the solitude of Suffolk, 16 years on from his Upton Park dismissal, John Lyall continued to revel in the tranquillity of the fishing lake in the grounds of his wonderful farmhouse, relieved that he was now detached from the cynicism and greed of the modern, money-grabbing, fun-challenged game.

Forget loyal Lyall's 34 years at the club, for despite getting Hammers back to the promised land of the Premiership, the demands of the top-flight dictated that Pardew – like the rest of his Premier League peers – would do well to endure even a 34-month reign at Upton Park.

As entrepreneur Kia Joorabchian insisted that he was considering a Roman

NEARLY REACHED THE SKY

Abramovich-style bid for West Ham United Football Club, chairman Brown could but wait to see the colour of the Iranian's £200m that would, reportedly, buy him out for £30m, repay debts of £30m and provide £30m working capital. A mind-blowing £100m-plus transfer budget would also, apparently, be made available.

Meanwhile, as he contemplated a return to the Premiership, Brown gave his manager an early vote of confidence. "I hope that Alan Pardew has now shut up all his critics," he said. "But I doubt whether I've silenced all of mine!"

And as he stood overlooking Green Street from the balcony of the Dr Martens Stand, just 24 hours after his Cardiff triumph, Pards milked the last ripples of applause from the remainder of the estimated 100,000 crowd who had lined the victory parade route from East Ham town hall to the Boleyn Ground.

From Macari's appointment in summer 1989 through to the 2005 victory over Preston North End at the Millennium Stadium, West Ham United had endured the most turbulent 16 seasons in its 110-year history.

But going into the 2005-06 campaign, despite the loss of half-a-dozen of the brightest young home-grown sparks in English football, plus countless other seasoned professionals, at least the decimated club would be kicking off the new term back where it belonged.

"We've had two years of darkness in the Championship," roared the ever-bullish Pardew, as he looked down towards the ecstatic gathering packed onto the forecourt below. "Now we're going to see some light in the Premiership!"

Acknowledgements

With a very big thank you to:

Billy Bonds MBE and those managers, players and officials of West Ham United Football Club, past and present, who have given their time and assistance down the seasons, especially, Lou Macari, Harry Redknapp, Frank Lampard snr, Eddie Gillam, John Green, John Helliar and Peter Stewart.

Tony McDonald and Danny Francis for their tremendous help, patience and friendship.

Lynn, Sam, Harriet, Len, Shirley and David Blowers – plus Rose Salmons – for their endless support throughout the years.

Susie Muir for her valuable input into this project.

The late Robert Main for giving me my Upton Park debut.

Tony Hogg, Terry Connelly, Philip Evans, Fred & Betty Jeapes, Pat & Bernard Blowers (no relation) and Graham Barrable for all their encouragement.

Ken Dyer, Trevor Smith and Steve Bacon for their press-room comradeship.

All those colleagues who have put a capital 'F' into Flexi-time on matchdays.

Marios Flourentzou and Vicky Kilby for their expert help with the cover.

Bibliography

Bonzo – Billy Bonds (Arthur Baker).
Boys of 86 by Tony McDonald & Danny Francis (Mainstream Publishing).
Broken Dreams by Tom Bower (Simon & Schuster)
Harry Redknapp – My Autobiography (Collins Willow).
Just Like My Dreams – John Lyall (Viking).
Paolo Di Canio – The Autobiography (Collins Willow).
Scoring: An Expert's Guide – Frank McAvennie (Canongate).
Terminator: The Julian Dicks Story by Kirk Blows (Polar Publishing).
Yours Sincerely – Ron Greenwood (Collins Willow).
Hammers News & *Hammers News Magazine*
EX Magazine
Newham Recorder and other local and national newspapers.

The Author

Born in Romford, Essex in 1961, Steve Blowers first went to the Boleyn Ground as a nine-year-old schoolboy. Within four seasons, he had persuaded his parents to let him spend his 30 pence per week pocket money on the return bus journey to Upton Park, admission to the South Bank and a match-day programme. Over the next 30 years he was to miss a mere handful of home matches. And upon jumping at the chance, in 1987, to write for *Hammers News* – the club's official monthly publication – the failed left-back was absent only twice as he went on to cover the next 800 or so West Ham United matches from Arsenal to Australia and Brighton to Bucharest. Now a veteran of over 1,300 Hammers' encounters, he has built countless relationships with a whole host of Upton Park players and personnel both past and present and has also written for national and regional newspapers, as well as the club's programme and official web-site. Married to Lynn, the couple have a West Ham season-ticket holding son, Sam, and a daughter, Harriet.